Other books by Thomas F. Waters:

The Streams and Rivers of Minnesota
University of Minnesota Press, Minneapolis
1977

The Superior North Shore:
A Natural History of Lake Superior's Northern Lands and Waters
University of Minnesota Press, Minneapolis
1987

Timberdoodle Tales:
Adventures of a Minnesota Woodcock Hunter
Riparian Press, St. Paul
1993

Sediment in Streams:
Sources, Biological Effects, and Control
American Fisheries Society, Bethesda, Maryland
1995

What others have said:

On *The Streams and Rivers of Minnesota:*
"Thomas F. Waters is a biologist who has turned the scientific paper into an art form, so when he produces a major piece of popular writing the result should be magical. It is."
St. Paul Pioneer Press
"Thoroughly researched and delightfully written. Human history and the landscape are intertwined, and Waters traces that connection with precision."
Minnesota History

On *The Superior North Shore:*
"...the book demonstrates ...the immensity of this inland sea, and the grand sweep of its Precambrian hinterland..."
Canadian Geographic
"This is an eminently readable history of the area and Waters has done a masterful job of writing and the result is wonderful."
The Forum (Fargo, North Dakota)

On *Timberdoodle Tales:*
"These are wonderful upland-bird tales, thoughtfully and vividly told." Nick Lyons, *The Lyons Press.*
"If you enjoy alder thickets, creek bottoms...and the edges of beaver ponds during nature's quality time of the year, then this book is must-reading ...The author has great credentials..."
New Hampshire Wildlife

On *Sediment in Streams:*
"A new book, Sediment in Streams...an excellent resource for fisheries managers, aquatic consultants, and pollution control specialists." *American Rivers*
"This book is an excellent treatise on the biological effects of soil erosion and sedimentation in streams...enjoyed reading this book. It is Tom Waters at his very best."
Journal of the North American Benthological Society

About the Author:

IN HIS EARLIEST YEARS, Tom Waters explored the local creeks of southwestern Michigan, an area of many lakes, streams, and wooded hills. Alone he fished for creek chubs in a nearby stream—with his father, further afield, for brook trout.

Waters maintained an addiction to flowing water, and after high school and service in the U. S. Navy, he entered Michigan State University, receiving his doctorate in 1956 in Fisheries. After a position with the Michigan Department of Conservation, in charge of the Pigeon River Trout Research Station (1956-1957), he joined the fisheries faculty at the University of Minnesota, for a total scientific career of thirty-five years. Waters taught fisheries biology and did extensive research on streams, concentrating on invertebrate and trout population dynamics, publishing in journals of the American Fisheries Society, Canadian Journal of Fisheries and Aquatic Sciences, Ecology, and Journal of the North American Benthological Society. He has received numerous awards for his research and became widely known internationally. His professional affiliations have included the American Fisheries Society, Ecological Society of America, North American Benthological Society, American Society of Limnology and Oceanography, and is a Fellow of the American Institute of Fisheries Research Biologists.

Waters has maintained a strong interest in the protection of streams and rivers. His popular works have provided sound scientific information with writing that is both accurate and easily readable. He is a long-time member of American Rivers, Trout Unlimited, Federation of Fly Fishers, National Wildlife Federation, The Nature Conservancy, a charter member of the new Rivers Council of Minnesota, and a continuing member of the Sierra Club, National Audubon Society, Izaak Walton League, Wisconsin's River Alliance and California's Friends of the River, among others.

His mission, Waters says, is "to interpret scientific knowledge on stream ecology to all those who love rivers and want to know more about them." As river scientist, avid fly fisher, and paddler, he meets his goal most effectively in this volume.

This is his fifth book.

Wildstream

Wildstream

North Umpqua River, Oregon

Wildstream

*A Natural History
of the Free-flowing River*

Thomas F. Waters

RIPARIAN PRESS
St. Paul Minnesota
2000

Published by RIPARIAN PRESS
            2551 Charlotte Street
            St. Paul, Minnesota 55113-2808
            1-877-953-7487

Text set in 12-point Adobe Garamond.
Printed in the United States of America on acid-free paper.
Cover design by Stanton Publications, St. Paul, Minnesota.
Book manufactured by Bang Printing, Brainerd, Minnesota.
Photographs by the author, except where credited.

Several chapters appeared in modified form in the following:
INTRODUCTION: THE MIRACLE OF RIVERS in *Midwest Fly Fishing*
        Volume 2, Issue 1, 1989 (same title*).*
CHAPTER 5 THE STREAM ECOSYSTEM in *Trout Unlimited*
        Minnesota, Winter 1997, as: The Ecology of a Trout Stream.
CHAPTER 12 SECONDARY PRODUCTION in *The FFF Quill,*
        A Federation of Fly Fishers Quarterly Journal, Spring 1994,
            as: Productivity of Streams.

Publishers Cataloging-in-Publication Data
Waters, Thomas F.
        Wildstream : a natural history of the
        free-flowing river / Thomas F. Waters.—1st ed.
        p.   cm.
        Includes bibliographical references and index.
        1. Rivers. 2. Stream ecology. 3. Natural history. I. Title.
        QH97.W37 2000   551.483
                            QBI99-500574

Library of Congress Catalog Card Number: 99-97785

ISBN 0-9637616-1-7 (pb)

                    FIRST EDITION 2000
                    FIRST PRINTING 2000

            Cover photograph: Thompson River, Alberta

DEDICATION

*To my many friends and colleagues
in the North American Benthological Society
and the American Fisheries Society
(who really wrote this book)*

Wildstream

A Natural History
of the Free-flowing River

TABLE OF CONTENTS

PREFACE   15

INTRODUCTION: A MIRACLE OF RIVERS   21

PART ONE   THE SEARCH FOR ORDER   27

Chapter 1 AN EROSIONAL LANDSCAPE   31
  RiverSketch *Ancestral Rivers*
Chapter 2 SUCCESSION   43
  RiverSketch *Coweeta*
Chapter 3 CONTINUUM   57
  RiverSketch *Northwest Passage*

PART TWO   THE LIVING VALLEY   71

Chapter 4 RHEOGENESIS   75
  RiverSketch *Springs and Tributaries*
Chapter 5 THE STREAM ECOSYSTEM   93
  RiverSketch *Mississippi Rising*
Chapter 6 A FLUX OF NUTRIENTS   111
  RiverSketch *Muddying the Waters*
Chapter 7 ALLOCHTHONY   125
  RiverSketch *River Pigs and Log Marks*

Wildstream

PART THREE   THE DYNAMIC RIVER   143

Chapter **8** SPIRALING   147
  RiverSketch *Killer Rain*
Chapter **9** PRIMARY PRODUCTION   163
  RiverSketch *River of Grass*
Chapter **10** HETEROTROPHY   183
  RiverSketch *Black Waters*
Chapter **11** FUNCTIONAL GROUPS   203
  RiverSketch *The Longest Refuge*
Chapter **12** SECONDARY PRODUCTION   217
  RiverSketch *Steamboat 'Round the Bend*

PART FOUR   LIFE AT THE BOTTOM   239

Chapter **13** BIODIVERSITY   243
  RiverSketch *A Different Drummer*
Chapter **14** MAYFLIES   273
  RiverSketch *Old Man River*
Chapter **15** CADDISFLIES   303
  RiverSketch *A Change in the Weather*
Chapter **16** CRUSTACEANS   327
  RiverSketch *Rivers in Darkness*
Chapter **17** MEIOFAUNA   349
  RiverSketch *Ghost of the Red River Valley*
Chapter **18** HYPORHEOS   367
  RiverSketch *"Rivers of America"*

PART FIVE   A FINE KETTLE OF FISH   385

Chapter **19**   *SALVELINUS*   389
    RiverSketch   *Castor canadensis*
Chapter **20** TROUT OF DESERT AND MOUNTAIN   407
    RiverSketch   *Fish out of Water*
Chapter **21**   *SALMO*   435
    RiverSketch   *The Avian Linkage*
Chapter **22**   PACIFIC SALMON   455
    RiverSketch   *The Blessed and the Dammed*
Chapter **23**   SMALLIES, MINNIES, AND CATS   483
    RiverSketch   *Ozark Rivers*

PART SIX   BY CLOCK AND CALENDAR   509

Chapter **24**   RETURN TO THE RIVER   513
    RiverSketch   *Aldo Leopold and the*
                  River of the Mother of God
Chapter **25**   INVERTEBRATE DRIFT   535
    RiverSketch   *Wild and Scenic*

AROUND THE BEND   551

GLOSSARY   557

INDEX   573

PREFACE

THE EVOLUTION OF *Wildstream: A Natural History of the Free-flowing River* was first set with the publication in 1964 of John Bardach's delightful *Downstream: A Natural History of the River.* Dr. Bardach was a professor of ichthyology at the University of Michigan, and I knew him slightly. Second was my growing perception of an increasing desire of many persons who had recently come to enjoy rivers for sound information about the natural history of their many aquatic organisms.

Downstream was descriptive in its approach. It illustrated types of rivers, their different sources, the plants and animals that inhabit rivers and their fascinating adaptations to life in water currents. Nearly four decades ago, *Downstream* reflected what science knew about rivers.

By 1964, I was settled into my profession of stream ecology and river fisheries, and Dr. Bardach's book seemed to me an important first step in informing the public about what stream scientists had been up to. I delighted in its reading.

The next step in summarizing the discipline of river ecology became a great stimulation to scientific research worldwide—Professor H. B. Noel Hynes's definitive treatise, *The Ecology of Running Waters,* published in 1970. He brought the world's knowledge about streams together in one volume, up to the vanguard of scientific knowledge at the time. In contrast to *Downstream,* Dr. Hynes's volume was a reference book for the professional. It was broad in scope and abundant in detail.

The Ecology of Running Waters marked a departure from earlier works. It was sweeping in its scientific scope, and it changed

15

the direction that river science would subsequently follow. Beyond early descriptive natural history, Dr. Hynes now addressed the *dynamics* of streams and their underwater inhabitants. He has been given the highly deserved title of "the father of stream ecology."

It is a combination of chemistry and biology interacting with the forces of water currents, in tune with daily and seasonal cycles, that has so fascinated stream researchers over the past three decades. The accumulated new knowledge has been immense, making the production of another one-volume, comprehensive reference work on stream ecology wholly impossible.

Recently summarizing this new knowledge, J. David Allan in 1995 published his *Stream Ecology: Structure and Function of Running Waters,* a modern reference text for scientists and students. Gathering that new knowledge has been an exciting effort on the part of many scientists, and I consider myself fortunate to have participated in it. Dr. Allan's book introduced to the discipline of stream ecology one of the most profound concepts in our new understanding of life science: *biological diversity*—the importance of the richness of differences among species, in their form and functions, their behavior and adaptations, their genetic makeup. Once the value of biodiversity becomes apparent, the need for protection of different forms becomes crucial, as does also the need for conservation of all genetic identities, embodied in current concerns about the endangerment of species.

◆   ◆   ◆

MY OBSERVATION OF THE PUBLIC'S increasing use and interest in rivers accelerated over the years and inspired my more urgent efforts to bring *Wildstream* to fulfillment. I suspect that, in a scientific study like stream ecology many academics are drawn by the same attractions that appeal to the broader public. We all know these attractions that impinge upon our senses: the sights and sounds of a clear stream set in a beautiful valley—the bird song, water rippling, whispering pines, colorful wild flowers, etc. Surely, these are strong attractions to all of us.

But just as surely, I felt, there exist other, deeper appeals, enticements that excite our curiosities, our hunger to know and understand. These attractions lure the scientist out to the stream with hip boots, chemistry sets, sampling nets, and fish shockers. I believe the same desire to know and understand also lures the canoe paddler, the angler, and the artist with pen and paint. An image of a lovely mountain trout stream might cause my audience to lean back with sighs of fond memories of past trips. But a slide of a caddisfly larva's capture net and gravelly retreat on a stone beneath the rushing water—with which the insect catches its food—may bring the same persons to the edge of their seats with eyes and minds wide open. And in those eyes I have seen the hunger to know and understand.

Therefore, this book is not for the scientist's reference shelf or the university curriculum. I hope it will serve all river lovers—the hiker and camper, artist and photographer, the poet, the river advocate. There is beauty in the gossamer sails of a mayfly as it glides down through a riffle, but there is beauty, too, in an understanding of the feeding behavior and mate seeking, and even the predatory attacks, of the creatures who live and die on the streambed.

I believe I have a potentially powerful, influential reading audience: students, young and older. As an educator, I saw the enthusiasm of young persons wanting to know about their natural world. Always they were inquisitive about the problems of pollution and misuse of our natural resources, eager to join the environmental conflicts. Often growing up in small or rural communities, they knew the value of clean waters and healthy wildlife populations. From a teacher or mentor, they learned that if they wanted to spend their life's work in protecting those values, they must first arm themselves with the most important weapon of all—*knowledge*—in order to make a difference in their lifetimes.

So, in writing this volume I kept in mind that I was trying to fill the armories that would later serve the battlefields of environmental activism: high school biology curriculums, extension classes for postgraduates, nature study courses for all ages, science project programs, community adult education systems. There must be no limit—or minimum—for those who love their natural surroundings and want to understand them better.

◆   ◆   ◆

I HAVE ADDED SOMETHING different into this book: brief articles at the end of each chapter as RiverSketches. These are
meant as short breaks in the thread of scientific material—sort
of "end bars." They can be read as end-of-chapter diversions, in
total as an addendum, or just selected now and then randomly.
They vary from the nonscientific (*River Pigs and Log Marks*) to
brief ecological supplements (*Springs and Tributaries*), and most
do not relate to the preceding chapter. Enjoy.

By the way, you will find many words throughout the book
that are printed in *italics*. Some of these are done this way simply for emphasis. But most are technical words or jargon that
also appear in the Glossary at the end of the book.

I hope my basic motive shows through. It's true that I write
to entertain and inform, but I believe that in deeper understanding come appreciation and a sense of proprietorship—and
ultimately a greater stewardship. Out of a new responsibility,
then, inevitably must emerge the force of citizen action to con-
serve and protect our natural resources—in particular, those
lovely, living, silver strands we call *rivers*.

◆   ◆   ◆

ANY SET OF ACKNOWLEDGMENTS must first credit my outdoor friends to whom I owe grateful thanks for companionship
afield, and for the students who made me aware of their yearn-
ing for sound natural history information and understanding.

Of course, I owe great debt to many others. The wide scope
of the entire discipline of stream ecology required the help of
scores of colleagues. I remain both gratified and humbled by
the professional competence and personal warmth they extended to me when I asked for assistance.

As usual, I benefited from the technical advice of my close
colleague, Raymond M. Newman; financial and operational assistance from the University of Minnesota's Department of
Fisheries and Wildlife; and the energetic help from the staff of
the University's Entomology, Fisheries, and Wildlife Library.

I received professional and common-sense advice on publishing, design, printing, marketing, and other aspects of the book's production from Patricia Condon Johnston, Director, Afton (Minnesota) Historical Press; Will Powers, Director of Design, Minnesota State Historical Society Press; and staff of the Department of Marketing, University of Minnesota Press.

Adding greatly to scientific accuracy throughout the work was a group of scholars and scientists who reviewed specific chapters and other sections on their own subjects of specialization: J. David Allan, University of Michigan; Norman H. Anderson, Oregon State University; Robert A. Bachman, Maryland Department of Natural Resources; Robert J. Behnke, Colorado State University; Ernest F. Benfield, Virginia Polytechnic Institute and State University; Arthur C. Benke, University of Alabama; Edwin L. Cooper, Pennsylvania State University; Alan P. Covich, Colorado State University; Kenneth W. Cummins, South Florida Water Management District; Colbert E. Cushing, Batelle-Pacific Northwest Laboratories, Washington; Stuart G. Fisher, Arizona State University; R. John Gibson, Department of Fisheries and Oceans, Newfoundland; Nancy B. Grimm, Arizona State University; James R. Karr, University of Washington; Paul C. Marsh, Arizona State University; W. Patrick McCafferty, Purdue University, Indiana; Judy L. Meyer, University of Georgia; G. Wayne Minshall, Idaho State University; Peter B. Moyle, University of California, Davis; Robert J. Naiman, University of Washington; Thomas G. Northcote, University of British Columbia; Margaret A. Palmer, University of Maryland; James A. Perry, University of Minnesota; Charles F. Rabeni, University of Missouri; Vincent H. Resh, University of California, Berkeley; Leonard A. Smock, Virginia Commonwealth University; Jack A. Stanford, University of Montana; Kenneth W. Stewart, University of North Texas; Bernard W. Sweeney, Stroud Water Research Center, Pennsylvania; J. Bruce Wallace, University of Georgia; Jackson R. Webster, Virginia Polytechnic Institute and State University; and Glenn B. Wiggins, Royal Ontario Museum.

Many of the above reviewers contributed additional literature, suggestions, photographs (credited in photo captions), and other materials. Similar contributions were received from Jennifer K. Hathaway, Ralph W. Holzenthal, Willard L. Koukkari, and Peter W. Sorensen, University of Minnesota; Tex Hawkins, Upper Mississippi River National Wildlife and Fish Refuge; Charles C. Krueger, Cornell University; and Thomas J. Kwak, North Carolina Cooperative Fish and Wildlife Research Unit. I am greatly appreciative of a field day with Elizabeth (Cassie) Gibbs, University of Maine, and her husband Harold, to her research site on Tomah Stream and along the wild coast of Maine; and for two days on Ozark Mountain rivers shared by Kenneth C. Chilman, Southern Illinois University. Dean Hansen, of *WetBugs Press*, Stillwater, Minnesota, provided photos of stream insects and fish through his skill in underwater photography.   Many thanks are due my copy-editor, Jan Z. Grover, not only for proper grammar and sentence constructions, but also for the *absence* of mispellings, wrong tenses, incomplete sentences, passive constructions, reflexive pronoun uses, and long and nonparallel series. It was a pleasure working with you, Jan.

Finally, most personally, I am deeply thankful for the constant support and assistance from my wife Carol—for help with the manuscript, looking up information on the internet, and, mostly, putting up with my many absences, whether I sat and clicked at a computer or (more often) wandered down some distant river with camera, paddle, or fly rod.

I am grateful to all.

Introduction

A MIRACLE OF RIVERS

ALL OF US, WHILE FISHING, paddling, or hiking, pause once in a while to polish a streamside log and enjoy the scenic beauty of a stream's valley. Probably few of us, however, stop to wonder what role the valley's soils and forests play in our day's pleasures. Naturally, a consideration of chemical and biological processes outside the river's borders cannot compare to the wonder of a leaping trout or the exhilaration of a successful run through a whitewater rapids.

And yet, without the basic physical and chemical processes that take place on the rocky slopes, woodlands, and grassy meadows that make up the valley, there would be little of life in the river. In fact, without all of the inocula and fertilizers injected from outside the water, a favorite trout stream would be little more than a freshet of rainwater running along a street gutter in spring—attractive, perhaps, but not a producer of trout.

Chemistry and physics may not have been our favorite subjects in the classroom, but applying them to the unraveling story of fundamental interactions between a stream and its valley has been both challenging and rewarding. The required research—by fisheries biologists, benthologists, chemists, hydrologists, and more—took place mostly in the past forty years. All researchers shared a common curiosity and fascination about flowing water. The result of their effort is an equally fascinating tale of exploration and successes.

In the early decades of the 1900s, fish scientists (and some anglers) realized that the *habitat* of trout was important in a trout stream. Prior to that time, professional managers, noting declines in fish populations, had relied almost wholly on hatcheries. But then biologists and anglers observed more trout under overhanging banks, behind logs and boulders that produced "pocket water," and in the deeper pools below small waterfalls. So they devised bank covers with logs and sod, emplaced logs and boulders into otherwise uninteresting stretches of stream, and built small dams that created plunge pools.

In the 1930s, a nation-wide management program of so-called "stream improvement" was initiated, facilitated by labor of the federal Civilian Conservation Corps (CCC) of the depression years. Unfortunately, this extensive activity of modifying stream bottoms rarely resulted in real "improvement," especially in terms of more trout. Nor did structures of concrete blocks, sheet metal, steel fencing, and dimension-sawn lumber measure up to expectations of improvement in an aesthetic sense, more trout or not. The real gap in our knowledge about stream ecology at that time had yet to be revealed: the fish's food. Somehow, it was difficult to realize that to produce more trout, more food had to be available.

New interests and innovative approaches did not materialize until after the Great Depression and the Second World War. In the postwar decades of the 1950s and 1960s, a new awareness of our environmental shortcomings resulted in a tremendous outpouring of scientific endeavor—yes, in trout streams as well as in satellites—and government and private institutions made sufficient funds available for research in all fields.

Universities took in war veterans and poured out newly trained graduates in all branches of science. State and federal agencies concerned with fish, wildlife, and other natural resources were created and enlarged throughout North America. Among this new army of scholars was a growing group interested in a relatively new field: the ecology of streams and rivers. The moving environment of water currents was attractive for many reasons. The science of limnology—fresh water—had previously emphasized lakes; the science of streams lagged far behind. (We will be using the term *lotic* frequently in this volume—it describes streams or flowing water, as distinct from *lentic*, which describes lakes and ponds or still water. Lotic science has now caught up!)

Not all of these new river scientists were interested in trout or canoes, but all were fascinated by the mysteries of flowing water. New questions were asked in this endeavor—and answers were intensively pursued. Some questions were recent; some old questions were approached in fresh ways. For example, if fish habitat was important in a stream, surely there was more to it than overhanging banks and the cover provided by logs and boulders?

Of course, we knew that fish fed upon mayflies, grasshoppers, and worms. Anglers for centuries had used natural baits and imitative artificials. But where did the mayflies come from? Getting further down to the bottom of it, what did mayflies eat, and where did that kind of food come from? What factors controlled the abundance of the mayflies' food, and the abundance of mayflies, and, ultimately, the abundance of trout? The solutions began to come in, beginning in the 1960s.

Some answers were obtained through serendipity—scientists stumbling upon them while researching something else. Most were obtained by systematic, deductive processes. For example, we looked carefully at the contents of fish stomachs. If a certain species of mayfly nymph could be identified, then the gut of the mayfly nymph was examined to determine its contents, and the mayfly was sampled from the stream bottom to investigate its own life history. We studied the problem of productivity intensively, attempting to measure the caloric content and rates of energy flow through invertebrate and fish populations.

Much of what we found in mayfly stomachs could not be readily identified. But some items—such as certain algal cells, particles of leaves, even small animals—were sorted out and identified. Then we looked even closer with ever-stronger microscopes which produced scanning electron micrographs, and we found items like fungal cells and bacteria. Then we were able to see and classify previously unidentified material in both fish and insect stomachs—all of which raised more questions.

In 1975, Professor H. B. Noel Hynes published a paper that concisely summarized the new understanding of natural streams. Entitled *The Stream and its Valley*, the paper outlined perceptions and imaginative projections that galvanized the science of freshwater ecology and underscored the dependence of the stream on the valley's soil and forest systems. We call this approach *holistic*, perceiving the system as a whole.

The postwar years were a period of great experimentation in lotic science. When we discovered that some stream bottom invertebrates were feeding primarily on decomposing leaves of deciduous trees and bushes, we conducted experiments in the laboratory to determine which species of trees were most beneficial, and why. Further experimentation showed us the chemical requirements for rapid decomposition of leaves, making them palatable.

Stream researchers conducted other studies of the nutritional requirements of organisms like aquatic insects and other invertebrates. They constructed complex artificial streams in laboratories to measure and manipulate important environmental factors. They directed portions of natural streams through experimental channels—some even indoors—for similar purposes.

With a new generation of scientific instruments, we measured dissolved oxygen, acidity, water temperature, and a host of other factors in natural streams, automatically transmitting data from remote locations by telephone line to the laboratory where the data were computer-analyzed. Chemicals labeled with radioactive tracers were added into the stream's biological processes to identify pathways and rates of flow of nutrients and metabolic byproducts.

Emerging from this broad, intensive research effort arrived a new portrait of the stream: an orderly, dynamic organism. In addition, like other organisms, it had to be fed, to breathe, and to have its metabolic wastes processed. The strong linkage between the stream channel and the terrestrial part of the valley became well understood as an integral part of the living stream, and a fresh view of the basic unit of stream ecology—the *stream ecosystem*—also emerged.

Autumn leaves provide a substantial part of the energy supply for woodland streams.

Many of the stream's visible elements have long been familiar to us. Mayfly nymphs, caddisfly larvae, and scuds prosper among the stream bottom's stones and gravel until discovered by foraging fish and eaten. We imitate these invertebrates with artificials. Sometimes, fish have to compete with other predators, like those stonefly nymphs that feed upon mayfly nymphs and caddis larvae, but then fish may eat the stoneflies, too. And the angler imitates the stonefly. Most stream bottom inhabitants are insects that, upon maturity, emerge as flying adults, and we imitate these with dry flies. So we come to understand the interdependence between the stream and its valley—reflected, in part, in our angling with terrestrial imitations such as beetles, jassids, and grasshoppers.

◆ ◆ ◆

CERTAINLY THE VALLEY SCENE with its meadows and forested hills offers beauty to the angler or canoeist resting at streamside. So, too, do the valley and stream processes in all their orderliness of chemistry and physics bring delight and beauty to the scholar who searches out their mysteries.

This, then, is the ecologists' story, told with hopes for bridging the gap between the river scientist and the river user, to bring a deeper understanding to us all, the young scholar, the angler and paddler, hiker, camper, and river advocate—all who love our free-flowing waters.

Part One

The Search for Order

Introduction to Part One

THE SEARCH FOR ORDER

IT SEEMS WE HUMANS have always been driven by the desire to categorize and classify—to arrange in some orderly fashion almost everything that touches us. All of our possessions, all of those elements of our lives that we love but cannot possess—such as songs, odors, and images—and all parts of our physical and natural environment, we try to arrange into compartments, some neatly, some with difficulty.

The best known classification in all of natural science is the *binomial system* of naming plants and animals. This scheme includes the two Latin (or latinized) words for genus and species (like *Hexagenia limbata),* always written in italic*s,* a system used worldwide so that, no matter in what language, the name of an organism is always the same. No exceptions.

Famous for the invention of the binomial system is Carolus Linnaeus, Swedish botanist, who in 1735 published his *Systema Naturae*, which attempted to label the genus and species of all plants and animals known to the world at that time. The names used today for many of our familiar animals, such as the brown trout (*Salmo trutta*), the northern pike (*Esox lucius*), and the common carp (*Cyprinus carpio*), were included in *Systema Naturae*. Of course, many names have been changed along the way as taxonomists discovered new information, but we'll see a lot of binomial Latin names in this book that have their derivation in Carolus Linnaeus's original classification.

The job of categorizing streams and rivers, it turns out, has been a particularly tough one. System after system were proposed, varying in the criteria with which the categories were created. The same system, it seemed, was never suggested by more than one proponent—which is another way of saying that almost everyone tackling the job of classification had their own, singular idea on how to go about it.

Landscapes, lakes, rocks, and even ice forms have been more amenable to categorization, and we may wonder why river classification has instead been so difficult. The probable reason is the same that makes rivers so attractive in the first place to scientist and layman alike: a great *biodiversity*. In fact, the variation is so huge that a rigid set of criteria would almost place each and every river in a single, unique category. Of course, this conclusion is indeed valid—each stream is unique, and no two are exactly alike. And this great diversity engenders a great fascination with many waters. Despite the difficulty with variation, several systems of river classification have appeared. All are interesting, and all help us, a little or a lot, to understand rivers better.

Within their variations, river systems nevertheless exhibit a certain unity of organization, laterally and longitudinally, that is shared worldwide. The unity, Dr. Luna Leopold of the United States Geological Survey tells us, is due to a delicate, physical balance between the forces of erosion and the forces of resistance to erosion.

One of the major discoveries of early ecological science was that the character of rivers changes throughout their lengths. That fact seems simple and self-evident to us today, but at the time (perhaps only a century ago), it must have been a brilliant deduction! Consequently, more effort has been put into classifying different reaches or zones of a river, than into comparing whole rivers. The changes in a river as it flows downstream—in its physical and chemical conditions, in size and temperature, and in biological features—are sometimes dramatic. River "zones," apparently, are easier to categorize than the diversity among whole rivers. Quite a few different systems of zone classification have been devised, but the one most useful and accepted today is the River Continuum Concept, a principle we will be hearing about often in following chapters.

A word of caution: No system is perfect. A classification or zonation system is created in the human mind, formulated usually within the limited experience of a single scholar. After developing a system, we should not expect nature to necessarily conform to it. It may be annoying, especially to a new student, to learn a satisfying new system and then find exceptions. But it just may be that those very exceptions, if followed up, can lead to new insights.

In our attempts to bring order to the seeming chaos that we encounter on a day astream, we will explore variation along with the streams' shared unity. Even while we seek orderliness, the diversity among streams is fascinating and exciting, and the exception to the rule may be the most exciting of all.

Chapter 1

AN EROSIONAL LANDSCAPE

Landmasses that include streams and rivers—what we may call valleys or watersheds—constitute terrains known as "erosional landscapes." The erosion of rock and land sediments is a process that moves the materials of high plains and mountains to the sea, while at the same time the eroding process moves headward, causing river valleys to migrate upstream.

The process may be rapid, as in a flood, or it may be exceedingly slow, consuming centuries or millions of years. The process is relentless. Over geological time, however, tectonic forces deep in the earth may uplift the land, then again subject it to erosion that will sculpt the landscape further.

Seemingly, a process that takes a million years will not touch our lives very much. That erosion has gone on for a long time before us, but it is responsible for the character of our present river systems, profoundly affecting our everyday lives, a legacy of erosional landscapes.

As we examine the many rivers in such a landscape, we first see a great variation in size and shape of rivers. In fact, the characterization of rivers by size would appear to be a logical first step. And we are soon struck by a seemingly insurmountable question: What criterion best indicates size? Width, depth, or length? Watershed area? Or the amount of flow, or discharge?

◆   ◆   ◆

IT WAS LOGICAL THAT OUR FIRST ATTEMPTS to classify streams applied the criterion of width, the most obvious, visible measure of a stream's size. Nearly a half-century ago, Belgian professor Marcel Huet laid the foundation for many of our early ideas of stream classification, for example:

	Brooklet	Brook	Little River	River	Large River
Width (meters)	0-1	1-5	5-25	25-100	100-300

Although Huet's table of quaint stream categories was part of an attempt to describe fish distribution in streams (which we will take up in the next chapter), the difficulty in quantifying river size is obvious. The attractive names and precise widths tell us little about the significance of these streams in the greater context of an erosional landscape.

Length is also a measurement of great interest, but it, too, has its drawbacks. For example, the Mississippi River is a mighty long river but not nearly as long as the Nile in Africa. If we followed down the Missouri River, however, from its source in the Rocky Mountains to the Gulf of Mexico, and called *that* the Mississippi instead, it would be the longest in the world!

About the same time that Marcel Huet was struggling with river distribution of fishes, other scholars were studying how rivers sculpture the land. Some scheme was needed to identify different reaches as a river changes and grows downstream. Streams may begin with little trickles and, over long geological times, grow larger as they erode headward. With that principle in mind, we used the terms *youthful, mature,* and *old* to designate upper, middle, and lower reaches, respectively, terms not used much anymore. Each of the three categories, however, can be associated with recognizable features: small, stony and tumbling in youthful stages, growing to large, silty, and meandering as senior citizen rivers. The aging process downstream on a single river recapitulates the aging of a river reach through time.

Still, this oversimplification of categorizing rivers by age called for further refinement, a means of quantifying different river zones. Led by Robert E. Horton of the United States Geological Survey in the 1940s, hydrologists developed the system of *stream order*. It was an elegant scheme in its logic, and it remains in wide use today.

This system designates the uppermost stream channel—usually small, stony, and shaded—as First Order. When two first-order streams join, their product is termed Second Order; when two second-order streams join, the result is Third Order. And so on downstream. But when a second-order stream is joined by a first-order stream, it remains second order, rather than progressing to third. Two second-order streams must join to create a stream of third order.

A second-order stream is formed by the junction
of two first-order streams.

Some general principles emerged from the stream-order system. For example, there are more lower-order stream reaches than higher ones. On the average, about ten times as many streams of any one order occur as those of the next higher order. Stream length increases with order, but the numerical relationship is not exact. And of course all other measurements—width, depth, discharge, and others—can be expected to increase, too. By far, streams of low orders (first through third) make up about 85 percent of total stream miles in the United States.

Some difficulties and exceptions inevitably occur with such a scheme, and the system has been criticized in some quarters. For example, a relatively straight river flowing through a long, narrow valley—like many in the Appalachian Mountains—offers an extreme case. Such a stream may have many small, low-order tributaries and may grow to a very large river, while never getting beyond second order, although its actual size may be as great as one normally designated at a much higher order.

Another extreme case is the *dichotomous* example of a broad drainage basin. In it, each pair of first-order streams forms a second-order stream, and each pair of second-order streams forms a third-order stream, etc. A very high stream order may be attained without the stream becoming large at all.

Sometimes it is difficult to decide which count as first-order streams—do we include every little drip and trickle? If so, we might have a tenth-order stream only large enough to dip a cup of cool water from on a hot day. Conversely, some fairly large rivers arise full-blown from springs and caves and may flow their full course as first order. Other conceptual problems are raised by intermittent streams, rivers passing through large lakes, and streams that arise but disappear in deserts. We'll take up the subject of stream sources in another chapter.

Despite these rather formidable obstacles, the stream-order system remains very useful. The reason for this acceptance probably lies in the fact that *in most cases* stream order can give us a fair picture of a stream's approximate size and general character, at least within a prescribed geographic region. The system is made more attractive by its simplicity.

Recently, scholars have pointed out that such quantities as *watershed area* and *baseline discharge* (or some ratio between the two) provide us with more accurate ideas about stream reaches within total drainage basins. Those measurements may tell us more of actual stream size and biological significance.

Some stream ecologists and stream fishery managers say, "Tell me the discharge and gradient, and I'll have a picture of the stream in my mind." But such accurate mind pictures require much expertise and experience. The stream order system, even though less accurate, and with all its exceptions, will no doubt stay with us as a means of rapidly categorizing stream size. Its simplicity is very useful as a guide to further studies.

How does stream order translate to a guide for the angler or paddler? Think of it this way:

Most anglers probably will not fish a first-order stream (except kids). Orders second and third may be fishable, but many fly fishers risk losing their duns and spinners in tree branches. Orders fourth and fifth may be just right—easy wading, nice clear water, and plenty of room for backcasts. But in such stream orders canoeists may come along to disturb the fishing. With higher orders, wading may become too deep or the rapids too rough. The highest orders may require boats to fish waters that may be too muddy to be rewarding anyway.

Paddlers are likely to find the middle orders just right, with exciting rapids and intimate riparian scenery, but they might find seventh- or eighth-order streams boring. In fact, these days, most sixth-order streams and larger are dammed or polluted. And a tenth-order stream may just find you on the lower Mississippi dodging barges and ocean freighters.

◆   ◆   ◆

THE UNITY SHARED BY ALL STREAMS and rivers is subtle. It is related to processes rather than to appearances, yet the unity is profound. Two processes shared by all streams are *meanders* and *gradients*, both of which are related to the hydrodynamic energy of water as it flows downhill. Both are important to river users.

For example, meanders, or bends in rivers, have great significance to the fish-holding capacity of a stream, as well as to the general stream attractiveness to anglers. Paddlers, maneuvering their canoes around fast bends, and photographers seeking S-shapes in their compositions, are also keenly aware of meanders.

A stream erodes against an outside bend, while inside the bend a gravel bar migrates in the same direction, forming a meander.

Owing to the hydrodynamic character of flowing water, the development of meanders seems to be controlled in proportion to the width of stream, regardless of its actual size. On the average, and with remarkably little variation, the radius of a river bend will be about three times the width. And a meander will occur, first to one side and then to the opposite, along a stream length equal to about eleven times the stream width.

Meanders occur in different shapes, varying in the "tightness" of the river bends, or *sinuosity*, as a fluvial geomorphologist would term it. But meanders that resemble a sine wave appear to be the way a river wants to go, and so the sine wave shape of meanders is the most common.

All of which translates to the fact that, without a map scale to go by, a drawing of a meandering lower Mississippi River will not look a whole lot different from that winding little pasture creek on your grandpa's back forty.

The *gradient* of a stream is measured as the drop in elevation per unit of stream length, such as feet per mile, or percentage or degrees. The gradient determines many important conditions that affect us, no matter how we may use a river.

First, it affects the current velocity. Is it too swift to wade? Will it be exciting (or dangerous) to paddle? What kind of organisms can adapt to swift current and prosper on the streambed? Can fish migrate up the rapids to spawn?

Second, the gradient helps to determine the bottom type (boulders and stones, gravel, or sand and silt) which in turn affects all of our activities. The kinds of organisms living on the bottom—the *benthos*—depend greatly on the bottom type. Typically, headwater reaches in all rivers tend to have high gradients with stony bottoms; farther downstream, gradients are lower, with more sand and silt deposits.

The *slope* (another term for gradient), when pictured over a river's entire distance, gives us the stream's *longitudinal profile.* The profile almost always begins with a steep gradient that levels out downstream.

The longitudinal profile is closely related to meanders. The more meanders, the longer the stream length—and thus the lower the gradient. The interaction of these two elements of river behavior is affected by several watershed features, such as the valley slopes responding to the action of moving water by erosion and sorting of sediments.

Visualize one extreme in river formation taking place in a region of unsorted glacial till, where the bedrock, whatever it is, lies so deep beneath glacial drift that it exerts no control on stream morphology. In this case, water erosion is the force acting on the valley landscape. We expect many such streams in the glaciated upper Midwest of North America.

We can predict that streams flowing through a region of exposed ancient, hard rock, like lava, will little erode streambeds. Here, control of stream morphology by bedrock placement is virtually complete. In such a case, runoff and tributary waters have almost no erosive effect, and the stream simply flows through its valley without having created it. We find examples of these kinds of streams, for example, in the long, narrow valleys of the folded Appalachians.

An Appalachian stream controlled by reisistant bedrock,
Eastatoee Creek, South Carolina.

Desert streams, which are often intermittent, may flow through valleys carved by wind erosion. Streams under some degree of bedrock control in limestone regions may exhibit rectangular shapes in their drainage patterns. And streams on the Precambrian Shield, a region of hard lavas billions of years old, may flow through channels scoured more recently into the ancient rock by glaciers.

And so migrating fish swim to the headwaters, where they find gravel and stony bottoms to build their nests and redds and swift currents that will bring oxygen-rich water to their incubating eggs.

◆   ◆   ◆

OTHER PHYSICAL QUALITIES OF RIVERS, such as chemical properties and water temperature, have also been used to catalog river types, but because of their close relationship to other biological matters, we will take them up in later discussions.

Probably owing to the economic and aesthetic interests of us humans, it was the biology of rivers that first drew the attention of scholars. But the size and shape of streams, it turned out, were of major importance to later scholars. And the characteristics of width and depth, current velocity and discharge, gradient and meanders, were all intimately associated with the biology of aquatic plants, insects, and fish.

TECHNICAL REFERENCES:

Leopold, Luna B. 1994. *A View of the River.* Harvard University Press, Cambridge, Massachusetts.

Rosgen, Dave. 1994. *Applied River Morphology.* Wildland Hydrology. Pagosa Springs, Colorado.

Montgomery, David R., and John M. Buffington. 1998. Channel processes, classification, and response. Pages 13-42 *in* Robert J. Naiman and Robert E. Bilby. *River Ecology and Management: Lessons from the Pacific Coastal Ecoregion.* Springer-Verlag, New York.

RiverSketch

ANCESTRAL RIVERS

T HOSE OF US WHO LIVE, FISH, OR PADDLE in the northern parts of North America know that the condition of our streams and rivers owe much to recent glaciation. Especially during melting of the huge ice sheets 10,000 years ago, all that coursing of icy water redirected and shaped new streams across a freshly formed landscape of glacial drift.

The trout stream we fish and the rapids we run in these northern areas now are really brand new, for ten thousand years is only a blink of an eye compared with the millions of years that went before. The species of fish we pursue with rod and line today weathered glacial storms many times, in rivers of ancient geological lineage. Where did these ancestral rivers run?

The mid-continent region, and the Mississippi as its largest river in both flow and watershed area, have received the most intensive study. Along with its two major tributaries, the Missouri and the Ohio, the drainage of the Mississippi underwent great change as the result of glaciation in the Pleistocene Epoch two million to about eighteen thousand years ago. Before the Pleistocene ice age, however, ancient rivers in bedrock valleys shaped the land in courses much different from today's, with significant modifications to the old network of valleys, drainage divides, and stream orders. Not that glaciers reshaped bedrock. Rather, massive amounts of glacial drift, such as sand and gravel, were carried by the one- to two-miles-thick ice that covered the region, creating new landscapes that shifted drainage patterns profoundly. The puzzles of the resulting ancient valleys can now be reconstructed using seismic data and well-drilling records.

Of course, some preglacial drainages remain where overlying glacial drift was thin, and many modern streams still flow along the paths of the old bedrock valleys. Nevertheless, many new streams were formed, mostly small, but some large. Some streams follow the course of old valleys but flow in reverse directions.

In mid-continent, drainages developed two major erosional landscapes: (1) in the northern plains, the Western Region, streams flowed north instead of joining the Mississippi, and (2) in the Central Region, the upper Mississippi, such as it was, flowed south.

The Western Region, including the upper Missouri and Yellowstone rivers, veered northeastward to join the north-flowing

Red River of the North, the Winnipeg in Canada, and eventually Hudson Bay. This is the pathway of the old bedrock valley.

The thick ice sheets that pushed south across the area of Montana, North Dakota, and South Dakota redirected this northward flow of the ancestral Missouri River to the south and caused it to cut the modern valley leading to the Mississippi River, where the two now join at present-day St. Louis. The primordial Mississippi did not collect the waters of the Missouri and Yellowstone, as mentioned above, nor those of the Minnesota and Illinois rivers. The only major streams reaching the old Mississippi were the plains rivers Niobrara, Des Moines, and Platte, all still much the same today.

Waters of the Missouri River now flow to the Gulf of Mexico, but once ran north to Hudson Bay.
(Photo courtesy of Thomas H. Helgeson.)

In the Central Region, the ancestral Mississippi River was unlike the "Old Man River" we know today. The lower river flowed into a huge embayment of the Gulf of Mexico at about the location of modern southeastern Missouri's "boot heel" (when the level of the ocean was some two hundred feet higher than it is now). Just there, a large preglacial stream, now named the Teays River (after the community of Teays, West Virginia), emptied into the Mississippi after draining large portions of West Virginia, Pennsylvania, Ohio, and Indiana. Later, the Teays drainage became the watershed of the Ohio, but when today's Ohio River was newly created, it did not exactly follow the old bedrock valley of the Teays.

By the time glaciation ended, two new drainages had formed: (1) in the west, glacial deposits had forced the previously northward flowing Yellowstone and Missouri southward, so that instead of flowing north to Hudson Bay, their waters now empty into the Mississippi; and (2) in the east, glacial deposits had pushed the ancestral Teays River southward to form the new Ohio River.

The modern Mississippi was left with its two major tributaries, the Missouri and Ohio, forming a huge west-to-east crescent that now mark the southernmost edge of glaciation in mid-continent. As ocean levels lowered, the saltwater embayment disappeared, and today's Lower Mississippi flows from St. Louis to its present entry into the Gulf of Mexico.

When you run a favorite river reach of Pennsylvania's famous "Yock," or cast an elkhair caddis on a mountain pool of the Yellowstone, the water beneath your canoe or pulling at your waders just might (a couple of million years ago) have flowed a hundred feet lower down and in the opposite direction!

SELECTED REFERENCES:

Bray, Edmund C. 1985. *Ancient Valleys, Modern Rivers: What the glaciers did.* Science Museum of Minnesota. St. Paul.

Darrel, Richard H., editor. 1977. A recycled landscape. *Quarterly* (Cincinnati Museum of Natural History). Volume 14, number 2, pages 8-15.

Chapter 2

SUCCESSION

ONE OF THE FIRST PERCEPTIONS of early stream observers must have been that the kinds and abundance of fish change along the course of a river. Fish were the largest members of the stream *biota*. Fish could be captured relatively easily, even a hundred years ago, with traps, nets, or hook and line. Furthermore, they were good to eat. We can imagine how early fishers would have reacted, in both the means of capture and in the quality of eating, to the change in kinds of fish through the length of a stream.

Science came later. The single work that stimulated so much research on succession in streams was that of Victor E. Shelford, professor at the University of Illinois. Shelford's paper, published in 1911, documented the "arrangement" of fishes in several streams tributary to Lake Michigan, near Chicago. Probably anglers and hikers also had observed a change in fish species as they came to know all reaches of a single stream.

During a day's fishing on one reach of stream—probably not much more than a quarter-mile—you probably will not notice changes in fish species. Trout or smallmouth bass will probably be much the same as where you started. But if you combined fishing with a canoe or backpack camping trip for a week, you may notice quite a difference. Going downstream and fishing here and there, you may catch trout at the start; but 25 miles farther and smallmouth bass may be the predominant species;

50 miles more and your catch might consist of northern pike and perhaps largemouth bass. Of course, this might not surprise you, especially if you are familiar with this, your favorite river. But it may surprise you that a hundred years ago science did not pay much attention to just *why* the fish species changed.

Professor Shelford produced two major concepts in stream ecology that, for nearly a century, have greatly influenced the thinking of later scholars and fish-watchers alike. The first was that each fish species has a unique set of habits and behaviors matched to a particular environment. Along the course of a stream, from headwaters to mouth, habitats available to fish change along with many stream characteristics: width and depth, substrate, gradient, temperature, pool-and-riffle spacing, and meanders. Different species "arrange" themselves along the stream course accordingly.

The second of Shelford's contributions was the observation that the fish community in a small, short stream near its mouth was the same as one found in the small headwaters of a larger, longer stream. From this he concluded that, as young streams erode and migrate headward and grow through time, the "young" fish community migrates headward, too. And other species and communities of plants and animals follow in turn.

Thus, stream succession can be viewed from two perspectives. First is the view through time—that is, successional changes occurring over long eras at a given point on a stream. Second is through space—that is, the longitudinal view from headwaters to mouth, at a given point in time. Ecologists thus differentiated between habitats going through *temporal* and *spatial* succession, respectively. Many hundreds of scientific studies have been conducted on the question of downstream succession since Shelford's time. His paper has become a true classic in ecology, still cited in scientific publications on stream succession.

Another aspect of succession is the series of "post-disturbance" changes that take place after a severe flood, dam construction, even just a beaver dam. Downstream biological processes essentially "start over," or *reset*.

A mountain meadow, legacy of a long-ago abandoned
beaver pond, causing a reset. Lucky Dog Creek, Idaho.

Along with the realization that rivers tend to shape their valleys, rather than just flowing through them, came a curiosity
about biological changes that occur when rivers erode headward.
Further questions arose about the differences between rivers and
about the need for an orderly classification system that would
reveal the diverse array of stream and river types.

◆   ◆   ◆

PROBABLY THE SIMPLEST STREAM classification meaningful to
the distribution of fish species is water temperature, which has
resulted in our use of *coldwater* and *warmwater* streams.

Fishery biologists seem to have emphasized trout streams in
modern ecological studies. The chief distinction made between
coldwater and warmwater streams has been that coldwater
streams are defined as trout streams and warmwater streams
(with warmwater fishes) are those too warm for trout! Despite
this admitted bias, the distinction is nevertheless useful, because

fisheries management generally breaks out along these two broad categories of thermal conditions.

Groundwater temperatures are typically close to the annual average of air temperature, which is usually a function of latitude, and they lie between high summer air temperatures and low winter air temperatures. In fact, the annual average water temperature of a coldwater stream may actually be higher than the average for a warmwater stream! Winter conditions in high latitudes (subarctic) or high altitudes (mountains) do not present the relatively warm water as those at lower latitudes and altitudes. The distinction between effects of cold winter stream waters in mountains and northern areas, and winter effects of warmer water in temperate zones has not been studied thoroughly.

A good trout stream will remain unfrozen in the most severe cold.
(Photo taken at −20° Fahrenheit.)

One good way to scout out potential trout streams that have their source in groundwater is to observe them at the coldest times of winter—if they remain unfrozen, chances are they will be coldwater streams in the summer.

A major difference in fish distribution between coldwater and warmwater streams is readily observable: there are fewer species occurring in coldwater streams. Trout streams may have only one or two fish species throughout their coldwater reaches, often only one species of trout and maybe a sculpin (muddler). But where a coldwater trout stream warms up farther downstream, the number of species increases.

Generally, water temperature rises from headwater to mouth (in summer), an important feature of downstream succession. In an Ontario study, for example, brook trout and sculpins were found in an upstream reach less than three miles from the stream's source, where it was shaded and cool. A lower reach over ten miles from the source contained smallmouth bass, rock bass, and many other warmwater species; this lower reach was sunny and eight degrees warmer than the upper reach.

Warmer water affects other aspects in the biological community, too, like aquatic plants and insects. Processes such as plant photosynthesis and insect metabolism are affected by water temperature. We will look at some of these processes in more detail in future chapters.

◆   ◆   ◆

BY THE TIME PROFESSOR SHELFORD began to record the arrangement of fishes in his study streams, other workers in Europe had made related observations. Of course, European stream fishes are different from those in the American Midwest. Nevertheless, it turned out that the principles determining succession of fishes were very similar. Marcel Huet published a paper in a North American journal in 1959, when a system of "fish faunal zones" had been studied and accepted in Europe.

Starting from the headwaters, four zones included:
• *trout zone*, with brown trout and sometimes an Old World sculpin;
• *grayling zone*, with a European grayling closely related to the North American grayling, but with temperature preferences

a little higher in Europe. A few brown trout remain, along with the occasional northern pike;

• *barbel zone*, named after a large minnow called the *barbel*. Other stream-adapted, large minnows and northern pike accompany the barbel;

• *bream zone*, named after another large European minnow, the *bream*, a fish of still waters. Other fishes are also like lake species—large slow-water minnows, including carp and the ubiquitous northern pike.

Some scholars felt that the four zones should be reduced to two; the *rhithron* (with cool, fast currents and trout and grayling) and the *potamon* (with warm, slow currents and large minnows such as carp, northern pike, and other lake-living species).

In contrast to North American rivers, the European experience is markedly different—mainly, in that more centuries of civilization resulted in more abuse and pollution. So, we may wonder how these European successional schemes fit North American systems, such as the Horton stream order system, previously described. With some imagination, we might equate the Trout Zone with first and second orders, Grayling Zone with third and fourth orders, Barbel Zone with fifth to seventh orders and Bream Zone with eighth to tenth orders.

For several decades following Professor Shelford's early work in Lake Michigan tributaries, little attention was paid to stream fish succession. But soon several patterns emerged.

In northern and eastern spring-fed streams, the upper headwaters could be termed coldwater. Such reaches are typified by the brook trout, often the only species present, but sometimes accompanied by one species of sculpin. In this type of stream, waters typically warm up slightly farther downstream, and the creek chub and some other "upstream" minnows, such as the blacknose dace, can be found. Warmer and larger, the middle reach may contain smallmouth bass and rock bass, two species frequently found together. Many darters (bottom-living fishes in the perch family) may appear in shallow riffles, whereas several suckers can be found in pools.

Even farther downstream, in reaches similar to the lower reaches of all warmwater streams, we are likely to find more minnows, sunfishes, suckers and redhorses, perch, bullheads, and the ubiquitous northern pike. Channel catfish, walleye and, rarely, muskellunge will be found in middle reaches. Of course, there will always be some exceptions.

Keep in mind that, in summer, the low temperatures in upstream reaches, closer to groundwater sources, are low *relative* to the air; downstream temperatures, which are farther from groundwater sources, are higher and near air temperature.

The point is that the annual swing in upstream reaches, from a little below air temperature in summer to a little above air temperature in winter, has a narrower range than it has downstream. In lower reaches, water temperature swings broadly from near air temperature in both the heat of summer and cold of winter.

Species in headwater reaches we term cold *stenothermic*, adapted to a narrow range of low temperature; those in downstream warmer reaches, adapted to the broader range in temperature, we call warm *eurythermic*.

The creek chub is a species typical of warmwater, first-order streams (small, steep-gradient, rocky bottom, shaded habitat). Where a trout stream warms just a bit, the creek chub may be the first warmwater species to join the brook trout. It rises readily to feed on floating insects, which no doubt accounts for the annoyance that dry-fly trout anglers frequently experience when encountering these moderately sized minnows, instead of the anticipated brook trout. (Shelford called the creek chub horned dace, a common name for the creek chub that persists in some regions today, because in its spawning finery the male creek chub sports tubercles or "horns" on top of its head!).

Many investigators have noted that although the number of species increases downstream, the new additions do not necessarily replace the upstream species. For that matter, upstream fish can sometimes be found throughout a stream's entire course. The longer the stream—and thus the more that aquatic habitats change—the more likely it is that upstream species will in fact drop out, new species start to appear, and downstream species will not be found upstream.

The reason for habitat changes downstream is related to the increase of water flow, depth, and width. When these measures increase, a greater variety of habitats are created—different sizes of stones and woody debris, more kinds of protective cover, a greater variety of streambed materials offering different kinds of invertebrate foods. This greater diversity in habitats, the result of greater flow, wider channels, and locations with varying current velocity, all lead to additional kinds of spaces for more fish—and invertebrate species, too.

Stenothermic fishes (like the brook trout) prefer temperatures with a narrow daily and seasonal swing; eurythermic fishes (like the common shiner) prefer wider temperature swings.

Often only one species of fish occupies a first-order reach, and this one is soon joined in a second-order reach by maybe two or three more; fifth- or sixth-order streams may have over 200 species. Interestingly, beyond that, the number of species appears to decline. However, trout streams that are coldwater through several orders have fewer species than warmwater streams through the same stream orders.

Mountain and desert streams present a different pattern of fish species than in the east. One obvious difference is that the native cutthroat occupies the uppermost reaches, like the brook trout in its native eastern streams). Other species—sculpins, muntain whitefish, some minnows, suckers—ecologically similar but of different species than in eastern streams follow.

Exotic species have resulted in some distressing problems. These fish may actually replace natives, or they may simply arrange themselves along a stream profile in much the same ecological roles that they filled in their native region. For example, the brown trout, notorious for its dominance over other trout species, has replaced the brook trout in many streams in eastern North America, but it seems to be a species best suited to mid-range reaches or as far upstream as second-order streams. Many brook trout populations have been replaced by the brown trout throughout many streams, except for the very uppermost reaches, where the brookie continues to hold fast.

In the West, the introduced brook trout has replaced the cutthroat in many headwater reaches. Where both brook trout and brown trout have been introduced in western mountain streams, the sequence is sometimes cutthroat-brook-brown, uppermost to lower. And the rainbow, native in the West but introduced widely, has replaced the brook trout in many Appalachian Mountain streams, although the brook trout still holds out in the uppermost reaches. In other regions where rainbows have been introduced, they appear to occupy some upper-middle portions, similar to brown trout.

We may logically ask about the abundance or total weight (*biomass*) of all fish species: does it also increase downstream? A few studies suggest that total fish abundance, expressed on an area basis such as pounds per acre of stream surface, increases with stream order. But basic productivity may be related instead to factors other than stream order, such as local geology and water chemistry.

We'll take up biological productivity in later chapters.

◆   ◆   ◆

DOWNSTREAM SUCCESSION in other parts of the community—algae and other plants, insects and other invertebrates—has also attracted much attention from stream ecologists in the past few decades. The downstream distributions of most insect orders, for example, have been intensively studied.

One of the major similarities between invertebrate and fish distributions is the increase in number of species downstream. Like fishes, invertebrate species increase in number downstream, also, apparently, in response to higher summer temperatures. Also, like fishes, invertebrates can be either stenothermic (in upper reaches) or eurythermic (in lower reaches).

One major problem comes up with insects and other invertebrates that we don't have with fishes: identification to species. Insect orders are easy: Ephemeroptera (mayflies), Trichoptera (caddisflies), and Plecoptera (stoneflies). Members of a single order may be found through a stream's course, but species within that order may change greatly, because different species have different habitat requirements, though in the same order.

◆   ◆   ◆

ATTEMPTS TO CLASSIFY WHOLE STREAMS into types have been largely unsuccessful. The downstream succession caused by changes in river characteristics seems to be the chief reason why we have difficulty in categorizing the whole stream, whereas the zonation concept has been more useful.

Lake classification has been more successful, particularly when based on productivity: *eutrophic* (highest productivity), *mesotrophic* (middle), and *oligotrophic* (low productivity). This "trophic state" system has been widely accepted by lake ecologists. Similar attempts to apply a chemical index, such as alkalinity or calcium content, to streams has met with some success.

Unfortunately, the search for order may lead to dangerous categorizing. The late English stream ecologist, Professor T. T.

Macan, warned us thirty years ago against confining *ideas* within a rigid framework, because "...a framework makes a cage." A cage, we must agree, is not the point from which we can extend knowledge through creative scientific exploration.

Throughout the history of attempts to delineate zones along a stream profile, almost all researchers have agreed that the zones are not discrete, that boundaries of zones are not distinct, and that overlap and intergrading exist. Of course, this "problem" may complicate matters, but it does not invalidate the concept of downstream succession.

We now may view changes in habitats, species, and processes from upstream to downstream, through time, or below a major disturbance in a logical *continuum*—fascinating in its complexity, but orderly in the dependence of the downstream upon the upstream—a unifying concept we will explore next.

TECHNICAL REFERENCES:

Fisher, Stuart G. 1983. Succession in streams. Pages 7-27 *in* James R. Barnes and G. Wayne Minshall, editors. *Stream Ecology: Application and testing of general ecological theory.* Plenum Press, New York.

Huet, Marcel. 1959. Profiles and biology of western European streams as related to fish management. *Transactions of the American Fisheries Society.* Volume 88, pages 155-163.

Shelford, Victor E. 1911. Stream fishes and the method of physiographic analysis. *Biological Bulletin, Marine Biological Laboratory, Woods Hole.* Volume 21, pages 9-35.

RiverSketch

COWEETA

TUCKED HIGH IN A REMOTE VALLEY of western North Carolina's Blue Ridge Mountains is a unique outdoor research facility of the United States Forest Service, the Coweeta Hydrologic Laboratory.

Established in 1934 as the Coweeta Experimental Forest, its name was later changed to reflect a mission that was evolving from experimental forest management to broader ecological objectives. The area covers more than 5,000 acres (eight square miles) and includes more than 45 miles of first- and second-order streams that flow in steep, **V**-shaped valleys.

Hill slopes are particularly steep in this mountainous region. Elevations rise to over 5,000 feet, and hillside gradients *average* 50 percent (45° slope). This extreme topography leads to striking results from almost any kind of land use involving surface disturbance.

The use of the term "laboratory" here may be misleading, for this is not an indoor facility of sterile lab benches and microscopes. Coweeta is an *outdoor* laboratory—a set of connecting experimental valleys, or watersheds, where studies in hydrology and stream ecology are conducted in the real world of sun and soil and tumbling streams.

By the mid-1930s, agricultural cultivation, livestock grazing, and unrestricted logging had brought devastation to much of Appalachia. The experimental forest was first established to assess the effect of such activities on water supply and quality. Practical objectives included developing improved forest management. Basic studies were soon added to measure the various fates and consequences of precipitation—runoff, stream flow, sediment transport, and groundwater conditions—resulting in more effective forestry practice.

The value of a facility that employs whole watersheds is that it provides an entire stream system as the basic study subject. Coweeta's large number of watersheds also provides a rare opportunity for making sound comparisons between them.

A small watershed at Coweeta is subjected to experimental logging methods, in order to study erosion.

The laboratory encompasses the major watershed of Coweeta Creek and its many tributaries. Each tributary flows through its own distinct watershed, sharply defined by ridgetops that separate contiguous, smaller valleys. Each of these small watersheds contains its own individual set of environmental conditions, characterized mainly by the type of vegetative cover or forest type. The overall result is a large, natural laboratory of some 50 small watersheds created over long ages of natural erosion, now available for both basic research and experimental manipulation. Small streams flow through most watersheds, many of these gauged and instrumented so that data like volume of flow, water temperature, chemical concentrations, and other information are automatically recorded. A typical experiment compares the water yield from a watershed with original hardwoods to a watershed where the forest has been converted to white pine.

In the 1970s and 1980s, researchers in many other disciplines from universities in the region came to take advantage of the facility's unique research opportunities in sedimentation, insect productivity, nutrient supply to microorganisms and invertebrates, and inputs of plant material from the watershed. One of the most important was the measurement of energy supply, both by photosynthesis in the stream and by the input of external organic matter from the land. In the overall program of Coweeta's basic stream research, benthic ecology has been the core area of study.

A few outdoor research facilities similar to Coweeta have been established elsewhere in the United States and Canada, where the effects of forestry practice upon streams are investigated. But none matches Coweeta's number of experimental watersheds and long-term background data. A great deal of the current knowledge of stream ecology in this book was gained at Coweeta.

SELECTED REFERENCES:

Wallace, J. Bruce. 1988. Aquatic invertebrate research. Pages 257-268 *in* Wayne T. Swank and D.A. Crossley, Jr., editors. *Forest Hydrology and Ecology at Coweeta.* Springer-Verlag, New York.

Webster, Jackson R., S.W. Golladay, E.F. Benfield, J.L. Meyer, W.T. Swank, and J.B. Wallace. 1992. Watershed disturbance and stream response: An overview of stream research at Coweeta Hydrologic Laboratory. Pages 231-253 *in* P.J. Boon, P. Calow, and G.E Petts, editors. *River Conservation and Management.* John Wiley & Sons, New York.

Chapter **3**

CONTINUUM

THE DEVELOPMENT OF A SYSTEM for classifying streams and rivers from headwaters to mouth was well underway by mid-twentieth century. So too was knowledge of fish distribution along the stream profile. After fish, we also came to know more about how other biological elements change. We now know that the kinds of insect species, the number of species, and the number of individuals all change in a downstream direction.

Beyond "what kind?" and "how many?" are questions about what these organisms do to survive and prosper: their feeding, reproduction, and migrations. How these animals respond to their surroundings is what makes up the science of ecology: the relationship between living organisms and their environment.

When Professor Shelford was studying the "arrangements" of fish along stream profiles, little was known about how fish and insects responded to variations in their environment. In stream ecology specifically, why do species and numbers change as the physical environment changes downstream?

The discipline of ecology made great progress in the early half of the twentieth century, but what made the study of streams so fascinating, so attractive to scientist, angler, and paddler alike, were the changes observed in downstream succession. The ecology of a particular riffle or pool may be thoroughly studied—but all bets are off around the next bend!

Might these downstream changes be predictable? In the 1970s, that query was a startling question. Building upon this question and their dissatisfactions with the imperfections of zonation schemes (for example, trout zone, barbel zone, etc.), a group of stream ecologists developed a theory that came to be known as the *River Continuum Concept*, or RCC.

Earlier efforts in the search for order were largely descriptive of the *structure* of stream communities, that is, the number and kinds of species. Stream segments had been identified by physical conditions, by the species structure for each segment, and then by laying out these segments or zones systematically, one after the other, in a downstream direction. Little attention at first was applied to how or why one segment or zone interacted or depended upon the zone preceding it.

The RCC was developed from an entirely different perspective. Recognizing the greater dependence of a portion of a stream upon its upstream, contiguous portion, the RCC ecologists examined the ideal stream as a whole, rather than a number of distinct parts. (The River Group, as it came to be informally known, in order, included: Robin L. Vannote, Stroud Water Research Center, Academy of Natural Sciences of Philadelphia; G. Wayne Minshall, Idaho State University; Kenneth W. Cummins, Oregon State University; James R. Sedell, Weyerhauser Corporation, Washington; and Colbert E. Cushing, Batelle-Pacific Northwest Laboratories, Washington.)

The stream-order system, developed earlier, provided an outline within which details change in a stream's course—about fishes and insects and their response to changes in currents, temperature, and food availability. It was a matter of filling in the blanks according to stream order in a downstream direction.

The RCC emphasized the idea that streams do not really exist in parts or zones, but rather in a predictable, continuous pattern that evolves downstream in accordance with physical factors. The RCC was intended as a *template*—a model—against which any stream could be compared and examined.

◆   ◆   ◆

THE RCC EMPHASIZED TWO major features of stream ecology. First, the *structure* of biological communities changes downstream—the numbers and kinds of plants, insects, and fish. Second, organism *functions* also change downstream—in accordance with food resources available.

Organisms can be classified by what they eat, how they interact with each other in competition, and how they may affect their own environment. So we can classify stream organisms further into *functional groups*, a subject we will take up in a later chapter. The important point here is that all functions vary along with structure in the downstream continuum.

Another feature of stream ecology newly emphasized in the RCC was the linkage between the river and the area of its watershed—the relationship between the stream and the size of its valley. Whether the terrestrial watershed is forest, desert, or grassland, the input of terrestrial organic matter—leaves, soil particles, grass, woody debris, or dissolved organic substances—is decisive to the ways in which stream organisms function along the continuum.

In later chapters, we will explore how terrestrially derived organic material gets processed, as well as how fresh plant matter (derived from photosynthesis in the stream) is used. For now, however, what is most important is recognizing the "heritage" aspect of stream communities along the continuum—that is, how biological communities reflect what they inherit from upstream: a legacy of water quality, organic matter, inorganic sediments, and even drifting live organisms.

◆   ◆   ◆

NEITHER STRUCTURE (number and kinds of species) nor function (what they do) evolves smoothly along the stream's continuum. The very fact that physical conditions and their dependent biological conditions change irregularly (but not randomly) is what led to zonation concepts in the first place. Some stream ecologists came to recognize that reaches with different characteristics contrasted with other reaches when conditions were altered downstream, but they also realized that these distinctions do not exist in isolation.

For example, the ideal stream would consist of three broad regions:
- headwaters, first through third orders;
- midreaches, fourth through sixth orders;
- large rivers, seventh through tenth orders.

These three regions approximate the older terms—youthful, mature, and old—mentioned previously. The *headwaters* region is typically small and shaded by streamside vegetation. Clear, cool waters tumble in riffles of steep gradients, often as trout streams. The main feature of the headwaters reach is the source of *energy*. Because intense shading occludes full sunlight from the stream surface, little photosynthesis by green plants in the stream is possible, and little fresh plant matter is produced. Instead, the major input of energy is from terrestrial organic matter contributed by nearby trees, bushes, and other vegetation. Insect species in the biological community are mainly those that can process leaves and other terrestrial vegetation. Headwaters reaches with stream orders first through third are most common. As mentioned previously, such headwaters make up a high percentage of all stream miles in the United States.

Farther downstream, conditions change significantly. The change is not abrupt but gradual; often intergrading sections will be quite long. These *midreaches* with stream orders fourth through sixth are typically wider and, most important, not shaded. Here a canopy of trees and bushes does not close over the stream or even shade the major part of the channel. The water is still clear but warmer, or at least its temperature varies more widely on both a daily and seasonal basis. The smallmouth bass, and sometimes trout, may be the chief sport fishes. Gradients are less steep in these midreaches, and pool-and-riffle sequences develop. In fact, it is often in the midreaches where creeks become rivers.

The three major regions of the River Continuum:
Top—Headwaters, stream order 1-3;
Middle—Midreach, stream order 4-6;
Bottom—Large river, stream order 7-10.

The greater amount of sunshine affects the roles played by stream organisms in midreaches. Penetrating clear water, light stimulates photosynthesis by stream-bottom algae and other plants. The predominance of such fresh plant matter constitutes major changes in the stream's energy availability and the kinds of food for invertebrates. In turn, species with different functions appear here.

Farthest downstream, in *large river* reaches (streams seventh through tenth orders) energy inputs and the organisms' functions change again. Because large rivers are wide, terrestrial material from streamside vegetation now becomes unimportant. Here water is turbid from suspended sediment, preventing sunlight from reaching the streambed and thus inhibiting photosynthesis. Here enrage is carried by organic particles drifting from upstream. Omnivorous fishes predominate in these reaches—suckers, buffalofish, and the introduced carp. Large rivers are more lake-like, so phytoplankton and zooplankton often develop and contribute to the drifting material in the river.

◆   ◆   ◆

STREAM ECOLOGISTS FOR DECADES have been seeking unifying concepts to bring order to their discipline. Many now firmly believe that the great complexity of physical processes, chemical reactions, structure of biological communities, and animal behaviors—all the intricate mixture of organisms and their environments—cannot occur haphazardly along a stream or river. In the biologists' search for order, they have sought a formula, a basic template, a unifying concept that will bring logic and organization out of seeming confusion.

The RCC is such an attempt. It was a bold step, but like many new ideas, it defied conventional wisdom and therefore attracted critical attention and skepticism—as it should. Some criticisms were petty, but others were important and constructive.

Many examples of variances from this basic template have emerged. For instance, some streams have essentially no headwaters region with streambank vegetation at all. These include mountain streams heading up above tree line, streams emitting from caves or lake outlets essentially as midreach-type streams, and streams originating in desert or prairie regions with little surrounding leafy vegetation. These streams, without headwaters, are termed *decapitated*.

Earth's climate and geology differ greatly around the globe, causing variations in rainfall and temperature regimes. Erosional landscapes can be found under control of bedrock, ranging widely in slope and chemical conditions. These *lithologic* controls, which shape the stream's course by bedrock arrangement, can create the variable character along a stream continuum. Lithologic controls may create a low-gradient, slow, deep reach in a stream's mid-course, and below that a return, or *reset*, to a steep profile with stony bottom and other characteristics of a headwater. Streamside trees may increase partway down a prairie stream, forming a *gallery forest* that reverses the usual pattern of shading, terrestrial input, and water temperature. In much of North America, beaver dams and the impoundments behind them have created many such discontinuities in the stream profile, causing stream continuums to reset.

Tributaries may affect the water of the receiving stream, particularly if they are large and different in character. Even without increasing stream order, they cause resets and temporary reversals and accelerate or decelerate downstream succession.

A major cause of variance from the RCC may be the *anthropogenic* factor of human activity. Damming, channelizing, deforestation by logging or fire, pollution, and a host of other such influences have created irreversible changes that mankind has made upon streams and rivers worldwide. All of these factors can produce deviations from the continuum template.

Variation among streams, however, does not invalidate the basic idea of a unifying concept. In fact, it is the search for the reason *why* they differ that helps us to understand the functioning of a stream ecosystem. Through the history of science, it has been the variance—the exception, the anomaly, the out-lier—that often has been the most interesting object of all—and the source of breakthroughs in knowledge.

◆   ◆   ◆

THE STREAM CONTINUUM is not an invariable thread of known events and processes winding its way through a valley. Compared with lakes and other stillwater wetlands, a stream is a vastly more heterogeneous entity. The stream's structure, in fact, may best be viewed as an array of *patches*.

The three major regions of the RCC—headwaters, midreaches, large rivers—are large patches; smaller patches include riffles and pools, beaver ponds, and debris dams; the stone in a riffle is a smaller patch yet.

At an even finer scale, a microscopic concavity on a grain of sand is also a patch, holding a few cells of bacteria or algae. These cells are survivors, perhaps, of a devastating flood—but they hold promise of a later flourishing patch of bacterial or al-gal growth on a stone in a riffle that will provide food for a grazing mayfly nymph.

Patches are not constant. They change in size and character, not only through a stream continuum, but also through time as flow levels increase with spates and decrease with drying. For example, desert streams depend heavily on photosynthesizing plants in their sunlit environments, so changes in the level of biological productivity can be dramatic.

The common thread that promises to bring order out of ap-parent chaos is the continuum's downstream flow of energy and matter. Occasionally, however, some caddisflies and salmon, migrating upstream, bring organic matter, nutrients, and new living cells to headwaters.

The patch mosaic concept complements the RCC. In fact, the study of patch dynamics can enhance the predictive capa-bility of the RCC and add immeasurably to the rich diversity of our continuously increasing understanding of free-flowing rivers.

◆　　　◆　　　◆

THE RIVER GROUP AND ITS ASSOCIATES pointed out that diversity can be defined in terms of *resolution,* or focus. At a coarse resolution, all streams are alike—all are made up of water and flow downslope. At the finest level of resolution, however, each is unique; it's true, you will never find two streams, like two fingerprints, *exactly* alike. Neither level of resolution is very useful in helping us to better understand—whether scientist or fly fisher—the functioning of streams. But between the two extremes in resolution lie levels that make visible interesting patterns: insect life cycles, fish feeding behavior, and all the other functions expressed in the interdependencies of stream organisms and their continually shifting environment.

The original RCC has undergone much fine-tuning. The 1980 model was admittedly a template, largely based on an eastern stream in a deciduous forest. When other streams in different forested or non-forested settings were examined against the original model, differences in detail emerged.

Again, we must not make the RCC a "cage" that would inhibit expansion or further definition. However, as a perception, a product of the human mind, the River Continuum Concept becomes a powerful unifying tool, a major stride in our search for order in the discipline of stream ecology.

TECHNICAL REFERENCES:

Minshall, G. Wayne, Kenneth W. Cummins, Robert C. Petersen, Colbert E. Cushing, Dale A. Bruns, James R. Sedell, and Robin L. Vannote. 1985. Developments in stream ecosystem theory. *Canadian Journal of Fisheries and Aquatic Sciences.* Volume 42, pages 1045-1055.

Vannote, Robin L., G. Wayne Minshall, Kenneth W. Cummins, James R. Sedell, and Colbert E. Cushing. 1980. The River Continuum Concept. *Canadian Journal of Fisheries and Aquatic Sciences.* Volume 37, pages 130-137.

RiverSketch

NORTHWEST PASSAGE

IN THE FEW DECADES AFTER Christopher Columbus landed on a Caribbean island shore, seeking passage to the Orient, other bold explorers probed the eastern coasts of North America, searching out an artery leading through the continental mass. French mariner Jacques Cartier was one of the first. In 1535, he penetrated the St. Lawrence River as far as the future city of Montreal—nearly a thousand miles from the Atlantic Ocean. But a little farther Cartier and crew met impenetrable rapids, and his search for a westward passage came to an end.

Then came a host of explorers, attempting to find a route through North America. The British searched the northern shores toward the Arctic, intuitively believing that a far northern route would eventually be the successful one.

But the French continued the search begun by Cartier, by river. Samuel de Champlain in the early 1600s followed up a major tributary of the St. Lawrence, the Ottawa River, and through other waters to Lakes Huron and Superior. Radisson and Groseilliers in the mid-1600s explored Lake Superior and some of its tributaries; Sieur du Lhut, in the later 1600s, continued the search throughout the Lake Superior country and even overland to connect with the Mississippi River by way of Lake Superior's headwater, the St. Louis River. Others penetrated farther north to Lake Athabaska and there established the legendary fur post, Fort Chipewyan.

For another century, French fur traders dominated the northern forests, lakes, and rivers of eastern North America.

However, after the close of the French and Indian War in 1763, English traders replaced the French on all their routes and trading posts, and France's influence upon the North American fur trade—as well as their search for the Northwest Passage—was extinguished.

One of the most notable attempts to force the wilderness barrier of mountains and wild rivers to the Pacific was that of the Scot, Alexander Mackenzie, an experienced river explorer. Following the long-established route from the St. Lawrence River to Lake Superior and Lake Athabaska, Mackenzie formed his western expedition at Fort Chipewyan in 1793. His route was upstream on the Peace River, leading toward the Rocky Mountains and the Pacific. In the rugged mountain headwaters of the Peace, Mackenzie's party was forced to travel on foot and found another river he thought was the Columbia. Instead, it turned out to be one of the most violent, wildest rivers on the continent, totally impassable. (Later it was named the Fraser, after another British explorer who followed.) Mackenzie capsized in the Fraser, and after a grueling trek westward, again on foot, the party reached the salt water of the Pacific Ocean.

Mackenzie's trailblazing trip was a momentous undertaking; it opened up new paths, expanded geographic knowledge, and enlarged the still-important fur trade. It was the first inland traverse, cross-continent from the Atlantic to the Pacific, by any means. But as a westward trade route to the Orient for European merchants, it proved impracticable; that goal remained elusive. The river search for the Northwest Passage had still not materialized.

Mackenzie published his memoir and journals of his trips in 1801 as *Voyages from Montreal*, which enlarged greatly mankind's knowledge of wild North America. The book was also to stimulate later expeditions—most notably one by two American army captains: Meriwether Lewis and William Clark.

◆   ◆   ◆

INITIAL PLANS FOR LEWIS AND CLARK'S "Corps of Discovery" were hatched in Washington by President Thomas Jefferson and Lewis. It was President Jefferson's favorite project. Negotiations with France were soon to result in the transfer of the Louisiana Purchase, comprising the entire western watershed of the Mississippi River, 800,000 square miles, including the entire drainage of the Missouri River. Jefferson saw it as a hugely significant addition to the United States, rich in natural resources, Indian connections, and trade potential—as well as the possibility of a water passage to the Pacific. Meriwether Lewis was the president's preeminent choice to head the expedition.

With his co-commander, William Clark, and a party of picked men, Lewis and the Corps of Discovery left St. Louis on May 14, 1804, headed upstream on the Missouri River to blaze the river trail to the Pacific. In the uncharted territory of the upper Missouri, Lewis and Clark and their party fought wild river currents, punishing portages, tense confrontations with natives, illness and injury, hordes of vicious mosquitoes, and finally, in the uppermost mountain headwaters, the high, snowy passes of the Bitterroot peaks. It was only with the assistance of friendly Shoshoni Indians—and their horses—that the party was successful in forcing the trackless mountains to the west slopes of the Columbia River drainage. After following the tortuous paths of its tributaries and steep valleys, on November 7, 1805, they finally reached the Columbia's mouth and Pacific shores. The trip west had entailed some four thousand miles.

Jefferson had wanted a "water communication," and Lewis and Clark had expended enormously difficult labors to find it. But again, the desired water route, open to easy trade, had proven elusive. Like Mackenzie's expedition in Canada, the track of Lewis and Clark's expedition was not the Northwest Passage of their dreams.

But the consequence of their discoveries in the western wilds of the United States was a seminal contribution toward future exploration, expanding geographic and scientific awareness of this new, huge portion of the nation, as well as of the new territory between the Rocky Mountains and the Pacific Ocean, then in British control. Jefferson gave high praise to the two captains.

◆   ◆   ◆

The Head Water of the Missouri River

Lewis and Clark became confused at the junction of Three Forks—the Gallatin, Madison, and Jefferson rivers (which they named)—but chose the correct one, the Jefferson, leading toward the upper Columbia River and the Pacific Ocean.
(Courtesy Murphy Library, University of Wisconsin, LaCrosse.)

IN THE LAST QUARTER OF THE 1500s, English navigators began to sail the far northern seas off the American continent, seeking passage to the Orient. These were the opening scenes of immense endeavor to find the Northwest Passage by sea. But three centuries of Arctic struggle, from both sides of the continent, were to pass before eventual success was attained.

Weaving through an incredible maze of islands large and small, dead-end bays and straits, icebergs the size of islands themselves, and at times frozen in thick ice, ships and men persevered in their quest, many never to return.

The final assault on the Arctic Archipelago, by young Norwegian mariner Roald Amundsen, was successful in the ultimate passage from ocean to ocean. Leaving Oslo in June of 1903, spending two winters locked in ice, Amundsen in August, 1905, entered the eastern end of the Beaufort Sea and there encountered an American whaler, out of San Francisco. Although his ship—along with the whaler—was to be locked in ice for one more winter, Amundsen wrote in his journal, "Victory at last!" The passage, entirely by water, although delayed three times by the ice of Arctic winters, had indeed been victorious, from the Atlantic to the Pacific.

◆   ◆   ◆

THE CONSUMMATE STRUGGLE to find a route across the North American continent, by river and sea a century apart, undeniably had been successful. Neither approach, however, resulted in a practical trade route, and soon after, a third means—by air—seemed to make these watery endeavors moot. But the river and sea struggles to find the Northwest Passage—with all the trials and tragedies that those pursuits entailed—remain among the brightest in the history of mankind's continuing need to explore the unknown.

SELECTED REFERENCES:

Ambrose, Stephen E. 1996. *Undaunted Courage: Meriwether Lewis, Thomas Jefferson, and the opening of the American West*. Simon & Schuster, New York.
Lehane, Brendan, and Editors of Time-Life Books. 1981. *The Northwest Passage*. Time-Life Books, Alexandria, Virginia.

Part Two

The Living
Valley

Introduction to Part Two

THE LIVING VALLEY

LONG BEFORE THE TERMS *ecosystem, landscape ecology, biome,* and other such words became popular in the field of ecology, human perception must have resulted in the realization that much of what fell into a valley as precipitation ended up in its river as flowing water.

We *knew* that, but we did not really *believe* it.

So when early settlers built their homes, farms, and towns on flat, verdant river floodplains, it seemed perfectly logical. After all: soils were rich and productive, river transportation was nearby, water supply handy—logical, that is, until some wild, wet spring night when the heavens opened and the reason why it was called a *flood*plain became painfully apparent.

Destructive floods are not our main object in this Part Two, which examines the interrelationships between the stream and its valley. But floods have long been some of the most obvious manifestations of a valley's influence on its river. We'll deal with floods and other disasters in later sections. Our larger objective here will be to explore the stream in a more "normal" state, especially how the valley influences the stream's condition.

Somewhere within a valley a stream begins, a point or a process that continues to fascinate us. Sometimes this beginning is discrete and sometimes unfocused; the beginnings are many and varied in kind. Although our main thrust in this part is on the relationship between the stream and its valley, we will first focus on the influence exerted upon the quality of its upper reaches by the stream's source. I have chosen to coin the term *rheogenesis* to use in describing a stream's birthing (rheo- = current or stream; genesis = origin or beginning). Many factors within a valley determine a stream's rheogenesis.

Much has been said and written about the term *ecosystem*, and much of it has been inaccurate. Technically defined, an ecosystem is a space on Earth where organisms interact with each other and their physical environment in an orderly manner.

Around the beginning of the 1900s, the term "microcosm" was popular, at the time meaning a natural community of organisms that operated "as a world within itself," independent from the rest of the world, like a closed lake isolated from all other influences. We soon came to know that a lake did not, and could not, function as if it were completely isolated.

We have come to view an ecosystem as a space with a community that is not truly independent, but rather as a functioning, orderly community with a source of energy (usually sunlight) and a logical pattern of energy flow through successive trophic levels of living plants and animals.   Our world has many such orderly systems, rather than having organisms scattered randomly across Earth's surface. The ecosystem concept brings sense and organization to what would otherwise be a hopeless jumble. There are many sizes and kinds of ecosystems, all of which overlap at their edges; large ecosystems contain smaller ecosystems within them.

We can easily conceive of an individual lake as an ecosystem; sunlight provides energy for photosynthesis that is passed through an orderly system of plants and animals. A river, however, cannot be viewed the same way, although some scholars tried valiantly to fit streams into the same set of physical formulas that seemed to control lakes. Flowing water made such attempts unreasonable; the stream system was simply too "leaky."

The stream does fit the idea of an ecosystem in many respects—sunlight, algae, invertebrates, fish, and so on. However, even this definition seemed to demand revision when studies of small woodland streams revealed that almost no photosynthesis occurred in their heavily shaded waters! Yet, these streams had normal populations of invertebrates and fish. What was their energy source? What did aquatic insects and other invertebrates feed on?

It was at this point that ecologists came to realize that stream banks could not be the borders of stream ecosystems, and necessary energy was soon identified as having a terrestrial source. In valley uplands, sunlight provides for photosynthesis—in trees, shrubs, grasses, and other plants—and energy to serve the needs of the stream's biological community. In valleys, everything runs downhill, and all kinds of terrestrially derived organic matter moves down valley slopes to stream channels, providing energy and nutrients to the stream's inhabitants. Stream ecologists came to understand that although the stream may sculpt its own erosional landscape, its character is also the product of its valley.

We'll fine-tune this process of energy supply from the valley and later explore some other interdependencies of valley and stream—water, chemicals, water temperature—that are important in all ecosystems.

And so it is the *valley* that has come to be viewed as the defined stream ecosystem, the basic unit of our river world. This is the holistic view, which considers the system as a whole. In a stream ecosystem, the valley slopes, tributaries, and the channel itself all contribute to the nature of the stream. The borders of this ecosystem are not the stream banks, but the high rims of the valley—the ridge tops where the landscape falls off to a neighboring valley, which is another, contiguous ecosystem.

We'll dig into the concept of the stream ecosystem more fully as we go along. It's a principle that concerns us more than any other in this entire book, a basic idea that is fundamental to the discipline of stream and river science.

Chapter 4

RHEOGENESIS

T HE SEARCH FOR THE ORIGIN OF RIVERS has long fascinated. mankind. Indeed, the question of just where all that seemingly unending water comes from occupied some of the greatest intellects from the beginnings of ancient science.

Over two millennia ago, Aristotle perceived some of the basics of the hydrologic cycle, and later philosophers in the first century suspected that rainfall was the source of river water. For the most part, however, the great thinkers of the Middle Ages perceived the *ocean* as the source, believing that it entered the groundwater of Earth's landmasses to become the fountainheads of inland, freshwater streams.

Not until the late 17th century was it proven to the satisfaction of contemporary naturalists that rainfall was indeed sufficient to provide water for the Earth's rivers on a sustained basis.

Even now, when modern scholars of streams set out to examine the changing character of a river or stream throughout its course, it seems only natural and logical to begin at the beginning: at the stream's source. The journey downstream encompasses all the processes and alterations, leading to a final, complete image of the mature river.

Logical, to be sure—but historically the major explorations of rivers did not proceed that way. Exploration began at the mouth, or at least at some significant downstream point, and worked upstream—in some cases to search for riches, in others to search for beginnings.

In 1832, geologist Henry Rowe Schoolcraft paddled and poled north from the civilization of midwestern United States to the wilds of northern Minnesota, where he discovered (albeit with the help of a local Ojibway guide) the source of the mighty Mississippi, naming it Lake Itasca. Englishmen Sir Richard Burton and John Speke struggled upstream from Egypt through central Africa's deserts, swamps, and hostile native populations to seek the source of the Nile, which Speke, in 1862, declared to be Lake Victoria. Nearly 140 years later, however, the world is still unable to agree on the Nile's ultimate source.

There is good reason for this seemingly reverse plan of exploration. Ancient cities were located at mouths of rivers, the crossroads of river transportation, not on first-order trickles in the wilderness. Explorers, traders, settlers began their travels at downstream sites because that's where their first, new forts and habitations were located. The discovery of new continents began at the mouths of rivers that could be approached by sailing ships from across the sea. Rivers were the only practicable means of transportation into the hinterlands.

The famed discoverers in history have had their detractors. Lake Victoria has tributaries, for example: Does that make them or the lake the Nile's source? Some folks claim that a raindrop, falling from a pine needle high up above the first noticeable trickle in the north woods is the ultimate source of the Mississippi. Of course, Minnesotans familiar with Lake Itasca know that such a raindrop must flow quite a ways—including through another lake—before it traverses Lake Itasca and its rocky outlet. Even so, most of us agree in our maps and songs that it is in the riffled effluent where the greatest river in North America really starts.

Our purpose in this book is not to explore new lands, but to discover the nature of rivers and streams. To accomplish this goal, we'll begin at the source: the birthing of a river, its *rheogenesis*.

However, the ultimate source—the absolute debut of a flowing stream—may not be easy to find. It may even move around a bit. Our raindrop falling from a pine needle may indeed enter the Mississippi drainage, depending on the vicissitudes of wind and forest litter. But it might as easily fall to become the source of the St. Lawrence River leading to the North Atlantic, or the Red River of the North leading to Hudson Bay. A slight rise of land and a small monument near Hibbing, Minnesota, mark the spot. Such triple origins occur wherever the boundaries of three separate drainages meet. But try to find the source of your favorite stream, then chances are you will become totally frustrated as smaller and smaller rivulets simply disappear!

Just as the nature of the valley determines the nature of the stream, we will find that the origin of a river is likewise determined by the valley: its geological formations, its vegetation and soils, its slopes and gradients.

◆   ◆   ◆

IN AN EARLIER ERA of attempts to classify streams, the invention of terms and graphic names was very popular. In a previous chapter, we mentioned the rhithron and the potamon, the upstream, swift reach with stony bottom, and the downstream reach with slow, silty bottom, respectively.

Upstream from the rhithron, it was believed, lay another kind of origin—the springs, pools, and collections of trickles that feed the rhithron but do not by themselves constitute a distinct reach of stream. Because many streams originate in springs, the term *crenon* was coined in the mid-1900s for this zone, generally meaning a spring or system of spring brooklets. Such a term could be used to help understand the organisms living in these habitats.

Not entirely satisfied with crenon, however, early stream scientists continued to refine their ideas about headwaters with ever more specific names. These terms are little used today, probably to the relief of most stream ecologists. In the Horton system, the designation of the region of tiny stream sources has been proposed as *Zero Order* in modern usage. The development of this lexicon of origins illustrates our struggle to communicate an increasing understanding of the birth of streams. In all probability, that struggle is not yet over.

♦   ♦   ♦

THE SOURCE OF MOST STREAMS is groundwater. And now that we are agreed that the source of groundwater is not the salty oceans, but rather rainfall and other forms of precipitation from the atmosphere, it seems appropriate to consider a few basic principles of groundwater.

Most of us are already familiar with the *hydrologic cycle* in which water falls from the atmosphere as rain or snow, runs down landmasses in rivers to the sea, and there evaporates back to the atmosphere. Some hydrologists prefer the term hydrologic *sequence* to *cycle*, because the broad concept of a cycle obscures so many interceptions, time delays, subordinate cycles, and other details that a great deal of interesting information can be missed.

For example, not all precipitation reaches land surface; some evaporates before it reaches the surface. And much does not run down rivers at all; some is intercepted by tree leaves and other vegetation, or by the forest litter on the ground, and evaporates. Our concern with groundwater is with that which gets through or around these obstacles and reaches mineral soil.

There is one more withdrawal before precipitation becomes groundwater-*cum*-river: all stemmed plants take up water from the soil through their root systems. Some is used in the production of plant tissue, but a good deal more is lost through transpiration, which is what we term the loss of water vapor from the plant into the atmosphere. Transpiration losses from certain forests are large enough to decrease stream flow (or to increase stream flow after these forests are cut).

The water remaining after these withdrawals is now available as groundwater or runoff to continue through the hydrologic sequence toward the sea. Surface runoff includes overland flow that is usually very minor, but runoff is mainly by streams and rivers.

There are other exceptions. Some precipitation freezes as snow and ice during Temperate Zone winters, temporarily delaying runoff, or freezes as glaciers in polar regions and high mountains through longer periods. Some is delayed in our many small natural lakes, in reservoirs, and in large cul-de-sacs like Lake Michigan.

But most of the precipitation remaining is available to infiltrate the mineral soil in large quantities, where it percolates downward through rock and porous soil material finally to become groundwater.

The fate of almost all groundwater is to become discharged onto the land surface again, somewhere downhill, as springs or, as hydrologists call them, *groundwater outcrops.* Now the former groundwater becomes available to enter (or to initiate) streams and rivers.

This chapter could end at this point. We have, after all, covered at least briefly the genesis of rivers. But the stream ecologist—as differentiated from the hydrologist—is interested in other, more detailed aspects of groundwater and its relationship to living organisms. For example, we are concerned with the quality of spring water. Its temperature, oxygen content, and nutrient concentration are some of its most important qualities. All of these reflect the nature of the valley and help to determine the quality of the stream.

Groundwater flow does not depend upon recent rainstorms. Rather, it is the result of long-term accumulation in the valley, integrating inputs of precipitation over long periods of time. Groundwater flow is slow and its quantity stable, and its upper surface is the actual water table. The stream flow produced entirely by groundwater is what both the hydrologist and stream ecologist call *base flow* in a stream. To biological communities in streams, base flow is the norm. To the stream angler, baseflow conditions mean low, clear water, where insect emergences and fish-feeding orgies occur as expected—to the angler's great delight, of course.

But when a summer thundershower erupts and rain falls, drowning emerging mayflies and raising water levels, it is the increase in groundwater flow, above the water table, that is mainly responsible and that affects both stream-bottom communities and angling success. This subsurface flow moves much more rapidly, flowing through unsaturated soil and fractured rock above the water table, than does the groundwater below the water table. Entering springs and stream channels, subsurface flow raises and roils streams in spate, and may even raise a stream's level above its banks in flood.

A valley's uplands of plateaus and hills constitute the *recharge* area, and the lowlands of valley floor and floodplain are the *discharge* areas of springs, or groundwater outcrops. These waters are fairly constant in their temperature and chemistry. As such, springs can function as refuges for stream organisms in times of flood and drought. Typically, the recharge area is large, constituting up to 95 percent of total drainage area, but it is in the smaller discharge areas that we find our rheogeneses.

◆　　　　◆　　　　◆

ALL OF US HAVE SEEN SPRINGS, small or large. Some are notably large, like Silver Springs of Florida or Kitchitikipi in Michigan's Upper Peninsula. But more commonly we are used to the little boils of water and sand on the streambed of a creek. Most of these groundwater outcrops are just that: groundwater emerging onto the land after having flowed slowly downhill, underground, from its recharge area.

Across most of northern North America, landscapes are the result of glacial till, the debris left from the continental ice sheets of the Pleistocene Epoch. Lying upon lower strata of impermeable rock, saturated glacial till of sand and gravel constitutes an *unconfined aquifer*, through which groundwater flows easily, under little pressure.

In the discharge area of the valley's lowlands, where the surface of the unconfined aquifer (that is, the water table) meets the open air springs are formed. Sometimes these springs arise in a discrete basin, and a spring pool, the *limnocrene*, forms, becoming the origin of a small stream.

More often, however, the spring is not discrete and only occurs as a seep—a wet, boggy area. And out of the seep may eventually flow a tiny rivulet—also the origin of a stream. The area of a seep may be variable through time: becoming larger after several years of wet, rainy weather, or smaller after several years of drought. The search for the ultimate source of this kind of stream can be greatly frustrating.

In karst topography, many "sinks" are formed on the surface, connecting to cave-ins leading to subterranean regions.

An artesian spring occurs when a *confined aquifer* reaches the land surface. Such an aquifer occurs between two impermeable layers of rock or compressed sediment, so that considerable water pressure builds in the confined aquifer, the result of the downward trending water mass farther "uphill" in the aquifer. In this case, the spring has a definite upward movement, in some cases becoming literally a fountain and creating the most identifiable source of stream: the artesian spring.

In arid regions, spring headwaters may develop into sizable streams that disappear into a permeable land surface to become groundwater again. This event constitutes sort of a *restart* to the process of rheogenesis. The upper stream thus constitutes an island of sorts, its aquatic plants and animals isolated from other water bodies. If the isolation lasts long enough (for example, thousands or millions of years) and remains unmodified by human activities, natural evolutionary processes may create new strains or species, like the many subspecies and other genetic stocks of cutthroat trout inhabiting the high mountains of western North America.

Some of the most evident and distinct sources of streams occur in what is known as *karst* landscapes. The term is taken from a locality in Yugoslavia and refers to a landscape dominated by features that occur above soluble, sedimentary bedrock, such as limestone. In this type of landscape, the dissolution of limestone underground creates caverns (some very large, like Mammoth Cave in Kentucky), surface "sinks" or cave-ins, and underground rivers.

About 20 percent of Earth's land surface is karst topography, underlain by large deposits of limestone bedrock. The fact that the limestone is subject to dissolution by percolating rainwater has left a great legacy of karst landscape and some of our most distinctive systems of stream and river origins.

Natural, uncontaminated rainfall is always slightly acidic, due to diffusion of atmospheric carbon dioxide into water droplets (creating the weak carbonic acid). The acidic nature of percolating rainfall, however weak, dissolves limestone, albeit slowly. From the caverns that form, flowing waters eventually open to the surface, sometimes as a full-blown river large enough to canoe or fish.

(Here is an example of an anomaly in the Horton stream-order system. Such a stream would by definition be a first-order stream but actually may be as large as a stream of a much higher order, perhaps by several levels.)

Underground flow from a cave is termed a *conduit spring;* this underground flow leading to the surface opening is like water flowing confined within a large pipe. Being exposed to the air of a cavern's atmospheric oxygen, conduit springs are usually well oxygenated.

A cave source of a highly productive trout stream,
Forestville Creek, Minnesota.

A primary factor affecting stream water is the chemical
makeup of the water in the stream's source. Most springs in karst
topography are of the conduit type, but all springs resulting from
groundwater that saturates limestone bedrock will be high in dissolved limestone. Thus, one of the more important chemical factors of spring water, particularly in the conduit springs of karst
topography, is a high concentration of calcium, in the form of
calcium bicarbonate. Calcium gives water the attribute we call
hardness and bicarbonate the quality we call *alkalinity*. Calcium

bicarbonate, the soluble product of carbonic acid dissolving the calcium carbonate of limestone, is often responsible for high biological productivity. Many of the trout angler's beloved limestone streams have a conduit spring genesis.

By accident, perhaps, much of Earth's karst topography occurs in temperate and southern regions. For chemical and climatic reasons, these are the world's great agricultural areas. Consequently, modern-day effluents of agriculture, such as organic matter, nutrients, and pesticides, now affect streams and rivers flowing through karst topography.

A conduit spring gushes from a hillside bordering a small stream in the karst region of southeastern Minnesota.

Under storm conditions, some large conduit springs carry quantities of surface wastes—fertilizers, herbicides, and crop residues—from sinks located among cultivated fields. Unfortunately, although surface effluents may include fertilizing nutrients that increase the productivity of a prized trout stream, they may also include field pesticides that can destroy a valuable fishery.

In contrast to the conduit spring is the *diffuse spring,* in which the groundwater leading to a surface opening flows slowly through compacted, though permeable, soil materials like sand

and gravel, or even through highly permeable sedimentary rock. An important difference is that the diffuse spring's water may be devoid of oxygen, especially if it has remained below ground for a long time, a condition important to aquatic life in the immediate vicinity of the spring opening.

The temperature of stream origins often is the primary factor determining fish species. Because groundwater is cooler than air temperature in summer, the temperature of spring water also remains low. If tributaries along the stream's course are near groundwater sources, the stream may remain *summercool* for its entire length. This type of thermal regimen produces conditions suitable for trout and other salmonids or, if just a little warmer in summer, smallmouth and rock bass.

But in streams originating mainly from surface or subsurface drainage or dispersed seeps, water temperatures follow seasonal changes in air temperature more closely, and therefore are not low enough in summer for coldwater fishes. Instead, warmwater species may predominate, often starting with the creek chub in headwaters, a result when seeps of cool groundwater, draining into a trout stream, are destroyed by agricultural cultivation.

When spring water is devoid of oxygen, it often contains soluble *ferrous* compounds, that is, dissolved iron-containing chemicals. When these waters emerge into open springs and the atmosphere, oxygen diffuses rapidly into the water, reacting with the ferrous compounds to create *ferric oxide*, which is not soluble. The precipitate of ferric oxide floats on the water surface to produce a glimmering, rainbow-hued sheen, much like an oil slick. This slick is not indicative of subsurface oil riches. To tell the difference, poke a twig into the slick, and if it breaks up into discrete segments, it's only ferric oxide. On the other hand, if it simply swirls around without breaking up, you may become wealthy!

Many streams exit from lakes, but a lake outlet is not likely to be the ultimate headwater. Tributary streams entering the lake always lead upstream to technically more legitimate sources—like our raindrop on a pine needle. Nevertheless, the character of the flow from a lake is more likely to affect stream conditions below the lake than the upper sources do. One of the major factors is the release of lake-produced organisms into the stream: phyto-plankton, zooplankton, and larger invertebrates, including insects. Although organisms evolved to lake conditions may not indefinitely survive the stream environment, they nonetheless serve as an abundant food supply for stream animals below the lake outlet. This somewhat anomalous food source continues sometimes for miles downstream, resulting in an extremely productive fish population. Similar conditions are obtained artificially in the tailwaters of some dams and reservoirs, where some of our most popular fisheries have been created, particularly trout fisheries in near-bottom releases of cool water from reservoirs and dams.

The beginning of a stream on the surface of a mountain glacier,
a headwater of the North Saskatchewan River, Alberta.

We have not exhausted all of the possible means by which streams and rivers begin. The glacial stream, for example, is common in polar regions. In temperate zones, this type of stream arises as meltwater from mountain glaciers. When a small stream begins to flow on the surface of ice, it is crystal clear (and, of course, very cold); this melting takes place more in summer than in winter, and more in daytime than at night, for it depends on seasonal and daily changes in air temperature. Farther downstream, the glacial rivulet picks up more meltwater and becomes larger, until it finally resembles any other large stream or river of the Temperate Zone that flows through forest land or prairie. Glacial meltwater also emits from beneath glaciers, where the moving ice grinds along on a mineral soil surface, creating friction and much heat. These streams may not be clear, but instead appear whitish or milky from the grinding of rock under the ice.

Meltwaters occurred in enormous quantities during the period of glacial retreat 10,000 years ago, when cold continental climates were warming. These waters often carried massive amounts of sand and gravel that spread out over the landscape to create extensive sand plains and water-sorted gravel. The meltwaters also formed vast glacial lakes. Streams emitting from them were also very large and flowed for long periods—hundreds or thousands of years—during which deep valleys were formed. Today we can see the result of these long-ago natural events in some of our major river valleys, where streams may now be relatively small but flow through wide, deep valleys—a puzzle to early geologists. Such streams are known as *underfit*. An outstanding example was the Glacial River Warren, which emitted from huge Glacial Lake Agassiz, the largest in North America, in portions of present Manitoba, North Dakota, and Minnesota. Today, the Minnesota River winds through a valley much too large to have been carved by the present stream.

◆   ◆   ◆

ALTHOUGH THE CHEMICAL COMPOSITION and temperature of a stream's source water are extremely important, they only jumpstart the biological processes and events in the larger stream. In other words, springs, trickles, and other sources provide only an initial nourishing environment.

It is into this initial chemical and thermal mix that other products of the valley now inject additional vital elements. Included are the chemistry of oxygen, alkalinity, and nutrients. Temperature of tributaries and groundwater, the kind and abundance of riparian vegetation (determining shade or sunlight), and—most important of all—the energy that drives the biological engines of animal communities, invertebrates and fishes, all affect the nature of the stream through its entire course.

TECHNICAL REFERENCES:

Gordon, Nancy D., Thomas A. McMahon, and Brian L. Finlayson. 1992. *Stream Hydrology: An introduction for ecologists.* John Wiley & Sons, New York.

Troelstrup, Nels H., and James A. Perry. 1989. Water quality in southeastern Minnesota streams: Observations along a gradient of land use and geology. *Journal of the Minnesota Academy of Science.* Volume 55, issue 1, pages 6-13.

RiverSketch

SPRINGS AND TRIBUTARIES

DID YOU EVER WONDER WHY THE WATERS of a good trout stream stay cool—even under the blazing sun of a late summer afternoon? Of course, you will remember that big springwater cave, or shaded, swampy wetland out of which trickled many tiny rivulets of icy, clear water. But all the way downstream from the main source, you've probably stepped over, or staggered into, other small trickles that emit almost unseen from the stream bank, a rocky cliff, or just a sticky mud hole at the main stream's edges. Or maybe an actual but tiny stream by itself, perhaps almost covered by watercress, leads away from the river into shaded woodlands.

These small seeps and dribbles of springwater we term *springs and tributaries*, a legal phrase that has important implications to the continued health of summercool streams, creeks, and rivers.

State statutes that define springs and tributaries usually give them full protection against row-crop cultivation and other land uses that would destroy these important sources of cool, clean water. Most states do not have such laws, especially in the West, but should.

In the Ozark Mountains, Alley Spring supplements the Jacks Fork River in a region where many large springs provide source waters.

Springs and tributaries make up an extremely important component of the *riparian zone,* a "thin green line" of wetter, greener, and richer belt of unique vegetation along almost all streams. Natural resources scientists have given a great deal of study to the concept of the riparian zone. Much research has been directed not only to the zone's natural beneficial influence on the stream, but also to the various practical safeguards. When implemented, those protections help to preserve the riparian zone and thus the natural values of the river.

Buffering the stream against degrading influences from upland activities such as cultivation, grazing, and logging, the riparian zone—if left undisturbed—filters out sediment, logging debris, livestock wastes, and non-point pollutants of many kinds. It is here in this dynamic, energizing, and productive corridor so vibrant and biologically diverse, that the microorganisms, unique animals, and highly active photosynthesizing plants can change destructive chemicals and degrading substances into benign or useful organic matter. Protected by both biology and law, the riparian zone nurtures and shields the cool waters of springs and tributaries, sustaining the high quality of water in the rivers you wade or float.

Science has a special name for such an interfacing corridor—*ecotone*—where two different ecological systems collide and overlap. These create a third system, greatly dynamic, interjected between the other two. There, gradients continually change and produce a transition zone that protects the two original systems. The riparian zone, an ecotone, also prevents the stream water from widening and shallowing. Similarly, the riparian zone protects trickles and cool, clean springs and tributaries from spreading and warming. Natural disturbances from both sides of a stream riparian zone create an environmental mosaic without parallel among the Earth's ecological systems—dynamic, mitigating, protective.

The physical dimensions of riparian zones vary greatly and are difficult to generalize. One definition is the area influenced by flooding. More specifically, three principal reaches of a stream with springs and tributaries can be described:

• headwater reaches completely embedded into woodlands, where surrounding trees and bushes may constitute the major riparian function;

• middle reaches that have the largest and most dynamic riparian zone, determined by river flow;

• large rivers with broad floodplains, often alternating between one side of the river and the other.

Within any riparian zone, tiny trickles of emerging groundwater in springs and tributaries may penetrate the immediate terrestrial surroundings, places that, compared to the stream itself can be isolated from harsh conditions that threaten aquatic life. These extensions of the riparian zone must be protected, by law if necessary, if we wish to maintain the natural values of coldwater inputs from the groundwater. In large gravel-bottom rivers, water that flows in subsurface (hyporheic) gravel aquifers may emerge farther downstream as surface springs thus returning to the river. During its underground passage, water becomes cooled to groundwater temperature and picks up dissolved nutrients from microorganisms that prosper beneath the floodplain surface.

Springs and tributaries can serve as essential refuges for invertebrates that might be extirpated by sediment or pulses of toxic agricultural chemicals. For example, watercress often holds huge quantities of *Gammarus,* and even short reaches of gravel harbor many mayfly, caddis, and stonefly immatures. After toxic conditions dissipate in the stream, organisms protected in small tributaries can soon reinoculate the entire stream and restore its former invertebrate populations. Such refuges also serve trout or other fishes, protecting them against total losses in times of floods or high temperatures in droughts.

Springs and tributaries help keep trout streams cool in summer, but also relatively warm in winter, an advantage to brook and brown trout eggs incubating in gravel redds. Springs and groundwater tributaries are especially important for thermally marginal streams that become too warm in summer and make the main stream untenable for short periods.

Rampant destruction of riparian zones is common in the arid West, where livestock grazing along streams is common. When cattle are allowed unrestricted access to small streams, spring seeps become trampled, spread out, and unshaded, where intense sunlight warms the water, which then loses its cooling effect on the main stream. Fencing cattle back from riparian areas has shown striking improvement in stream conditions, and some advances in implementation have been made. On some public lands, new rules and regulations have been effective; some ranchers have been cooperative and have seen for themselves the advantages of riparian area protection. Nevertheless, huge difficulties remain.

Successful management schemes to protect the stream ecosystems everywhere must pay attention to three components:
- land use in the uplands of the catchment;

- riparian zones to buffer stream edges, with their springs and tributaries;
- proper management of the stream itself, nurturing entire native biological communities.

In the past we emphasized first the stream channel, and secondly the quality of the uplands. Now a greater appreciation of the riparian system is critically needed, recognizing this important linkage between water and land—with its spring seeps and cold tributaries that help protect the natural attributes of our valued streams and rivers.

SELECTED REFERENCES:

Gregory, Stanley V., Frederick J. Swanson, W. Arthur McKee, and Kenneth W. Cummins. 1991. An ecosystem perspective of riparian zones. *BioScience.* Volume 41, pages 540-551.

Naiman, Robert J., and Henri Décamps. 1997. The ecology of interfaces: Riparian zones. *Annual Reviews of Ecology and Systematics.* Volume 28, pages 621-58.

Chapter 5

THE STREAM ECOSYSTEM

Probably the mention of a *valley* brings to mind a clear, pleasant image to most of us. A wide open scene with forested hills on either side, a winding stream in the center of a green floodplain covered with rich, natural vegetation or perhaps a field of corn, is just one possibility of such an image. Another might be a grassland prairie set deeply between mountain ranges, a rancher's delight. Or a Shangri-la. We also may equate the valley with terms like watershed, or drainage basin.

And now, *catchment*, the scientist's term. Why yet another label?

We now use the term *catchment* for several good reasons. For one, although *valley* is perhaps the most colorful word, it is vague in its dimensions; for most folks, *valley* does not necessarily convey an area with distinct borders. *Watershed* can mean something quite different—a milepost, a change of plan or life style, a ridge between two valleys. And *drainage basin* is the hydrologist's term—a label defining a valley with distinct borders of dashed lines and an emphasis on how many acres it contains.

Catchment adds a different emphasis. Its significance in stream ecology is that it "catches" two elements vastly important to any stream: precipitation and the sun's rays. Looking back to our definition of an ecosystem, we know that for an aquatic ecosystem, an abundant source of water is required; for any ecosystem, an external source of energy is required. For any stream ecosystem, everything within the catchment becomes of importance—the rain and snow that provide water for the stream's source, groundwater to maintain stream flow throughout its length, and mechanisms for transporting nutrients and organic matter from the uplands to the stream channel. Sunlight permits photosynthesis in the riparian zone and upland forests, as well as in the stream channel itself.

But the stream channel alone is not a complete ecosystem. Only when the entire catchment is included, along with all the processes taking place throughout, do we have a biologically functioning ecosystem. More than anything else, the term *catchment* accentuates the terrestrial part of the valley as an essential component of the stream ecosystem. When we enlarge our perspective from the stream channel alone to the landscape of the catchment, we are immediately led to a broader perspective. The riparian zone is the most obvious new component, with its inputs of water, chemicals, and organic matter. But the entire landscape also influences the stream, if not so obviously, affecting the shape of the channel, water supply and temperature, sediment inputs, and nutrient delivery.

At the end of the nineteenth century, scholars of the natural world had little understanding of the importance of a terrestrial influence on streams and rivers. This was long before the terms *ecology* and *ecologist* were invented; the subject was *natural history*, and the scholars were *naturalists*. Although they were interested in describing living organisms and their life histories, just as scientists are today, their accumulated knowledge of function and dynamics was sparse. They lacked a major element in their understanding of natural history: the critical dependence of a stream's condition upon its terrestrial surroundings.

This oversight was due in part to researchers' emphasis on headwater reaches. Their bias was perhaps understandable: headwater reaches are most often small and clear, unpolluted, frequently attractive trout streams, easy to wade and sample. But naturalists' appreciation of the entire stream continuum was too often missing, and this narrow view did not allow room for a broader emphasis on function and dynamics in the entire stream system. This bias is still present to some extent today.

Whether the mountain wilderness valley of Alberta's Bow River
or the pastoral Whitewater Valley in the hills of southern Minnesota,
ecosystem processes and functions are much the same.
(Whitewater photo from David Palmquist,
Minnesota State Parks Interpretive Services.)

During the first few decades of the 20th century, however, appreciation of the terrestrial influence increased, albeit slowly. By mid-century, the idea of the stream life's dependence upon water, organic matter, and energy inputs from the terrestrial environment was becoming more acceptable. Even so, in his pioneering text on stream ecology in 1970, Professor Hynes emphasized the fact that accumulated data on the subject was inadequate.

With the publication of his "The Stream and its Valley" in 1975, however, Professor Hynes provided a stimulation to research that swept the scientific community of stream ecologists worldwide. Outcomes of this increased effort include the River Continuum Concept and many other topics that we deal with in this volume.

◆　　　　◆　　　　◆

FIRST, LET'S LOOK AT THE STREAM'S fundamental morphology: the channel's shape and size, affected by its terrestrial surroundings and the nature of its streambed. In previous sections, we discussed such physical characteristics of channels that together create the morphology of a stream. These include slope or gradient, current velocity and discharge, bottom type, and stream order. Of course, these traits vary from stream to stream, and few streams conform exactly to the idealized profile.

We have previously considered the valley as an erosional landscape, the result of work done by the stream and its tributaries. But these erosional results are best viewed along a gradient. In other words, the shape of a valley may vary with the degree of erosion. Underlying bedrock, for example, exerts some control over the catchment shape; the slope, hardness, erodibility, permeability, depth below overlying soil or glacial deposits, all affect the valley landscape to varying degrees. The properties of the catchment determine the properties of the stream.

◆   ◆   ◆

A stream's morphology is controlled and
strangely molded in a hard lava catchment:
Temperance River, a northern tributary of Lake Superior.

WHEN A STREAM AND VALLEY OCCUR in a natural, vegetated state,
overland runoff from precipitation may be very slight, and true
overland flow is rare. Most rain penetrates the soil and permeable
bedrock and may remain there for a long time as groundwater.

When heavy precipitation falls, it displaces the "old" water in the ground, which then moves downward and laterally to stream channels.

As groundwater, the "old" water has had a chance to reach a constant, relatively low temperature. In summer, it will be cooler than air. Furthermore, the stored water has had a longer time to dissolve chemicals from the subsurface soil and rock than from surface soils—calcium, as an example.

We can view the entire catchment as a huge reservoir containing soil and rock saturated with water. It discharges water underground to the stream, slowly at most times, more rapidly when augmented by recent rains that have infiltrated the land.

Exceptions occur when extraordinary rainstorms exceed the valley's reservoir capacity and cause heavy overland flow, or when slopes and floodplain surfaces have been disturbed and made impermeable by activities like heavy equipment use and the laying down of urban streets.

Catchments composed largely of impermeable igneous rock do not hold large quantities of groundwater, for obvious reasons, and more surface runoff occurs. Runoff water contains less calcium and other nutrients; it will be "softer"—as well as warmer (in summer). Igneous rock landscapes such as South Dakota's Black Hills, the Canadian Shield, and the Appalachian ranges are all examples that have softwater streams.

Groundwater moving underground picks up and carries quantities of essential elements and nutrients, including calcium, necessary for life in streams. Silicon is a necessary element for the production of *diatoms* (as well as for computer chips!*)*. These are the algae responsible for the slippery surfaces of streambed stones and sometimes make your wading unstable. But diatoms also provide valuable food for some fishes and many grazing aquatic invertebrates, especially the mayfly *Baetis* (blue-winged olive, to you dry-fly fishers). So, don't knock diatoms, even if they do make you slip and become *wet* fly fishers once in a while.

Rainwater also contains small amounts of various chemicals, although with the advent of "acid rain" in the latter half of the twentieth century, the chemical constitution of rain changed dramatically.

We'll take up the very important topic of nutrients and chemical elements in more detail in the next chapter. Right now, it's most important that we know where these materials come from and that the stream depends upon the nature of the catchment for the quantity and quality of their supply. When rains fall upon a catchment, the water divides into several components. Much of it is lost to the atmosphere, some directly by evaporation into water vapor and some through transpiration by plants. About half of precipitation is lost to the atmosphere by the sum—*evapotranspiration*—of these two losses.

Sometimes evapotranspiration from deciduous woodlands may be so great that a substantial increase in stream discharge can be noted after the fall of leaves in autumn. Similarly, streams may increase their flow after logging, because of the decrease in evapotranspiration losses.

Other portions of rainfall reach the ground and have other destinations. A relatively small amount arrives at a stream over the ground's surface as *runoff.* This amount is particularly small where the ground surface is heavily vegetated; significant amounts of runoff probably occur only during extreme storm events and floods. A greater amount reaches the stream as water that passes through the soil above the water table directly to the stream.

By far the greatest proportion of precipitation reaches the stream by *groundwater discharge.* In this case, water infiltrates the soil and other permeable material, enters the water table, and arrives at the stream by the slow, lateral movement of groundwater toward the channel.

A stream can thus be visualized as actually flowing at the surface of the water table, receiving water from it in the form of small, invisible springs. This is what is called an *effluent* stream. (The hydrologist's *influent* stream is one flowing above the water table and losing water into the groundwater, a less common occurrence.)

An effluent stream takes on the chemical characteristics of its source groundwater. In a drought, when all or most of a stream is supplied by groundwater as its source, it is likely to be more alkaline, because more carbonate is dissolved from the soils and bedrock than that reaching the stream directly. After a storm or flood, stream water will be more acidic, owing to greater surface runoff over vegetated land surfaces.

A recent concept in patterns of water flow is the *interflow* of groundwater *between catchments*. This increased interest in subsurface flow—"substreams," if you will—has broadened our concept of the catchment. Hydrologists and river ecologists now view this great volume of groundwater as running beneath the streambed, down valleys along with the surface flow but beneath it. We have recently learned that this "below the stream" region—the *hyporheic zone*—contains a distinctive animal assemblage that also interacts with animals in the visible stream above. This is a dynamic aspect of the stream ecosystem that promises new ideas and theories about groundwater interflow between stream catchments. That changing perspective interjects a new dimension into catchment hydrology.

◆   ◆   ◆

WATER TEMPERATURE is another aspect of the stream ecosystem, closely associated with the valley's reservoir of groundwater. Generally, the temperature of groundwater is at or near the average local air temperature. In north-temperate regions—about 45 degrees north latitude (from Oregon, east to the upper Great Lakes, to Maine)—this temperature will be in the neighborhood of 45 to 50 degrees Fahrenheit. If the catchment soil and bedrock contain large quantities of groundwater (and if a stream has groundwater in a high proportion of its water source), then that stream is likely to be also at or near 45 to 50 degrees. The closer a stream reach is to the groundwater source (that is, a spring), the closer the stream temperature will be to groundwater temperature. The farther downstream from a spring, the more the stream water temperature will reflect the air temperature. In summer drought, when the stream is at *base flow* (all groundwater), it will be cooler.

After a storm, stream water containing more surface runoff will be warmer.

A stream with copious amounts of groundwater as its source will thus tend to be relatively cool in summer (probably a trout stream) but relatively warm in winter. We tend to call such a stream a *coldwater* stream, when actually its annual *average* water temperature may not be any lower than that of a so-called warmwater stream. There is a tendency among biologists to call a stream fed mainly by groundwater *summercool*, rather than *coldwater*.

The so-called warmwater stream is one where a higher proportion of its groundwater enters from nearer the land surface, or perhaps in overland runoff. Such a stream will tend to be near air temperature at all times—thus, warmer in summer and colder in winter than the summercool stream—and probably a stream with warmwater fish species.

A number of factors tend to move stream water temperature toward air temperature: beaver ponds create larger surface areas exposed to air and sunlight, and lack of streamside shade also allows more sunlight to reach the stream. Disturbance and compaction of land surfaces such as cultivated fields and urban streets cause warmer runoff. The effect of higher altitude is similar to that of higher latitude; streams in mountainous regions are cooler than those at lower altitudes.

Just about everything we have discussed in this chapter (and much more) is embodied in the scientific discipline of *hydrology*. The catchment's hydrology is an engrossing subject, for the stream is indeed the product of hydrologic events throughout the entire catchment.

On the broadest scale, the catchment can be viewed as the integration of several sets of environmental factors, one set being dependent upon another:

• climate and geology—our heritage from the Pleistocene ice age—set the boundaries of the catchment's physical features;

• soil and vegetation, results of biological activity, respond to those static factors and vary within their boundaries;

• the stream—the "bottom line," if you will—is shaped both in quality and form by its response both to the relatively constant factors of climate and geology and to the varying biological factors of soil and vegetation.

Between the channel banks, the living community of aquatic plants and animals develops as the final, integrated functioning unit. We are now becoming painfully aware that human activity influences both climate and weather, and that these global conditions can change soil and vegetation—drastically sometimes—to alter the stream, often to its detriment.

The importance of vegetation in the catchment may be the most important ecosystem component. For example, the marked differences between forested valleys and grassed plains set the boundaries within which pristine streams developed in the distant past. In the central and upper Midwest regions, the original vegetation was prairie—vast expanses of perennial grasses, whose roots penetrated the deep, rich soils and resisted recurrent fires.

Today, prairie regions exhibit modifications more extensive than those in any other major region, mostly by agricultural cultivation. Although the fundamental morphology of prairie streams may remain essentially the same, biological communities, including fish, have been altered greatly by sediment, nutrient inputs, and toxic components like pesticides. These streams have been changed so much from presettlement conditions that they little resemble original streams today.

Prairie streams are open in upper reaches but sometimes flow in woodlands farther downstream. These so-called *gallery* forests cause an apparent inversion of the RCC, or river *reset*, where the continuum starts over again. The inversion does not invalidate the basic concept of the RCC, but the contrast between streams in prairie and in forest underscores one way in which the nature of the catchment as a whole exerts a profound influence on its channel and the stream ecosystem.

◆   ◆   ◆

An example of a river reset: Upper—plains in headwaters;
Gallery forest downstream; Plains below forest.
Cottonwood River, Minnesota.

FIFTY YEARS AGO, the classic *trophic level* concept of ecosystem structure was popular and widely accepted. Originating in lakes, the concept was believed to apply to streams as well. And even more broadly, the theory was applied to all Earth's ecosystems—terrestrial, freshwater, and marine.

The trophic level concept basically states that at the bottom of the trophic food-chain (or pyramid) the primary producers, or green plants, produce the most tissue; herbivorous animals, such as most insects and other invertebrates, feed upon green plants and produce less; carnivores—most fishes, and many birds and mammals—feed upon the herbivores and produce even less; and so on. This decreasing productivity of successive trophic levels accounts for the concept's *pyramidal shape.* In fact, the laws of thermodynamics (physical principles relating to conversions of energy) say that it could not be otherwise. Of course, many variations to the simple trophic pyramid concept occur. As an example, omnivorous animals feed in several trophic levels, and many animals change feeding habits and trophic levels during their life cycles. But the basic concept remains a valid and useful template.

A few decades ago, evidence from studies in stream ecology led to a disturbing finding: primary production by algae and other aquatic plants simply was not high enough to produce enough plant tissue to support the herbivorous animals!

The solution to this apparent paradox lay with several creative stream ecologists who theorized that input of terrestrial plant matter (deciduous leaves and other vegetable detritus) in other parts of the catchment accounted for a high proportion of the energy supplied to many streams. This supply of terrestrial energy, particularly in headwater reaches, is now one of the major tenets of the River Continuum Concept.

External detritus adds enough primary production in the channel to resolve the paradox. Thus, the pyramidal shape of the trophic level structure is restored, but only when we consider the entire catchment as the defined stream ecosystem.

Most nonliving organic matter consists of plant or vegetable detritus, entering the stream at the primary trophic level much as if it had been plant matter photosynthesized by algae and other plants in the stream. But we must add the external matter that enters at the secondary trophic level, too—that group made up of herbivorous animals from the surrounding land. Every stream fly fisher knows about these terrestrials, which fall or fly into a stream and are fed upon by fish—and which they imitate with fur-and-feather creations resembling ants, beetles, hoppers, and other insects occupying streamside vegetation.

◆   ◆   ◆

OVER THE PAST QUARTER CENTURY the study of these externally produced organic materials and how they are used in the stream by living organisms has produced one of the great advances in stream ecology. These discoveries have had a profound effect in helping us understand how the stream's living components function and what their connections are to the rest of the catchment. In fact, when we come to managing a stream or river (for fisheries or any other societal interest), we find that in order to manage it effectively, we must treat the entire catchment—*ecosystem management*, in other words.

The boundary between a stream and the terrestrial part of a catchment is the *riparian zone*—the linkage, or interface, between land and water. We use the term *ecotone* to describe a special corridor where important ecological changes take place. The riparian zone acts as a great protector of the stream. Of course, when the riparian zone is destroyed by cultivation, livestock grazing, or logging, disaster strikes in the stream. We'll have more to say about how land use and management affect stream quality in later sections.

And so we have meandered our way through the morphology of valley and stream, come to understand more about water supply and water temperature, and hinted at the energy source that must be made available to fuel living stream communities. We'll take up this fascinating new view of energy supply from the riparian zone and the rest of the catchment in later chapters.

Most profoundly, we have come to understand that *energy supply* depends heavily on the nature of the catchment—the stream ecosystem that extends not just from stream bank to stream bank, but from ridge top to ridge top.

TECHNICAL REFERENCES:

Cummins, Kenneth W. 1992. Catchment characteristics and river ecosystems. Pages 125-135 *in* P.J. Boon, P. Calow, and G.E. Petts, editors. *River Conservation and Management.* John Wiley & Sons, New York.

Hynes, H.B. Noel. 1975. The stream and its valley. *Proceedings of the International Association for Theoretical and Applied Limnology.* Volume 19, pages 1-15.

RiverSketch

MISSISSIPPI RISING

EACH SPRING, AT THOUSANDS of riverside locations across the nation, concern arises about flooding. Snowmelt from the north and the usual heavy seasonal rains, especially in the country's midsection, combine to raise river levels. The threat becomes palpable when waters rise above normal—and sometimes the worst fears are realized. Nowhere in North America is the threat of flood-generated disaster more feared than along our largest rivers, those that drain North America's most expansive watershed—the Mississippi and its major tributaries.

When rain falls or snow melts, the water can take one of two paths: penetration into the land surface—likened to a great sponge—or flow through stream and river channels to the sea.

The sponge of surface soil often absorbs all of a single rainfall. But when the absorbing capacity of the soil and its groundwater is exceeded, river levels must rise.

When immigrants first settled the Mississippi's huge catchment, they began to reduce the absorptive capacity of the land surface by filling and draining wetlands, disturbing soils that then promoted more runoff to streams, and covering much of the land with impervious materials. The absorbent sponge got smaller—and flood intensities increased.

◆   ◆   ◆

BY SPRING 1927, THE MISSISSIPPI had already experienced many severe floods. So by then, various flood control structures had been put in place up and down the Mississippi's shores and tributaries: levees along the river, dams on tributaries, and newly excavated channels and diversions. Everything that could possibly be imagined and devised by the engineers, it seemed, was in place. Confidence ran high in the ability of instream, physical *structures* to tame a wild river.

In March and April of that year, torrential rains like none other in human memory lashed the Mississippi watershed. From the Rocky Mountains, from the North Woods surrounding the river's source, from the gentle wildernesses of the Alleghenies, the rushing waters poured down onto the Lower Mississippi.

All normal criteria defining a flood were exceeded. River discharges rose into the hundreds of millions of cubic feet per second; crests rose far above levees that would, it was believed, hold back anything the river had to offer. Losses exceeded all those in the past—26,000 square miles inundated, 250 million dollars in damage, more than 200 lives lost. This was The Great Mississippi Flood of 1927.

In the aftermath, nature gone wild was blamed again. Orators railed against the untamed river. Commissions were appointed; congress passed new laws and authorized more dollars for more structures.

The engineers returned to their drawing boards. Levees were heightened. More floodways were dredged. More "cutoffs" eliminated river bends, shortening the river by 150 miles in order to speed high water downstream—to someone else's shores.

To the north, the draining and filling of wetlands continued unabated. The sponge shrank still further. More floods followed in 1937, 1965, 1969, 1979, and 1983.

◆   ◆   ◆

THEN IN 1993 CAME THE BIG SPRING MELTDOWN of winter's lingering ice and snow in the upper river, along with torrential rains that exceeded even those in 1927. The reduced sponge in the headwater region could not hold these quantities of water, and The Great Mississippi Flood of 1993 was underway. Once again, the tamed river broke its human bonds and went wild.

Along the Upper Mississippi a levee fails, and water from The Great Flood of 1993 pours out over farms, homes, and riverside towns. (Photo from Dennis Anderson, U.S. Army Corps of Engineers.)

The first alert of potential flooding was forecast in March by the National Weather Service in Minnesota. Once the snowmelt and rains began in April, the worst flood in this part of the world since the glaciers melted 10,000 years ago unfolded (as far as we know).

The deluge centered over the upper Midwest, from Minnesota to Missouri—an area 900 miles north to south, 600 miles west to east.

The wild rains that started in April continued almost steadily for three months. Rainfall records were shattered in the upper states by more than 40 inches of precipitation. All told, the great deluge savaged nine states—North and South Dakota, Minnesota, Wisconsin, Nebraska, Kansas, Iowa, Illinois, and Missouri. It passed down the Mississippi and its major tributaries, the Missouri, Ohio, and Illinois rivers, producing an inundation of twenty million acres (31,250 square miles, almost exactly the same size as Lake Superior).

The two floods of 1927 and 1993 are not strictly comparable. In the spring of 1927, floodwaters engulfed the Lower Mississippi, mainly from St. Louis to the Gulf, bypassing the city of New Orleans through a diversion to the Atchafalaya River and salt water. It was the worst flood n the *lower river's* history. In 1993, the flood inundated the *upper river* valley, from St. Paul to St. Louis, including major tributaries. In 1927, the Lower Mississippi's discharge at its mouth reached a peak of about 300 million cubic feet per second, but the Upper Mississippi's discharge at its 1993 crest in St. Louis reached an unheard-of one billion cubic feet per second.

Economic losses exceeded 10 billion dollars. Crops were destroyed on millions of acres. Some 50 persons lost their lives.

◆   ◆   ◆

THE CRISIS—AND THE CRESTS—eventually passed. Cooler—and drier—heads asked profound questions. Such as: *Have we been doing it wrong all along? And can we change our ways?*

The levee system came under the most severe criticism. Levees had been a logical remedy: build a wall and keep the water out.

But the levees, we realized, constricted the river and raised water levels!

If one silver lining showed at all in the darkness of disaster, it was the understanding, at last, that yes, we had been doing it wrong. Enormous economic losses were incurred because we built dwellings and planted crops in harm's way—and surrounded them with levees that failed. With drainage of natural wetlands, *we created the huge flood ourselves.*

The wide Mississippi Valley is a good place to seek solutions like relocations, retiring floodplains of crop cultivation, and other nonstructural measures. It must be far more appropriate to send floodwaters to the great earthen sponge of natural wetlands and floodplains, than to our homes and farmyards.

SELECTED REFERENCES:

Barry, John M. 1997. *Rising Tide: The Great Mississippi flood of 1927 and how it changed America.* Simon & Schuster, New York.

Mairson, Alan. 1994. The Great Flood of '93. *National Geographic.* Volume 185, number 1 (January 1994), pages 42-81.

Chapter 6

A FLUX OF NUTRIENTS

IN PART OF THE HYDROLOGIC CYCLE, water of precipitation falls upon the land surface and makes its way from the land to the sea. During such a journey, a variety of events converge to provide stream communities with the chemical ingredients fundamental to biological productivity: a flow, or flux, of elements that are the building blocks of living organic matter. Biologists now agree that it is the sum of processes in the entire catchment that defines the supply of essential elements and nutrients to a stream.

Rainwater itself contains dissolved chemicals, and these are important, too. But most chemicals in streams have their source in the land, from which water dissolves or otherwise releases many substances. In addition, biological processes on land contribute greatly to the forms that nutrients take, so important to stream organisms.

An illustration of a simplified hydrologic cycle may show the water of precipitation flowing over the land as surface runoff, but most water reaches the stream passing into and through the land subsurface, eventually reaching the stream as groundwater. Very little overland flow contributes to stream water on a regular basis, although during floods and spates, runoff from riparian zones and floodplains may be substantial. Such irregular pulses provide nutrient inputs that, if not physically damaging, may be thought of as occasional "subsidies," rather than as a regular supply.

Three major processes act as sources of stream chemicals in a catchment:

- precipitation carrying dissolved compounds and elements;
- dissolution of soil particles and rock in the subsurface;
- generation of byproducts from biological processes.

Photosynthesis, animal metabolism, and bacterial decomposition, all generate by-products from the land that are important to streams. Each of these products on the land is subject to infiltration and subsequent downward movement of groundwater or surface transportation to the stream channel in runoff.

At this point, however, we should distinguish between two major groups of chemicals important to stream life: dissolved inorganic compounds and gases.

As products of the vegetated uplands, dissolved inorganic compounds are extremely important in the link between land and stream. Some dissolved gases, particularly oxygen, nitrogen, and carbon dioxide, are essential to the plants and animals of aquatic systems. Virtually all biological processes involve these substances. Plants use carbon dioxide and produce oxygen, and animals use oxygen and produce carbon dioxide, both of which can diffuse across the air-water interface. Nitrogen becomes transformed into available nutrients. We'll deal with the interesting aspects of oxygen and carbon dioxide in other discussions, but here we'll explore the source of dissolved chemicals from the land.

As you might expect, the soil and rock of land surfaces are great mixtures of solid substances—some from the sky, such as volcanic dust accumulated over millions of years; some previously deposited under ancient oceans; some brought down by past glaciers. Much of it is the result of transformations brought about by heat, frost, and biological activities. We might expect, therefore, that water percolating through the land surface would be a veritable chemical soup. And so it is.

Some trace elements, occurring in very minute quantities, are important in special circumstances. But we will pay the greatest attention here to a few of the major elements—calcium, nitrogen, phosphorus, and silicon—because these four are essential in all circumstances. In this chapter, we will focus on how groundwater and runoff provide these major elements to the stream.

Sedimentary rocks of the relatively young Rocky Mountains erode more easily than igneous formations. Athabasca River, Alberta.

◆   ◆   ◆

CALCIUM IS ONE OF THE MOST ABUNDANT and widespread elements on Earth's surface. It occurs most commonly as calcium carbonate, or limestone rock. Limestone is the result of precipitation and deposition on the bottoms of ancient oceans. More than any other chemical, calcium in its several compounds affects the kinds and quantity of aquatic organisms in streams. Remarkably, we don't know exactly why. The tale of calcium is an engrossing story.

Through hundreds of millions of years past, layers of calcium-containing rock continued to form on ocean bottoms. From time to time, uplift raised plateaus thousands of feet high, and a large area of midwestern North America—including the central plains and the Ozark Plateau—is the product of such processes.

Where topography is eroded and rugged, limestone outcrops of bluffs and ridges are readily visible, through the eroded hills of glacial moraines. Beneath the glacial drift and leached surface soils, dissolved limestone bedrock provides copious amounts of calcium to groundwater.

The water of precipitation is a chemically active agent. Although carbon dioxide makes up only a tiny proportion of the atmosphere, it dissolves readily in water. So when raindrops form, the combination with water creates carbonic acid. This is a "weak" acid, to be sure, but still capable of reacting with calcium carbonate to form calcium bicarbonate, which reaches open streams through springs and groundwater seeps. Calcium bicarbonate is the most common calcium compound found in surface waters.

Calcium bicarbonate does several things for us in stream water—mostly good things. So usually we appreciate large quantities of it:

• Calcium is chiefly responsible for the attribute of water "hardness," which may be defined as "soap-reacting power," and it prevents us from getting a good suds in sink or shower. Water treatment procedures "soften" water either by eliminating most of the calcium bicarbonate, or by substituting sodium for the calcium, which does not cause hardness. It is sodium bicarbonate in small, medicinal pills and powders that is good for the digestion! Calcium, though, is better for streams.

• Calcium bicarbonate causes the water to be more alkaline, that is, less acidic. (Among other effects this acts as a buffer against acid rain.) Alkalinity (which more recently has been termed *acid neutralizing capacity,* or ANC) accelerates recycling of nutrients by decomposer bacteria, thereby increasing productivity.

• Bicarbonate provides a great reservoir of carbon dioxide available for photosynthesis by all plants, including the slippery algae on stones that mayfly nymphs like to feed upon. When plants extract carbon dioxide from the bicarbonate, they leave calcium carbonate (or *mono*carbonate), which in large concentrations precipitates out into small solid particles sinking to the bottom as marl (in lakes) or as more limestone (in oceans). This is a happy cycle of events, albeit requiring millions of years.

• Because hardness (from calcium) and alkalinity (from carbonate) occur together in calcium bicarbonate, highly alkaline waters are often term *hard* water. This is not technically true, of course, but OK for picking out a good fishing stream. We call the hardwater, high-alkalinity stream a "limestone" stream, most alkalinity deriving from limestone bedrock; similarly, we call the softwater, low-alkalinity stream "freestone," also OK for deciding on whither a day's fishing. Calcium carbonate is required by several invertebrate animals such as crustaceans (scuds and crayfish) and mollusks (snails and clams), which produce crusty exoskeletons and hard shells.

◆   ◆   ◆

AMONG THE SEVERAL ELEMENTS and nutrients essential to stream organisms, nitrogen and phosphorus are at the top of the list. Nitrogen originates in the atmosphere, but it is modified by biological processes at the Earth's surface; phosphorus occurs naturally in minerals present in the rocks of Earth's crust and becomes available either through natural weathering of rocks or commercial mining.

In stream waters, nitrogen and phosphorus occur in much lower concentrations than calcium. Both are important elements in instream photosynthesis and other biological processes. We will take up those processes later, but for now, we'll consider how these two essential nutrients are acquired from the valley and transported to the stream.

Nitrogen is the most important element in water quality and stream life. It plays a prominent role in all streams as a major component of protein and thus of all animals, and therefore it can often become the environmental factor most limiting to insect and fish productivity.

Although nitrogen is one of the most common elements on Earth (making up 80 percent of our atmosphere), its gaseous, elemental form is scarcely available in most biological processes. Gaseous nitrogen must be transformed to other compounds, primarily *nitrate.*

The first step in making nitrate available from nitrogen to stream organisms is the *fixation* of gaseous nitrogen by certain bacteria—termed *nitrogen-fixers.* The first product of nitrogen fixation is *ammonium,* containing nitrogen and hydrogen (but not oxygen). Nitrogen-fixers occur mainly in the terrestrial part of a catchment, in bushes such as alders, a few coniferous trees, some deciduous trees, legumes, and the algae in lichens.

Nitrogen fixation is also accomplished by bacteria in stream sediment; including the gravel bars that frequently develop along the sides of the channel; the greater amount of stone surfaces in the interior of gravel bars provides for more structure for bacteria.

The second step is the transformation of ammonium to *nitrate,* the oxidized form, produced by *nitrifying bacteria* in a process termed *nitrification.* Ammonium is also produced as a by-product of the decomposition of animal wastes and remains. It, too, is transformed to nitrate by nitrifying bacteria, in both terrestrial and stream environments.

Lightning strikes can also cause nitrification, delivering significant amounts of nitrate to the catchment in dust and rain. But most nitrate production is accomplished through bacterial processes of nitrogen-fixing and nitrification.

Gravel bars that form along the sides of channels provide for more underwater stone surfaces for nitrogen-fixing bacteria.

Other, human-caused inputs of nitrate to streams can have detrimental effects. For example, excess nitrate can result in *eutrophication,* an overproduction of algae and other plants that create nuisances and oxygen depletion. Most fertilizer applied to crops actually ends up in streams or the groundwater. So a stream in an agricultural catchment may receive large quantities of nitrate fertilizer, even to high levels that constitute pollution. Treated sewage and animal feedlot runoff that enters tributaries add excessive ammonium, which is toxic in itself, or which become transformed to nitrates in excess. Forestry practices can also affect nitrate levels in the catchment; clear-cut logging, for example, because it reduces uptake by forest trees and increases decomposition of the organic debris remaining on the ground, may increase the nitrate available to groundwater and thus to streams.

Overall, nitrogen in its nitrate form, is the most common nutrient in streams, as well as the most important element for synthesis of protein in streams. Nitrogen is so important that without a continuing supply of nitrate from the catchment to provide the building blocks of protein, little animal life as we know it would prosper in the stream.

Streamside alders may grab your fly or scratch your face, but they help to produce nitrate, an essential nutrient.

◆   ◆   ◆

PHOSPHORUS, IN ITS OXIDIZED FORM as phosphate, occurs in much lower concentrations in stream water than nitrogen, but it is nevertheless an essential factor in stream life. Unlike nitrogen, phosphorus is not present in the atmosphere but occurs in Earth's rocks and minerals. In some areas where natural phosphorus in soil and rock is lacking, phosphorus can also be a limiting factor in stream productivity. Many kinds of land use in the catchment are strongly related to the input of phosphorus to a stream.

Stream plants require other chemical elements and nutrients, but none are as crucial as nitrogen and phosphorus. For example, silicon, in the oxidized form of silica, is a major element required by the algae of periphyton. Fortunately, silica is richly abundant around the globe, making up about one-fourth of Earth's rocky crust. Silicon becomes available through weathering of rock and readily enters the stream, dissolved in water. The major use of silicon in streams is by the algal group *diatoms*, the principal photosynthesizing plants of periphyton. Diatoms (and the slippery streambed stones for which they are responsible) are common in all streams, but they require open sunlight to carry out photosynthesis efficiently.

Many other chemicals under the general title of trace elements occur in streams, also originating in the terrestrial part of the catchment. The need for these elements—aluminum, chromium, iron, manganese, zinc, to mention a few—have not received study nearly as thorough as have calcium, nitrogen, and phosphorus in natural stream waters. Some have been shown to be required for photosynthesis, some not; some at high concentrations or in certain formulations are toxic. Most occur in very low concentrations and usually appear to be present in sufficient quantities to meet biological needs in streams. Perhaps future research will point up some of their benefits or deficiencies.

Catchments differ from geological region to region in their quantities of available elements. Some land uses in uplands and floodplains may result in insufficient levels of chemical inputs to streams or, more likely, produce compounds and elements in excessive amounts, to the detriment of stream life.

◆　　　◆　　　◆

MANY RIVER AND STREAM USERS probably take the role of water chemistry for granted. After all, it is not likely to be a favorite subject to most of us. But the ecology of biological communities in streams depends upon dissolved elements and nutrients in the most fundamental way. Their chemical environment is a veritable jumble of what is needed to facilitate the essential processes of life.

The watery environment, in all its wonderful yet critical diversity of dissolved material, is the direct issue of its terrestrial catchment—bedrock, groundwater, surface soils, and biological processes of many kinds.

TECHNICAL REFERENCES:

Grimm, Nancy B., and Stuart G. Fisher. 1986. Nitrogen limitation in a Sonoran Desert stream. *Journal of the North American Benthological Society.* Volume 5, pages 2-15.

Meyer, Judy L., W.H. McDowell, T.L. Bott, J.W. Elwood, C. Ishizaki, J.M. Melack, B.L. Peckarsky, B.J. Peterson, and P.A. Rublee. 1988. Elemental dynamics in streams. *Journal of the North American Benthological Society.* Volume 7, pages 410-432.

RiverSketch

MUDDYING THE WATERS

Of all the injurious substances that daily pour into our streams and rivers, the worst, both for quantity and economic impact, is *sediment.* Sand, silt, clays—the smallest sizes—lead the list of pollutants that bring harm to stream life.

Ecologists often judge the quality of streams by the size of inorganic particles making up the streambed. Optimum sizes comprise gravel and cobbles where bacteria and fungi live and process organic matter, and where aquatic invertebrates find food and protection. Boulders and bedrock lack the tiny crevices essential for small animals and are thus merely unproductive. But the finest of particles that we call *sediment* spell trouble.

Sediment occurs naturally in all streams. In fact, to some extent, some sediment is necessary for successful functions by both invertebrates and fish. It is the *excess* that constitutes troublesome pollution.

We separate sediment into two forms: suspended and deposited. The suspended form—most often clay or fine silt—causes muddy water, or turbidity. Deposited sediment—most often sand

and coarse silt—can blanket the streambed. The two forms are not mutually exclusive, however, because particles in suspension deposit out, and vice versa, depending on water velocity and turbulence.

Suspended sediment produces many effects damaging to stream organisms. In high concentrations, turbidity blocks sunlight from the streambed, preventing photosynthesis by the algae of periphyton. Fine particles in the water are retained by the gills of fish and cause several forms of gill disease. We assume the same effect occurs with aquatic invertebrates that depend on gills for respiration. The most injurious effect of suspended sediment, however, is upon those fishes whose incubating eggs depend upon clean, oxygenated water—most particularly salmonids. When sediment collects in the interstices of the gravel, sediment shuts off supplies of water and oxygen. This factor alone has been responsible for the near-elimination of natural reproduction by salmon and trout in some of our western rivers.

Sediment deposition occurs when massive erosion removes great quantities of soil from catchment surfaces, subsequently reaching a stream. Its major effect is on streambed invertebrates, which may become partially or completely buried. Streambed habitat is then changed to promote burrowing forms not available to fish. When the streambed is completely covered, the food base for fish may be destroyed. Blankets of deposited sediment several feet thick have been recorded, mostly caused by improper logging practices in western mountains. Sediment deposits forming over salmonid redds can form an *armor* over the redd that also shuts off water flow, entombing new, free-swimming fry attempting to emerge from the gravel.

Many human activities produce *anthropogenic* sediment in excess. Agriculture in many forms produces by far the greatest proportion of anthropogenic sediment. Construction and use of logging roads and skid trails are the main producers of sediment from forest management operations, particularly in the steep terrains of the Pacific Northwest. Other sources include mining, urban development, road construction, off-road vehicles of many kinds, and overgrazing. All of these contribute sediment by disturbing land surfaces and allowing erosion to carry fine soil particles into streams.

Fencing the riparian zones along pasture streams (top) effectively prevents livestock trampling of stream banks (bottom).

A great deal of effort has been applied to the development of means that reduce or eliminate erosion in all of these industries. Agricultural scientists have devised cultivation procedures collectively called *conservation tillage*, virtually eliminating erosion. Sediment generated through unrestricted livestock grazing can be controlled by fencing riparian zones and providing livestock with water in other ways.

Logging roads often generate huge quantities of sediment, especially when built in locations vulnerable to landslides. Building roads too steeply, too close to streams, and fording or inappropriately bridging streams, generates large quantities of sediment. But careful planning for location, road shape, and steepness has demonstrably reduced erosion. Eliminating logging roads altogether—by removing cut logs with overhead cable or helicopter—can bring sediment generation down to almost zero.

An eroding bank, caused by loss of the riparian zone,
a major source of excessive sediment.

The big problem with these new procedures is *implementation*. And the big problem with implementation is that some of these preventive measures are costly. But the ultimate cost in damage to natural resources in the long run may be much greater, as recent research concerned with sediment and other pollutants has discovered.

Sediment generated by eroding stream banks makes up an especially high proportion of sediment pollution in streams. Streams and rivers everywhere have eroding banks, almost to the point where casual observers may view them as parts of the natural landscape. In fact, eroding stream banks, to some extent, are normal, and erosion of banks is the functional factor that causes all streams to meander.

But when stream banks are disturbed by human activities, natural erosion becomes accelerated, or newly eroding banks are created. Channelization and cultivation too close to streams greatly increase the generation and transport of sediment to streams and rivers.

Type of land use on natural floodplains affects the extent to which streambank erosion eats into a floodplain. Any disturbance that destroys the natural vegetative surface close to the edge has the potential to develop eroding banks. Some resource managers today recommend *no surface-disturbing activity on floodplains at all.*

An eroding bank can be restored by techniques like riprapping and reshaping the bank, but these methods are also costly. By far, the best means for preventing streambank erosion is protecting healthy riparian zones along the stream. The best solution for control of sedimentation, whether from crop field, forest, or construction site—is to *stop erosion at its source.*

SELECTED REFERENCES:

Bjornn, T.C. 1974. *Sediment in Streams and its Effects on Aquatic Life.* Idaho Water Resources Research Institute, University of Idaho, Moscow.

Waters, Thomas F. 1995. *Sediment in Streams: Sources, biological effects, and control.* American Fisheries Society, Monograph Number 7, Bethesda, Maryland.

Chapter 7

ALLOCHTHONY

THE SUPPLY OF ENERGY to a stream's living inhabitants is one of the most crucial components of stream ecology. The major dynamic force for all elements of the stream ecosystem is energy—the fuel needed for all ecosystem functions. Energy drives the processes of all life in the stream—microorganisms, green plants, aquatic invertebrates, and the many species of fish. Just as we humans require calories in our food for our bodies to grow and to carry out all bodily functions (albeit that sometimes we indulge ourselves with too many!), so too do all other living organisms require calories to grow and function.

That energy originates in two major sources:
- photosynthesis from sunlight falling directly onto the stream;
- energy-containing material produced outside the channel and transported to the stream.

Of course, both sources use the sun's radiation as their ultimate origin. And energy from both sources can be measured in *calories*, just as we watch our own caloric intake on our breakfast Wheaties box.

(The calorie is defined as the amount of heat energy required to raise a cubic centimeter of pure water one degree Celsius, under specified standard conditions. The calories we see posted on our cereal box, however, are really *kilocalories*, or a thousand times our defined calorie. Roughly, one gram (about four hundredths of an ounce) of fish or insect tissue contains about one kilocalorie. Thus, one quarter pound of fresh fish (four ounces) will give us a little more than 100 kilocalories, not counting the butter and corn meal in which the fish is fried.)

Sunlight falling directly onto the stream surface permits photosynthesis by aquatic plants—algae, mosses, rooted "waterweed." In ecology, we term this process *primary production*. It will be the subject of a later chapter, but here we deal with the second source of energy—material originating in the terrestrial environment outside the stream channel. This material we call *allochthonous* matter, which means "formed elsewhere." Many headwater streams or upper stream segments, shaded from the sun, depend almost wholly on such allochthonous organic matter for energy.

The study of the kinds, sources, and transport of allochthonous matter is a relatively new endeavor in stream ecology. Research efforts over only the past two to three decades by many scientists worldwide have greatly broadened our understanding of how allochthonous energy influences a stream ecosystem. In fact, the study of *allochthony*, in all its many aspects, has probably contributed the most to our knowledge of the biological functioning of a stream. Allochthony clearly underscores the importance of the connection between the terrestrial part of the catchment and the stream.

Even though John Bardach's *Downstream*, published in 1964, included no mention of terrestrial contributions to streams' energy supplies, a few papers on this subject were reaching the scientific literature in the early and middle 1960s. Most of them arose from stream scientists' burgeoning interest in *productivity*, that is, how plant and animal tissue is formed in flowing waters. For example, they found that much of the food eaten by fish not only came from the land in the form of terrestrial insects, but that the food of aquatic insects was also derived from the land. A substantial proportion of the energy production of stream fish has since been traced to terrestrial origins. And productivity became a subject that engaged many more scientists later on.

Professor Hynes, in a 1963 publication, made the novel suggestion (at the time) that, although all animal tissue has its productive origin in energy derived from plant material, much of the plant matter consumed by animals feeding in streams comes from the production of plants outside the stream. Dr. Hynes went on to promote this concept in further publications, including his book, *The Ecology of Running Waters* (1970) and his seminal paper, "The Stream and its Valley" (1975).

An understanding of allochthony must be divided into two parts. First is the generation of energy-containing organic matter in a terrestrial catchment (uplands, floodplains, riparian zones) and its transport to the stream. Second is how this material is used within the stream to produce the many organisms that make up biological communities—including that fighting trout on the end of your line!

The first part—the formation of allochthonous material on land—is the subject of this chapter. How allochthonous matter is used in the stream will be explored in a later chapter, on *heterotrophy*.

◆   ◆   ◆

AS CAN BE IMAGINED, the size of pieces of allochthonous matter varies greatly. In the early 1970s, a system for treating organic matter by size was introduced by Professor Kenneth W. Cummins, then with Michigan State University. His proposed scheme of particle-size classification revolutionized stream ecology and brought order to a seeming chaos in the great diversity among kinds and sizes of allochthonous organic matter.

The first step in classifying sizes was to divide organic matter into two major categories: particulate and dissolved. Roughly, *particulate organic matter* (POM) is visible, whereas *dissolved organic matter* (DOM) is not. When Dr. Cummins began partitioning POM into still finer categories, his task must have seemed daunting: his categories ranged from a half-micron to a forest log. (A micron is one-millionth of a meter, about 1/25,000-inch.)

The largest visible pieces are termed *coarse particulate organic matter*, or CPOM. These particles are the most obvious, ranging from one millimeter in length (one thousandth of a meter, or about 1/32 inch) up to a fallen white pine or Douglas fir trunk, a range of about 50,000-fold. Not very many aquatic organisms are prepared to handle pieces as large as tree trunks, although some microorganisms and insects do tackle such jobs and eventually bring about their decay over the course of decades or centuries.

Organic matter within the CPOM category includes deciduous leaves and coniferous needles; flowers, fruit, and seeds; and woody debris from twigs to tree trunks.

Particles smaller than one millimeter are classified as *fine particulate organic matter*, or FPOM. These range from one millimeter down to one-half micron, a range of 2,000-fold. At the lowest end of this range are particles too small to see without special microscopes. FPOM includes the finest of soil particles, "crumbs" from animal feeding, fecal pellets from aquatic insects, and pieces remaining from the abrasion and decay of CPOM.

The smallest particles, smaller even than one-half micron, constitute *dissolved organic matter*, or DOM. These include microscopic material resulting from leaching and decomposition of all kinds of plant and animal remains, including even large organic molecules. Aquatic animals are generally not able to use DOM directly, but through further instream processes, DOM from the terrestrial catchment provides a substantial proportion of energy input to stream inhabitants.

The identification and description of CPOM, FPOM, and DOM were largely responsible for bringing about a classification needed for the study of stream animal productivity. We will be making many references to these three classes of allochthonous organic matter when we explore the lives of stream animals, both invertebrates and fish, in later chapters.

Classification of organic matter by size was only part of the solution to the problem of how greatly diverse stream life is organized. Needed also was a parallel system that matched the sizes of POM to the kinds of stream organisms that feed upon them. The subject of animal *functions*—that is, how different animals use the different kinds and sizes of allochthonous particles for food and growth—was also studied intensively by Dr. Cummins, his associates, and many others. The system of invertebrate functions that they identified became another of the great contributions to our present knowledge of energy supply to streams. That system will be discussed in detail in a later chapter on *functional groups*.

◆　　　　　◆　　　　　◆

FOR MANY STREAMS, the major source of allochthonous energy is the autumn leaf fall from deciduous trees. Leaves make up the greatest proportion of CPOM. In the central Temperate Zone of North America, this autumnal pulse of energy is huge. Some leaves fall on the water surface and are immediately subjected to a series of processes that "condition" the leaf material into nutritious food for stream animals. Many more leaves fall instead to the ground outside the channel. Here, too, by coming into contact with rainfall, ground moisture, and soil microorganisms, they are exposed to the same conditioning process. Eventually, many reach the stream channel.

Some trace elements, occurring in minute quantities, are important in special circumstances. But we will pay the greatest attention here to a few of the major elements—calcium, nitrogen, phosphorus, and silicon—because these four are essential in all circumstances. In this chapter, we will focus on how valley slopes, tributaries, and downhill-moving groundwater and runoff provide these major elements to the stream.

Of course, most leaves are quickly swept downstream toward other streams and lakes. But many are caught on obstacles in the channel—gravel bars, projecting stones, and sticks and branches. We can usually see such *leaf packs*, particularly along riffles in the fall, and even later as they decompose.

The autumn leaf pulse has been likened to a huge meal, or pulse of energy, that continues to provide nutrition to stream organisms long afterward. In northern regions with heavy snowfall, spring melt often results in a second pulse of energy that has lain dormant beneath deep snowpacks through the winter.

The nutritional quality of leaves varies greatly among tree species and is closely related to how rapidly the leaf can be processed by microorganisms. As we shall explore later, both the leaf fragments and the tissue in the bodies of these microorganisms serve to nurture the animals that ingest the leaf fragments.

The autumn fall of deciduous leaves forms leaf packs that provide food and energy to stream invertebrates through the following year.

"Soft" leaves—elm, hickory, maple, willow, and aspen—provide the greatest quantities of nutritious food to aquatic invertebrates. Harder or resinous leaves—for example, oak, beech, and rhododendron leaves, and especially conifer needles—are *refractory* and are much more difficult for microorganisms to process into palatable food.

◆   ◆   ◆

WHAT HAPPENS TO A TYPICAL DECIDUOUS LEAF when it first hits moist soil in the terrestrial catchment? The initial process is *leaching*. Leaching occurs when rainwater or soil moisture dissolves the soluble portions of freshly fallen leaves or other plant matter. The percentage of the leaf's total weight that is soluble and subject to leaching is large—perhaps a quarter or more of the leaf's total mass. The leaching process is rapid; it starts as soon as a leaf becomes wetted and is often completed in the first twenty-four hours.

Rhododendron leaves, common along many Appalachian streams, are particularly resistant to conditioning by microorganisms.

The resulting solution, or *leachate*, contains much DOM, which rapidly infiltrates the soil and becomes incorporated into groundwater. Subsequent input of groundwater into the stream, DOM with it, becomes a major source of allochthonous energy reaching the stream. This product of autumn leaf fall becomes yet another input of terrestrial matter transported from the valley to the stream.

On the water surface, a fallen leaf undergoes the same conditioning process, and DOM is immediately infused into the stream water.

We have already discussed the difference in productivity between hardwater, high-alkalinity streams (limestone streams) and softwater, low-alkalinity streams (freestone). A most intriguing reason for this difference in productivity is the relationship between alkalinity and DOM leached from deciduous leaves: in high alkalinity, DOM is leached faster. We will take up this fascinating subject again later.

The rate of leaching, whether on moist ground or in the stream, varies with leaf species. Rhododendron leaves and conifer needles leach very slowly. Even when they are present in large quantities, they may wash downstream before dissolved organic matter becomes leached out. Add the fact that streams in the Appalachian Mountains (where rhododendron thickets are common) and in northern forests (with conifers) are often softwater, freestone streams, and we find more reason to explain the low productivity in so many softwater streams.

◆   ◆   ◆

The needles of coniferous trees—pine, spruce, fir—are slow to decay and provide little nurture to stream invertebrates.

RECOGNITION THAT WOODY MATERIAL makes up an important part of a stream's allochthonous energy source came a little later. This may have been because we had become so used to viewing logjams and branches as nuisances, especially for canoeists and flyfishing anglers in heavily timbered catchments.

Specific assemblages of organisms on submerged wood have now been identified and analyzed. These are the groups responsible for the decay of wood in water and, in the process, for providing food for many kinds of carnivorous stream animals. Like leaves and DOM, woody debris is respected as a substantial source of allochthonous energy.

As you float a river or fish through a favorite stream reach year after year, you probably note how an old log or a particular pile of branches gradually becomes smaller and then moves about. As an obstacle, this pile of woody debris thus becomes less and less obtrusive until finally, some year after a spring freshet, you may notice that it has disappeared altogether.

Woody debris along and in streams provides large amounts of organic matter available for conditioning.

Not surprisingly, woody contributions to rivers are more important in forested catchments, especially compared with prairie and desert streams. Although decomposition of woody material may be slow, its contribution to total energy supply is substantial, especially in small, shaded streams in either deciduous or coniferous catchments. In mature forests, wood contributes 50 to 70 percent of the total energy supply to stream invertebrates. But virtually any stream collects some quantity of wood, whether it consists merely of bits of plains cottonwood or desert mesquite.

The processing or conditioning of allochthonous matter in water is much the same for woody debris as for leaves and other less resistant organic matter—just slower. A combination of fungi, bacteria, and invertebrate animals is largely responsible for releasing the energy in woody debris, like that in leaves. Later, we'll discuss the dynamics of the many species of aquatic insects that inhabit wood—all of which may end up as fish food!

As in leaves, the rate of breakdown of wood varies. Generally, deciduous hardwoods are processed more rapidly than conifers. The size of pieces determines the time required for complete breakdown: small twigs may take up to a year or two; larger branches several inches in diameter might require a decade; and the largest tree trunks may need centuries.

Although the "Big Woods" of eastern North America is greatly diminished now, rich deciduous tracts remain in ravines, floodplains, and wooded valleys surrounding many streams and rivers. These individual woodlands continue to produce calories to supply the energy needs of mayflies and caddisflies, scuds and crayfish—and fish of many species.

Some "preconditioning" of woody debris through partial decomposition takes place on the forest floor, which speeds up the overall process of releasing energy to stream organisms. Wood that is alternately wetted and dried, such as tree trunks or brush along stream banks, decays more rapidly than wood continuously under water. However, in all cases the process is inexorable and continues until the wood and its populations of microorganisms and insects totally disappear.

◆   ◆   ◆

AMONG THE ALLOCHTHONOUS INPUTS so far discussed, we have considered only those at the *primary producer* level—material produced by green plants—trees, bushes, and grasses outside the stream channel. Organic matter of plant origin makes up the greatest proportion of allochthonous organic material reaching a stream.

However, another element of allochthonous energy input—at the *secondary producer* level—is also important. Allochthonous animal input consists of many kinds of terrestrial invertebrates: grasshoppers, leafhoppers (our familiar *jassids*), earthworms, ants, and a host of others. Falling, flushed, or wind-blown onto the water surface, these animals can sometimes account for the major source of available food for fish, particularly stream fish that readily feed on the surface. In fact, this "discovery" is nothing new to flyfishing anglers, who have employed imitations of "terrestrials" for a long time.

Fisheries biologists also have been aware of the importance of terrestrials as fish food. Pioneer trout biologist Dr. Paul R. Needham, of New York State, made many studies of surface-drifting terrestrials long before intensive studies on allochthony and stream invertebrate drift were made. In the 1920s, Dr. Needham's investigations of stream drift emphasized terrestrial invertebrates in surface drift samples and their significance to the trout's food resource.

More recent studies on energy budgets for stream ecosystems have measured the *inputs* by instream aquatic plants as well as nonliving allochthonous energy versus *outputs* such as down-stream drift, emergences of insects, and predation on fish by terrestrial mammals and birds. Balanced budgets were attainable only when terrestrial invertebrate inputs—that is, allochthonous secondary producers—were included.

In terms of proportional contributions, terrestrial invertebrates may sometimes make up the highest percentage of available food. In many studies, the percentage found of allochthonous foods in fish stomachs have been on the order of 10 percent. In streams with low productivity of aquatic invertebrates, however, such as low-alkalinity freestone streams, terrestrial inputs are much more important and may make up almost all available fish food. (Hint to fly fishers: terrestrial imitations may be most successful in free-stone streams.)

The species, quantities, and timing of inputs by terrestrial invertebrates are generally unpredictable. Most such inputs occur, of course, in summer months. But weather—wind, rain, temperature, sunshine or cloud—plays such an important role that the input of terrestrials is as unpredictable as weather itself.

A few correlations between terrestrial conditions and terrestrial invertebrates can be hazarded. The proximity of grassy plains or meadows would suggest grasshoppers in late summer; overhanging trees and bushes would suggest ants, beetles, and caterpillars. Heavy rains sometimes result in incredible quantities of terrestrial earthworms (use a San Juan Worm after a thunderstorm?).

This small floodplain along a Maine river produces quantities of carnivorous mayflies that later return to the channel. Tomah Stream.

Flying adults of aquatic insects are not considered allochthonous. In fact, the loss of such airborne adult insects into surrounding uplands constitutes a reversal of the allochthonous process—an energy loss to the stream. Such losses have been rarely measured, but they may turn out significant at times.

Sometimes aquatic invertebrates move in both directions across channel-floodplain boundaries. When a floodplain is flooded, insects that normally drift from a stream may end up on the floodplain in new habitat. Invertebrates produced on the floodplain may later move to the stream, accounting for a substantial source of energy input to the stream and an important source of fish food.

Energy inputs from terrestrial invertebrates and floodplain-produced aquatics are difficult to quantify. Some biologists have compared terrestrial input with benthic production, with aquatic adults in surface drift, and with percentages in fish stomachs. Some studies relate terrestrial input to the individual species of riparian trees and shrubs, from which insects are assumed to fall. But calculating the rate of terrestrial energy input per unit area of stream (in order to compare it to aquatic invertebrate production in the same units) seems extremely difficult, although potentially greatly important.

◆   ◆   ◆

LEARNING TO APPRECIATE THE IMPORTANCE of allochthonous organic matter to streams was one of the most significant advances in the history of stream and river investigations. Almost every stream relies on the input of energy-rich material derived from the terrestrial part of the catchment. Whether the input consists of deciduous leaves, woody debris, or a mixture of fine plant and animal remains, the stream communities of invertebrates and fish benefit from it.

As we continue to explore instream processes, productivity, and other dynamics and functions of stream organisms in this book, we will often refer to allochthony as a crucial element in the ecology of rivers. The great supply of energy through allochthonous material—such as leaves and woody debris—is the greatest source of energy and nutrients for many streams. Our enjoyment of the rivers we love will be enhanced, in print and on the water, by an understanding of these terrestrial contributions to stream life.

TECHNICAL REFERENCES:

Cummins, Kenneth W. 1974. Structure and function of stream ecosystems. *BioScience.* Volume 24, pages 631-641.

Webster, Jackson R., and Judy L. Meyer, editors. 1997. Stream organic matter budgets. *Journal of the North American Benthological Society.* Volume 16, pages 3-161. (Various articles.)

SPECIAL NOTE:

    As we close Part Two, *The Living Valley*, recall that the terrestrial portions of the catchment have been discussed in several ways. We've dealt with the land's influence on a river's origins; with the entire catchment as the basic unit of stream ecology, the stream ecosystem; with the terrestrial part of a catchment as a source of chemical elements and essential nutrients; and finally, with the importance of allochthonous organic matter—primarily leaves and wood—as sources of energy. In Part Three, *The Dynamic River*, we shift to the stream channel itself and explore the processes by which stream organisms are produced, feed themselves, and in turn provide food, energy, and nutrients to the rest of the living community.

RiverSketch

RIVER PIGS AND LOG MARKS

IN LOGGING'S BROAD SWEEP across North America, vast forests of coniferous trees one or more centuries old were virtually eliminated. The process consumed hundreds of human lives and produced fortunes for a few. It was a matter of "cut-and-run," and it left huge areas of devastated, eroding hill slopes and wildfires. But it also produced the lumber that built ships and cabins, and later the homes and factories of some of the nation's major cities.

    In the beginning, the great forests stretched from horizon to horizon; they were firmly believed to be inexhaustible. But the entire enterprise of logging off the North Woods required only the last half of the 19th century. By 1920, the inexhaustible had been exhausted.

The crucial factor in removing and transporting the felled forest giants was the *river*. Rivers small and large provided the energy and the highways to bring wood to sawmills and to float huge rafts of sawn lumber to developing cities.

The river drive was a spring event. Felled, sawn, hauled, and piled at a riverbank rollway during the winter, the big logs were sent tumbling into rushing river currents once rising temperatures brought on the spring thaw. Then it was the job of the driving crew—inelegantly called river pigs—to guide the rumbling mass of pine trunks down to the mills. It was a rousting, brawling, dangerous job. Every "jack" thought *he* was the most skilled, toughest man on the river. But on many a stream bank, a crude cross marked the spot where a river pig met sudden death amid crushing logs and freezing water.

Many lumber companies sent their logs downstream simultaneously. In the turbulence of a river, masses of logs belonging to a single owner could not be contained in booms as they could on large lakes. A system had to be devised to identify ownerships of mixed logs once they arrived at the mill.

The system was the *log mark*. Much like cattle brands on the open ranges of the West, the designs for log marks created a magnificent variety. When logs were cut and stored in the winter, marks were driven into them by the scaler (who measured and recorded his estimate of board feet in a log) with a forged iron die and a stamp hammer. Most marks were applied to log ends and were called *end marks*. Because the ends frequently became damaged in the drive downriver, *bark marks* were also made instead on the sides of logs, or in addition to end marks.

Designs of log marks ranged from simple geometric shapes to elaborate pictures. Arrangements of letters (acronyms, initials, nicknames); simple drawings (animals, trees, wheels, guns, and faces); dollar signs and hearts—all were used, often in combination. Many log marks were fanciful and intricate creations.

The necessarily large number of distinctive log marks produced a huge collection of primitive art. Across the country, literally thousands of marks were recorded; sometimes several hundred were used on a single river.

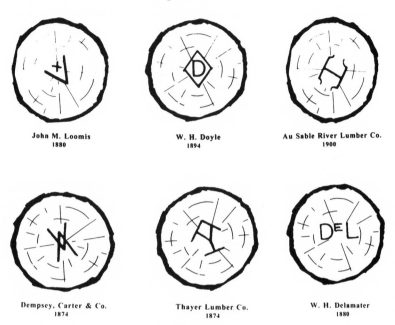

Some examples of log marks
used in the harvest of Michigan pine timber.
(From Titus 1941.)

The American logging industry began in Maine and churned westward through a broad belt of northern coniferous forest, mostly of white pine. As the cut-and-run operations depleted eastern forests, logging frontiers progressed west through Pennsylvania, Michigan, Wisconsin, and Minnesota, bringing with them some of the same companies, lumberjacks, and place names to establish new towns and cities in the upper Midwest.

When the last of the white pine had been depleted in Minnesota, loggers leap-frogged the north-central plains to the great conifer forests of the Rocky Mountains and the Pacific Coast. The mountain hillslopes were steeper, the trees larger, the rivers wilder. Although by the late 1800s some steam-powered machinery had been added to the loggers' tools, the river drive remained important. In the Rockies, wild rivers delivered the abundant ponderosa pine from the mountain forests of Idaho to sawmills at lower elevations. Douglas fir was preeminent in the coastal forests, driven down to the ocean on streams running out of the Cascade Mountains and the Coastal Range in Washington, Oregon, and northern California. Both ponderosa pine and Douglas fir were larger and grew taller than eastern white pine. Coastal western redwoods exceeded all others in size, and these were logged, too, but they were not as broadly distributed.

The western timberlands were not logged as completely as the eastern pinelands. Modern logging continues today, but the old brawling river drive is gone. On balance, the cessation of scouring river drives meant greater stability for all living stream inhabitants.

With each river drive, some logs were lost—cast aside by swift currents into sloughs, stranded on mud flats, waterlogged and sunk. Some of these "deadheads" were picked out and returned to the main drive by the rear crew, but not all of them. Sometimes the loss was substantial, perhaps five percent of the drive. The crush of logs scoured and shifted riverbeds and banks, and the resulting streambank erosion in some regions buried the deadheads downstream.

In succeeding decades, lumber companies sought to salvage the old deadheads, which was often a profitable enterprise. But the salvaged logs belonged to the owners of the registered log marks. If the marks became indistinguishable, to establish ownership salvage operators in a given river had to acquire *all* the old marks!

Eventually, state natural resource agencies prohibited further salvage in order to protect stream banks, fish spawning beds, and cover habitat. The era of the river drive was over, and hundreds of North American rivers began the process of recovery.

Today, some of the buried logs occasionally become visible when stream channels incise and meander. Almost any river paddler or stream angler today on such old logging rivers has encountered these old deadheads, projecting from an eroding bank or recently released and deposited on a new gravel bar.

Like the eras of the mountain men, cowboys, and forty-niners, the era of the river pigs was lusty, colorful—and short. Although in its westward march the river drive lasted a half-century, in a single locality it may have lasted only a few years. The limitless forests of large conifers turned out to be short-lived indeed, once they were assaulted by the log fallers, sawyers, and river crews.

The industry left a legacy of scoured-out rivers and modern cities. But in county records across the nation, its history is stored in an inheritance of frontier art in thousands of log marks.

SELECTED REFERENCES:

Titus, Harold. 1941. *Michigan Log Marks.* Michigan Agricultural Experiment Station, 89 pages. East Lansing.
Rector, William G. 1953. *Log Transportation in the Lakes States Lumber Industry 1840-1918.* Arthur H. Clark, Glendale, California.

Part Three

The Dynamic River

Introduction to Part Three

THE DYNAMIC RIVER

CENTRAL TO THE GROWTH AND DEVELOPMENT of a stream's biological community is *energy*. It is the energy of *calories* that drives and sustains all biological functions.

Just as food provides the energy of human metabolism and gasoline energizes the complex operations of an automobile, so too do the calories of energy that enter a stream's water provide the intricate array of dynamic forces that nurture and control the functions of all living entities in the stream.

We use the term dynamics here to describe the forces that result in growth and development of plants and animals. Synthesis of green plant tissue, the increase in animal protein, and recycling of minerals and nutrients by microorganisms—all contribute to the dynamics of the total ecosystem.

Functions within stream communities are profuse and intricate, and endlessly fascinating to stream ecologists. Insect and fish feeding, reproduction, growth, and survival—all are dynamics that together constitute the total performance of the community. Because of the interdependence of their life processes, stream communities have been likened to a complete organism.

Functions of all organisms change continuously. Photosynthesis reverses to respiration with the alternation of sunlight to darkness—as does the behavior of insects and fish. The pulses of

144

allochthonous energy input follow a seasonal cycling. Rates of energy flow required for reproduction accelerate and decline through the year with unceasing regularity. In fact, all functions follow patterns that oscillate through daily and seasonal cycles, in step with cosmic and climatic events. These are the events that cause variation in a rapids' roar, lift the chill of morning mist on a streamside camp, or create the brilliance of a leaping trout.

Less exciting, perhaps, but still essential to an understanding of stream dynamics are the numerical measurements that must accompany our understanding of these processes. We express these measurements in units of rates. Growth of a fish can be expressed as grams per day; decline of an insect generation as numbers lost per square meter per week; production of fish tissue as pounds per acre per year.

Such numerical expressions give us powerful tools for making comparisons and assessing trends, good or bad. In this way, we can measure differences between streams of different water quality—for example, limestone versus freestone. We can measure with precision the biological effect of a city's pollution load, of an instream flow reduction due to a dam's operation, and of different land uses within a catchment. Much of the great research effort in stream ecology over the past four decades has concentrated on developing methods for assessing dynamics and expressing their quantitative properties in numerical terms.

In these next few chapters, we'll explore the many dynamics that represent the recent advances in stream ecology. They represent a dramatic move from the static descriptions and species lists that characterized conventional natural history in the past.

Scientific perceptions have changed, resulting from a more intensive study of chemical elements and nutrients, which determined that these components are not constant, either in time or along the stream course. A further important realization emerged: green plant production in the stream channel was not the only source of plant tissue available to herbivorous invertebrates and fish. The importance of allochthonous organic matter became adequately defined, a resource that provides food and energy in large quantities to animal consumers in the stream. The essential role of microorganisms such as bacteria and fungi was proven in many laboratory experiments, describing their means of converting nonliving organic matter to palatable food, the subject of *heterotrophy*.

Another major advance was the precise categorization of animal consumers by the kind and size of organic food particles—functional groups—probing the complex maze of food types and feeding behaviors that were never imagined a half-century ago. These past few decades also saw the advance of methodology to measure secondary, or animal, production as rates that expressed how much is produced, in calories or biomass, in a given interval. Previously, the productivity of a stream's living community was expressed only by what was measured by static counts and weights.

Where we can, we'll put numbers on these measurements, numerical expressions that are the scientific equipment enabling us to properly manage and protect our valued stream resources.

Chapter **8**

SPIRALING

M ANY ELEMENTS CYCLE as they pass through plant and animal populations. Photosynthesis, for example, is one path through which plants provide elements and nutrients to the rest of the community. Animals, in turn, consume plants, assimilating the same elements and nutrients into their own tissue.

These elements return to the soil and water when plants and animals die and decay. Such cycling is similar in lakes and streams in all living communities: aquatic dust to aquatic dust, so to speak.

In the days when the trophic pyramid was a popular model, the transport of elements up the pyramid and through decomposition back to earth was celebrated as an important principle. We use the term *mineralization* to describe the return of these elements from organic matter back to inorganic, mineral form, in which they can be absorbed and used by plants again.

The passage of energy, in the form of calories, is another important component in the cycling of chemical elements, with one important difference: calories do not return to earth with the elements. Rather they dissipate in the form of heat through living organisms' respiration at every level of production and decomposition. So, in each cycle, ever-necessary energy must be renewed, in almost all cases from sunlight.

The principle of cycling—or recycling—is well established in the field of aquatic ecology. However, when stream ecologists began to look critically at element recycling in flowing water, a frustrating paradox emerged: downstream flow of water, along with all its dissolved and suspended material, suggested that before a cycle could be completed, water carrying its elements and organic matter disappeared downstream. A "cycle" literally could not happen. Could it?

◆   ◆   ◆

OBVIOUSLY, CYCLING IN STREAMS must involve an interaction between simple nutrient cycling and downstream transport. This process we now view as *nutrient spiraling*.

The concept is not really new. In 1941, Aldo Leopold described the "rolling motion" of nutrients as they progressed through soil and streams from uplands to ocean. But as a principle, spiraling has become newly appreciated in streams only in the past few decades.

Spiraling happens to all chemical elements, from their initial input to passage downstream, through all biological processes along the way. Elements taken up by microorganisms, plants, and animals are later released downstream, and taken up again still farther down, creating the spiral. Thus, a nurturing supply of nutrients is provided to primary producers, to insects and other invertebrates, to fish and, finally, to decomposing bacteria and fungi, and then over again, through a stream's course.

In stream reaches with fast currents, where the downstream passage stretches out faster than biological processes, the stream length of one complete spiral increases and the spiral is called "loose." In slower water, the downstream movement is reduced and the spiral "tightens." As currents may decline further, the spiral becomes tighter and tighter, until eventually, in still water (like a lake), the spiral closes to become a perfect circle.

Few precise estimates have been made of the length of spirals—that is, the stream distance required to complete one complete spiral. One investigator estimated an average distance of about 550 feet for phosphorus in a first-order, Tennessee mountain stream in summer, and a shorter distance in the fall.

Several estimates have been made of spiral lengths of carbon, a major ingredient of all organic matter, in some larger streams, where estimated spiral lengths were up to several miles.

Element spirals are loose and spiral lengths long in swift water; but in slow water, spirals become tight and lengths shorter.

◆   ◆   ◆

MANY MATERIALS—ELEMENTS, nutrient compounds, and organic particles—are involved in the spiraling process. Here we'll take up just a few of the most important elements: phosphorus, nitrogen, silicon. In a previous chapter, we discussed how these three elements could occur in the form of compounds that are usable by living organisms.

Phosphorus, in its oxidized form of phosphate, is primarily used by aquatic plants in production of tissue through photosynthesis. Phosphorus is a necessary component of nutrition for both invertebrates and fish. Phosphate (the oxidized form of phosphorus) occurs in very low concentrations in stream water, and thus it may sometimes be the main factor limiting biological productivity.

We can readily visualize the initial uptake of dissolved phosphate by the algal cells of periphyton in a headwater reach. These cells are then consumed by invertebrates, either in place or downstream when algal cells drift. The invertebrates may be eaten by a predaceous insect farther downstream, and this insect then may be eaten by a fish even farther down. At each step, phosphate may be released to the water during feeding and voiding of feces. Finally, in a still lower reach of the stream, decomposer bacteria mineralize the organic phosphorus in dead organic matter to the inorganic phosphate form, thus completing a spiral.

Because phosphorus is an essential component of all life in streams, it plays a major role in producing the myriad living forms we see beneath and on the surface of our favorite stream or river. Repeated spiraling of phosphorus throughout the length of a stream is good conservation!

Nitrogen, like phosphorus, also becomes available to aquatic organisms only in forms other than elemental nitrogen, but its use is more complex. Nitrogen in its elemental form is a gas, and although it makes up the greatest portion of normal air, it cannot be used in its gaseous form in green plant photosynthesis. So it must be transformed into compounds—principally ammonium and nitrate—through the activity of nitrogen fixers and nitrifying bacteria, mostly in the terrestrial environment.

Some aquatic microorganisms, notably the *cyanobacteria* (blue-green algae), are capable of fixing nitrogen instream, that is, transforming elemental nitrogen into usable forms. These organisms are commonly present in periphyton and in organic accumulations on the streambed, such as in leaf packs and debris dams. Ammonium and nitrate are forms that can be used by microbes, such as fungi that produce protein, essential in the production of the animal tissue of invertebrates and fish. The process adds greatly to the availability of nutrients, especially nitrogen, in streams.

Nitrogen occurs in higher concentrations in streams than phosphorus, but it still can be limiting in some streams, particularly in volcanic soils. A shortage of nitrogen reduces the ability of fungi to process organic detritus, like leaves and wood.

Like phosphorus, nitrogen spirals downstream. From its initial input as nitrate and ammonium in surface or groundwater, nitrogen spirals downstream through the trophic pyramid of fungi, plants, and animals. At every step in spiraling, nutrients re-enter the water through their decomposition and mineralization. In its use and reuse, nitrogen is recycled efficiently and conservatively through a stream's course.

Losses of nitrogen from the stream occur by *denitrification,* a process that changes nitrate back to gaseous nitrogen, which then diffuses to the atmosphere, a loss to the stream. Denitrification is accomplished by special *denitrifying bacteria* that function in deoxygenated conditions, like thick organic matter accumulations. The effect of such losses on stream productivity has not been thoroughly investigated, but the process does not seem to limit productivity.

Uses of silicon by stream organisms, though less complex than either phosphorus or nitrogen, are particularly important. The usable silicon compound in water, silica, is the result of rock weathering in the terrestrial catchment and transport in small quantities in groundwater and runoff. The main reason silicon is so important in streams is that it is used directly by *diatoms,* the group of algae that make up much of the periphyton. Although silicon itself is not very important to invertebrate nutrition, the diatoms are particularly nutritious for grazing insects and other invertebrates. Silicon is later released through mineralization of animal feces, to spiral downstream and be used again.

◆   ◆   ◆

MANY STREAM BIOLOGISTS have been concerned with how spiraling nutrients are transported through stream systems. After all, the availability of nutrients to biological communities is an essential factor affecting productivity.

Budgets of nutrient input (mostly from the land) versus nutrient output, or loss from the stream (at some downstream point) help us to visualize the biological health of stream communities. If input is greater than output, it means that nutrients that have been taken up by plants and animals have remained pretty much in place, and growth and production remain high. But output higher than input means that biological communities are losing nutrients and may be in poor health or even in senescence. Thus, we are concerned with nutrient retention versus nutrient transport out of the system. Developing an energy budget becomes most complex in the case of nitrogen because instream nitrogen fixation and denitrification occur along the length of a stream.

When a stream is recovering from some disaster, such as drought or flood, the input-output budget for nitrogen is particularly important. During the recovery period, input of nitrogen should exceed output—that is, biological communities will be using large quantities of nitrogen to grow and restore their normal population levels.

Budgets can be determined for nutrient use by invertebrates. For example, some results indicate that of the total nitrogen ingested (in food), about 50 percent is egested (in feces), 25 percent is lost by excretion (in urine and other fluid losses), and the remaining 25 percent is used to produce additional animal tissue. Of that tissue produced, nearly 75 percent goes to predators and other mortality, and 25 percent goes toward increasing the population. Only about 5 percent leaves the stream as emerging and flying insects. Thus, a great infrastructure of nitrogen utilization and re-use is necessary to produce those hatches of duns and spinners we anxiously await in the spring!

High rates of plant growth, grazing by invertebrates, animal production, and processing of CPOM and FPOM by microorganisms—all of which result in faster cycling—are reflected in tighter spirals and higher biological productivity. This condition becomes most evident in autumn after the seasonal fall of deciduous leaves, when higher populations of microbes that process the organic matter take up nutrients faster—and spirals become ever tighter.

The term *nutrient storage* refers to capture and retention of nutrients in both living organisms and nonliving organic matter on the stream bottom. Greater roughness of the streambed (stony riffles and woody debris) leads to greater retention, or storage, of nutrients. Conversely, severe storms and high flows may greatly reduce storage of nutrients and can temporarily lower productivity.

In streams (as opposed to lakes), biological processes are closely associated with streambed surfaces rather than to upper water strata. In streams, most biological processes and organisms occur at the stream bottom, and consequently, more retention and storage occur there. Therefore, streams that are wider and shallower have greater potential for retaining nutrients than do streams that are narrower and deeper, with equal flows. The broader streams tend to retain more nutrients with greater interstitial flow (that is, among deep gravels beneath the streambed), because they have more bottom surface available.

Nutrient retention also depends on whether streams are *effluent* or *influent* (to use the hydrologist's terms). Effluent streams are more common; these receive groundwater input that often carries dissolved nutrients. The less common influent streams are perched above their water tables and lose water (and nutrients) to groundwater; the resulting deficits probably represent permanent losses to instream communities.

◆   ◆   ◆

DOWNSTREAM TRANSPORT of nonliving, particulate organic matter, especially FPOM in water currents, is a major contribution to downstream spiraling of nutrients. Any process that facilitates the transformation from CPOM to FPOM, such as shredding by insects or particle-size reduction by any means, increases the rate of nutrient transport through the stream system, the looseness of spirals, and the spiral length.

With their abundant surfaces, debris dams provide shelter
for invertebrates and greater retention of nutrients and FPOM.

Animal production, which retains nutrients, and animal death and decomposition, which release nutrients, are extremely important in nutrient dynamics. For example, consumption of food and growth of tissue contribute to storage of nutrients. However, egestion of animal feces and decomposition of animal bodies after death transform nutrients into a more mobile condition and facilitate downstream transport by water currents.

Migrating invertebrates carry stored nutrients in their tissues, from which nutrients are released by decomposition of feces and their dead bodies. Such movements may be either upstream or down. Fish that feed on insects and then migrate themselves, or die and drift downstream, can carry nutrients far away from their original feeding site, upstream or down.

Many riparian birds—for example, dippers, sandpipers, waterthrushes—prey on stream insects and then fly even farther upstream or down, where they will deposit feces rich with nutrients far from original locations. In highly productive streams, downstream drift of insects and other invertebrates may turn out to be a mechanism for transporting large quantities of nutrients, but we do not yet know the full effect of invertebrate drift on nutrient transport. As flying adults of aquatic insects migrate upstream to lay eggs, they carry with them elements and nutrients that will be released in their decaying dead bodies. This migratory behavior (a subject taken up along with invertebrate drift in a later chapter) has been observed mainly in caddisflies.

The caddisfly *Oligophlebodes sigma* migrates upstream
for egg-laying, transporting nutrients to upper reaches.

Flying adult insects after emergence often die on land rather than on the water, thus removing nutrients from the stream. As a loss, however, such removal of nutrients is probably low. Besides, such nutrients may make their way back from the riparian zone to the stream after rain and runoff.

The effect of upstream-migrating fish can be enormously significant. This is true particularly during the spawning runs of Pacific salmon, which die after releasing their eggs. Their deaths are responsible for a substantial release of nutrients to upstream reaches. In fact, the decay of these large fish, the tissue of which has been produced by the uptake of nutrients in the ocean, represents a net income of nutrients from the salty sea to the stream, rather than a mere recycling. Decomposition of many large fish in a small stream can also cause pollution with their decomposing bodies that deplete the stream's oxygen.

◆   ◆   ◆

THE DYNAMICS OF NUTRIENT INPUT, utilization, and transport are basic to all living organisms in streams. Indeed, the entire chemical milieu of spiraling nutrients sustains all biological communities and their processes.

This nurturing environment of water and nutrients spirals around and around downstream to serve a highly complex system of organisms and their processes. Spiraling serves to focus our attention on the principle that living stream communities and their sustaining environment of nutrients are longitudinally coupled and interdependent along the stream's course. The concept of spiraling is a major advance over previous studies that were limited to short reaches. In summary, spiraling helps us to view the dynamics of a stream as a whole—as an integral part of the functioning of an entire ecosystem.

TECHNICAL REFERENCES:

Elwood, Jerry W., J. Denis Newbold, R.V. O'Neill, and W. Van Winkle. 1983. Resource spiraling: An operational paradigm for analyzing lotic ecosystems. Pages 3-27 *in* Thomas D. Fontaine, III, and Steven M. Bartell, editors. *Dynamics of Lotic Ecosystems.* Ann Arbor Science, Ann Arbor, Michigan.

Meyer, Judy L., William H. McDowell, Thomas L. Bott, Jerry W. Elwood, Chanel Ishizaki, John M. Melack, Barbara L. Peckarsky, Bruce J. Peterson, and Parke A. Rublee. 1988. Elemental dynamics in streams. *Journal of the North American Benthological Society.* Volume 7, pages 410-432.

RiverSketch

KILLER RAIN

EARTH'S PRECIPITATION HAS NOW CHANGED from a relatively pure and nourishing quality to rain so toxic that it can deface and kill almost anything it touches. That outcome is so profound that it is hardly comprehensible. Acid precipitation is right up there with climate change and ozone depletion in its potential to wreak destruction upon Earth and its ecosystems.

That acid precipitation is *anthropogenic* (caused by human activity) is undeniable. Ironically, the predicament we face is directly related to some of civilization's greatest needs: electric power, manufactured goods, and vehicular transportation.

Among the strongest and most destructive acids are sulfuric acid and nitric acid. These have tremendous power to combine with other substances and alter them—and kill living cells. Not all acids are equally destructive, however. Carbonic acid, which is naturally found in unpolluted rain, is a weak acid formed when atmospheric carbon dioxide combines with droplets in the air. Carbonic acid causes us virtually no problem. But when sulfur compounds are released by the burning of coal, which contains much sulfur, those particles, too, dissolve in water droplets to form the very strong sulfuric acid. The result is acid rain. In a similar way, nitrogen compounds are released in car and truck emissions, forming nitric acid in precipitation.

Sulfuric acid is present in rain in the larger percentage. But destruction results whenever either or both of these strong acids fall on forest leaves, crops, millennia-old monuments—and lakes and streams.

Environmental damage from acid precipitation does not occur equally on all parts of the globe. The amount of damage done varies in accordance with the *buffer* effect of alkalinity in natural waters (often called *acid neutralizing capacity*, or ANC). Alkalinity, commonly the result of dissolved calcium carbonates or similar compounds reacts with any acid to bring the acid/alkaline quality of water toward a neutral condition. Regions underlain by limestone, such as karst landscapes, have a high buffering capacity, and as a result their waters experience little effect from introduced acids. Sedimentary rock outcrops along a stream, such as limestone bluffs and streamside ledges, suggest a stream well buffered against acidic precipitation.

Limestone rock outcrops in the karst topography of the central Midwest exemplify streams well buffered against acid rain.

In areas underlain by igneous rock, often naturally acidic, soft waters may be extremely susceptible to acid precipitation. Many landscapes with underlying igneous rock are in northern, recently glaciated regions.

Surface waters with alkalinity less than 10 parts per million (ppm) are considered highly sensitive; waters between 10 and 20 ppm are moderately sensitive; waters above 20 ppm are generally safe from the effects of acid rain. Limestone streams often run to more than 200 ppm.

The distribution of sulfur emissions from smoke stacks also varies by region, with greatest concentrations located in the southern Great Lakes area—the industrial states of Illinois, Indiana, Ohio, southern Michigan, and Pennsylvania. With prevailing westerly winds, the greatest deposition of sulfur occurs east and south of this industrial area—New England, southeastern Canada, and the southern Appalachians. This association of highly sensitive areas downwind from an area of industrial emissions is a deadly combination.

Specific impacts of acid rain in softwater streams constitute a litany of death and destruction. Degrading effects at the basic levels echo up through the trophic pyramids of all stream life. Increased acidity severely affects bacteria and fungi, reducing the rate at which they decompose organic matter, thereby reducing food production for invertebrates. Primary production by periphyton is reduced or changed to nonpalatable products such as filamentous algae. Growth, production, and diversity of invertebrates—especially mayflies and scuds—may be reduced or eliminated. Fish of many species suffer slowed growth, reproductive failure, or death.

Elevated acidic conditions release several toxic metals normally stored in inert form in streambed sediments, especially aluminum. Aluminum is the most common metal in soils worldwide and is highly toxic to aquatic animals; it may be the major killer of brook trout in softwater, acidified streams. Data collected through the year show low annual averages of acid, but acid strength can vary seasonally. For example, snowpacks at the end of winter may be extremely acidic. When melting snow enters streams, it might be acidic enough to kill fish and invertebrates that will remain just as dead after acid levels improve during the following summer. It is extremely important to evaluate seasonal changes, even brief pulses.

Case histories of acid-caused stream damage abound. The State of Pennsylvania, in addition to producing huge quantities of sulfur emissions, also has suffered some of the worst acidic impacts. Pennsylvania contains few lakes but a great abundance of streams, including many with native brook trout. The state's Adirondack region receives the highest sulfuric emissions in the United States, and it has the greatest number of acidified streams in the nation. In one mountainous area, 20 percent of headwater brook trout streams have become so acidic that they now contain no fish at all.

The boreal forest of eastern Canada, a vast area of acid-sensitive soils and waters from Lake Superior to Hudson Bay, a quarter of the area of Canada, is predicted to suffer huge losses in its aquatic ecosystems because of acidification.

Softwater streams in the boreal forests of eastern Canada
are severely threatened by acidic precipitation.
Steel River, Ontario.

Appalachian streams in Virginia have suffered greatly. Ten percent of that state's brook trout streams have been acidified, and future estimates predict that 20 to 30 percent will not hold fish in the future.

Acid rain damages lakes as well as streams, by changing the environment of plants, invertebrates, and fish, and most evidence so far indicates that impacts are greater in lakes. Hundreds of lakes in New England and eastern Canada have been acidified, and many have experienced extirpation or declines of fish and invertebrates. In New York's Adirondacks, 180 brook trout lakes have been made sterile. Damage to lakes in Scandinavia, which receives heavy sulfur emissions from England and other northern European countries, has been even greater, where hundreds of thousands of lakes have been acidified.

Although some local improvements have been effected, acidification of natural waters continues. Stricter regulations on industrial emissions have somewhat reduced acid deposition, but the cost of scrubbers—devices to reduce emission from smokestacks—are expensive and often resisted by industry. Stricter standards on nitrogen emissions from automobiles have also been effective, but the continual increase in number of vehicles in the United States has largely countered the reduction of emissions from individual cars. Americans' love affair with the automobile will have to change, along with its fuels, in order to resolve the internal combustion engine's contribution to the production of acid rain.

Some experimental remedial measures have been developed. The application of lime to acidified lakes and the application of limestone rocks on the bottoms of acidified streams has shown some promise, but these measures, because of cost, aesthetics, and huge areas involved, are not practicable as permanent management operations.

Genetic development of resistant strains of brook trout has been attempted, but this measure probably cannot be successfully implemented on a broad scale. Replacement of wild trout with continuous stocking of hatchery fish may provide recreational fishing, but fisheries of second-rate quality. Current measures to eliminate the threat of acid precipitation are simply band-aid treatments; they do not address the greatest necessity—*elimination of sulfur and nitrogen emissions altogether.*

In order to reduce the killer rains, the burning of fossil fuels—coal, oil, and gas—eventually must cease. More effective scrubbers and automobile exhaust systems will not be sufficient to solve the persistent problems of climate change, ozone depletion, and acid precipitation. Other sources of energy must be found or developed if we are to avoid further reduction in our quality of life. Continued viability of our heritage of natural waters, including our esteemed streams and rivers, depends upon attaining these goals.

SELECTED REFERENCES:

Camuto, Christopher. 1991. Dropping acid in the Southern Appalachians: A wild trout resource at considerable risk. *Trout* (Trout Unlimited) Winter 1991, pages 16-23, 26-33, 36.

Haines, Terry A. 1981. Acid precipitation and its consequences for aquatic ecosystems. *Transactions of the American Fisheries Society*. Volume 110, pages 669-707.

Chapter 9

PRIMARY PRODUCTION

FUNDAMENTAL TO THE SUCCESS OF ALL LIFE in a stream is *energy*. Essential to the completion of functions and processes, to the survival and growth of all organisms, to the systematic removal of organic waste, energy in biological functions means a ready supply of *calories* available to the stream community. The supply of energy is the most critical factor fueling the stream ecosystem. It is the thread that ties biological elements together at all levels of the system.

The sun's radiant energy is the basic source of all energy. We have discussed in previous chapters some external, or allochthonous, sources of energy, mainly the calories stored in leaves and woody debris. But energy stored by plants within the stream itself also provides energy to the system. On much of the stream bottom, plant material is the major source.

Primary production—the creation of plant tissue from carbon dioxide, water, and energy from the sun—is the term we use in ecology as synonymous with *photosynthesis*. Primary production is also closely related to *autotrophy*, meaning, "producing its own food," which plants do. Autotrophy is distinct from *heterotrophy*, meaning "using food produced by other organisms," as all animals do.

In the next chapter, we'll examine heterotrophy. But here we'll take a close look at primary production, the process by which aquatic green plants provide food to other organisms.

We'll also try quantifying primary production—that is, applying some numbers. Science has made many attempts to measure primary production in streams, but results have not been wholly satisfactory. Nevertheless, we will try for some rough estimates in terms of pounds of plant matter produced per acre per year. We can later follow these units through all communities in streams, production by invertebrates and fish.

◆   ◆   ◆

FIFTY YEARS AGO, a popular principle in ecology was the *trophic level*, or *trophic pyramid*, theory. This concept viewed natural communities in different levels, with plants as the primary producers at the bottom of the food chain, the first trophic level. Each higher trophic level depends on the one below it for food (trophic = food or feeding). Herbivorous animals compose the second level, carnivorous animals the third, and so on. Because the transfer of food energy from a lower to the next higher level is never totally efficient (or even close), each successively higher level is always smaller—fewer individuals, fewer calories, and lower production. So, a graphic display of these various levels, stacked one upon the other, resembles a pyramid.

With the usual zeal of scientists exploring a new principle, someone calculated the maximum number of trophic levels that could be supported on Earth. The result was about 20 levels, with one large individual at the top. The theorist did not reveal how large the animal would be, or what it would look like.

It was scientific fun, of course. But the reality in most of Earth's ecosystems, including streams and rivers, is that the number of trophic levels is usually three or four. In most streams, algae and other plants make up the primary producers; herbivorous insects, other invertebrates, and some fish make up the primary consumers; and carnivorous insects and fish make up the third and fourth levels. We could even go outside the stream for additional trophic levels that include carnivorous birds and mammals, and fly fishers who did not practice catch-and-release!

However, a problem emerged when stream ecologists learned that their hypothesized pyramid did not fit the usual stream communities. In shaded woodland streams, for example, where plants did not have sufficient sunlight for photosynthesis, primary production did not appear high enough to support the abundant animals found there. The pyramid concept seemed questionable.

Before this seeming paradox was fully described, however, the concept of *allochthony* was developed and widely researched. Once allochthonous plant material, with all its calories, was added to the bottom level, the trophic pyramid was restored, and order was returned to the discipline of stream ecology! It was almost like finding the answer before the question had been properly set forth.

Allochthony became popular among stream ecologists; it was widely felt that most streams, if not all, were predominantly dependent on the energy provided by nonliving plant material generated outside the stream.

It soon became apparent that the universality of allochthony was a rush to judgment, that it was only part of the source of energy to streams. True, it was all-important in many streams, but not all. We came to realize that *autotrophy* (the production of food energy by photosynthesizing plants) still predominated in many streams or stream reaches. As so often happens in science, the resolution of controversy led to further knowledge. We better understand now that many stream communities rely on autotrophy *and* allochthony in varying proportions. In some reaches, instream primary production is the almost sole source of energy, in others allochthony is most important. The unraveling of the reasons for this diversity has occupied stream ecologists ever since.

The river continuum concept (RCC) greatly furthered our understanding of the role of primary production in many streams. In this model, the midreaches of the RCC—about fourth through sixth order sections—are autochthonous and primary production becomes increasingly important. Although some degree of photosynthesis takes place throughout a stream, the bright, sunlit, clearwater reaches in the middle are those most dependent upon primary production of plant matter, especially to nurture and feed some of our most esteemed herbivorous mayflies and caddisflies!

◆   ◆   ◆

ALL ECOLOGISTS ENJOY ARRANGING and describing categories and sometimes develop intricate classification schemes. Actually, such efforts are fundamental to the systematic organization of all scientific information. Stream scientists are no exception.

Primary producers in streams have been classified according to several different systems. We'll keep it simple and consider just two groups: *periphyton* and *macrophytes*.

Periphyton is somewhat of a catchall term meaning roughly "plants around some other object." Most of the periphyton we are concerned with are algal cells attached to stones on the streambed. These algae include mainly *diatoms*, a class of algae having many species. Through their photosynthesis, these algae provide the major source of food to some of our most important stream insects. Periphyton has been termed the *pastures* of the streambed, and diatoms have been likened to the "grasses of the water world." The diatoms of periphyton indeed provide the basic forage for all grazing invertebrates.

Another group of plants in the periphyton are the filamentous green algae, a conspicuous member of which is *Cladophora*. This common stream plant produces strands of bright green filaments, often several feet or yards long. You can see these in slower, sunlit, highly fertile streams, or when a late, hot summer results in warm water.

Periphyton, however, contains much more than algae, despite its name. Included also are fungi and bacteria, so important in conditioning nonliving organic matter. Microscopic animals are common in this coating on stones and other substrates, including a group of mostly invisible individuals under the general name of *meiofauna*. (We'll take up this fascinating group of animals, exceptionally important in the trophic structure of streams, in a later chapter.)

Periphyton sometimes is further subdivided into organisms attached to stones, to silt and mud surfaces, and to surfaces of leaves and stems of living higher plants. Periphyton often occurs in patches—a mosaic of life including microorganisms and grazing insects on gravel or stony streambeds. Whereas periphyton is found in almost all stream conditions, it prospers best in open, sunlit areas, such as in the middle reaches of the RCC.

Two other terms that similarly describe the community of organisms on stream substrates are *biofilm* and *epilithon*. *Biofilm* is another catchall term meaning a thin organic film containing a mix of living organisms, mainly microscopic. The term can be applied to an organic coating on any substrate, including sticks and stones and leaves of aquatic plants. *Epilithon* means specifically "on the surface of stones." Both terms include not only photosynthesizing algae, but also fungi, bacteria, and a microfauna comprising protozoans and tiny insects as well. All of these components in biofilm or epilithon are embedded in a matrix of large organic molecules that is "slimy" and has led to use of the term *slime community* (presumably familiar to any angler sitting and sputtering on the streambed, having just lost his footing on some slippery biofilm or epilithon).

Biological processes in biofilms and the epilithon include algal photosynthesis, invertebrate feeding, and fungal and bacterial decomposition of organic matter. Either term may seem the better choice than periphyton, but the latter is more commonly used in the ecological literature. So mostly we'll continue to use periphyton, too.

In a later chapter, we'll discuss the fascinating subject of stream invertebrate drift, but here we should mention the similarly interesting *drift of algal cells* in streams. Although this subject has not been investigated as widely as invertebrate drift, enough information has been published to at least outline the salient points.

Botanists have collected drifting algal cells and noted a regular daily pattern, with peaks at midday. They conclude that the greatest drift corresponds to the times of day when cell division of algae in the periphyton is at a maximum, presumably when photosynthesis—and cell division among the algae—is at its daily peak under high light conditions. The ecological effect of such drift is to provide a constant source of colonizing algal cells that settle in available spaces on substrates such as sticks and stones downstream, along the stream's entire course.

The process of drifting to a new site and colonizing it occurs rapidly, within hours or less, apparently assisted by the adhesive character of the slimy epilithon on stones. We can be glad that this process makes the stream's primary production more efficient, serving up energy for growth of stream invertebrates.

The second major category of primary producers comprises the higher plants, or aquatic *macrophytes* (= large plants). This group includes the mosses, rooted flowering plants, and floating plants. Mosses are shade-loving, headwater plants that are strongly attached to stones and boulders in riffles, rapids, or even waterfalls. They could even be called part of the periphyton. We often see them as dark, almost black, patches where currents are moderately swift.

Interestingly, mosses cannot extract carbon dioxide from their otherwise rich source in the bicarbonate of high-alkalinity streams. They can use only dissolved carbon dioxide abundantly available in the highly aerated water of riffles and rapids in headwater stream reaches.

A common genus of moss is *Fontinalis*, which is also the species name of brook trout (*Salvelinus fontinalis*); the word means "inhabiting springs or brooks," which seems most appropriate for both of these coolwater, headwater inhabitants.

Other aquatic macrophytes include rooted, flowering plants described as "waterweed" in some terminologies. Most of these are common in the slower, warmer midreach waters farther downstream. Generally, rooted macrophytes are not specialists to flowing water, and only a very few occur exclusively in streams. But in England, riverkeepers are often kept busy removing waterweed from streams on their employers' estates.

Because they are rooted in the streambed, with large leaves and stems trailing languidly in the current, macrophytes are more often seen by both river runners and anglers as nuisances. Common are the genera *Ranunculus* (water buttercup) in moderate current, and *Potamogeton* (pondweed) in slow currents. Many other macrophytes are common to different geographic locations.

Macrophytes prosper in many streams, often in slow reaches, warmer waters, and streams slightly polluted with agricultural wastes.

Rooted macrophytes often trap silt and sand. This process creates patches of sediment, which in turn provide additional substrate for more plants. Continued growth of sediment deposits can cover large areas and greatly modify stream shape and flow.

Aquatic macrophytes perform beneficial services to the stream community, providing habitat surfaces for algae and other microorganisms in periphyton and biofilms. In turn, these are available to grazing invertebrates that scrape the macrophyte leaf and stem surfaces for food. Furthermore, macrophytes are effective at filtering and trapping drifting FPOM, which also becomes available as food for invertebrates. These find sheltering habitats in accumulations of moss, emergent plants, and submerged rooted plants, such as watercress (genus *Nasturtium*). In some limestone headwaters, watercress can almost drip with scuds (*Gammarus*). (By the way, watercress is tasty in a salad, with a flavor something like a spicy radish. It is not a native of North America, however, but an exotic imported from Europe.)

The third category of higher plants, the floaters, is much less common, although they may occur in huge masses. Most conspicuous are the tiny discs of *Lemna*, or duckweed, measuring only about one-eighth inch in diameter, some with equally tiny rootlets extending down from the underside of the floating disc. They are rarely found in streams, usually only in pool eddies or in quiet water along stream banks. And yes, ducks eat duckweed!

Interestingly, although insects and other invertebrates are commonly associated with macrophytes, plant material is rarely eaten in its fresh state. Probably animals eat less than 10 percent of the fresh, living macrophyte production, and these may be mostly crayfish, terrestrial mammals and birds, and some fishes such as the foreign grass carp.

Instead, the major contribution made by higher plants to the dynamics of successive trophic levels is by contributing nonliving organic matter formed after dieback in late summer or early autumn. (This is a topic we will take up in more detail in the next chapter.) The ultimate fate of macrophytes is to become processed as part of the detritus pool and then to be eaten by aquatic invertebrates. And so we have come to understand that the great supply of energy stored by primary producers is of both allochthonous (on land) *and* autochthonous (instream) origins.

A third group of aquatic plants that is sometimes included among stream primary producers is *phytoplankton*, composed of floating, free-living algal cells drifting in the current. We say "sometimes included" because many stream scientists do not consider true phytoplankton to be present in streams. True phytoplankton is not attached to substrates or to the streambed. Phytoplankton in lakes and oceans is the major, almost sole source of energy realized from primary production in lakes and oceans. In streams, however, it seems unlikely that free-floating algal cells could contribute on a sustained basis to the stream's supply of energy because of their rapid movement downstream. Phytoplankton emitted from lake outlets or backwaters rapidly disappears in streams.

Sampling with plankton nets in stream currents, however, frequently does result in collecting algal cells. Upon close examination, however, they are usually found to be diatoms that have been scoured from the streambed, or that have been produced in daily rhythms from the periphyton, discussed previously.

In the lower reaches of the RCC, where waters are wide and deep, or in backwater sloughs and floodplain lakes, true phytoplankton may indeed develop, especially if the water is not turbid. Phytoplankton found in these environments seems to be a matter of lake organisms in lakelike habitats.

◆   ◆   ◆

ALTHOUGH MANY INVESTIGATORS have attempted the measurement of rates of primary production, attaining comprehensive, accurate data on primary production in streams remains elusive.

We can divide the methods that have been used into four types:
- direct measurement, counting or weighing plant material;
- use of the chemistry of photosynthesis;
- an indirect method involving chlorophyll;
- use of radioactive isotopes.

The direct measurement method is limited to macrophytes and involves sampling by pulling, cutting, or scraping all plant material at the end of the growing season (autumn). It is much like harvesting a crop at the end of summer, and it is in fact called the "harvest method."

Primary producers absorb carbon dioxide and produce oxygen. Changes in these gases resulting from photosynthesis can be converted to both energy and weight of plant matter. Measurements made in the open stream can be difficult, because both carbon dioxide and oxygen diffuse into and out of the water; in some circumstances, corrections can be approximated. Of the two gases, oxygen is more commonly used, and thus the technique is customarily termed the "oxygen method."

Incidentally, the idea that streams can be improved by installing small waterfalls to increase the oxygen content of water (as well as the belief that the more oxygen, the better) is incorrect. Adding turbulence this way only serves to keep oxygen content at equilibrium with air, and a cool, healthy stream naturally contains oxygen at equilibrium anyway. Most fishes require oxygen content in the range of about 5 to 8 parts per million (ppm), and equilibrium levels remain within or above this range. A neat evolutionary result.

Oxygen, by the way, is more soluble in cooler water (the opposite of most chemicals). Consequently, despite the seeming likelihood of low oxygen at night, when both plants and animals respire and take up oxygen, streams often have the *highest* oxygen at night, because that is the time when stream water temperatures are the *lowest.*

The third method of measuring primary production makes use of the fact that chlorophyll, the pigment that colors plants green, acts like a catalyst to the plant's rate of photosynthesis. The concentration of chlorophyll in periphyton can give us at least an approximation of primary production.

The fourth method of estimating primary production involves the use of radioactive carbon. Measuring the uptake of radioactive carbon by algae in a bottled sample, along with knowledge of the amount of radioactive carbon that has been added to the bottle, allows us to calculate the rate of normal carbon uptake. This method is now the one of choice in lakes and oceans, but the bottling of stream water is likely to produces errors.

◆   ◆   ◆

THE ECOLOGIST'S USE OF THE TERM *production*, whether it is for plant, invertebrate, or fish, refers to the rate of tissue elaboration. The unit most meaningful in a practical sense is "weight per unit area per unit time"—for example, pounds per acre per year. This unit can be readily compared between trophic levels, whose different units of chemical content may not be directly comparable. Scientists also distinguish between weight as expressed as wet (that is, fresh) and dry. Although dry-weight measurements are more consistent for use in statistical analyses, most of us are probably more familiar with fresh weight, especially when used to describe the lost trout or bass that had just broken off and would have weighed, say, at least five pounds!

From here on in this book, the measure we'll use is *pounds per acre per year*. The pounds measure will be wet weight. The acre is a convenient size to describe a stream section we can all relate to (a square area about 210 feet on each side). A section of stream about one acre in area is a reach about 50 feet wide and a little more than 800 feet long—a piece of water that any stream angler can visualize when stepping into a favorite stream for the evening rise.

The time unit of one year is an obvious best choice because it embodies one cycle in the annual rhythms of fish spawning, feeding and growth, emergence of insects, and fluctuations in stream flow.

Many factors enter the equation when we estimate primary production rates. By "estimating," we biologists do not mean just a guess off the top of someone's head. Rather, an *estimate* is the result of comprehensive *sampling* and intricate computation expressed within a range of probability. The fertility of the water (dissolved nutrients), sunlight, water temperature, nature of the streambed, and a host of other factors all contribute to the resulting level of tissue elaborated by the plants, as so many pounds per acre per year.

When this author some years ago attempted a summary of production rates in lakes and streams across the state of Minnesota, the result was necessarily a combination of many factors—and some uncertainties. Few totally accurate estimates of primary production in streams had been made and published in scientific journals and other literature at the time. But by combining the few available estimates with conversions from the worldwide published literature, I could formulate some generalizations.

Minnesota is an extraordinarily diverse region with a complex of natural resource factors. Across this huge complex, a notable ecological gradient is evident in the terrestrial catchments from northeast to southwest. Vegetative types vary from boreal forests of spruce and fir, to (previously) huge forests of lumber-producing white and red pine, to deciduous forests of oak, maple, and other hardwoods (the "Big Woods"), and to western prairies where buffalo roamed.

The gradient includes changes in geology (lava to limestone), vegetation (conifer to deciduous to prairie), and climate (wet/cool to dry/warm). Changes in the productivity of aquatic resources, low-to-high, northeast-to-southwest, can also be found across this gradient.

In previous sections, we mentioned the positive relationship between the alkalinity of water and biological productivity. Perhaps nowhere else is the relationship better illustrated than along this environmental gradient in Minnesota.

Stream waters in the coniferous forests of northeastern Minnesota range in alkalinity from near zero to about 35 parts per million (ppm) (average, 25 ppm); in central parts of the state, alkalinity is about 35 ppm to 85 ppm (average, 50 ppm); and in the southwestern plains region, alkalinity ranges from about 85 ppm to 275 ppm (average 125 ppm).

Top: a softwater stream in northeastern Minnesota;
Bottom: a hardwater plains stream in the southwest.

And instream (autochthonous) primary production? Northeast: about 10,300 pounds per acre per year; central: 36,900 pounds per acre per year; and in the southwest: 42,800 pounds per acre per year. The positive relationship between alkalinity and productivity is clearly evident.

Unfortunately, data were not available to separate these primary production figures into groups such as periphyton and macrophytes. It is likely that primary production in streams of forested areas is largely from periphyton; in more open streams in the southwest, macrophytes probably contribute the most.

These results are for autochthonous primary production only. When allochthonous matter was added at the primary production level, numbers increased, and we would expect the relative increase to be greater in woodland streams than in open streams.

Incidentally, it is interesting to compare the above numbers from streams with those from lakes located along the same ecological gradient. Primary production in lakes, where all primary production is autochthonous, was as follows: Northeast: 3,350 pounds per acre per year; central: 12,500 pounds per acre per year; southwest: 22,200 pounds per acre per year. As expected, primary production in streams was higher than in lakes. When allochthonous plant matter is added to the primary production level in streams, the disparity becomes even greater. Primary production has been observed to be higher in streams than in lakes by many times.

◆   ◆   ◆

CAN WE EXPECT THE SAME RESULTS elsewhere in North America? Elsewhere on Earth? Where geology, vegetation, and climate are fairly similar, *yes*. Where ecological conditions are greatly different, we should expect different results. At the same time, if the correlations between alkalinity and productivity are consistent, we should be able to explain differing productivity levels on the basis of documented ecological conditions.

Conditions that affect the rate of primary production in streams can be condensed to mainly two: nutrients and light.

The combined effect of these factors, especially in streams, is mediated by water currents and water temperature. Conditions fluctuate in streams—in time, through the RCC, in annual cycles, and sometimes unpredictably—which is what makes the study of stream ecology so very interesting!

As we work our way upward through the trophic pyramid, from plants to invertebrates to fish, we'll continue to add production data, as best we can. And when we're done, we'll compare all stream data together—which can then help to give us a larger view of the dynamics of life in streams and rivers.

TECHNICAL REFERENCES:

Benfield, Ernest F. 1981. Primary production in stream ecosystems. Pages 82-90 *in* Louis A. Krumholz, editor. *The Warmwater Streams Symposium.* Southern Division, American Fisheries Society, Lawrence, Kansas.

Minshall, G. Wayne. 1978. Autotrophy in stream ecosystems. *BioScience.* Volume 28, pages 767-771.

RiverSketch

RIVER OF GRASS

UNIQUE IN ITS EXTRAORDINARY STRUCTURE, the Everglades of south Florida were once characterized as a river fifty miles wide and six inches deep. In her classic history of the Everglades, published in 1947 as a component of the *Rivers of America* series, the late author Marjory Stoneman Douglas described them as "...the green and brown expanse of saw grass and of water, shining and shimmering below, the grass and water that is the meaning and the central fact of the Everglades of Florida. It is a river of grass."

Of course, the greater ecosystem of the Everglades is much more than the expanse of shallow, fresh water imperceptibly moving through a vast prairie of saw grass. Peatlands, pinelands, cypress swamp, hardwood islands, creeks and sloughs, and the brackish-water mangrove forests at the ocean edges—all make up the Everglades ecosystem in the holistic sense. And the "saw grass" is not a true grass, but a sedge, with sharp, sawlike teeth on its leaf edges.

The "glades" are magnificently diverse, incompletely known, still daunting and mysterious, and incomparably profuse in their diverse forms of life.

The Florida Everglades extends to a horizon of saw grass
in slowly moving currents (with alligator partly hidden)
(Photo courtesy of U.S. Department of the Interior,
Everglades National Park.)

The source of water is the headwaters of the Kissimee River, which flows south through the middle of the Florida peninsula to huge Lake Okeechobee, a collecting basin for water draining down the interior of the Florida peninsula. In early historic time, water flowed from Okeechobee across nearly the width of south Florida. Back then, water spilled out of the lake over its rim like a large, flat pan overfilling its capacity to spread gently southwestward toward Florida Bay and the Gulf of Mexico. The island-studded bay is a 40-miles-long triangle of part-water, part-land, lying between the mainland on the north and the Florida Keys on the southeast. From Lake Okeechobee to Florida Bay, the glades' water flowed about one-quarter mile per day, for a hundred miles.

The flow of water pulses seasonally: low in the dry months of winter, greater in the wet season of spring to late fall. Over eons, the Everglades evolved to depend on this pattern.

The water, this river, is the dynamic life force of the region. As Douglas so perceptively put it, it is indeed the "central fact of the Everglades."

The biodiversity of the Everglades, especially its bird life, is one of the richest on earth. The assemblage of water-dependent birds—herons, egrets, ibises, storks, pelicans, spoonbills, cormorants, and others—is unmatched. Mammals, reptiles, amphibians, fishes, migratory waterfowl, and many categories of aquatic invertebrates make up an astonishing variety of interacting life forms. The once so plentiful American alligator, severely reduced but now partially restored, remains as a charismatic icon of the Everglades.

Rare and endangered species have been of special interest. The Florida panther (subspecies of the western cougar) and the American crocodile (distinct from the more common alligator) are the best known. The multicolored tree snails of the genus *Liguus*, occurring in over 50 varieties with unique color patterns, have attracted collectors' attention to the point of rarity.

Always to the detriment of native life, exotic species have interrupted long-established ecological patterns. For example, the melaleuca tree (from Australia), grows rapidly and profusely to overwhelm indigenous vegetation. The walking catfish (from South America) has spread rapidly to many water bodies across land, where it competes with native fishes. The Brazilian pepper tree continues to threaten the Everglades pinelands, and the now-ubiquitous water hyacinth, with its beautiful flowers and an overwhelming propensity to choke waterways, shades out other aquatic plants with its profuse growth.

But the most important endangered component of the Everglades today, catastrophic in its new rarity, is *water* itself.

In the year of Douglas's book publication, 1947, President Harry Truman signed the act creating Everglades National Park, preserving the unique communities of life, even then recognized as threatened. The park encloses some 1,500 square miles, including Florida Bay, but it contains only about one-seventh of the entire Everglades ecosystem.

Canoeing among the Everglades mangroves.
(Photo courtesy of U.S. Department of the Interior,
Everglades National Park.)

Fortunately, Everglades National Park includes some of the most diverse elements of the "river." Unfortunately, the park does not include the source of water so essential to the river and its wildlife—Lake Okeechobee and its drainage.

In the concluding chapter of her book, "The Eleventh Hour," author Douglas issued a provocative warning that the water source was in danger. But since the time of her unheeded warning, the Everglades' water has been used, not to nurture the varied ecosystem of saw grass, mangrove, and wildlife, but as a *commodity* for human conquest and increase.

Our engineers have ditched and diverted its water for "flood control"; drainage along nearly 1,500 miles of water-constricting canals and levees has created and now irrigates new farmland. Lake Okeechobee's outlets now stand dammed behind a dike 40 feet high.

Currently the only natural water flow is south of the Tamiami Trail, US 41, which runs from the city of Miami west across the peninsula, effectively cutting the Everglades in half. Along with the resulting severe reduction in water quantity came the deterioration in water quality. As the result of runoff from agricultural areas, Lake Okeechobee's waters are now polluted, as is the Everglades itself. With a lessened flow of fresh water into Florida Bay and a consequent increase in saltwater influence, the Bay's salinity is now twice the level of the surrounding ocean water, destroying estuarine mangrove forests and producing green blooms of marine algae.

A huge increase in new homes, industries, and bustling cities, with their enormous thirst for water, has severely diminished the river that once served a thriving Everglades.

The losses in animal life, especially of wading birds, have been catastrophic. Over half of the original Everglades' wetland has disappeared. Nesting and feeding habitats for bird life have been reduced to less than half; total numbers in many bird populations have decreased to a mere 25 percent of predrainage times.

The controversy between agriculture/urban development and preservation of the Everglades continues to heat up. But at last, the concept of *restoration* seems to be tipping the balance with public sentiment now favoring renewal. Political pressure mounts, and governmental administrators from Washington to the State of Florida increasingly call for a change in environmental treatment of the Everglades.

The main thrust of restoration involves a return of the region's natural water supply—both in quantity and in its natural seasonal fluctuations. No one expects restoration to be easy or cheap; it will require a major reconfiguration of the current water-control system of dikes and canals and pumping stations, as well as substantial changes in water allocation. But even economic predictions now suggest that a revitalized Everglades has greater worth to the economy of Florida from tourist income, than from the present Everglades so compromised by the agricultural industry.

A restored flow of fresh water across the Everglades wetland, nurturing such a great diversity of plant and animal wonders, now may become a reality. Perhaps soon we will stop treating the Everglades water as a commodity and realize its value as a catalyst to sustain the productivity of one of Earth's most complex and threatened ecosystems.

Indeed, there is new hope for the river of grass.

SELECTED REFERENCES:

Davis, Steven M., and John C. Ogden, editors. 1994. *Everglades: The ecosystem and its restoration.* St. Lucie Press, Delray Beach, Florida.
Douglas, Marjory Stoneman. 1947. *The Everglades: River of grass.* Rinehart & Company, New York.

Chapter **10**

HETEROTROPHY

T HE PROVISION OF ENERGY to the biological communities of the stream is the most critical factor affecting their health and productivity. It is the fuel that powers all life functions. The previous chapter on primary production was concerned with green plants that use the energy of the sun to fuel their own body functions and to photosynthesize body tissue containing stored energy. In the last chapter, we defined the process of autotrophy as primary production; as green plants, they are autotrophs.

However, all animals and some other organisms must obtain their energy from food—for example, green plant tissue. This latter process of obtaining energy we term *heterotrophy* (other feeding). All animals are thus *heterotrophs*, from the tiniest midge larvae to humans to the largest of Earth's ocean mammals.

An important distinction between autotrophs and heterotrophs is one ecological difference: Whereas autotrophs (or plants) constitute a single trophic level, heterotrophs occupy several trophic levels, each one providing food for the organisms at the next higher level. Eventually, we will calculate some rates of production for heterotrophs (secondary production) just as we did for autotrophs (primary production). But because heterotrophs include several trophic levels, we need to estimate production rates separately for each. We'll get around to providing some secondary production rates later on.

Right now, we'll deal with the organisms and functions that make up one of the lowest trophic levels among heterotrophs. These are not animals, however. Rather, they are a separate group of *decomposers*—more specifically, fungi and bacteria.

A half-century ago (when this author was getting his college education!), stream biologists did not concern themselves with fungi and bacteria. Even as late as 1964, there was no mention of decomposers in Bardach's *Downstream*. Microorganisms simply did not seem to be of importance in the system of stream life, and no one gave much thought to the broader significance of heterotrophy. One reason for this early oversight, no doubt, was that they are invisible to the human eye and, probably, to the fish's eye as well. Stream biologists were mostly fishery biologists in those pioneer decades, and although we were vitally interested in the invertebrates that fish ate, little attention was paid to what the invertebrates ate.

An even greater reason for the lack of attention to the concept of heterotrophy, however, was probably because science had not yet appreciated the importance of allochthonous material produced outside the stream channel. And biologists used to think that the stream ecosystem was bordered only by stream banks!

Even so, we now know that heterotrophy does not involve only allochthonous matter. Much organic matter important to the rest of the stream community is produced instream by autotrophy—green plants, or macrophytes—and then consumed by heterotrophs after the plants die back in the fall and begin to decay. In fact, nonliving organic matter from any source—animal remains, for example—also proceeds through microorganisms toward its ultimate fates of decay and provision of energy to other forms of life.

In the discipline of stream ecology, the study of these microbes over the past few decades has resulted in major advances in our understanding of how stream life functions. Fungi and bacteria are particularly important in shaded, headwater streams, where little sunlight reaches.

Coursing through the lowest path of material transport along the bottom of a catchment, the stream collects the catchment's discarded waste and litter. Deciduous leaves and coniferous needles; flowers, fruit, and seeds; twigs, branches, and trunks—all of these allochthonous sources of energy blow, fall, or tumble downslope from uplands, hillsides, and riparian bottoms to the stream.

Upstream reaches with dense wooded canopy
supports little photosynthesis. Otter River, Michigan.

However, the stream is not just a "sewer carrying the earth's waste to the sea," (as one observer once put it), but rather a living organism in itself. Let's take a closer look.

◆   ◆   ◆

WE NEVER SEE THEM WHEN WE'RE ON THE WATER, but fungi and bacteria are some of the most important life forms in all streams. These primitive, microscopic organisms rejuvenate the waste and debris of biological communities into fresh, new life.

They are responsible for mineralizing, or liberating, elements and nutrients temporarily locked up in the molecules of nonliving organic matter, which had once ran their course through life to death. Mineralization makes phosphorus, nitrogen, calcium, carbon, and other elements available again for synthesis into living cells and bodies.

Fungi and bacteria are thus intermediaries between dead organic matter and new stream life. They are the first organisms in a progression of trophic levels leading to new plants, invertebrates, and fish, as well as to a few birds and mammals.

All nonliving organic matter, both allochthonous and autochthonous, requires *conditioning* before it becomes useful as food for invertebrates. Conditioning includes two processes: first, colonization by decomposers on the surface of the organic matter, and second, partial digestion of the organic matter itself so that it becomes more palatable to feeding invertebrates. Invertebrates obtain their nutrition from both the microbial biomass and the conditioned organic matter. In this conditioning process, fungi are often more important than bacteria to the rest of the stream community, making up 90 percent of the microbial biomass. However, under some less common conditions, bacteria show a higher rate of production.

Fungi make up one of several *kingdoms* of multicellular organisms on Earth. We see evidence of fungi everywhere—on dead trees or mushrooms on the forest floor (some edible to us humans, some not!), the visible parts of the fungus. A certain class of fungi, the Hyphomycetes, will concern us most here. Some are terrestrial and some aquatic; obviously, the aquatic hyphomycetes will interest us the more. In addition, streams are the primary habitat for this fungal group.

Absorbing nitrate from stream water, fungi synthesize protein, which is especially important to the function and growth of all animals. Thus, fish receive their protein from insects and other invertebrate animals, which in turn receive theirs from the fungal bodies that have colonized dead organic matter.

As it turns out, fungal growth is greatest in hardwater (limestone) streams, which frequently have high levels of nitrate. Additionally, hyphomycetes better perform their functions in headwaters with shallow, swift riffles—typical of low-order streams that are frequently shaded and therefore depend more on sources of energy in allochthonous organic matter.

Bacteria are single-celled organisms, with which our most common human association is through many diseases. Bacteria are the oldest known forms of life on Earth, as recorded from our fossil record of more than three billion years. They perform many beneficial services to humankind, not the least of which to us river lovers is the mineralization of the dead organic wastes in streams into useful elements and compounds.

◆   ◆   ◆

BY FAR, MOST RESEARCH EFFORT on stream heterotrophy has been in the ecology of deciduous leaves. For Temperate Zone streams in deciduous woodlands (where most stream ecological research has been concentrated), we find deciduous leaves, among all allochthonous energy sources, to contribute by far the most energy to a stream. The input of leaves is seasonal, following the cycle of autumn leaf fall. This autumn "pulse" of energy has been likened to a huge meal that must fulfill the energy requirements of the stream's biological communities for most of the following year.

Great significance has been assigned to the conditioning of deciduous leaves after they reach stream water. The fresh leaf, newly fallen, has little value as food for invertebrates. Furthermore, leaves comprise coarse particulate organic matter, or CPOM, not immediately useful to small invertebrates. The material of carbohydrate in fleshy parts and hard support structures of lignin hold little nutritive value. The raw leaf appears neither attractive nor palatable to feeding insects or other invertebrates.

The conditioning of a fresh leaf consists of three processes. First, the leaching of dissolved organic matter (DOM) removes a good deal of the leaf's mass, beginning the process of decay.

Second is the colonizing of the leaf by fungi and bacteria. These microorganisms, especially fungi, improve the quality of leaf material as invertebrate food by producing protein and by partially digesting the leaf material. Professor Kenneth Cummins likens the conditioned leaf to a cracker with peanut butter—the invertebrate consumer eats the cracker but receives lip-smacking good nutrition from the peanut butter!

The fall of deciduous leaves in autumn provides a huge pulse of energy to the stream in the form of allochthonous organic matter.

Third, fragmenting of the leaf is brought about both by microorganism growth that softens the leaf matter and by the shredding feeding of certain invertebrates. Many shredders that feed on CPOM do not assimilate or digest all of these larger pieces of organic matter. The material that is not digested then becomes available in the form of fecal pellets to other organisms downstream, filtering or gathering FPOM. Thus, the process of reducing particle sizes benefits a diversity of organic matter feeders and increases the overall use of the CPOM resource.

Leaf conditioning converts the energy-rich but indigestible maple or willow leaves into nutritious, palatable food, adding the peanut butter to the cracker, for many species of insects, crustaceans, and other invertebrates. Soon an abundant food supply is created from the catchment's leaves, eventually to sustain fish and other animals.

The quality of stream water—its temperature and concentration of elements and compounds—affects the rate and quality of leaf conditioning. The greater amounts of nitrogen, phosphorus, and alkalinity in calcium-rich limestone streams contribute toward the production of an abundance of nutritious food for invertebrates.

Leaf conditioning proceeds more rapidly at a higher water temperature. However, this does not necessarily mean that the warmwater stream will be more productive than the summer-cool stream. Rather, different animals have different optimum temperatures at which growth rates and other survival factors are optimal.

Tree species vary substantially in their rate of conditioning. Some species are much more receptive to conditioning—for example, basswood, maple, elm, willow, and aspen. Others, such as oak, alder, beech, walnut, and sycamore, are more resistant to conditioning. Rhododendron leaves and conifer needles are particularly resistant, a condition that contributes to the low productivity of softwater, freestone streams that flow through boreal forests of pine, spruce, and fir, and the rhododendron of the Appalachian Mountains. The species of leaf that break down most rapidly (that is, those with highest rate and level of conditioning) are those that are the most readily consumed, or preferred, by the feeding invertebrates that contribute to conditioning.

In the first stage of leaf conditioning, much organic matter is lost when dissolved organic matter (DOM) is leached from the leaf. However, this loss does not result in the wastage of energy. The energy in DOM is returned to the biological community in two ways: first, dissolved organic molecules are absorbed by the microorganisms in the organic matrix on the surfaces of stream-bed stones, the periphyton, which is subsequently fed upon by grazing invertebrates. Second, when DOM is subjected to turbulence, as in a riffle, organic molecules flocculate creating discrete particles (FPOM), which are then also subject to colonizing and conditioning by fungi and bacteria.

Flocculation proceeds more rapidly in the high alkalinity water of limestone streams. After colonization and conditioning by decomposing microorganisms, the FPOM thus formed is then readily available to many insects. Bacteria on these FPOM particles are also a good source of nutrition. Life—as well as energy and elements—continues on, always in a downstream direction.

We've all seen collections of leaves accumulated on the upstream side of stones and branches in our favorite streams, in late summer and early autumn. These leaf packs are a veritable storehouse of biological dynamics. Energy transformations, leaching and removal of DOM, colonization by fungi and bacteria, growth and production by fungal bodies, the synthesis of protein, and, of course, insect feeding—all constitute biological activities that support additional animal life of all kinds in streams.

A major scientific effort has gone into examination of the leaf pack. Many studies have been conducted in the field using natural leaf packs; other field studies have involved the use of simulated leaf packs with natural leaves tied into bundles, packages of many leaves fastened to bricks, and leaves enclosed in fine-meshed bags and baskets.

Other experiments have been conducted in the laboratory. Different water chemistry and temperatures, fresh versus dried leaves, inoculations with fungal and bacterial cells, exposure to invertebrate feeding (compared with exclosure of invertebrates), and comparison of different leaf species, have all been included in laboratory studies. These studies have yielded a treasure trove of new findings. A great proportion of our knowledge about heterotrophy has been gained through the study of leaf packs.

Forming in autumn along with the major pulse of leaf fall, packs may persist for a long time, sometimes over winter and into succeeding seasons. Spring floods and spates may remove leaf packs, however, depriving upper reaches of considerable energy and nutrients. However, such scouring may be just the kind of event that provides essential energy and nutrients to downstream communities!

The importance of leaves, particularly deciduous leaves, as a source of energy was a major element in formulating the river continuum concept (RCC). Professor Hynes placed an early emphasis on deciduous leaves as allochthonous energy sources in his *The Ecology of Running Waters* in 1970, and further studies in the following decade soon established a firm base of data and conclusions on the contribution of leaves to the headwater reaches of woodland streams. Researchers discovered that CPOM, in the form of leaves, was processed in the stream through size-reduction to FPOM, which then flowed on to support and nurture downstream communities. What followed was the hypothesis of a predictable system that changed from headwater streams to rivers—in other words, the river continuum concept.

◆   ◆   ◆

THE INPUT OF WOODY DEBRIS to a stream sometimes constitutes the main contribution of allochthonous energy, especially in forested catchments. Microbes and invertebrates condition wood, much as they do leaves, with a few important differences. First, although both leaves and woody material are classed as CPOM, wood is usually much larger—for example, big branches and tree trunks. Second, as might be expected, these very coarse "particles" of organic matter require a much longer time for conditioning and final decay.

The kinds and sizes of woody debris vary greatly, from almost invisible twigs to huge trunks. Anglers and paddlers may not be aware of twigs, but they will find a Douglas fir or white pine trunk across the river a great nuisance. For many stream animals, however, the presence of wood in streams constitutes a great resource of available energy.

For example, in the Pacific Northwest where forests are largely coniferous and deciduous leaves less available, woody debris in streams may account for 75 percent or more of the total allochthonous energy. Wood is an important source of allochthonous energy in virtually all streams, especially in headwater reaches shaded by riparian trees.

Woody debris in the form of branches, stumps,
and fallen trunks add energy and nutrients to a stream.
Upper Manistee River, Michigan.

The influence of wood upon the stream's biological community begins with its use as a stable substrate for insects and other invertebrates. For example, some caddisfly larvae take up position on woody edges to filter and feed upon FPOM drifting in the current. The sheltering habitat of brushy debris attracts many invertebrates.

Second, algae and decomposers, fungi being the most important in the conditioning of wood, colonize submerged wood surfaces. The effect of fungi begins necessarily on the wood surface, where they establish a highly nutritious and palatable biofilm.

Third, after the wood material becomes softened by microbes, insects are attracted to the biofilm. In addition to ingesting algae and fungi, some insects feed upon wood itself, creating cavities and channels deep into the wood's interior. Such spaces allow water, oxygen, and nutrients—and further activity by microorganisms—to penetrate deeper into the wood. It is interesting to note that some insects—for example, *xylophages* (xylo = wood; phages = feeders)—have evolved to bore, gouge, and feed specifically upon submerged wood. Which, of course, is very fortunate in providing food and energy to the rest of the stream community. Benefactors include the juveniles of Pacific salmon and steelhead trout, common in streams of the coniferous catchments of the Pacific Northwest.

The longer time required for conditioning of wood is particularly evident with large tree trunks, which may take one or two centuries. Branches two to four inches in diameter will need a half-century. Even small twigs less than a half-inch might take five to ten years. But even with these low decay rates and long conditioning times, the total energy contributed by such immense wood quantities is very high.

From shaded upstream reaches, input of wood declines in importance downstream. In first- to second-order streams, mostly in forested areas, perhaps one-fourth of the streambed is woody substrate; in stream orders third to fourth, probably about half as much will be wood. Farther downstream, woody debris occurrence may be negligible, because in the larger streams of higher orders, high flows move branches and tree trunks to the banks or out of the river channel altogether.

Still, much wood may be available as *snag habitat* in lower reaches. Submerged branches and twigs, or snags, constitute the most important—or sometimes the only—stable surfaces for invertebrates. In these lower stream reaches, the major allochthonous energy arrives in drifting FPOM from upstream, and the snag habitat has a great beneficial effect by providing stable surfaces up in the current where filtering insects can intercept drifting FPOM. Here, larvae of caddisflies and black flies gather FPOM from the water—and produce truly immense quantities of food for fish.

The development and influence of so-called *debris dams* has recently attracted much attention among stream ecologists. These thick, tightly woven accumulations of woody debris, interlaced entanglements of trunks, branches, and brush, occur commonly in small, high-gradient forested streams. In these headwater reaches, they profoundly influence the rest of the stream community.

Some effects of debris dams are physical. These may impede the migration of fish or create slow, stagnant reservoirs upstream from the dam. On the other hand, they create structural habitat for invertebrates, provide holding pools for fish, and bring about new spawning gravels.

Beaver dams function as debris dams,
providing shelter and food for a host of invertebrates.

Debris dams also exert profound biological effects. The major influence of such accumulations of woody debris is to enlarge greatly the stream's capacity to utilize allochthonous energy and nutrients, thereby leading to production by invertebrates. Within the interior spaces of the dam exists a profusion of surfaces on twigs and branches and other kinds of CPOM, and these provide shelter, substrate, and food for a host of invertebrate species. The density and biomass of invertebrates within the interior of debris dams have been estimated at from five to ten times the abundance of invertebrates on sedimentary and stony streambeds, because of the huge increase of surfaces that provide both living space and food.

The debris dam acts to retain and store the energy of CPOM that would otherwise flush downstream. The capture and retention of deciduous leaves is a major effect. With the action of fungi and invertebrates, the interior of the dam becomes a dynamic factory in which the leaves, as CPOM, are converted to FPOM, which then drifts downstream as *seston* to provide food to filter-feeding insects. Furthermore, debris dams store large amounts of FPOM, which later may be flushed out during storms, to nurture invertebrate populations downstream.

Debris dams do not occur nearly as commonly in high stream orders, where rivers are wider, gradients are less, and swift, deep flows prevent accumulations. In these reaches of the lower river continuum, streambeds are often lined with finer sediments that are less productive of invertebrates.

◆   ◆   ◆

THE ABUNDANCE OF LARGE AQUATIC PLANTS, or macrophytes, is often taken as an indication of high productivity in streams. However, as a source of autochthonous energy, while seeming a very large source, macrophytes are fed upon very little in their live state by invertebrates. Thus, live macrophytes do not contribute directly to the sustenance of invertebrates. Less than 10 percent of the macrophytes' primary production is consumed by invertebrates.

When these plants die back in late summer, however, their dead organic matter becomes a part of the stream's *detritus pool* of CPOM. Then, like allochthonous leaves and wood, autochthonous organic matter undergoes conditioning by microbes.

The dead plant material is made more palatable and nutritious for invertebrates and adds its calories to the rest of the stream's biological system. In contrast to leaves and wood, bacteria, rather than fungi, are more important in conditioning dead macrophyte matter.

This late summer timing of energy input is important. The seasonal pulse may constitute a significant link between the spring/summer production of autochthonous algae and the later autumn leaf fall, contributing to a continuous supply of energy through most of the year to stream invertebrate populations.

A few exceptions to the above general model of macrophytes and heterotrophy may be noted. Rooted macrophytes are more important in the middle reaches of a stream course, where sunlight is abundant and the water is slower and perhaps warmer in summer. In faster currents and open sunlight, however, the algae of periphyton remain the most common. In the swift currents of shaded, upstream reaches, patches of *moss*, usually attached to stones, may be an important source of autochthonous energy to the few invertebrates that feed on it. Mosses do not die back in winter, as do other macrophytes. As living structure on streambeds through winter, they provide attachment substrates for insects and other invertebrates. With their finely branched leaves, mosses retain large quantities of FPOM, offering abundant food for invertebrates that reside among the moss stems.

In some stream reaches with superabundant macrophytes, conditioning of dead macrophyte material may be the primary source of sustenance to the stream animal community. We have studied this aspect of stream ecology much less than other heterotrophic forms of energy supply. When further research results become available and rates of heterotrophic energy supply from macrophytes can be estimated, we may find that this source of autochthonous energy is extremely important, indeed.

◆　　　　◆　　　　◆

MODELS OF HOW ENERGY is supplied to the stream's biological community have changed greatly over the past few decades. Earlier theories of energy passing up through the trophic pyramid, or food chains, have not been discarded, but rather fine-tuned.

The earlier, simplistic concept—solar radiation *to* plant photosynthesis *to* feeding by herbivorous animals *to* feeding by carnivorous animals—still holds generally true. But now we know that much of the capture of solar energy by photosynthesizing green plants takes place outside the stream channel: deciduous leaves, woody debris, nonliving matter of all kinds, instead of just by aquatic plants in the stream. This more expanded system of heterotrophy, which includes nonliving organic matter from the land and conditioning by decomposers, providing palatable food to invertebrates, is more complex and much more interesting.

All organisms must undertake respiration—that is, they must use oxygen to metabolize organic matter and give off carbon dioxide as a waste compound. Green plants first absorb carbon dioxide and water to synthesize organic matter and give off oxygen; but then, especially at night they, too, use oxygen to metabolize organic matter, giving off carbon dioxide. Heterotrophic organisms—animals and decomposers—absorb oxygen from water to metabolize their ingested food and also give off carbon dioxide. In the *autotrophic* process, and over the long term, green plants produce more oxygen than they use, releasing much of it into water for use by a host of heterotrophic organisms.

Streams or stream reaches can be considered as mainly either autotrophic or heterotrophic. In the river continuum concept, headwaters (first to third orders) are typically heterotrophic: oxygen is consumed above the rate of production by plants and a net production of carbon dioxide is released. Middle reaches (fourth through sixth orders) are autotrophic: producing a net excess of oxygen. And large rivers (seventh order and higher) are again heterotrophic, being turbid and deep, where little light penetrates to the streambed to provide the energy required for photosynthesis.

Recognizing that the stream ecosystem encompasses the entire catchment, the holistic view of the stream and its valley proceeded hand-in-hand with the appreciation of allochthony and heterotrophy. We now know the value of both instream autochthonous primary production, some of which enters the detritus pool after its death, and of external allochthonous input as well. Our intellectual view has been expanded from the stream channel to its entire enclosing catchment.

The principle underlying the trophic pyramid remains valid. But the unfolding of its details through heterotrophy has advanced the discipline of freshwater ecology immensely—and provided us with a fascinating scientific adventure.

TECHNICAL REFERENCES:

Anderson, Norman H., and James R. Sedell. 1979. Detritus processing by macroinvertebrates in stream ecosystems. *Annual Review of Entomology*. Volume 24, pages 351-377.

Wallace, J. Bruce, Jackson R. Webster, and W. Robert Woodall. 1977. The role of filter feeders in flowing waters. *Archiv für Hydrobiologie*. Volume 79, pages 506-534.

RiverSketch

BLACK WATERS

ACROSS THE BROAD COASTAL PLAIN of southeastern United States, through expansive floodplain swamps thick with water-loving undergrowth and trees, slowly flow numerous streams known as blackwater rivers. To first-time visitors, they may appear dark and mysterious.

Many blackwater rivers originate in the Coastal Plain swamps. They range from first- to sixth-order streams. Darkly stained with brown swamp-water, sinuously meandering in the half-light beneath heavy tree canopies, these streams may indeed give the impression of rivers from the nether regions.

At first glance, the blackwater rivers would seem to be starkly unproductive. The waters are soft, low in alkalinity. Stream bottoms are composed mainly of shifting sand and mud. With little sunlight, primary production is almost nonexistent. The only structure in the streams is woody debris composed of decaying twigs and branches.

Such seemingly somber prospects, however, mask ecosystems of surprising biological productivity, conditions that have come to be appreciated over only the past two decades. In fact, blackwater streams are rich and teeming with aquatic life. Invertebrates appear in diverse communities that in turn support a thriving assemblage of warmwater fishes. Paradoxical as it may seem, its explanation revealed a fascinating connection between river and riparian floodplain.

With the holistic appreciation of the broader ecosystem—linkage to the land—the solution to the paradox became evident. Here, where sunlight and photosynthesis were all too absent, another energy source was eventually identified: the massive input of organic matter from riparian swamps and wet, richly vegetated floodplains. Unlike the infertile streams of northern coniferous forests, which are also darkly stained, the Southeast's blackwater rivers are biologically rich.

In these subtropical regions, winter is the season for replenishment. While northern boreal catchments are locked in snow and ice, these southern black waters flood and divert across surrounding swamps and floodplains. The inundations remain for several months. During this time, aquatic primary production flourishes in the swamps. Bacteria and fungi process organic matter, and the biomass of a rich, microscopic fauna literally explodes. Even after water levels decline in springtime, permanent pools remain as fecund sources of aquatic life. Allochthonous organic matter now becomes more plentiful in the streams, providing the energy that drives the biological systems evolved to use it. Woody debris, consisting of roots, trunks, and branches that have resulted from undercutting of banks provides the major structural habitat for macroinvertebrates, ultimately food for microorganisms, invertebrates, and numerous fishes.

A blackwater river with woody debris winds through
a southeastern coastal swamp. Cedar Creek, South Carolina.
(Photo by Leonard A. Smock, Virginia Commonwealth University.)

Woody debris, accumulating along stream banks, in debris dams, and on stream bottoms provides major habitat that offers both structure and sustenance to invertebrates. Upon its surfaces, filtering caddis larvae build their retreats with capture nets, and black fly larvae extend their filtering head fans to collect the abundant FPOM drifting in the slow currents. Upon these same wood surfaces, biofilms rich with microorganisms thrive and provide food for another group of insects, collector-gatherer mayflies that find nurture from the biofilms.

All three of these insect groups are subject to drifting in large quantities, thereby providing a rich supply of food for fish. Many small fishes—warmouth bass, spotted sunfish, pumpkin-seeds, redbreast sunfish, and bluegills—consume up to 60 or 70 percent of their diet from the drift of aquatic insects originating from the snag habitat. Furthermore, snags also offer essential protective cover for smaller fish. Total annual production for all fishes in these waters easily reaches levels comparable to the most productive of limestone streams.

The other major habitat for invertebrates is the shifting sand and mud. Rich with decomposing FPOM, these substrates also have their origin in riparian swamps. Huge populations of midge larvae, microcrustaceans, and tiny aquatic worms feed on the FPOM mixed in the bottom sediments. Although very small, these invertebrates are so numerous that secondary production rates calculated for their community are as high or higher than for the snag insects. Most of these "microinvertebrates" have life histories with several generations per year, increasing their annual production. They, too, provide food for fishes—minnows, catfishes, and suckers—that gain their food from the unstable bottom. Larger predatory fish—largemouth bass and pickerel—feed in turn on the smaller fish. Because the coastal plain topography presents little local relief, blackwater rivers have low gradients of only about one foot of drop in elevation per mile of stream. Consequently, the coastal plain rivers have largely escaped dams; some run free-flowing for hundreds of miles.

This lack of impoundment has made possible scientific research on the natural, full length of long streams—a rarity in modern times. Thus, these blackwater rivers have broadened our perception of the diversity within the river continuum concept (RCC). Originally, the RCC was developed on clear streams in temperate zones, where wooded, shaded headwaters were *heterotrophic* but middle reaches sunlit and *autotrophic*. Blackwater streams, in contrast, are heterotrophic in their entire course.

The blackwater river has given us a new model for studies in stream ecology. Its linkage with the surrounding land is exceptional, demonstrating the importance of surrounding floodplains that bring richness to a stream that otherwise would be unproductive. Blackwater rivers give us a broader understanding of the ecosystem concept.

Blackwater rivers have their own beauty, different from that of northern or highland trout streams, but equally important in an increasing public use for river enjoyment.

Much of the Coastal Plain is under attack by urban development, logging of valuable swamp timber, and draining for agriculture. Few significant protection programs are in place to balance these kinds of development. Only one blackwater river is now included in the National Wild and Scenic Rivers System—the Lumber River in North Carolina. No other blackwater river has received federal or state protection in the region. More special blackwater rivers will need such protection soon, if their individuality and productivity are to survive.

SELECTED REFERENCES:

Meyer, Judy L. 1990. A blackwater perspective on riverine ecosystems. *BioScience.* Volume 40, pages 643-651.

Smock, Leonard A., and Ellen Gilinsky. 1992. Coastal plain blackwater streams. Pages 271-313 in Courtney T. Hackney, S. Marshall Adams, and William A. Martin, editors. *Biodiversity of the Southeastern United States, Aquatic Communities.* John Wiley & Sons, New York.

Chapter **11**

FUNCTIONAL GROUPS

Hand in hand with recognizing and classifying organic matter in streams, in all its many forms and sizes, stream ecologists soon came to realize the need for understanding how this potential food matched up to the different kinds of animals that feed upon it. Different kinds and sizes of organic matter particles, we soon realized, were eaten by animals that employed distinctive strategies for feeding.

The feeding behaviors exhibited by insects and other invertebrates can be arranged into categories or groups that describe the functions, or roles, they play in the ecosystem. Thus, the term *functional group* followed logically.

This term should not be confused with that of *feeding guild,* which applies to a group of animals that eat the same kind of food. Functional group applies to those species that exhibit *the same method* of feeding, even though the food resources may vary. Feeding guilds are described by *the kinds of food* eaten; the functional group is described by the animal's method for acquiring it. In this chapter, we'll deal exclusively with the functional group.

◆　　　◆　　　◆

NOT LONG AGO, THE INVERTEBRATE FAUNA of lakes and streams was simply described by lists of major taxa—that is, by order and family. We knew about mayflies, caddisflies, midges, scuds, and other taxa. Little thought went into classifying these animals by their ecological functions: We did not ask what role each group played in events in the lake or stream.

With the practice of making lists of taxa, we sometimes used the broad categories of feeding modes: *herbivore, detritivore,* and *carnivore.* Later came the realization that these animals must have evolved to match the great intricacies of food type, quality, and particle size in an aquatic system. The organization that followed—functional groups—became one of the most elegant and stimulating advances in the history of ecological theory. The system that finally developed applies to streams, lakes, and other water bodies, but in this book we will explore only those functional groups that inhabit streams.

As with so many other major advances in stream ecology, Professor Kenneth Cummins played the initial and central roles in developing the organization of functional groups. About the same time that Hynes's classic reference book *The Ecology of Running Waters* was published, Cummins was wrestling with these new concepts of how a stream system functioned. An immense amount of work by Cummins, his associates, students, and colleagues followed.

The classification of stream animals based on their trophic (feeding) functions begins with the three general broad categories of herbivore, detritivore, and carnivore. In this chapter, we will be dealing almost exclusively with invertebrate animals, mainly insects and crustaceans. Herbivores are those invertebrates that feed on green plants; detritivores, on nonliving detritus. Carnivores prey upon other animals. Within each of these broad classes, however, there is important variation.

Another broad category that we can consider is *omnivores,* those animals that feed on all kinds of food, particularly when they are in their immature stages. All stream organisms are omnivorous to some extent. A herbivorous insect, for example, while grazing on algae, may ingest some fungi and bacteria, a few smaller insects, and some organic detritus, along with the algae. Detritivorous invertebrates may be wholly nonselective in their feeding. And the carnivore, or predator, although actively foraging on other, smaller animals, may very well ingest some plant or detrital matter, either incidentally or deliberately. But for simplicity's sake, we will concentrate on the first three groups, keeping in mind that some divergence of feeding occurs.

Although the functional groups that follow are based fundamentally on the three broad groups, our earlier consideration of the trophic level concept must be modified. The basic trophic pyramid does not reveal the specific linkages between a given animal or group and its food resource. This does not mean that the trophic-level theory is invalid, even though each group feeds to some extent on all kinds of food. It is the *principal* food use that determines the functional grouping in the ecosystem.

The functional group provides fine resolution and rich detail about a specific group's influence upon the rest of the community.

◆   ◆   ◆

THE CATEGORIZATION OF INVERTEBRATES into functional groups is based on two factors. First is the location of the food item, whether attached to a substrate, drifting in the current, deposited on or within the streambed sediments, or alive and swimming. Second is the size range of the food item, whether coarse particulate organic matter (CPOM), small leaves to trees, or fine particulate organic matter (FPOM), less than one millimeter in size.

To those herbivores that feed actively by grazing or scraping the periphyton from substrates, we apply the functional group *scrapers*. Although their chief food is algae in the periphyton, they also consume FPOM, bacteria and fungi, and microscopic animals in the organic matrix of the biofilm. Scrapers include many species of aquatic insects, but chiefly mayfly nymphs, caddisfly larvae, midge larvae, and most snails.

We divide the detritivores into two major categories, *shredders* and *collectors*, which feed mainly on CPOM and FPOM, respectively. Shredders have evolved with unique mouthparts especially adapted to rasping, chewing, or "shredding" large particles of organic matter. Large particles predominate in forested, headwater reaches (first- through third-order streams). Large-particle matter consists mostly of conditioned leaves and wood, and so the shredder functional group is most commonly found in these upper stream reaches.

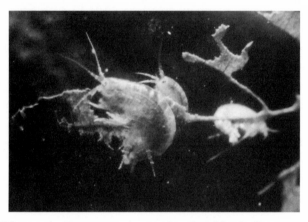

The scud, *Gammarus*, is a major shredder in limestone streams, feeding freely on conditioned deciduous leaves.

Shredders are subdivided into two groups by their principal food: leaves and wood. Shredders that feed on leaves include amphipods (scuds), many case-building caddis larvae, many stonefly nymphs, and "water worms" or "leather jackets" (crane fly larvae). Those shredders that colonize and consume wood are *borers* and *gougers*, which include a small number of insect species, among them larvae of beetles and caddisflies.

Shredders create large quantities of FPOM in two ways. First, "crumbing" the leaf or woody material is an incidental result of their rasping or chewing mode of feeding, an important process of particle-size reduction. Second, shredders egest fecal pellets that retain much energy-containing organic matter and fall within the size-range of FPOM. This is also a size-reduction process. The particles of FPOM thus produced in low-order stream reaches make up an important source of food and energy deposited on the streambed or carried downstream in the current, there to be consumed by other invertebrates in the middle and lower reaches.

Fine particulate organic matter that is generated by shredders and mechanical breakage in turbulent water is used by the second major functional group, the *collectors*, which garner fine particles in a variety of ways.

Thus, we have the two major groups processing detritus. Shredders use the leaves and wood (CPOM) to produce their own tissue, and in so doing, they generate FPOM. Collectors use the FPOM as food for their tissue production and create even finer FPOM in their fecal pellets.

Collectors are further divided into two subgroups—*gatherers* and *filterers*. Gatherers are unspecialized. They glean FPOM deposits from the streambed, from other surfaces, and from interstitial spaces in riffles and gravel deposits. They constitute a large group of invertebrates, including all orders of aquatic insects and many other invertebrates.

Filterers, on the other hand, are highly specialized in their feeding habits. As their name suggests, they are adapted to strain drifting FPOM from water currents. Drifting fine particles, however, include material besides nonliving detritus, such as algal cells and other microorganisms. The whole assemblage of drifting FPOM is sometimes termed *seston*.

Many filterers strain FPOM with specialized body parts, such as antennae, leg hairs, and certain mouthparts, including larvae of black flies and caddisflies, as well as a few mayflies and midges. Another large group of caddisflies spins fine-meshed nets, or capture nets, at the openings of stony, loosely attached cases called *retreats*. The larvae glean FPOM and other particles from the meshes of the capture nets. Others build fine-meshed sacs and some string silk threads across the interstices of gravel beds.

A final functional group consists of carnivores, or predators, which really belong to the next higher trophic level. Predators do not feed upon detritus and thus do not contribute to the size-reduction process, but among the total community of stream bottom invertebrates, they are an important component, so they are classified along with the rest of the functional groups.

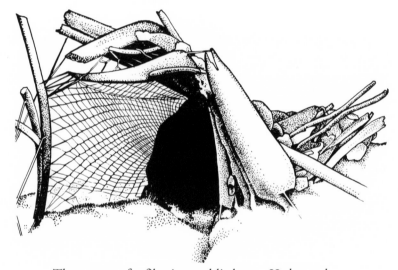

The retreat of a filtering caddis larva, *Hydropsyche*,
and its fine-meshed capture net at the opening.
(From *Larvae of the North American Caddisfly Genera* [*Trichoptera*],
by Glenn B. Wiggins. Courtesy of the Royal Ontario Museum).

Predators common in streams include nymphs of dragonflies and damselflies, some beetle larvae, the brightly-colored nymphs of stoneflies in the genus *Acroneuria*, and the formidable dobsonfly larva, *Corydalus*, common in smallmouth bass streams. Filtering caddisfly larvae glean small animals from their capture nets, and so function to some extent as predators. A few other caddisfly predators do not build capture nets or even cases, but are instead free-ranging, such as the genus *Rhyacophila.*

Predators are divided into two further functional groups: *engulfers* and *piercers.* Most predators are engulfers that catch prey with their legs or mouths and chew or swallow them. Engulfers include many stoneflies, caddisflies, beetles, and some crane fly larvae. The piercers, such as the true bugs, have specialized mouthparts that pierce their prey's bodies to extract energy-rich body fluids. (Life is sometimes hard on the stream bottom!)

The larva of the dobsonfly *Corydalus,*
a common predator in many warmwater streams.
(Photo by Dean C. Hansen, *WetBugs Press,* Stillwater, Minnesota.)

A few insects pierce the stems of aquatic plants to extract fluid foods, so these are functionally classified as herbivores, rather than predators. These plant-piercers consist mainly of very small caddisflies, the "microcaddis."

◆   ◆   ◆

THE FUNCTIONAL GROUPS OCCURRING in a given reach of stream depend upon the kind of food present. Thus, different groups predominate according to vegetative types in riparian zones. In the basic model of the river continuum concept (RCC), shredders in headwater reaches (first through third orders) are particularly well represented in the exploitation of allochthonous inputs of leaves and wood. The ratio of shredders to collectors will reflect the predominance of shredders by perhaps 2:1, or higher.

Farther downstream in open, sunlit midreaches (fourth through sixth orders), we find that shredders are less important and the ratio of shredders to collectors becomes about even, 1:1, or less. In these middle reaches, primary production becomes of greater importance and the ratio of shredders to scrapers will show a predominance of scrapers, 2:3.

These processes continue to change downstream. The abundance of FPOM increases, and the importance of collectors, both gatherers and filterers, likewise continues to rise. In the lowest reaches of large rivers (seventh through tenth orders), the filterers attached to woody snag habitat are the major functional group, straining the drifting FPOM that was generated in upstream reaches. The lower reaches are also prime habitat for clams and mussels, filtering FPOM as food.

Changes downstream in the basic RCC result in varying distributions of functional groups. For example, in upper stream reaches in coniferous forests, such as the mountainous Pacific Northwest, the ratio of shredders to collectors favors the shredder group even higher, perhaps by a margin of 3:1, because of the greater abundance of woody debris. In arid or desert catchments, without woodlands, where upper reaches are open and sunlit, shredders are less important, and scrapers (feeding on periphyton) are more abundant. Prairie streams without wooded catchments vary from the model RCC by their frequent paucity of shredders and an increase of scrapers and collectors. Sometimes prairie streams enter wooded areas in midreaches, where a reversal of the RCC model occurs. The distribution of functional groups corresponds with scrapers in the upper reaches and shredders in the middle, wooded sections.

◆   ◆   ◆

KNOWLEDGE OF FUNCTIONAL GROUPS may not increase your catch of trout. But if you fish a scud or a woolly worm in an upper wooded reach to imitate an amphipod or a crane fly larva, both shredders, you may produce more strikes.

In a sunlit middle reach, you may see a heavy hatch of blue-winged olives (the adult mayfly *Baetis*), a scraper.

In broader reaches downstream on some summer afternoon, a huge fall of adult caddisflies may stimulate you to change to a Henryville Special (simulating the caddisfly adult of a filter-feeding caddisfly). Good luck!

TECHNICAL REFERENCES:

Cummins, Kenneth W. 1974. Structure and function of stream ecosystems. *BioScience*. Volume 24, pages 631-641.

Cummins, Kenneth W., and M.J. Klug. 1979. Feeding ecology of stream invertebrates. *Annual Review of Ecology and Systematics*. Volume 10, pages 147-172.

Merritt, Richard W., and Kenneth W. Cummins, editors. 1996. *An Introduction to the Aquatic Insects of North America*. Third edition. Kendall/Hunt Publishing Company. Dubuque, Iowa.

RiverSketch

THE LONGEST REFUGE

ALONG THE VALLEY FLOOR of the Upper Mississippi River for more than 280 river miles, runs a special band of river and floodplain rich in aquatic resources, a refuge for natural communities and a humankind seeking connection to its natural environment. It is a corridor of immense biodiversity.

The Upper Mississippi River National Wildlife and Fish Refuge, from Alma, Wisconsin, to Rock Island, Illinois, 280 river miles. (From *Big River*, July 1999, by permission.)

Shifting in width from two to five miles, between bluffs over 200 feet high on both sides, the nature of this floodplain was created by the Glacial River Warren about 12,000 years ago and, later, modified by the Army Corps of Engineers. It remains a strip of river, lakes, marshes, and islands that provides a veritable Eden of diverse habitats for wildlife of many kinds.

By the early 1920s, much development of the Upper Mississippi for navigation had already been completed—the four-and-a-half-foot and six-foot channels, including emplacement of wing dams and closures to block flow through backwater lakes and side channels. Residential and industrial development lined parts of the shoreline and floodplain, and little attention had been paid to problems of water quality and pollution. Recognizing these and future threats to the fisheries of the river and its variety of many productive waters, the Izaak Walton League began vigorous promotion of a refuge concept. A conservation-minded Congress passed enabling legislation in 1924, establishing the Upper Mississippi River National Wildlife and Fish Refuge within the national system—today numbering over five hundred refuges—administered by the United States Fish and Wildlife Service. The refuge grew over the years, to reach a current total area of 200,000 acres (over 300 square miles). It is not the largest of national refuges, but in terms of its single dimension in length—bordering parts of Minnesota, Wisconsin, Iowa, and Illinois—at 280 miles it is the longest in the lower 48.

Fish, bird, and mammal faunas are impressive, by any measure. Huge numbers of migrating game and nongame birds using this route, where the refuge provides secure places for resting and feeding on their fall flights south and return springtime migrations north to summer breeding grounds.

The Mississippi refuge boasts something like 270 bird species, counting both seasonal migrants and residents. Many of these are ducks (both dabbling and diving groups), geese of several species, eagles and ospreys, marsh species including herons, egrets, and bitterns; a huge number of upland birds occupy the forested islands. Fifty-some species of mammals inhabit the refuge—most prominent are the white-tailed deer, furbearers such as beaver, otter, and mink, upland species, and a host of small, seldom-seen nongame mammals. Sport hunting is permitted over most of the refuge, under state laws, for all legal

species and seasons, except for the closure of 14 designated areas during waterfowl migrations in the autumn.

The refuge contains hundreds of marshes, islands, wooded peninsulas,
and backwater lakes, a rich mix of aquatic and terrestrial habitats.

Fishing is a major use of the refuge; half of the some three
million public visits per year are for sport fishing and boating.

Nearly 200 species of fish occupy the river and its associated side channels, backwater lakes, beaver ponds, and tributaries, and most of these habitats occur in the refuge either permanently or intermittently.

Fishing opportunities are many and diverse. Most sport fishing is for walleyes, smallmouth and largemouth bass, channel catfish, and panfishes such as bluegills, yellow perch, and crappies. The fish fauna also includes some unusual and rare species, like sturgeons, gars, eels, the huge blue catfish, and the ancient, endangered paddlefish. Some 35 species of minnows (including the superabundant carp) are found here, about a dozen darters, and 15 species from the sucker family.

Winding slowly through the center of the refuge is the navigation system of locks and dams. Twelve units are located in the refuge. The current nine-foot channel, accomplished by dams and dredging in the 1930s, changed the nature of the river and floodplains, and the system of dams and locks remains as a point of controversy among the shipping industry, natural resource managers, and river users. Despite this intrusion in the center, the profusion and complexity of natural areas on the sides provide solitude and adventure among hidden passages, sandy beaches, and wooded retreats. Locks transit recreational boats and canoes, as well as commercial traffic.

Almost all national refuges welcome public use. (A few are set aside for scientific research and for protection of rare or endangered species.) Fishing, hunting, hiking, boating, camping, and other recreational uses are all facilitated by a huge array of maps and guides. The complexity of the many habitats often means you can have an island all to yourself!

The events of November 11, 1940—Armistice Day—wrote a tragic footnote to the history of the Upper Mississippi. In southern Wisconsin and Minnesota, the morning was mild and foggy; temperatures were in the 50°s, unseasonable for that time of year. Hundreds of waterfowl hunters, many literally in shirtsleeves, ventured out into the maze of duck and goose hunting sites. But weather forecasting was not available then and the weather changed, drastically. During the day and following night, an unprecedented blizzard with sharply dropping temperatures, heavy snow, and extreme winds descended upon the Mississippi Valley. Some hunters were blinded by snow and lost, surface waters became storm-lashed or frozen solid, and many hunters were without sufficient clothing. The day rapidly developed into one of death by freezing and drowning—and some heroic rescues. Some 20 persons perished. The tragedy occupies a place in history that, each year on November 11, is reprised in local newspapers as the Great Armistice Day Blizzard of 1940.

◆   ◆   ◆

TODAY, THE UPPER MISSISSIPPI is being increasingly recognized as an ecosystem in the holistic sense, where a new, broader perception of ecosystem management is emerging. Many complex problems have arisen, and funding is an ongoing dilemma. But a host of citizen organizations continue to be focused on the Upper Mississippi River and refuge.

Located in the middle of the continent's spreading plains where agriculture dominates land use, the refuge remains as an oasis, an elongated ecosystem that serves as a centerpiece of protection for diverse natural communities and public involvement.

SELECTED REFERENCES:

Moore, Rick. 1999. A case study in conflict: The Upper Mississippi Wildlife and Fish Refuge celebrates its 75th anniversary. *Outdoor America* (Izaak Walton League of America). Summer 1999, pages 36-40.

Wise, Madalon. 1999. A long refuge history: Upper Mississippi River Wildlife & Fish Refuge celebrates 75 years. *Big River* (A monthly newsletter on the Upper Mississippi River). Volume 7, No. 7 (July 1999), pages 1-3.

Chapter **12**

SECONDARY PRODUCTION

MANY MATERIALS AND PROCESSES combine to produce the aquatic animals, mainly insects and fish, that we see or seek in streams. Most often, we assign worth to a stream based on the abundance and variety of fish. Anglers may value abundance and biologists diversity, but from either perspective, the final judgment is usually based on our perception of a stream's capacity to produce these living organisms.

So far in this volume we have discussed many of the dynamic components of a stream ecosystem: chemical elements, provision of energy, autochthonous and allochthonous organic matter, and invertebrate feeding functions.

All of these components come to a final focus in the stream's *productivity*. The living tissue produced is an integration, the cumulative effect of all the dynamic processes of the ecosystem. Productivity represents the final measure of success for a population of invertebrates or fish—the bottom line.

But productivity is only an abstract concept until we describe it in quantitative terms—that is, with numbers. An invertebrate or a fish can be weighed, to determine its *mass* (as scientists term it) in units such as grams or pounds. To describe the whole population of invertebrates or fish quantitatively, however, we must relate them to a given area, such as a square meter or acre. So when we sample or collect the living organisms in a known area of stream bottom, we can compute the mass of a mayfly population, for example, as so many grams per square meter or a trout population as so many pounds per acre.

We term this measurement the *standing stock* (as in "stock on hand") or, increasingly, *biomass*. A common standing stock for a *Baetis* mayfly may be about ten pounds per acre; the standing stock for all invertebrates combined may be a thousand pounds per acre. In the same stream, the standing stock of brown trout may be about a hundred pounds per acre. Many folks consider standing stock an adequate indication of productivity, and that's OK for a start. But standing stock is only a measure of what's "on hand," or present at any given moment—say, on a particular date. The dynamic measure of productivity, however, is the mass of tissue grown, or produced, by an animal population *per unit time*, on some unit area. Thus, we use the term *production rate*, or more commonly *annual production*, in pounds per acre when the interval is one year. And because we consider photosynthesis of plant material as *primary production*, we now designate the rate of all animal production as *secondary production*. If we know the total area of a stream in acres, we can then calculate the total mass of invertebrates or fish produced by the entire stream during a year.

◆   ◆   ◆

IN ADDITION TO EXPRESSING secondary production in terms of the mass of tissue, we can also express it in terms of energy, or calories. For example, one gram of fish tissue contains about 1,000 calories, or one kilocalorie (kcal), of energy. There's about to 450 grams in one pound, so eating one pound of fish is equivalent to an intake of about 450,000 calories, or 450 kcal.

The research and estimation of secondary production have often been characterized as *bioenergetics*—the study of energy flow through living organisms. When a population of fish feeds, for example, some of the food energy is lost in fecal waste and some as respiration. The remainder of the calories is stored into body growth, or production.

We usually measure fish production first in terms of mass (grams or pounds) and then calculate production in terms of calories simply by multiplying the grams or pounds by an appropriate conversion factor: multiply grams by 1,000—or multiply pounds by 450,000—to obtain the production in terms of calories. If we wish to have it in kcal, we then divide by 1,000.

Some researchers have worked out energy "budgets" for single species of insects or fish, a whole population in a trophic level (such as herbivorous invertebrates), or for an entire ecosystem.

Let's work out a hypothetical example. We'll use some real figures and some that, although assumptions, are realistic. We'll start out with the calories in solar radiation and work up through a typical trophic pyramid in a stream, ending with fish production.

Solar energy reaching Earth is about 1.5 billion calories per square meter per year. The light energy available to plants, however, is about one-third of that, or 500,000 kcal per square meter per year. After the process of photosynthesis and all the losses involved in that process, only about one percent ends up in plant tissue, or 5,000 kcal per square meter per year, a measure of average worldwide primary production. These are real figures, but they are averages that vary over the earth's surface and with the change of seasons, and they exclude polar regions in permanent ice.

Now, to get our spatial unit up from square meters to acres, we multiply by 4,000 (because there are about 4,000 square meters in an acre), to arrive at a mean primary production of about 20,000,000 kcal per acre per year.

Let's now assume that the primary production of periphyton on the bottom of a stream is about half that much. The stony riffles in which periphyton grows cover only part of the streambed, and we'll assume about half. This gives us about 10,000,000 kcal per acre per year for this lowermost trophic level of the stream's trophic pyramid. Now we'll assume that aquatic insects eat about half of this primary production, mostly diatoms. Again, this is a realistic assumption, so we will place their food consumption at 5,000,000 kcal per acre per year.

With losses in feces and respiration, resulting in a metabolic efficiency of 20 percent (again, realistic), the remainder—or production—is 1,000,000 kcal per acre per year, the production of the second trophic level or herbivorous insects.

Now we come to fish. Again, we'll say the fish eat about half of the insects produced, placing their food consumption at 500,000 kcal per acre per year. Again using an efficiency of 20 percent, the fish, our third trophic level, produce about 100,000 kcal per acre per year. To obtain fish production in pounds now, rather than calories, we divide by 450 (about 450 kcal are contained in one pound of fresh fish) and come up with 220 pounds per acre per year for fish production.

After all these rather fuzzy calculations, you may be surprised to know that many studies of fish production, from around the world, in different bodies of water, have resulted in estimates around 200-250 pounds per acre per year!

An annual production in that range reflects a highly productive system, and those numbers are usually found only in limestone streams. Freestone streams may produce only 5 or 10 pounds, sometimes up to 50. In contrast, a warmwater fish population in fertile water may yield an annual production of 500 pounds per acre, although this figure would be for the sum of many species. A good smallmouth bass stream may have a total annual production of 500 pounds for all species, but because the smallmouth must share its habitat and food resource with many other fishes, the smallmouth production itself may be only about 10 or 20 pounds per acre.

The development of methods for estimating secondary production by stream invertebrates and fish has been one of the most challenging efforts in stream ecology. Even the basic concept of production and its terminology were so difficult to comprehend that they occupied a long series of attempts, over many years, to straighten out the confusion. And often, each attempt simply made things worse!

Two major methods eventually emerged. For invertebrates, Professor Noel Hynes initiated a method of measuring losses of organisms between age and size groups, and assuming that the sum of all losses for a generation was equal to the total production, the final summing of losses provided the production of the generation. After some modifications, this method was termed the *size-frequency method*.

For fish production, two prominent fisheries biologists, K. Radway Allen of New Zealand and William E. Ricker of Canada, independently developed formulas based on growth rates of fish over a single year, providing annual rates of production. After some modification, this method resulted in the current *instantaneous growth rate method*.

Today, a large database of production rates for both fish and invertebrates has been accumulated from around the world. Knowledge about invertebrate production helps us understand how various stream management strategies, land-use practices in catchments, and pesticide inputs from agricultural lands affect supplies of fish food. Fish production data can assist managers in determining fishing quotas or needed angling regulations.

◆   ◆   ◆

IN REPORTS IN THE SCIENTIFIC LITERATURE on annual fish production, mostly for stream trout, we find a wide range—from less than one pound per acre to a very few over 300 pounds per acre. A wide range of results has also been observed for invertebrates, ranging up to several thousands of pounds per acre.

Why this great span of results, with the highest more than a hundred times the lowest? Do streams really vary this much—or are the results artifacts of imprecise measurements?

The truth is that, yes, production values do vary that much. We have no reason to believe that energy-flow rates should range narrowly around some standard mean. That being the case, we might—and should—ask why? Why does this great variation occur in streams? And in this question lies one of the greatest challenges encountered in the subject of production.

We mentioned previously that production integrates many dynamic factors in the ecosystem, both aquatic and terrestrial. It is a complex network of energy pathways and processes.

Limestone streams with sedimentary rock ledges (top)
are much more productive than freestone streams
in an igneous rock catchment (bottom).

The environment of living organisms influences all dynamic factors. Therefore, the multitude of answers to the question posed above can be assembled under a broad topic labeled the *ecology of production.*

Two major factors constitute the main divisions of production ecology: food and space. Each is an integration by itself; behind each lie more specific environmental factors, which we'll explore in turn.

First, the significance of food (which contains energy) seems self-evident. All living organisms need the energy of food; the search for food is a continuous activity for virtually all animals living in the wild. So here we take up this all-important aspect of the ecology of stream invertebrates and fish: acquiring food.

For streambed invertebrates, we know that the two most important sources of food are the algae of periphyton and conditioned allochthonous organic matter.

We've already discussed the conditioning of allochthonous organic matter by bacteria and fungi. Some researchers have made advances in developing methods for estimating bacterial production by modifying the instantaneous growth rate method, but little progress has been made in estimating the total input of calories made available to invertebrates from bacteria and fungi.

Furthermore, although we know that nitrate is an important nutrient for fungal production, we have little quantitative information about what sources of nitrate are most important. Are the alder branches that hang over stream banks (and continually snag our flies and leaders) important in the nitrate supply? Alternatively, if the branches were removed, would more sunlight be available to increase primary production?

Many attempts have been made to budget the calories in allochthonous organic matter and its various fates, such as storage, consumption, and eventual transport out of the system. The use of such organic matter and its colonizing fungi has been thoroughly studied. We have also attempted to measure the caloric uptake by grazing invertebrates that feed primarily on the periphyton on the stream bottom. But seldom have these numbers been correlated to the animals' levels of production. Many quantitative details of energy flow between trophic levels have yet to be determined.

We have often regarded the stream fish's food resource as the production of a stream's invertebrate population. For the most part, this is true. Not so very long ago, we believed that the fish used the entire invertebrate community. However, after examining this relationship more closely, we now realize that the food the fish eat must be *available* to the fish—and many invertebrates are not, or are only sometimes available to fish. For example, an insect species may live its entire nymphal life burrowed in mud or silt, and therefore unavailable to fish except when it emerges to the flying, aerial stages (the actual case of the mayfly *Hexagenia*).

The usual method of measuring fish production in trout streams involves collecting samples by electrofishing.
Howard Creek, North Carolina.

We now know that invertebrate production does not constitute the entire food supply to fish. Fish are opportunistic—they take different kinds of food as they become available. So while immature insects (mayflies, caddisflies, stoneflies, and others on the streambed) may be the main entrees, fish may also chow down whenever an unusual abundance of terrestrials shows up—grasshoppers, for example, on a windy, late summer afternoon.

In sum: although we find it relatively easy to estimate the production of stream invertebrates, we still find it difficult to identify and measure the total food supply available to fish.

◆   ◆   ◆

THE WIDELY HELD BELIEF that streambed invertebrates provide the only food for fish resulted in one of the most fascinating problems in production ecology: When production is measured for both the invertebrates and fish, in virtually all cases the estimated production of invertebrates has not been sufficient to supply food for the estimated fish production!

Collection of samples of streambed invertebrates with this kind of sampler allows the eventual estimation of annual production.

This discrepancy was first noted by fisheries biologist K. Radway Allen in his studies of fish production in a New Zealand trout stream—and it became subsequently known as the *Allen paradox*. Allen compared the annual production of brown trout to the invertebrate population and found that the fish production required about 150 times the observed abundance of invertebrates! His estimate of invertebrates, however, was of standing stock, not production. Production estimates would have been higher, but in Allen's study still not high enough.

Some scientists felt that Allen underestimated the abundance of the streambed invertebrates (perhaps with inadequate sampling methods in use at the time) and also that he probably overestimated fish production (again, with primitive sampling equipment, not electrofishing). But speculative corrections only partially corrected the discrepancy. Even after better methods for estimating production were developed for both invertebrates and fish (including electrofishing), the error has remained. After a multitude of research efforts worldwide and many published production estimates, the paradox has persisted.

Theoretically, of course, we must conclude that the fish are taking additional food from *somewhere*—sources other than streambed invertebrates. This is an unassailable hypothesis—but what are the other sources?

We know some of them: terrestrial insects that fall or are blown into the water; plants such as algae eaten by some fish species; small fish of other species such as sculpins and creek chubs; macroinvertebrates that live unnoticed and unsampled deeper in the substrate. Undoubtedly there are invertebrates other than the usual ones sampled on the stream bottom. For example, some invertebrates that enter the stream from floodplains during floods, some that are normally burrowed into woody debris (the *snag habitat*), or deep in the gravel substrate (the *hyporheos*, which we'll take up later), or in the mud and soil under overhanging stream banks. The list can go on further.

An almost unexplained factor affecting the paradox is the *quality* of food. Some recent studies indicate that some food is more nutritious and contains more calories than others. The efficiency of food digestion by fish is another factor. Some foods are more digestible than others—and some fishes digest their food more efficiently than other fishes—adding to the available energy that we might not otherwise calculate.

Recently published research is narrowing the gap. Some reports have come close, but none, so far, have unequivocally shown production rates of available food high enough to support the measured fish production. Some time in the future we may look for that to happen. But for now, the Allen paradox remains.

◆   ◆   ◆

THE EFFECT OF SPACE on the production of invertebrates and fish may be similar to the effect of food. The quality of space, however, differs greatly over the total streambed, and it cannot be measured accurately as a simple area expressed in square feet or acres.

We can gaze upon a wide, deep river—perhaps a reach that seems to be devoid of fish—and think that surely there is no shortage of space. What we may not realize is that living aquatic organisms need *suitable* space. And the apparently spacious reach of river may be regarded by fish in the same way as we humans may view a featureless, wind-swept desert—space unsuitable for our living. Convert the desert to a lush forest, build houses, and develop all the infrastructure of utilities, and humans would prosper. If the featureless river reach were converted to a winding channel of bends and runs, with alternating pools and stony riffles, with woody debris and a vegetated riparian zone, the otherwise barren reach would be replete with finny, happy campers, as well as a bounty of invertebrates.

Two elements of space necessary for fish in a stream are a roof and sufficient turf. Translated, fish need overhead cover as visual protection against predators and enough personal foraging room on the streambed to provide food.

Fish appear to be strongly territorial in a riffle or rapids where the streambed is broken by cobbles and boulders. A riffle with large gravel or cobbles holds many more fish fry than a streambed that is flat and smooth. For a small fry, the interstitial space between stones provides suitable space, including foraging room with available food that is isolated from sight of a potential competitor, sometimes only inches away. As the fry grows, its territory must expand to larger and larger stones or other substrates and eventually, perhaps, to a large boulder or pool of its own.

Here's where space and food interact, for if food is abundant, individual territories can be small. When invertebrates are scarce, fish need larger territories for foraging room.

Space in pools is another matter. Here, fish appear to take up hierarchical arrangements. Several or many fish may occupy a pool, but the largest or most aggressive individual will hold down the choice position, perhaps to intercept drifting food. Many an angler has experienced taking a large fish from the head of a pool, and then coming back later to take another, almost as large, from the same spot. The number two fish in the hierarchy simply moved up to the choice position.

As with many other areas of fish ecology study, the behavior of trout and salmon has received the most intense research. Observations from elevated blinds at streamside, by underwater viewing with SCUBA, and from studies in artificial, laboratory streams, have revealed much information about salmonids and their spatial requirements, including interrelationships between space and food.

The management application of so-called "stream improvement" is based on providing more suitable space for stream fish, mostly trout. The installation of bank covers, plunge-pool dams, and other structures has been a large part of stream trout management for over a half century.

The objective, of course, was to improve on nature by increasing suitable space and, consequently, fish production. Most of the early work was done without adequate knowledge of either stream hydraulics or fish production ecology, and it failed in its objectives. Although it seemed as if additional cover and territory would increase production, most failures occurred because we did not appreciate the need for increasing available food at the same time.

Today, where such structures of good hydraulic design are planned to restore damaged streams, and where invertebrate production is already high enough to provide the additional food, fish production can indeed be increased to a semblance of production levels originally in the natural stream. Fortunately, we have largely abandoned the practice of trying to improve on nature.

Success with higher fish production has been attained only in streams:
- that were small and productive, such as high-alkalinity limestone streams;
- that had large areas of riffles favorable for invertebrate production;
- that had little suitable space for fish, such as pools and cover.

In these circumstances, adding space to hold more fish can increase fish production. Long before we had methods to measure production rates, fish managers perceived the benefit of a good pool-riffle arrangement in trout streams. The alternation of pools and riffles is still held to be beneficial—only today we know why, and we can put numbers on invertebrate and fish production.

Like fish, insects and other invertebrates have interesting behaviors related to territoriality, feeding strategies, and needs for protection against predators. We commonly find more insects under stones, for example. Some recent research on insect behavior in the bottom darkness beneath streambed stones using fiber-optic technology has provided close-up images of some of the most specific activities of these animals.

Tiny, newly hatched insects may occupy a small stone surface in great abundance. But as larvae and nymphs grow, the stone sustains fewer individuals, resulting in the phenomenon of *drift*—the movement of invertebrates downstream in sometimes enormous numbers, usually at night. The idea is that as the animals grow and require larger and larger territories, some leave their stone (perhaps voluntarily, perhaps kicked off by a cohort) to drift downstream and find new lodgings. The subject

of drift—its causes and effects—has been one of the larger subjects of stream ecological research. We'll take it up in more detail in another chapter.

One of the most fascinating underwater sights is a view of
the larvae of the caddisfly *Brachycentrus* lined up on the edge of
a stone or stick, evenly spaced like birds on a telephone wire,
snatching fine bits of organic seston from water currents.
(*Brachycentrus*, by the way, is the caddis larva that builds a long,
slightly tapered case from short bits of wood or other vegetation, square in cross-section like a log cabin). Look for these log-
cabin cases with your face close to the water, and you may find
them lined up in their territorial banquet convocations. Incidentally, the adult *Brachycentrus* can be imitated with a size 18
Henryville Special or, on the Bighorn River, a size 16 Black
Caddis.)

◆   ◆   ◆

IN PREVIOUS CHAPTERS, we discussed productivity at several
trophic levels—primary production by plants (instream and allochthonous), production by streambed invertebrates, etc. In
those sections, I promised that later we would acquire numbers
with some real values of production at all trophic levels.

Some unpublished data from the State of Minnesota were
used in these calculations wherein production rates varied across
the state from northeast to southwest. Along this line, Minnesota varies in vegetation, local geology, and stream water chemistry (especially alkalinity), from forests north of Lake Superior,
to plains in the state's southwestern corner.

In the northeast, vegetation is mixed coniferous and deciduous woodland, local geology is wholly igneous, and there is low
nitrate and alkalinity in the streams. In the southwest, vegetation cover was originally prairie but is now largely in row-crop
agriculture. Local geology is calcareous glacial drift over sedimentary bedrock, and stream chemistry features high nitrate
and alkalinity. Streams in this southwest region are tributary

mainly to the Minnesota River and, to a small extent, to the Missouri River. Conditions in central Minnesota are between the other two extremes, but are more similar to the southwest; most streams are tributary to the headwaters of the Mississippi River. Thus, the three regions constitute a wide strip with a gradient of productivity—low in the northeast, high in the southwest.

Very few actual estimates of annual production were available in the scientific literature for this region. To provide meaningful values and averages for the calculations, I made an extensive search in the world literature for production values at all trophic levels in relation to nutrients, local geology, and water chemistry, especially alkalinity. Averages from the worldwide values were then applied to the Minnesota streams. Matching up geology, vegetation, water chemistry, and the few actual production estimates available, I roughed out production values for streams along the gradient.

Production values were averaged for the three geographic regions: northeast, central, and southwest, and for the four trophic levels: primary production (both autochthonous and allochthonous), invertebrates, first-fish carnivores (small fish feeding on invertebrates), and top-fish carnivores (large fish feeding on small fish). To relate production values to water chemistry, alkalinity from my measurements were correlated with the production values. Alkalinity averaged around 25 parts per million in the northeast, 50 ppm in the central region, and 125 ppm in the southwestern plains.

Several relationships and principles emerged. Production at all levels across the gradient clearly increased from the northeastern region of mixed conifer-deciduous woodland, igneous geology, and low alkalinity, to the southwestern region of open plains vegetation, agricultural crops, calcareous geology, and high alkalinity.

Furthermore, the shape of the trophic level arrangements was clearly pyramidal, with production values decreasing successively from the highest for total primary production, to the least at the top-fish carnivores in all three regions. Although total primary production increased along the gradient, allochthonous proportions decreased, in accordance with the change from woodland to open-canopied streams.

Roughly, total annual primary production (the sum of allochthonous and autochthonous) ranged from about 19,000 pounds per acre in the northeast, to 42,000 in the central region, to 47,000 in the southwestern plains. A higher proportion for allochthonous material was found in the wooded northeast.

Invertebrate production ranged from 750 pounds per acre per year in the northeast, to 2,300 in the central region, to 2,700 in the southwestern plains.

Annual production for first carnivore fish ranged from 80 pounds per acre in the northeast, to 200 in the central region, and to 230 in the southwestern plains streams.

Top carnivore fish production ranged from only 5 pounds per acre per year in the northeast, to 30 in the central region, to 35 in the southwest.

The relationship between production and alkalinity was clearly positive among these numbers.

◆   ◆   ◆

AN ENGROSSING QUESTION related to secondary production arose in the river continuum concept (RCC). We have a few reasons to think that the annual production of both fish and invertebrates increase in a downstream direction, but no definitive conclusion.

Some studies correlate secondary production with functional groups. Recall that in the RCC, the main source of energy in the headwaters is allochthonous organic matter, such as leaves and wood; the middle reaches are well sunlit and photosynthesis by plants high; and in large river reaches fine particulate organic matter (FPOM) drifting down from upstream is the main energy source. The functional group of shredders, which feed on conditioned leaves and wood, exhibits its highest production in the headwaters. Scraper production is the highest in middle reaches, grazing on the highly productive periphyton. And in the lower reaches, filtering caddisflies, straining FPOM in their fine-meshed capture nets, show their highest production. In only a few studies has total invertebrate production been measured through a stream's course; even so, those studies suggest that production increases in a downstream direction.

Few similar studies on fish production have come forth. One factor that would suggest higher production downstream is that fish populations there often include a greater proportion of omnivores and herbivores, such as suckers, catfishes, and carp. At a trophic level lower than carnivores, such fish have more food available in primary producers and benthic food materials in soft substrates, and fish production is consequently higher. Furthermore, large floodplains often associated with lower river reaches can contribute much greater quantities of allochthonous organic matter than is available for headwater or middle reaches.

To conduct production studies on both invertebrates and fish over a full stream course, even a river of moderate length, would be greatly labor-intensive and expensive. But such endeavors would result in wonderful contributions to our understanding of overall stream productivity, as well as secondary production, in the natural history of streams and rivers.

◆   ◆   ◆

NOT LONG AGO, the main theme of fisheries management was to increase the catch—"the more the better." A common goal was "to shorten the time between bites." The main criterion of success for management was the catch per unit effort (CUE), when the emphasis was on increasing the number of fish caught per hour. If management programs increased the fish catch, then management was deemed a success. Often, hatchery trout were stocked to increase the CUE.

But a change in perspective away from the "more-is-better" emphasis is in the wind. As we change to a view of *stewardship* of natural resources, rather than trying to *improve on nature*, we come to know that a deeper understanding of productivity serves us well both to protect and restore the quality of our natural streams and rivers. Instead of more fish, our goal will be a higher quality of the total recreational experience.

Perhaps some day we will obtain the means to accurately measure energy flow through all components of a stream ecosystem. We are close to it now. The components must include autochthonous photosynthesis, allochthonous inputs from terrestrial areas, and all the transformations of energy from consumption of food to growth of new tissue.

To tie together the many pathways of energy flow we need to know the various efficiencies of energy passage between trophic levels, between prey and predator, as well as the details of the loss of energy from the stream.

Armed with knowledge about these pathways of energy flow, researchers and managers alike will be able to better identify problems and predict results of both neglect and corrective action. Then we can take early remedial steps to maintain healthy energy-flow systems that will give us the highest quality of recreational returns from our river resources.

TECHNICAL REFERENCES:

Benke, Arthur C. 1993. Concepts and patterns of invertebrate production in running waters. (Edgardo Baldi Memorial Lecture). *Proceedings of the International Association for Theoretical and Applied Limnology.* Volume 25, pages 15-38.

Waters, Thomas F. 1977. Secondary production in inland waters. *Advances in Ecological Research.* Volume 10, pages 91-164.

RiverSketch

STEAMBOAT 'ROUND THE BEND

WE ALL KNOW THAT RIVERS WERE THE HIGHWAYS of the North American frontier. Our history of river transportation can be related in just a few words: the native Americans' canoe—the fur traders' bateau—the loggers' raft of pine trunks and lumber—the flatboat and the merchants' keelboat. And then: the steamboat—that glorious, uproarious mix of luxury, smoke, speed, and deadly danger.

The "Golden Age" of steamboating lasted only 75 years. But during its era, it enraptured America—at least that part within earshot of its ear-piercing but enticing whistle—a siren song to gamblers, story-telling old men, and footloose boys. The Golden Age ended only when commercial river transportation was brought to a virtual halt by the railroad.

The cradle of steamboat invention in the United States was Pittsburgh, where the Allegheny and Monongahela rivers join to form the Ohio. Following some earlier ventures on eastern rivers, Nicholas Roosevelt (a business associate of Robert Fulton) captained the *New Orleans* onto the Ohio in the fall of 1811, bound for the Mississippi and the steamer's namesake town at the Gulf of Mexico. In a remarkable coincidence, the *New Orleans* steamed into the most violent land-shaking event in midwestern North American history: the New Madrid (Missouri) Earthquake. The earth opened and filled up with the Mississippi's waters, creating Reelfoot Lake. Huge chunks of landscape fell into the river; the streambed buckled and heaved, and so did the *New Orleans.* But miraculously, the steamer survived it all and pulled into New Orleans, Louisiana, on January 12, 1812. The steamboat era on western rivers had truly begun.

Steamboats flourished in all sizes, in all degrees of luxury and embellishment on the Mississippi and its major tributaries, the Ohio and Missouri. Upstream they carried tools, cotton, plow shares, and immigrants; downstream came produce from the western plains and lumber from northern forests.

Packets, the workhorses of the steamboat fleet, which regularly carried freight, mail, and passengers on reasonably reliable schedules, plied virtually every river that could float the smallest steamer, from coast to coast. Some ran only when spring spates raised water levels above rapids. The Tennessee, Kentucky, and Cumberland rivers floated steam vessels from the southern Appalachian Mountains filled with lumber, coal, and whisky. Smaller steamers towed logs on northern Maine's Allagash; in Florida, St. John's River boats worked the lower Atlantic coast during the Civil War, carrying supplies to coastal towns. In the West, little Humboldt, a desert river in Nevada's Great Basin with no outlet, served a silver boom with steamboats.

The palatial excursion steamboat, the "*J. S*", carried passengers
on the Mississippi in the years 1901 to 1910,
and burned in the latter year with loss of two lives.
(Courtesy Murphy Library, University of Wisconsin-LaCrosse.)

Construction of the steamboat was simple but effective. Because a shallow draft was essential on rivers, there was no hold; rather, their two engines, furnaces, and boilers were mounted on the lowest level, the main deck. The engines drove two side-mounted paddlewheels independently. Freight and fuel were also stored on the main deck. Above this, the boiler deck held the passenger cabins, each named for a state of the Union—the source for our term *stateroom*. The roof of the staterooms was the floor of the hurricane deck, which was used for promenades. Atop that was the Texas, which housed the quarters for the steamer's officers, over which loomed the pilot house, where the captain and pilot could get the best view of the entire boat and the river ahead. Sidewheelers comprised the great majority of steamboats, because they could be maneuvered most easily on twisting rivers; sternwheelers were developed primarily for towing operations across lakes and open water.

Some of the grandest steamers, the excursion boats, carried only passengers for pleasure cruises. They were huge, with giant salons that served up to a thousand passengers rivaling the most luxurious hotels on land, complete with crystal chandeliers, gas lights, thick carpets and tapestries, and a cuisine of the rarest and most exotic foods. Some boats were over two hundred feet long, with paddle wheels exceeding forty feet in diameter. The Golden Age years included the Civil War, when steamer traffic came almost to a standstill on the lower Mississippi. Steamer traffic started up again after the war, but it did not last much longer.

The average life of a steamboat was only four to five years, and by 1850 more than 4,000 persons had been killed in steamboat accidents. The litany of collisions, sinkings, and fire, reported in rivertown newspapers, had no effect on the public's accelerating love of the gingerbread palaces. The worst accidents were boiler explosions, sometimes brought on by overzealous captains in a race. Safety valves, when the boats had them at all, were removed to get more pressure from the primitive wood-fueled furnaces.

The most tragic accident of all was the destruction of the *Sultana*, bringing Union soldiers up the Mississippi from Confederate prisons at the close of the Civil War. The steamer had been greatly overloaded to collect the generous passage fees paid by the U.S. Army. Built for only 376 passengers and 85 crew, she carried over 2,500. When three boilers blew at once, on April 27, 1865, near Memphis, Tennessee, the steamer literally flew apart. The central area of the vessel became a cauldron of fire, through all decks. Estimates of men burned, drowned, and blasted to bits rose to 1,800 (300 more than the number lost on the *Titanic*), most of them Union soldiers. It was, and remains, the worst marine disaster in United States history.

By this time, iron rails had sliced across the continent in their narrow, shiny ribbons. Railroads already carried as much freight as steamboats, including the war materiel that had fueled the clashing armies of the North and South. Soon, thousands of rotting hulks rested in the nation's river backwaters. By 1887, the steamboats, palaces and packets alike, surrendered to new federal regulations and competition from the iron horse. They left a colorful and exciting legacy, still mourned by old-timers now, who remembered their fathers' and grandfathers' tales of piloting the huffing, puffing, whistling palaces that, despite the tragedies, they had loved so well.

SELECTED REFERENCES:

Andrist, Ralph K., C. Bradford Mitchell, and the Editors of American Heritage. 1962. *Steamboats on the Mississippi.* American Heritage Publishing Co., Inc, New York.

Havighurst, Walter. 1964. *Voices on the River: The Story of the Mississippi Waterways.* Macmillan Company, New York.

Part Four

Life at
the Bottom

Introduction to Part Four

LIFE AT THE BOTTOM

)

MANY OF THE EARLIEST STUDIES IN STREAMS were on the small aquatic creatures inhabiting the crevices among stones in riffles. To young, budding biologists turning over stones at creekside, the creatures were fascinating creepy-crawlers. To fishery biologists a half-century ago, stream bottom invertebrates were collectively viewed merely as "fish-food," a sort of nutritious soup. Now, however, after several decades of scientific study, this bottom fauna, whether in stream or lake, has become the scholarly domain of the *benthologist*.

Derived from the Greek (*bathos*—at the bottom of the sea), *benthos* refers to the total assemblage of all organisms associated with the bottom of a body of water. Included are plants (such as algae), a host of invertebrates (lots of insects), and a few fish (such as sculpins and some darters).

But in these next few chapters, our discussions concern mainly invertebrate animals, ranging from the scarlet integument of a living San Juan Worm to the refractive glimmer of a mayfly spinner.

Many biologists refer to benthic invertebrates as *macroinvertebrates*—organisms large enough to see, like scuds, snails, worms, and most aquatic insects. Also important, however, are the *microinvertebrates* and the *meiofauna*—creatures too small to see, at least easily with only our unassisted eyes. These tiny animals play an ecological role much like the zooplankton of lakes, providing food to newly hatched fish fry and to larvae of some predaceous insects. Big fish have to live first as small fish, and we often fail to realize that down there among the smaller pebble particles on the bottom, there must be an ever-renewable supply of microscopic food items for the small fish. We'll take up the importance of these tiny benthic invertebrates, too.

The scientific study of the benthos is *benthology,* and the principal professional organization for benthologists is the North American Benthological Society. In fact, it is from the pages of this society's professional journal that much of the stream ecological information in this book has been acquired for both plants and animals.

In numbers, the benthic invertebrate community predominates in the stream fauna. There is good reason for this condition in flowing water. In no other habitat can life be so precarious. The everyday environment of these stream organisms is always in a state of flux, shifting as swift currents carry projectiles of pebbles, stones, and boulders. And we may wonder why the organisms do not eventually all get washed out!

The myriad ways in which living organisms deal with their running-water environment, however, are fascinating as well as effective. True, these are ways that enable them to stay in place, but there *is* much else. The stream bottom is not merely a safe place for a small animal to hang out, more than simply protection against the aquatic storms that could carry it away. Adaptations to currents include many other benefits as well, such as foraging areas and protection from predators.

Floods and sedimentation, the two principal scourges to stream life, it would seem, could almost totally destroy the benthic community at times. But aquatic invertebrates adapt with remarkable resilience to these natural disasters. Recovery, if disturbance is not continual, is certain to occur.

Streambed habitats provide an equally important environment for the production of the invertebrates' food. Here, in these greatly diverse and patchy surroundings of stone surfaces, micro-eddies behind stones, and organic debris such as leaf packs and debris dams, an intricate system of specialized strategies exists. Foraging for food, reproductive behavior, and many interactions between stream-bottom inhabitants, are all sustained by a great diversity of species and ecological functions. On a microscopic scale, the stream bottom is a treasure house of life. We term this great variety *biodiversity*.

Water currents have many beneficial physical effects on the stream bottom community. The surface of turbulent water, for example, has such intimate contact with the atmosphere that a deficiency of dissolved oxygen almost never occurs, even in the bottom gravels. Deadly winterkills due to loss of oxygen do not happen in the substrate environments of unpolluted, free-running streams and rivers. Furthermore, water currents flowing through streambed materials carry away the byproducts of growth and decomposition, like carbon dioxide and animal feces, which are used farther downstream by other invertebrates.

In the next few chapters of this Part Four, we'll take up those many adaptations of stream invertebrates that allow life at the bottom—the benthos—to thrive so productively.

Most river users see only the obvious: flying insects during an emergence, crawling mayfly nymphs and caddis larvae under stones, scuds darting among the watercress. We'll discuss these in some detail, but we'll also look into groups seldom seen, but equally important, the microinvertebrates and some animals that live hidden deep in stream gravels.

So enjoy a trip to the bottom, where we'll see what's going on down there among the benthos. Our excursion promises to be an enchanting journey into that hugely intricate system churning with life, growth, death, and renewal.

Chapter 13

BIODIVERSITY

SINCE THE BEGINNING OF SCHOLARLY INQUIRY into stream and river science, research effort into the life history of aquatic invertebrates has predominated. Early field observations on distribution, abundance, and behavior were among the first, and intricate experimentation in field and laboratory followed. Experiments and observations included the fascinating seasonal occurrence of insect emergences, foods of nymphs or larvae, the growth and progression of generations, and predation, or who eats whom.

The term *life cycle* is closely related to life history. Although the two concepts overlap somewhat and often are confused and incorrectly interchanged, they are really quite distinct. For example, the single, bare-bones life cycle of insects includes but three major life stages:

- egg;
- immature stage;
- adult.

Some variation occurs. Immatures differ in kind, such as nymphs and larvae. In mayflies, the flying *subimago* precedes the adult; in caddisflies, the encapsulated *pupa* precedes the flying adult. There are other differences, and major variations occur among noninsect invertebrates.

The sequence of stages and the interval between the time when eggs are laid by one generation, and when the new generation matures and lays its own eggs is the *life cycle*. In the progression of generations, a set of life stages—or one generation—is one cycle, one link in the chain in continued life.

On the other hand, life history is the *quality* of life, the story of how a species accommodates to the limits set by its life cycle. A particular kind of life cycle may be fairly constant for a large group, such as an order or family, but life history characteristics vary among species and often within the same species. Life history can also be viewed in *quantitative* terms: number of eggs, growth rate, and final size. Life history is genetically determined but flexible and responsive to the environment; a species' life cycle is tightly fixed by genetics.

Life history, then, includes an infinite variety of adaptations that enables a species to complete all parts of its life cycle:

- kinds of food;
- mode of oviposition, or egg-laying;
- duration of egg incubation;
- seasonal timing of the egg hatching, emergence, and egg laying;
- behavior in dispersal and migrations.

In order to persist, each species must have evolved to survive and reproduce in a unique mixture of environmental relationships distinct from all other species—that is, in its own *ecological niche*.

This resulting complex of the many species in an ecosystem we have come to appreciate as one of the most valuable traits of any living community—*biodiversity*.

In the forthcoming pages, we will explore the life histories of many groups of stream animals. But what you find here is neither a field guide nor a scientific treatise. Instead, I hope you will experience something that leads to a greater enjoyment as you observe in the stream some of these many complexities of life at the bottom. In addition to the memory of a leaping trout or a tough rapids successfully run, you will, I hope, carry home from the river a greater sense of appreciation and wonder—and some questions you never before thought of asking!

◆   ◆   ◆

IT IS APPROPRIATE TO TAKE A SHORT BREAK at this time and review how we identify and classify the many species making up the benthos. This is the subject of *taxonomy*, the classification of organisms. This term derives from the Greek word *taxon*, which refers to any distinct group within the classification. Thus, every category, from class to species, is a taxon. So there are taxa (plural), which have taxa. We'll use these ideas frequently in following sections and chapters. Taxonomy may be a boring subject at first glance, but it may be useful when we come to select an imitation from our fly box!

Most of our artificial flies and nymphs imitate insects, which make up the *class* Insecta. The Insecta is only one of several classes in a larger group of animals having exoskeletons. Another example with exoskeletons is the class Crustacea, which includes crayfish and scuds. The next subdivision within a class is *order*, such as the order Ephemeroptera (mayflies). In turn, orders are divided into *families*, such as the mayfly family Baetidae (pronounced *bee'-ti-dee*). A common name for a family member is created by deleting the "ae" (always as "*ee*") at the end of the family name—and thus a member of the family Baetidae may be referred to as a "baetid" (pronounced *bee'-tid*).

A family is further subdivided into genera (plural of *genus*) such as *Baetis*, a mayfly genus with which we're all familiar. But now we see that the genus is *italicized*. Why? So professional entomologists as well as fly fishers can keep track of their taxonomy! Note, however, that all names of groups so far are first-letter capitalized. But when we see a taxon name that is both capitalized and italicized, we know it's a genus!

The next step, and final one, is the species. In each genus, we have one to several species ("species" is spelled the same for singular and plural). One species is the familiar mayfly *Baetis tricaudatus* (formerly *Baetis vagans* in eastern United States). But now we see another difference—the species name, like the genus, is also italicized but, unlike the genus, is *not capitalized.* Another way to help keep track.

In summary: class (Insecta), order (Ephemeroptera), and family (Baetidae) are always capitalized but not italicized; genus (*Baetis*) is always capitalized *and* italicized; and species (*tricaudatus*) is always italicized but not capitalized. Another example is the black caddis of Montana's Bighorn River fame: class Insecta, order Trichoptera, family Brachycentridae, genus *Brachycentrus,* and species *americanus.*

It is professionally conventional to always identify a species with both genus and species names—the *binomial system*—for examples, *Baetis tricaudatus* and *Brachycentrus americanus.* Sometimes the genus may be abbreviated, as *B. tricaudatus* and *B. americanus,* but only when a previous mention of the genus name is completely spelled out. Otherwise, how does the reader know for certain whether *B.* stands for *Baetis* or *Brachycentrus?*

Now something special. The order Diptera, or "true flies," includes some of our better-known common "fly" names, such as crane fly. When the common name of a true fly contains the word "fly," it is spelled as two words, as "crane fly" (and black fly, horse fly, etc.). But when the common name in an order other than Diptera contains "fly," it is spelled as one word—like "caddisfly," "mayfly," and "stonefly."

Bell rings, class over. Let's move on to more interesting subjects in which we'll use some of the rules spelled out above—and understand why.

◆   ◆   ◆

ONE OF THE MOST IMPORTANT FEATURES of an invertebrate's life history is its *voltinism,* that is, an expression of the number of life cycles per year. Many aquatic insects in temperate zones are synchronized to one annual cycle of seasonal events and are thus *univoltine*—a life cycle length of one year. In this case, emergence and oviposition often occur in the spring, the eggs incubate for a month or so, and then hatch into tiny immatures. The nymphs or larvae feed and grow during the summer, fall, and some in winter (especially in good trout streams, which you will remember are likely to be *relatively warm* in winter). Then adult emergence occurs again in the following spring.

Many mayflies, caddisflies, and stoneflies are univoltine. We refer to an actual group of individuals with a given life cycle as a *cohort*; thus, a univoltine species produces one cohort per year.

Some species are *bivoltine* or *trivoltine*—producing two or three cohorts in one year. *Multivoltine* simply means having several cohorts per year. Midges (family Chironomidae) are notable for being multivoltine; in some cases a new cohort (that is, life cycle) hatches every few days!

In all of the voltinisms described above, one cohort follows another theoretically with no overlap. If one cohort should totally fail to mature and lay its eggs, conceivably the cohort's progression would be interrupted and the species extirpated from that stream. Fortunately, some overlap of cohorts often occurs.

Voltinism may vary within a widely distributed species and seems to be related to latitude, with multivoltinism more common in the south and univoltinism in the north. Presumably, higher temperatures at more southerly latitudes promote faster growth and development of cohorts and thus more cohorts per year.

Another form of life history is the *semivoltine* type ("half" a cohort per year), in which a life cycle covers two or more years. This is the case in northern regions with our familiar mayfly, *Hexagenia*. Other species show semivoltinism everywhere, regardless of geographic location: the stonefly *Pteronarcys*, the famous "salmon fly" of the West, and the dobsonfly *Corydalus*, whose immature larva is the *hellgrammite* often found in smallmouth bass streams.

In semivoltinism, two or more cohorts typically coexist at any point in time, each of them present at a different point of their life cycle. Thus, the cohorts do not progress one after the other, but rather overlap by one or two years. That is, one cohort may emerge and oviposit in the spring of one year, the progeny of which emerge in the spring two years later. But in the meantime, another cohort emerges and oviposits in the intervening spring. Sort of like leapfrog.

This design, however, is not firm and inviolable. Often a small percentage of individuals delays development and emerges along with the following cohort, affording some insulation against a failed cohort. If such overlap between cohorts never occurred, and the cohorts were completely and permanently separated, they would (in a million years or so) become two separate species!

Semivoltinism is the rule also for most fishes—spawning every year, although the cohorts (fishery biologists use the term *year class*) overlap greatly. We'll take up fish later on.

The flexibility in voltinism, by the way, demonstrates a difference between life cycle and life history: A species may have a multivoltine life history that consists of two or more life cycles.

Voltinism is extremely important in estimating annual production by invertebrates. For example, the higher the voltinism (more cohorts per year), the greater is the population turnover—what biologists call the *production-to-biomass ratio* (*P:B*). The more cohorts per year, the higher the *P:B* ratio, which means that total production for the year is greater than would be predicted from observing the average quantity (standing stock, or biomass) throughout the year.

In one method, the length of life cycle is crucial to estimating the production—in fact, the length of the "producing period" becomes most important. This is the time during which the organism is growing as a nymph or larva. It does not include the time spent in the egg or pupal stage, so the producing or growing period is always shorter than the voltinism would suggest. We call this period the *cohort production interval,* or CPI (no relationship to business economics). For example, the CPI for a univoltine species would be less than 365 days, and the CPI for a trivoltine species would be shorter than 122 days (one-third of 365 days).

Voltinism affects your fly fishing. A univoltine mayfly, such as *Ephemerella subvaria* (the Hendrickson) has one period of emergence and so is available on the water for only a single, short period of each year. Small mayflies, such as those species in the genus *Baetis* (Blue Dun, Blue-winged Olive) are often bivoltine, sometimes trivoltine; *Baetis*, for example, has two or three emergence periods, often stretched out over the year, affording good dry fly-fishing for much of the summer! Somewhat the same situation is provided by the tiny mayfly *Tricorythodes* (our "trico"), with the first of two cohorts hatching from overwintering eggs in the spring. Growth occurs during the summer, the first emergence takes place in midsummer, and the second cohort emerges in late summer and on into the fall, thus providing a long time for fishing.

With an asynchronous, multivoltine life history,
The mayfly *Tricorythodes* may emerge every day for many weeks.

Synchrony is another important aspect of life history. When all individuals of a species hatch from their eggs at approximately the same time and later mature as adults at the same time, their life cycle stages are said to be *synchronous*. When egg hatching, adult emergence, and oviposition are each spread out over time, we call such a life cycle *asynchronous*. This factor affects your fishing, too. With synchronous adult emergence, you have to be Johnny-on-the-spot to meet the hatch; with asynchronous emergence, your window of opportunity in meeting the hatch is spread out over a long season. The life cycles of many *Baetis* and *Tricorythodes* are asynchronous; the life cycle of the Hendrickson (*Ephemerella subvaria*) is synchronous.

Different life history traits contribute greatly to the diversity of stream life. Different voltinisms spread out the timing of benthic invertebrates' use of their resources, sustaining the multitude of insects, crustaceans, and other taxa in all their needs. Some cohorts prosper in the sunlit days of springtime when benthic algal populations explode; some thrive in the cooler environments of late autumn and even winter.

Some cohorts are so different in size and appearance from season to season that they may not even seem to be the same species. An example is the mayfly *Baetis tricaudatus*, which sometimes produces three cohorts per year (trivoltine). When so, the early spring cohort consists of large adults (maybe hook size 16), the summer cohort of very tiny adults (perhaps 22), and the autumn cohort back up to 16. This size difference is so striking that in decades past, the several cohorts were thought to represent different species.

Just the opposite may occur among truly different species that share the same stream but in different seasons. Whether collected in the fall or spring, both samples may appear to include the same species. But the larvae of one species of caddisfly may do better in spring/early summer, while another, but different species utilizes the late summer/fall environment. In effect, two species divide up the seasonal supply of resources, using the same habitat but at different times. Some biologists refer to a *winter fauna* and a *summer fauna* of ecologically similar but taxonomically different species. This seasonal distribution of resource use maximizes the use of a stream's resources and results in both greater biodiversity and higher annual productivity.

◆   ◆   ◆

ANOTHER IMPORTANT ASPECT of species diversity is molting or *metamorphosis*, the changes that take place in the form of an insect as it grows and matures from the egg to mature adult. Great variability and complexity best describe the processes of growth and metamorphosis.

To begin with, entomologists divide insect life histories into two major groups, those with so-called *incomplete metamorphosis* (more primitive in evolution) and *complete metamorphosis* (more advanced). Both result in the change from swimmer to flyer.

The group with incomplete metamorphosis is described as *hemimetabolous* (only "half" changed). It is in this group that the immatures are technically termed *nymphs.* The changeover from swimming nymph to adult is gradual, and the adult appears very much the same as the nymph, with the notable addition of wings. Hemimetabolous insects include mayflies and stoneflies, among others.

Complete metamorphosis produces a radical change in form, from an encased or burrowing larva to a delicate flying creature freed from its earthly and watery bonds—truly a remarkable transformation. This group is described as *holometabolous* (wholly changed metabolism), and the immature form is always called a *larva* (plural is *larvae*). The changeover from larva to adult takes place during a non-mobile stage, the *pupa* (plural is *pupae*), which is sealed in a stony or organic case. Holometabolous insects include those with a wormlike larva, such as the caddisflies, true flies, beetles, and dobsonflies.

Hemimetabolous nymphs are capable of swimming, whereas holometabolous larvae are usually sessile, contained in a self-constructed case. Nymphing anglers might twitch their lures that imitate swimming, hemimetabolous nymphs—but use a dead drift to imitate holometabolous larvae!

The degree of variation in life history details among invertebrates seems infinite. The time and period of emergence and the site of egg-laying vary greatly (spring, summer, fall) and the site of egg deposition (under water on stones, broadcast on the water surface, on overhanging vegetation, on the backs of other animals). This variation is less within a family, even less within a genus and a species. Voltinism, growth rate, kind of food, size of adults—all vary even within a family. Adult emergence may occur while the nymph or pupa is floating downstream, climbing up or attached to a stone or stick, or burrowing in riparian soil. Midge pupae (Chironomidae) molt to adults under water and rise to the surface using their cast pupal shucks as temporary platforms at the water surface. Some true flies (black flies, for example) also emerge as adults under water and then rise to the surface enclosed in gas bubbles. (Try that for an emerger on your vise!)

We'll take up many of these variations in following sections about more specific taxa.

◆   ◆   ◆

OF SOME THIRTY TO FORTY INSECT ORDERS worldwide (containing more than a million described species), only about a dozen orders are considered aquatic or semiaquatic. Semiaquatic orders are mainly terrestrial but live near the water. However, a few of these partially terrestrial orders have one or more taxa that are truly aquatic.

Heteroptera and Coleoptera

Aquatic bugs and beetles are some of the most conspicuous of stream insects, although most species in these two orders are terrestrial. Some are the largest of the aquatics, almost all are predaceous, and some can bite or stab you (a defense behavior—they don't really think you're good to eat!). Both orders are only partially aquatic. There are about 400 species of aquatic bugs, and about 1,000 species of aquatic beetles (including semiaquatic species in both orders) in North America.

"True bugs" used to be classified as the order Hemiptera ("half wings"), but recently taxonomists have tended to use the order name Heteroptera. They are hemimetabolous, with incomplete metamorphosis. Beetles—order Coleoptera—are mostly terrestrial and holometabolous and make up the largest order of insects on Earth. We may often confuse bugs and beetles, because they appear similar to a casual glance.

Most aquatic bugs are predaceous and feed with mouthparts modified into a tube called a *rostrum*. The stinging bite of a giant water bug (family Belostomatidae) can be painful. Other bugs include the backswimmers (family Notonectidae) which are more common in lakes than in streams. As their name implies, they swim upside-down in the water, the better to attack their prey from below, like a fighter plane attacking the soft underbelly of a bomber. Water striders (family Gerridae) are common to all kinds of water bodies, skating along the surface near shores and banks like spiders. One would think them to be susceptible to surface-feeding fish, but they do not seem to incite rises. Water measurers (family Hydrometridae) and water scorpions (family Nepidae) resemble sticks or twigs, are more common in ponds and slow streams, and may be confused with the similar "walking sticks" in the terrestrial order of grasshoppers and crickets.

Water boatmen (family Corixidae) are perhaps the most common and abundant fish-food items in warmwater streams. Mostly small (one-fourth inch), these bugs nevertheless appear in great abundance in sandy shallows. With their paddle-like legs, they often explode in an expanding shower at the approach of a paddle or booted foot. Water boatmen are often consumed in great numbers by fish, especially by young smallmouth bass, but unlike most bugs, water boatmen are themselves herbivores, feeding by piercing plants. Some have an unusual seasonal migration, living mostly in lakes and ponds during the summer and then migrating as adults to overwinter in open streams that do not freeze.

Closely related to the aquatic order Heteroptera is the terrestrial order Homoptera, the leafhoppers. This order includes the Family Cicadellidae (previously Jassidae)—the "jassids," to anglers a familiar terrestrial imitation.

Coleoptera, the beetles, includes the most species of any order in the insect world—350,000 species, 150 families, some one-third of the one million insect species worldwide. Some beetles are common in streams, but most are terrestrial.

Common aquatic families include: Dytiscidae (predaceous diving beetles), with large adults (two to three inches long) that rise from the water surface to fly like a flushed mallard; Gyrinidae, the whirligig beetles, are often seen in summer wildly circling on the water surface; Psphenidae, water pennies, the larvae of which are greatly flattened and tightly attached to stones in swift water, presenting an oval or nearly circular appearance on the stone's surface; Elmidae, or riffle beetles, small in both larval and adult stages, occurring in gravel riffles or where swift water flows through vegetation and detritus. Unlike most aquatic Coleoptera, riffle beetles are herbivorous and detritivorous, and they are probably the most important among the beetles as food for fish.

Another dozen beetle families are aquatic or partly so but are not very abundant or visible, or are common only in lentic habitats, that is, lakes and stillwaters.

Many species of aquatic bugs and beetles are not technically part of the benthos, because they do not literally inhabit the stream bottom. For example, good swimmers like backswimmers and diving beetles are more properly included in the *nekton*—that is, swimmers in the upper water. Others that live most of their lives on the water surface, like water striders and whirligigs, are categorized as *neuston*—that is, supported in the surface film.

Diptera

The order of true flies, Diptera, is also large, with some 200,000 species worldwide, and about 3,500 aquatic and semiaquatic species in North America. It is a very diverse order and extremely important in both streams and lakes. As the order name implies, adult flies have only two wings. Midge larvae, family Chironomidae, are small-to-minuscule in size; they feed on fungi and detrital FPOM, and in turn serve as food for virtually all newly hatched fish fry and many predaceous insects, which in turn provide food for larger fish. Some midge adults are so small that their wings measure less than a millimeter long. As the huge taxon that it is, midges are ubiquitous in all suitable waters worldwide, and a hundred different species or more may inhabit a single reach of stream or river. Many species are multivoltine, producing several cohorts each year. Although many biologists have tackled the job of studying the Chironomidae, the task is always daunting, and we still do not know the full significance of the role that midge larvae play in the stream ecosystem. Even taxonomists have difficulty in identifying Chironomidae species in larval stages. There are more than 160 genera among the midges, with thousands of species.

A few other Diptera families are common—and some are notorious when they bite. The lake-living family Ceratopogonidae, known as "pogies" to benthologists and "no-see-ums" when, unseen, they give us campers annoying bites. A fully lake family, Chaoboridae, consists of the only planktonic fly—the "phantom midge" that lives in deep water and makes nocturnal migrations to the oxygen-rich surface of lakes. They get their name from the fact that the larvae are almost transparent and can be seen only by their two black eyes flitting about in a sample bottle of water. They are not found in streams, however. Larvae of the family Dixidae ("loopers," named after the way they double their bodies while "inching" along) inhabit stream edges and frequently are a component of nighttime stream drift. Simuliidae is the black fly family, the larvae of which occur in profuse aggregations on stony surfaces in the swiftest water. Probably we have all been plagued by the biting adults. Certain black fly species make some regions of the world almost uninhabitable, not only by biting but also by transmitting serious diseases. Similar to black flies in their pestilential character are members of the family Culicidae, the mosquitoes, which have annoyed river travelers since time immemorial. Most do not breed in running water. Another family of biting true flies is Tabanidae—horse flies and deer flies—that include some semiaquatic species but are not abundant in streams. Finally, among aquatic true flies, is the family Tipulidae, or crane flies, commonly with large larvae, which are often used as bait in streams. These "water worms" can usually be found among accumulations of organic detritus, such as large leaf packs. Although some are large, worm-like, and long-lived (semivoltine), and menacing-looking, the worm-like larvae do not bite and are not predaceous but detritivorous. The adults sometimes resemble monster mosquitoes but do not bite (fortunately). The artificial "woolly worm" is probably mistaken by fish for the tipulid larva.

◆   ◆   ◆

WE ARE NOW LEFT WITH FIVE ORDERS OF INSECTS that are truly aquatic: Megaloptera, Odonata, Plecoptera, Ephemeroptera, and Trichoptera. All are readily fed upon by fish, and all can be imitated with artificial flies or nymphs. We'll take up the first three in this chapter, but the Ephemeroptera and Trichoptera will come along later in separate chapters.

Megaloptera

Megaloptera is one of the smallest orders of all insects, with only two families and less than 50 species in North America. They are all holometabolous with aquatic larvae, but their egg and pupal stages are, interestingly, terrestrial. Larvae of the family Corydalidae are the more conspicuous—large, semivoltine, and predaceous—easily found among boulders in rivers ideal for smallmouth bass. Adults of *Corydalus*, a common genus, are known as dobsonflies and sometimes are mistaken for large stoneflies. Larvae of the alderfly, family Sialidae, are smaller and univoltine, commonly inhabiting lakes, ponds, and streams, particularly in eastern North America.

Odonata

An ancient order with a long fossil record is the Odonata, divided into two suborders—Anisoptera (dragonflies) and Zygoptera (damselflies). The order prefixes refer to different structure of wings. About 450 species have been described in North America.

This order includes some of the most fascinating life history elements in all the insect world. Yet the behavior of this group as a whole remains little known to most of us who angle or paddle in flowing water. Many species inhabit lakes and ponds, but the few that we see in streams and rivers are well worth the attention of river devotees. Both suborders are predaceous feeders, in both immature and flying adult stages.

Although classed as hemimetabolous, many immature forms undergo drastic changes during metamorphosis to the adult, and consequently they are sometimes referred to as *naiads* (old usage) or *larvae* (recent usage) rather than nymphs. Voltinism is variable: a few damselflies are bivoltine, whereas some dragonflies can take up to four years for development. At least one species, a dragonfly, migrates south for the winter, returning as sexually mature adults in spring to lay its eggs.

In both appearance and habit, the two groups are aptly named. Anisoptera larvae are truly the dragons of the streambed, while larval Zygoptera can swim about like fairy naiads, members of the nekton.

Short and robust, dragonfly larvae are benthic marauders that stalk their prey along the stream bottom, or lie in ambush, half burrowed in sediment, for passing victims. Smaller insects, crustaceans, even small fish, provide their living menu. The dragonfly nymph owns a strong, hinged, prehensile organ called a *labium*, which consists of a pair of parallel, wide blades, like forceps, attached beneath its head. When potential prey passes by, the labium is extended in a lightning-like snap to grasp its quarry. Holding its catch in its labium, the larva crushes it with strong mandibles, and then—in an unusual gastronomic twist—masticates its food with an internal gizzard.

Besides crawling, a dragonfly larva has an auxiliary method of movement—a jet engine, of sorts. Its rectal chamber contains internal gills that serve for respiration, with water pumping in and out. But the pumping action can be strongly pulsed, vigorously propelling the animal forward for both escape and attack. This behavior can be easily observed by placing a dragonfly larva in a shallow white pan and sharply disturbing it.

In the air, adult dragonflies are strong and swift predators, and their incredible maneuverability is a treat to watch. They are said to be beneficial because they feed on mosquitoes (although mosquitoes never seem to diminish!) Some dragonfly adults have been known to fly for more than a 100 miles at a time, reach speeds up to 35 miles per hour, and sometimes fly backward. Fossil dragonfly adults have been measured with wingspans of nearly two feet, making them the largest insects yet discovered to have taken flight. However, today you can see these aerial hunters patrolling the skies over almost any stream on a sunny afternoon. This dragon, moreover, is fully capable of attacking the artificial fly on the end of your flailing line (as it did with mine, one time)—so if it does, be prepared for a good fight!

In contrast to dragons, damsels at least appear to be more genteel and delicate. The larval body is long and slender, and many species are good swimmers. They use their swimming maneuverability rather than the dragonfly's stalk-and-ambush mode. In the air, the adult damselfly appears to be a weak flyer, compared with the dragonfly, but still it is an efficient predator.

Both groups emerge as adults by first crawling out of the water and up some streamside stone, branch, or stem, where their final metamorphosis takes place. The cast *exuvium*, or shuck, is often left attached to the object on which the last instar has rested and molted, easily observed along most stream banks. A concrete bridge abutment is also a good place to look.

The body shape of adults in both groups is similar, with long, slender abdomens resulting in the sobriquet "darning needles," with the dragonfly's usually longer. The two can be further distinguished when at rest on limb or twig: dragonfly wings are spread horizontally, whereas damselfly wings are cocked upright.

Angling imitations for these insects are not as common as for others. Artificial nymphs imitating the swimming damselfly can be a good choice, both for trout in streams and for warmwater fish species in lakes. But tying an imitation of a stalking dragonfly larva can be a challenge!

Plecoptera

Among all aquatic insects, the order Plecoptera, the stoneflies, is especially associated with two very important environmental factors: running water and low temperatures. Their preference is thus for cool streams. In fact, the aquatic nymphs of some species are never noticed by those of us who visit streams mainly in the summertime, because many species undergo a hidden, resting stage known as *diapause* to escape the warmer waters of summer. About 500 species of stoneflies inhabit the United States and Canada.

Stonefly nymphs' demand for oxygen is high, yet the gill structures for many species are small and inconspicuous, or even lacking altogether. Because of this condition, they require the cool, running water that is rich in oxygen, continuously washing over their body surface, where oxygen is absorbed. Of course, this predilection for cold, swift streams makes the Plecoptera almost an icon for trout streams!

Many species of aquatic invertebrates have evolved ways to cope with swiftly flowing water—swimming ability, streamlined or flattened bodies, attachment organs, burrowing habit. But stoneflies appear to be the only major group that has not only evolved to *survive* swift water, but also to *depend* upon it.

Yet, there are always exceptions to the rule. For stoneflies, the stream habitat is a rule, but some are found along shores of cold, windswept lakes, where this often-turbulent habitat may not be so different from cool, swift streams. Some other exceptions, however, may not be so easy to explain. For example, some have turned up from Lake Superior's depths of over 200 feet, and one species of stonefly apparently enjoys an entirely aquatic life history, including the adult, in the 300-foot depths of California/Nevada's Lake Tahoe.

Stoneflies are hemimetabolous. Despite the fact that they do not have a pupal stage, the change in their appearance from immature to adult in some families is a bit radical. They do not have a pupal stage but we refer to the immature as a larva. Voltinism is variable across the order—from univoltine to semivoltine, with up to four years per cohort life.

With some exceptions, adult stoneflies are not easy to observe. All are weak fliers, reclusive in streamside vegetation, and drab in coloration. One of the exceptions is the adult of the genus *Hastaperla*, only medium in size but colored in a pale, glistening lemon-yellow—the namesake of the Yellow Sally. Larvae can occur in great numbers in small, summercool midwestern streams.

Of special interest are the so-called "winter stoneflies." They characteristically have a life history that is cold-adapted—that is, the major period of larval growth and adult emergence occurs in the winter. Adults are seen only in the winter, perhaps walking about on the surface of the snow at streamside. The larvae are not visible in summer because, after hatching from eggs in early spring, they undertake *diapause* to wait out the heat of summer. They then begin their major growth period in the fall.

Plecoptera is a relatively small order, with only nine families in North America. These nine are divided by taxonomists into two major groups. One group of four families has relatively small larvae, all species of which are univoltine and which feed as herbivores and detritivores. This group includes the winter stoneflies and the deep-living species in Lake Tahoe. We are unlikely to see the larvae of this group, in view of their summer diapause.

The other major group is much more variable across its five families. Some are of the winter stonefly type with summer diapause; some are abundant and present as larvae in summer. Some feed upon the algae and fungi on decaying leaves, and some are voracious predators. Voltinism, as mentioned above, is also variable.

Two special stonefly families are the most visible and meaningful to us human river habitués. First, the family Perlidae is common in many trout streams: roach-like and medium-sized, the flat-bodied larvae can be found in abundance under riffle stones, particularly in the spring. These are among the main predators, feeding on other small invertebrates, and in some streams, they may be the primary predators. Many species that used to be in the genus *Acroneuria*, common across most of North America, are now collected into Acroneuriinae, a subfamily of the Perlidae that now includes several new genera. However, whether *Acroneuria* or Acroneuriinae, these larvae are very important in streams and as imitations in the angler's fly box. The flattened larvae often have striking, colorful patterns of yellow and brown on their backs and thorax, and highly visible filamentous gills at the base of their legs. Most species in the family are semivoltine.

Pteronarcys
A large stonefly adult, the salmon fly of the West.

Second, the Family Pteronarcyidae includes the well-known genus *Pteronarcys*, the most visible of all stoneflies when emerging and ovipositing. The larva is large and fierce-looking but is only vegetarian, feeding mainly on large CPOM and associated microorganisms.

These stoneflies are semivoltine, with a life cycle of up to four years. When the adults are on the water, they appear like small birds in distress, raising a ruckus. The western species, *Pteronarcys californica*, is the famed "salmon fly" of mountain rivers, the adult hatch inciting an animated response from both trout and anglers. In midwestern streams, the emergence of *P. pictetii* and *P. dorsata* may not be so abundant and conspicuous, but these species are common, and probably most large, dark-colored artificials used in fishing, such as the Woolly Bugger, serve to simulate these enticing larval detritivores.

Mollusca

An important group of invertebrate animals in almost any stream or river is the mollusks, phylum Mollusca. Snails and clams are placed respectively in two classes: Gastropoda and Bivalvia. Both snail and clamshells are constructed of crystalline calcium carbonate (secreted by special organs of the animals inside the shells), so both groups require alkaline waters.

Gastropods, or snails, make up the most diverse group of mollusks, with about 500 species in North America. Two subclasses are placed in the Gastropoda: Prosobranchia and Pulmonata. Aquatic snails are prosobranchs, found in both ocean and fresh water, whereas the pulmonates are mostly terrestrial, with some aquatic. Interestingly, the pulmonates, as the name may suggest, have effective lungs that permit their respiration on land. It is thought that the aquatic pulmonates evolved by dispersing from land to water, retaining the lung attribute; in disturbed, oxygen-depleted stream conditions, pulmonates can respire air at the water surface, while prosobranchs must move to conditions that are more suitable underwater. Of the 500 species in North America, prosobranchs number 350, and pulmonates 150.

Snails are among the most important invertebrates feeding on periphyton, abundant in many streams. Some snails possess a *radula*, a scraping organ that enables them to feed on detritus, microorganisms, diatoms, and other algae in the periphyton. In turn, they are fed upon by many fishes, including pumpkinseed sunfish and redear sunfish in warmwater streams, the latter known as "shell-crackers," for their preferential feeding on snails and clams. Of course, only the flesh inside the shell is digested.

Eggs of snails can often be observed attached to the undersides of stones in stream riffles, with a number of eggs clearly visible in gelatinous masses. If you are in the habit of turning over stones in small streams, you are sure to see many snails and the packets of snail eggs.

All snail shells are spiraled. Three major forms can be easily recognized:

• simple-conical—may appear something like a single clam-shell, but flat and open on the bottom, gradually spiraled up toward an apex. These animals are known as *limpits,* usually attached to stone surfaces; *Ferissia* is a common stream genus.

• whorl—"like a doughnut," but with the outside ring spiraling toward the center. Most are dwellers of ponds and lakes; *Armiger* is a common genus in northern United States and Canada.

• spiral—with a bulbous body spiraling upward to a sharp apex. This spiral may be either *sinistral* (left) or *dextral* (right), in different species:

—*sinistral*: when viewed toward the aperture (the entrance into the internal body), its opening is on the left side. *Physis* is one of the most common snails in streams; sometimes you can feel their presence in the fish's intestine like a string of beads along the fish's lower flank. Some species of *Physis* have the ability to secrete gas within their shells, which causes them to float and drift away from unsuitable conditions, such as high temperatures and low oxygen.

—*dextral*: like sinistral except with the aperture opening on the right side. *Lymnaea* is a common genus, mostly found in ponds, marshes, and lakes.

The reproductive mode of snails is diverse. Most prosobranchs are *dioecious*, having separate sexes; all pulmonates are *monoecious* (or *hermaphroditic*), with both male and female sexual organs in the same individual. This latter trait enables these snails to reproduce by fertilizing themselves under conditions of low abundance, when mates would be difficult to find. Many prosobranchs are *viviparous*, with eggs hatching internally and incubated in the female's *marsupium*; juveniles are later released as miniature adults, fully formed, onto the stream bottom. Many life histories are *semelparous* (one breeding period in its lifetime), and some *iteroparous* (breeding repeatedly).

Snail shells make good collections, because they occur in a great variety of types, some colorful (especially terrestrial ones). The shells do not spoil and are easily arranged in display cases.

Bivalves, or clams, have about 260 freshwater species in North America, mostly in two families: Unionidae and Sphaeriidae (formerly Pisidiidae). Many species of bivalves are endangered, declining, or extinct. Both groups have many colorful and expressive common names. The class name, Bivalvia, suggests the general form of clams—a matched pair of shells (or valves) connected by a muscular hinge on the dorsal edge.

The two families are very distinct in their life history, distribution, and ecology. Many unionids are large (up to three to four inches in shell length, some larger), long-lived, with limited, scattered, and discontinuous distributions, although they occur across the continent in different species.

The sphaeriids, on the other hand, are widely distributed, small in size, common and abundant in lakes and streams, as well as in stillwater sections of rivers, often on mud bottoms. Some of the smallest of these are called "pea mussels" or "fingernail clams." Like some snails, these small spheriids are preyed upon by fishes like the shell-crackers.

The two families differ greatly in their mode of reproduction. Unionids produce *glochidia*, tiny larvae that also have bivalved shells, which are held in the female's *marsupium* until released in the presence of a fish (any fish species). Glochidia are then carried as encysted parasites on the fish's gills. After growth and metamorphosis to a juvenile size, they drop off their fish host and become settled on the stream bottom. The number of glochidia produced by a single female is huge, but with high mortality at every step, only the rare individual becomes a settled juvenile. While the glochidia are attached to a fish, their dispersal into new areas is limited by the fish's ability to disperse; consequently, their distribution is minimal.

The reproductive mode of sphaeriid clams is quite different, for these are *ovoviviparous;* the eggs hatch internally and are "born" as live juveniles that resemble adults in miniature form. These then settle immediately to the stream bottom. Sphaeriids disperse much more widely than unionids, because the juveniles are capable of being carried by birds and mammals, sometimes over great distances.

These different life history features mean different survival rates of eggs to adults. Unionids have longer life spans (with longer time to reach maturity), reduced dispersal, greater selectivity toward high quality habitat (stable sand deposits), combined with extremely low survival to settlement. Consequently, unionids are much more sensitive to human-caused disruptions than are sphaeriids.

Many unionids are at risk of extinction (or already gone), the result of commercial overfishing and human-caused habitat degradation. Major disturbances affecting unionids include river navigation, stream channelization, and dams and diversions. Combined with overharvesting by the button industry and low reproductive rate, these species are much more subject to population declines and extinctions. Furthermore, all bivalves feed by filtering algae and other seston from passing water, so they are susceptible to excessive suspended sediment and toxic pollutants in water.

North America has been plagued by a couple of exotic clams causing havoc to native species: the Asian clam, genus *Corbicula*, now throughout the continent, and the zebra mussel, of the genus *Dreissena*, in the Great Lakes. These introductions have probably resulted from ocean-going freighters that came from foreign ports, where they took on fresh water for ballast—and a few juveniles of clams native to the foreign port. Exchanging ballast water in mid-ocean would kill the freshwater organisms with salt water, but obviously such an operation would slow the transport and cost time. The exotics have damaged domestic and industrial water supplies. The Asian clam has devastated native clam populations in southern rivers. Severe competition by the zebra mussel in the Great Lakes, where it was introduced from the ballast water of foreign ships, also interferes severely with other mollusks and fish spawning. It furthermore clogs industrial intake conduits and water treatment facilities. The zebra mussel appears to be rapidly expanding its range across the continent.

◆   ◆   ◆

SOME OF THE OTHER ANIMALS you are likely to meet, if you were to sample the benthos in your favorite stream, may seem unimportant. Some are strange, even weird. Others, like crustaceans, can be extremely important in the web of benthic life. Some crustaceans are large, like crayfish, some so tiny they can't even be seen with the naked eye. Later, we'll devote an entire chapter to these crusty fellows, because they can account for very high rates of energy flow through benthic communities. They also make abundant, nutritious food for fish.

We'll skip most microscopic animals for now, however, such as protozoans and rotifers, and some others that you are likely to encounter only in pursuit of a degree in zoology. Although few and small, they can still open fascinating views of life at the bottom.

For now, we'll take a quick look at the fly-fishing lure called the San Juan Worm. It's a popular nymph, of course, but what does it really imitate? Several possibilities are among some old friends like the earthworms. We dug garden hackle from Mom's petunia patch, hunted nightcrawlers on a well-watered golf course, and dug "red worms" from a manure pile. A red worm could very well be what that twenty-incher thought it was getting when it ate your San Juan Worm last spring. After a heavy rain, many terrestrial worms are washed into streams and provide a sudden, lavish banquet for fish. No wonder they are good bait for stream fish.

Many aquatic worms closely resemble terrestrial earthworms, some reddish or red-brown in color. The aquatic worm in the family Tubificidae is one of the best bets for the San Juan Worm. In this family, members of the genus *Tubifex* occupy oxygen-depleted waters, including sediments in deep lakes. Perhaps in the deep, anoxic waters behind Navaho Dam on the San Juan River live high densities of *Tubifex*, which then wash downstream from the dam to tickle the gastronomic palates of the trout in this famous tailwater fishery.

Another possibility for the San Juan Worm, though not an earthworm, is the insect larva of the midge genus *Chironomus*—a bright red "worm" smaller than *Tubifex*, but one that also thrives in anoxic waters in deep sediments. Its red color is from *hemoglobin*, which stores oxygen in the blood and thus permits the animal to live in low-oxygen conditions for long times. This arrangement also results in their common name: bloodworm. Red worms, *Tubifex*, bloodworms—imitated by a San Juan Worm—make for good fishing in the San Juan River, and in other tailwaters, too.

Another group of worms important to nymph fishing is the leeches. We often abhor these blood-sucking parasites, which sometimes attach themselves to our boots, but they probably provide another reason for the success of the Woolly Worm, especially when it is tied with a long tail of marabou. They are good swimmers, moving with graceful undulations, and therefore attractive to a hungry fish. Leeches are inhabitants mainly of ponds and lakes, but they can also be found in some slow streams.

If you take some stream samples with a very fine-meshed screen or net and empty the contents into a white enameled pan with clear water, you may see some red specks, about the size of pepper flakes, zipping about in the pan. Under a microscope, they appear almost perfectly round, bright red or orange in color. These are water mites, related to spiders in the class Arachnoidea. We casually call these Hydracarina, which is not a specific taxon but a loose collection of several families in the class. Mites have eight legs, like spiders, in contrast to the six of insects. Their preferred habitat is in springs or summercool waters and—consequently—in trout streams.

◆   ◆   ◆

BIODIVERSITY AMONG STREAM ANIMALS is a reflection of the great variety of ecological *niches* in streams. The niche describes not only the physical locations of animals but also their *functional* positions in the system.

The physical location includes stream bottom particles of different sizes from silt grains to boulders, the open spaces among the particles, and the velocity of water flow through the spaces. But the niche also embodies a complex of interactions with other living forms. Interactions among species interjects a large, separate formula into the ways in which individual animals conduct their life activities, such as foraging, feeding, and protecting themselves against predation. The patchwork mosaic in stream bottom populations, both plant and animal, thus becomes an intricate and engrossing web of life.

The many spaces, small and large, in a stony stream bottom provide a great host of ecological niches for benthic animals.

Still it is remarkable that life cycles and life history features among stream organisms still closely resemble each other in a worldwide uniformity. Functional aspects of the stream ecosystem are similar on all major continents. For example, species of the mayfly *Baetis* and the scud *Gammarus* often occur together in small, summercool brooks in an ecological relationship. In

Europe and midwestern North America, only the species will be different and then only slightly in the same kind of habitat, where the niche, function, and genus are the same.

Today's aquatic insects began their evolutionary progression as primitive, terrestrial animals, then "invaded" freshwater habitats hundreds of millions of years ago. Their life histories have adapted to the complexity of niches on the stream bottom. Varying from stony riffle, to leaf pack, to sandy bar, these niches and life history accommodations nevertheless have remained virtually unchanged through the long life history of Earth itself—at least for the last several hundred million years!

We are fortunate to witness this complexity. Whether turning over riffle stones, playing a fighting fish, or witnessing a mating flight of adult aquatic insects from a riverside campsite, we are privileged indeed to be able to understand and appreciate this wondrous mixture of cycles of life we call biodiversity.

TECHNICAL REFERENCES:

Butler, Malcolm G. 1984. Life histories of aquatic insects. Pages 24-55 *in* Vincent H. Resh and David M. Rosenberg, editors. *The Ecology of Aquatic Insects.* Praeger Publishers, New York.

Stewart, Kenneth W., and B.P. Stark. 1988. *Nymphs of North American Stonefly Genera (Plecoptera).* Thomas Say Foundation, Entomological Society of America, No. 12.

RiverSketch

A DIFFERENT DRUMMER

ALL OF US WHO ENJOY AND VISIT THE OUTDOORS have heard the drumming of the ruffed grouse, the most widespread of upland game birds. The grouse signal is given only by the male, for bordering his territory and for mate finding. The grouse is enshrined in sporting literature by upland author Burton Spiller as the "drummer in the woods."

But did you know that adult stoneflies drum? The "ritual" is performed by both males and females, for mate finding. The signal is transmitted by beating on a substrate (like a small branch) with the abdomen. The male's signal is returned by the female, which he then seeks out through the direction of her responding signal. Unlike the grouse drum, the stonefly's is only a vibration across wooden limbs in bush or tree, or in the ground.

Many signals are given by mate seekers throughout the animal world. The wolf howls, the cricket chirps, the elk bugles, the loon yodels. And high in the springtime sky of a dusky evening the snipe emits his haunting, quavering winnow.

And so the stonefly drums, creating good "vibes." These cannot be heard by human ears; instead, sensitive microphones in the laboratory can send them to a recorder for translation into pictures on an oscilloscope.

The scene at streamside proceeds something like this: Within a day after emergence from the water as a flying adult, the male begins his searching signal while pausing on a twig or small branch of a bush or small tree. The signal, a vibration that is transmitted for some distance through the woody substrate. If somewhere within two or three yards a female receives it, she responds with a signal of her own; the male replies, differently now, for he means to have her know that he has received her response. Soon both sexes drum alternately to each other in a *duet*; all the time the male is approaching closer and closer. When contact is made, copulation and fertilization take place immediately. The male will leave to search for other mates, but the female, now pregnant, will not respond to another searching drumbeat.

Signals are specific to a single species. A female will respond only to the signal from a male of her own species, and likewise the male's reply to her. Variations include: duration of the signal interval—up to two or three seconds for the male, usually under a second for the female; number and configuration of pulses within that duration; the frequency and amplitude of beats within a pulse. The number of combinations and arrangements appear infinite, each one recognizable by the receptors of the opposite sex. When air temperatures drop to a few degrees above freezing, drumming will not occur. Above that minimum threshold, higher temperatures will result in higher frequencies in the drumming pattern, still recognizable by the opposite sex of a given species.

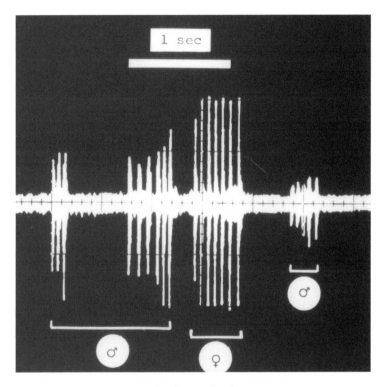

Oscillograph of stonefly drumming.
First two segments by male are a searching call;
second is a reply of female; third is a confirmation call by male.
(Courtesy of Kenneth W. Stewart, University of North Texas.)

Many stonefly species have been studied for the nature of their drumming signals, and so far, it seems all species of the order Plecoptera—including our familiar ones in *Pteronarcys* and *Acroneuria*—exhibit this form of communication, each species having its own language. Other, terrestrial insects also drum—some leaf hoppers, beetles, termites, others—but as far as we know

now, the Plecoptera are the only members of the stream benthos that do so.

Entomologists call the drumming behavior "intersexual vibrational communication." But by whatever name, this different kind of drummer in the woods, that which we now understand but probably will not hear, will result in more stoneflies—and more rises in our favorite evening pool—in two or three years' time.

SELECTED REFERENCES:

Abbott, John C., and Kenneth W. Stewart. 1993. Male search behavior of the stonefly, *Pteronarcella badia* (Hagen) in relation to drumming. *Journal of Insect Behavior.* Volume 6, pages 462-481.

Stewart, Kenneth W. 1997. Vibrational communication in insects: Epitome in the language of stoneflies? *American Entomologist.* Volume 43, pages 81-91.

Chapter 14

MAYFLIES

OF ALL INSECTS, THE MAYFLY HAS LONG HELD mankind's greatest fascination. More than two millennia ago, scholars remarked about the mayfly's ephemeral life, and mayfly imitations on a hook were among the first, primitive attempts at fly fishing.

The mayfly order name itself, Ephemeroptera ("short-lived flight"), evokes a delicate and fleeting portrait, an image of its odyssey down the swirling waters of a stream riffle. It is the product of a long evolution.

The mayfly is indeed ancient, the most primitive of all insects. The fossil record is replete with mayfly remains, much larger than today's, dating back to the coal-accumulating, reptile-roaming ages of the Mesozoic Era, two hundred million years ago. One of the most primitive characteristics of mayflies is their cocked wings or, more accurately, their inability to fold their wings back along the tops of their bodies. Mayflies share this feature with the Odonata, the ancient order of dragonflies and damselflies, who also cannot fold back their wings. On the other hand, the more "advanced" stoneflies and caddisflies can indeed fold back their wings when at rest, as well as fly with wings outstretched, a fact the discriminating fly tier knows well.

To the riverbank hiker trudging back to camp in the dusk of a spring evening, swarms of mature males and ovipositing females may be a surprise and a delight. Females carry yellowish clumps of eggs at the tips of their abdomens, seeking a suitable glide of current upon which to deposit the seed of the next generation. To the flyrod-wielding angler seeking an expected "hatch," the moment becomes one of keen anticipation.

The whole art and culture of fly tying and fishing the "dry fly" is *mostly based on imitating the mayfly.* The very earliest accounts of fly-fishing in the angling literature of several centuries ago reveal attempts to simulate this gossamer vision during its brief flight. To meet the anticipated emergence at just the right time of year and day, armed with an adequate supply of accurate mayfly imitations in the fly-box, is to savor the consummation of the fly fisher's most ardent fancy.

◆   ◆   ◆

THE ORDER EPHEMEROPTERA comprises nearly 30 families worldwide, 21 in North America with 675 species. We'll investigate about a half-dozen families among the streambed nymphs that represent different and interesting life histories. And we'll discuss how their diverse life strategies may influence your fishing strategies!

Throughout the Ephemeroptera, the life history features that characterize the order are the same, but many vary within families and genera, and some even within a single species. A great diversity in life history traits appears among the mayfly species that occupy stony-bottomed, low-order, headwater streams.

The succession of two flying stages, the subimago and adult (dun and spinner, respectively) is typical of mayflies, and unique among insects. Only the adult is sexually mature. (Even here, there occur a few exceptions.) Both stages are important to insect watchers and fly fishers, but it is the subimago, or dun, that is most imitated by the dry fly. The duration of both stages is relatively brief. The subimago's existence may be as short as a few minutes, but most persist for one or two days. The adult lives a bit longer, from a couple of hours to several days. Throughout the order of Ephemeroptera, it was this short adult life that led to the order name.

Another typical attribute of mayflies is the swarming behavior of adults during mating. Males swarm above the water and females enter the swarm, where copulation takes place on the wing. The size of swarms varies from a few individuals that can barely be called a swarm to huge congregations that give the impression of smoke above the water.

Mayflies have a hemimetabolous life cycle, changing not very much from nymph to adult. Although much variation appears in the morphology and behavior of the nymphs, all adults are similar in their gross characteristics, regardless of species, varying mainly in size and coloration. Color variations appear slight. Which leads to the question: Is there a "generic" dry fly pattern that needs only to vary in hook size and hue? Or, do we really need to carry all those fly boxes?

Mayflies have two or three tails (*caudal filaments*, if you must), but nymphs of most have three. When the nymph molts into a subimago or, later, into the adult, these forms will usually have just two tails. However, if you look carefully at the base of the two tails with a magnifying glass, you will probably find a third, tiny appendage that is a vestigial middle caudal filament. It seems unlikely that hungry trout will notice this difference, and it is probably OK to even the most exacting of entomologists if you insist on tying a nymph imitation of *Baetis bicaudatus* with two tails and *Baetis tricaudatus* with three!

Mayfly nymphs are often organized by ecological groups, or life forms depending largely upon their means of moving around or staying put. Most taxonomists divide them into just four categories:

• swimmers—described as minnowlike in their actions, they dart swiftly and can swim in moderate currents;

• clingers—flattened in shape, they cling tightly to surfaces of stones and can withstand swift currents in riffles;

• sprawlers—more robust in shape, they are poor swimmers and occupy detritus accumulations on the streambed or under stones in slow currents;

• burrowers—large, with expansive gills, they construct **U**-shaped burrows in soft sediments and require moderate currents.

Top: *Baetis* subimago just emerged from nymphal shuck,
nymph with three caudal filaments, subimago (dun) with two.
Bottom: Adult (spinner) emerging from subimago,
also with two caudal filaments.
(Photos by R. J. R. Johnson.)

In *Aquatic Entomology* (1983), Dr. Patrick McCaffferty's wonderful book on aquatic insects, he divides these groups into some further categories. Based largely on shape and the more obvious anatomical features, these life form descriptions can be of great benefit to fly tiers concentrating on nymph fishing.

Adult *Baetis*, typically with cocked, transparent wings.
Shown here is the male with large protuberant eyes.
(Photo by Dean C. Hansen of *WetBugs Press*, Stillwater, Minnesota.)

Swimmers, like *Baetis*, are described as minnowlike, and although small, are often the most abundant mayflies in many streams across North America. The clingers, well represented in the family Heptageniidae, are the most common mayfly nymphs found in swift riffles, especially in western mountains. Sprawlers, typified by *Ephemerella*, are more robust but poor swimmers, and are rarely found in swift riffles. Burrowers, family Ephemeridae, dig their tunnels in silty streambeds and obtain their oxygen and drifting FPOM food from the water that flows through their burrows. Large, obvious gills typify these nymphs; the gills, waved with rhythmic undulations of the animals' bodies, create currents through the burrow. *Hexagenia* is our best-known representative among the burrowers.

Other life history attributes vary greatly among mayfly nymphs. Seasonal patterns in growth, emergence, and egg incubation are hugely diverse. Length of life cycle varies from as short as little more than two weeks to more than two years. So voltinism, as we have already discussed in the previous chapter, ranges from multivoltine to univoltine to semivoltine, with a tendency toward shorter life cycles (that is, multivoltinism) in southern latitudes and lower altitudes and, conversely, univoltine or semivoltine in the north and high altitudes.

Other life history traits—feeding habits and foods, ovipositing behavior, fecundity (number of eggs), duration of egg incubation, number of instars (12 to 45), susceptibility to drift, and many others range widely. We'll take up most of these variations in discussions that follow on families, genera, and species.

Three families concern anglers, and most particularly fly fishers, above all others. Baetidae is the most abundant in numbers and species (130) and in its widespread distribution, followed by Ephemerellidae (85 species) and Heptageniidae (105 species). These three families together make up most of the angler's dry flies. Three special groups include some genera and species that can become extremely important at certain seasons: the family Isonychiidae (Mahogany Dun, Slate Drake), the genus *Tricorythodes* (the Trico), and the family Ephemeridae (*Hexagenia*). Three more families are of special interest because of their unusual life histories: Polymitarcyidae (with *Ephoron*, whose subimago female is sexually mature); Siphlonuridae (with a carnivorous nymph); and Baetiscidae (an "armored" mayfly nymph that more resembles a spiny beetle!).

◆   ◆   ◆

THE FAMILY BAETIDAE is the most commonly encountered of mayflies in streams worldwide. Most nymphs are small, and the smallest of these (size 30 hook?) are seldom imitated by the angler's "nymph." Furthermore, studies by fisheries biologists suggest that these tiny nymphs are rarely preyed upon by adult trout; exceptions occur when extreme numbers drift *en masse* as sort of an underwater "hatch." The contribution of *Baetis* to the productivity of stream communities consists mainly of providing food to other, predaceous invertebrates, such as stonefly nymphs and scuds, and to larger fish when these mayflies emerge as subimagoes and adults. As early, tiny instars, these nymphs may be among the first foods taken by fish fry.

Most baetids (the professionally accepted common name for all members of the family Baetidae) are scrapers and gatherers, grazing on diatoms and fungi in the periphyton or collecting up organic bits from the streambed. Most nymphs inhabit stony riffles in small, swift streams, and are the most abundant mayflies in high-elevation streams. Across the entire family, however, the range of habitat quality is exceptionally broad: from pristine mountain trout streams, to slow-flowing plains streams, and even to streams slightly degraded by pollution.

Within the family Baetidae, the genus *Baetis* includes the most species, 41. One species—*Baetis tricaudatus* (formerly *B. vagans* in North Central states—appears across the continent. In later discussions, we'll see that *Baetis* is the genus most involved in the intriguing phenomenon of invertebrate drift.

It is during their emergence and oviposition that *Baetis* becomes an intriguing phenomenon of greatest interest to fly fishers. The spinner fall often results in an exciting trout rise. With a bivoltine or trivoltine life history, the spring emergence is the most obvious, with larger adults (perhaps size 16), followed by a midsummer emergence of smaller adults (size 20), and sometimes an autumn "hatch" of the larger ones again. *Baetis* species are not synchronous in emergence and oviposition, so flying adults can be seen almost continuously from early spring to late fall. This lack of strong synchrony, together with their multivoltine life cycle, results in the huge popularity of *Baetis* imitations throughout their long season.

Adult *Baetis* perform mating swarms, but not directly over the stream. An observant angler may see just a few, some flying upstream, some down. Their ovipositing behavior is one of the most complex of all, and one of the easiest to observe.

The gravid adult female of *Baetis tricaudatus*, for example, alights on some substrate, such as a stone projecting above the water surface. She immediately proceeds to crawl down the downstream side and lays a patch of 100 to 200 eggs, under water, on the side of the stone. The eggs are thus firmly attached to a solid substrate and protected from currents and moving sand for about a month during the incubation period. This method provides great protection to the eggs, compared with surface broadcast of eggs—common with *Ephemerella*, for example (the Hendrickson)—which may be subject to higher losses during the initial journey downstream.

Imitations of winged *Baetis* have received many common names, actually about 20. Most common are Bluewinged Olive and Blue Dun, used with modifiers such as Dark, Little, Minute, and Evening, all for the subimago. Rusty appears commonly in names for the adult. Not to confuse matters, however, many species in genera other than *Baetis* have received the same common names!

For some fun, try this:

Prepare yourself with an insect sweep net (butterfly net) and a quart mason jar. Fill the jar about one-third full with fresh, cool stream water and a stone placed inside with its top above the water. During a good "hatch" of *Baetis* (probably *B. tricaudatus*), notice the spinners flying and darting about over the water. (A trout rise may be going on at the same time.) A good time of day for *B. tricaudatus* is late afternoon or early evening, when spinners arrive. Low-slanting sunlight will make it easier to see their small flying forms. You will probably be able to see one or two alight on a stone partially protruding above the water, and if you're close enough, you may even see the female crawl down the side.

Now catch a flying female with your net, maneuver her carefully into the jar, and clamp on the cover. Quickly, the female mayfly will alight on the stone and attempt to crawl down the side. She will struggle a bit to get through the surface film, and as she succeeds, her wings, normally cocked upright, seem to snap downward and backward to cover the abdomen, enclosing a bubble of air, or *plastron*. The spinner's wings, unlike the dun's, are wettable upon contact with water, allowing them to collapse.

Underwater now, the mayfly looks more like a caddisfly adult with her wings laid back. The plastron appears silvery. Watch the insect under water through the side of the mason jar. She will probably search around on the side of the stone, as if she is looking for just the right spot (like a dog searching for a spot to lie down). When she is satisfied, she will begin to lay her eggs. She will move the tip of her abdomen back and forth, laying a row of tiny eggs with each sweep. As she moves forward, the curved rows of eggs, roughly parallel, will form a patch that ends up rather pear-shaped. During this time, the plastron provides her with oxygen. When done, she stops and remains motionless, her final act of life history completed.

The bubble of air, however, will keep the insect alive for a long time, for as she uses oxygen from the bubble, more oxygen diffuses into it from the water. Many other terrestrial or flying aquatic insects use the plastron to obtain oxygen under water. After the emergence is over, you can probably pick up stones from the stream riffle and note freshly laid egg patches, some with the female mayfly still attached.

The next morning, take another look, and you can probably find a female mayfly on a stone, still alive, with the tip of her abdomen attached to the tip of the egg patch, the plastron still surrounding her and providing oxygen. Try lifting the stone out of the water, let the spent spinner dry for a moment, then give her a good strong blow, and watch her fly away!

◆　　　　　◆　　　　　◆

THE TWO FAMILIES, EPHEMERELLIDAE and Heptageniidae, make up the most visible and commonly encountered mayfly species in North American trout streams. We'll take up these two families together. Because both can commonly be seen in stream bottom samples, they can be easily confused; they share some interesting attributes. Most anglers' dry flies are intended to imitate members of these two families, and most of the common names used by anglers for the winged forms of these two groups are used interchangeably. Although both families occur widely in distribution across North America, species vary among New England, the central Midwest, and the western mountains. Ephemerellidae contains 85 species, Heptageniidae over 100. Their robust bodies and a swimming performance that is ungainly and undulating make them distinct among all mayfly nymphs.

Many heptageniids are clingers (for example, *Rhithrogena*), with greatly flattened bodies. Other heptageniids are sprawlers (for example, *Stenonema*). If deprived of a roughened surface upon which to cling (for example, in a mason jar with water), they attempt to swim, but awkwardly. Pull up a stone from a riffle and look closely at both the top and the underside. If a heptageniid nymph is present on either side, it will move quickly with an easily recognized "scurry," and in most cases it will scurry right off the edge of the stone and back into the water.

Ephemerellidae is best exemplified by *Ephemerella* and *Drunella*, which have very widespread distributions. Most species in this family are sprawlers and inhabit organic detritus patches on the streambed.

In their classic *Mayflies of Michigan Trout Streams*, published in 1962, Justin and Fannie Leonard regarded *Ephemerella* as the only genus of Ephemerellidae in Michigan. Since then, however, many taxonomic changes have been made, and their species descriptions have been placed in other genera. These authors wrote passionately about *Ephemerella* and declared their high regard for this genus as the *par excellence* of trout stream mayflies. Let's just look at a few for discussion.

Some variation exists within the Ephemerellidae, but not much. Most nymphs are poor swimmers. Most are univoltine and collector-gatherers, their main functional group, but some species have been noted feeding on plant filament tips and engulfing small midge larvae.

Most *Ephemerella* species emerge and lay their eggs in spring, and the eggs incubate during most of the summer. Typically hatching in the fall, the nymphs grow through the winter months to mature in the spring, to oviposit and carry on the population.

The adults of the species group, *Ephemerella subvaria*, *E. invaria*, and *E. rotunda*, provide some of the most spectacular early spring "hatches" and trout rises among all mayflies. Some of the very first flurries of spring emergences are anxiously awaited. All three species have received the common name Hendrickson, one of the most popular dry fly names in the history of fly-fishing. Another related species is *E. dorothea*, whose emergence brings a bright splash of color to trout streams—yellow, accurately described in its common name of Sulphur, but also termed Pale Evening Dun and other fly-fishers' names. It shows up brilliantly in the dusk of an evening hatch.

Common names for winged stages of *Ephemerella* are many and varied. Many species of *Ephemerella* are the "olives," Blue-winged Olive, Graywinged, Ironwinged, Leadwinged, Slate-winged, and others (all presumably "gray," as most subimago wings are). Other common names for *E. subvaria* are Beaverkill and Lady Beaverkill (the latter, of course, for the female adult carrying a bright cluster of eggs at the tip of her abdomen).

The species *Drunella coloradensis* is a major component of the benthos in western mountains and present in many streams. Another western species with greatly different morphology is *D. doddsi*. This species is unusually robust in form and sports a "friction pad" on its ventral surface formed by its large overlapping gills, which enable the nymph to withstand extreme current velocities in swift streams. Interestingly, *D. doddsi* is one of the rare predaceous species in the order Ephemeroptera.

Nymphs in the family Heptageniidae are all clingers and sprawlers, strongly flattened. Some stick tightly to the tops of riffle stones and cobbles; some are more loosely active within the streambed, where they occupy the thinnest of cracks and crevices in a riffle. More than 100 species compose the family. All are univoltine. Many are scrapers, grazing stony surfaces; others are detritus feeders under stones.

If you are the type who occasionally turns over a few stones from a swift riffle and now and then see a flattened insect with three tails either holding tightly or scurrying rapidly across the stone's surface, in all probability it will be one of the family Heptageniidae. In the West, look for *Epeorus* and *Cinygmula*, short-bodied and very flattened. You'll find *Epeorus* (with some 20 species) on the tops of stones and *Cinygmula* (11 species) underneath. Emergence of *Epeorus* is largely through the summer; *Cinygmula* emerges only during spring months.

In the east can be found the genus *Stenonema* (17 species), flattened clingers that lie hidden under stones. *Stenonema* is the most common heptageniid in New England, the Southeast, and the central Midwest; very few are found in the West. Emergence is fairly long, through the summer, with mating swarms at dusk, lasting into darkness.

Most of two other common heptageniid genera are widespread across the continent, *Rhithrogena* (21 species) and *Heptagenia* (13 species). Like other heptageniids, these two are greatly flattened. The scurrying nymph you see under a stone from a swift riffle is most likely to be a member of *Heptagenia* or closely related genus. Their main emergence is in early summer, June and July.

Rhithrogena nymphs are found on tops of riffle stones, but if you try to pick one up, the nymph scurries away (like *Heptagenia*), but rather than dropping off it may whirl around to the bottom of the stone you hold in your hand, to hide from you. If it wants to stay, it can hold so tightly to the stone that you will have difficulty dislodging it.

Life histories vary among the family Heptageniidae, but most eggs hatch in late summer or fall, even in winter, and subimagoes and adults emerge in spring to summer. *Rhithrogena* nymphs have somewhat of a friction disk formed by their large gills, which together make a cup beneath its abdomen (but not as distinct as in *Drunella doddsi*). Nymphs can be distinguished from other genera by the presence of this disk, at least after you've had experience with several genera.

Fly-fishers' common names for the above two families vary greatly and, it seems, without much relevance. For example, many *Stenonema* species have been models for variants of the Cahill. Similarly, a number of *Heptagenia* and *Epeorus* species have contributed to the Sulphur. In the East, *Stenonema vicarium* inspired the famous March Brown as well as the Ginger Quill. In the West, however, other heptageniid species have been responsible for the March Brown and the Ginger Quill. Also in the West, the Pink Lady still practices her deadly mime of *Epeorus albertae*. In any case, we can exult in this rich variety of common names, sometimes even within a single species!

The flattened form of *Heptagenia* enables this mayfly nymph to maintain its position on the surface of stones in swift riffles.
(Photo by Dean C. Hansen, *WetBugs Press*, Stillwater, Minnesota.)

Together, species of *Rhithrogena* and *Heptagenia* make a great contribution to the color and diversity of mayflies. While not congregating in large mating swarms, their fluttering forms can be often seen just at dusk on most swiftwater streams and rivers.

◆   ◆   ◆

THE FAMILY LEPTOPHLEBIIDAE contains a number of genera and many species, distributed across the continent with different species locally. The largest genus, *Paraleptophlebia*, contains 35 species. Widespread as a genus, species are more locally distributed.

Small mating swarms occur mainly over the water in spring and early summer. The nymphs are slightly flattened, awkward swimmers, and could be confused with some *Ephemerella*. They often locate in detritus deposits on the streambed, although some are typically in riffles. The subimagoes and adults are variously known as Blue Dun and Blue Quill, with modifiers such as Iron and Dark; Brown Dun and Quill are also used for some species of *Paraleptophlebia*.

◆   ◆   ◆

THREE FURTHER MAYFLY FAMILIES are small but very important to us, one spectacularly so. The Ephemeridae includes the famous *Hexagenia*—or infamous, depending upon your perspective. On a late evening in the latter part of June or early July, the flight of *Hexagenia* adults can resemble a blizzard. The ovipositing adults are huge, their color beautiful, and the intensity of the trout rise incredible. Throughout the order Ephemeroptera, the "Hex hatch" is the most awesome and breathtaking.

The family Ephemeridae includes only three genera: *Ephemera, Hexagenia,* and *Pentagenia*. Most of all three genera occur in the central Midwest and eastward, with little dispersal into western regions of North America. All three share many life history characteristics. For example, all are burrowers as nymphs, digging out **U**-shaped tunnels that allow entrance of water carrying oxygen and FPOM food. Stout *mandibular tusks* project forward of the head, enabling the nymph to dig its burrow. Large gills are present in all three genera, assisting nymphs in absorbing oxygen in their burrows. All are large, both as nymph and as winged adults.

Ephemera nymphs inhabit lakes and slower sections of streams, in both cases in soft sediment or light stream riffles. Seven species in the genus are eastern in distribution, with only one species widespread across the continent. The genus as a whole, however, is most abundant on the other side of the world, especially in Asia, with one species in Africa.

On the other end of the distribution scale is *Pentagenia*, a form found only in large rivers in the central Midwest. In appearance and habit, *Pentagenia* is very similar to the other two genera and has been collected in latitudes throughout the Mississippi's course and in other large streams, north and south.

A Hexagenia mayfly hatch often reaches spectacular abundances,
exciting both trout and trout anglers.
(Photo by Calvin R. Fremling, Winona State University, Minnesota.)

The genus *Hexagenia* attracts the greatest attention from scientists, anglers, and the general public. *Hexagenia* inhabits streams and rivers, small and large, and inland lakes, including the Great Lakes, and large impoundments. Its geographical distribution is chiefly the central Midwest and regions to the east. The length of its life cycle is commonly one year, although that is dependent upon latitude and temperature. *Hexagenia* populations may thus be considered potentially semivoltine in some areas, but flexible in others.

Hexagenia members are divided mainly into five species in North America, but additional species occur in other parts of the world. Two species concern us most: *H. bilineata* and *H. limbata*.

Both occur in suitable locations in the Great Lakes but differ between their respective stream habitats.

Hexagenia bilineata is the major species inhabiting large rivers. Anyone who has traveled much around the shores of the Mississippi River in summer on a late evening will be familiar with the mass emergence of *H. bilineata*. A heavy emergence can coat a car windshield with a gelatinous icing that resists all manner of windshield wipers, ice scrapers, and vigorous washings with detergents.

The mass emergences of *H. bilineata* on the Mississippi River have taken on a legendary character akin to nature's wrath, but they are nevertheless human-induced. The history of this species in the Mississippi has been studied intensively by Dr. Calvin R. Fremling of Winona State University (Minnesota), located on the river about 120 miles downstream from the Twin Cities of St. Paul/Minneapolis. Fremling attributes the huge emergences and their fluctuations to a succession of navigation developments on the Upper Mississippi from St. Paul, Minnesota, to St. Louis, Missouri, and to pollution from the Twin Cities.

Certainly, mayflies were present in the river in presettlement years, but when the U.S. Army Corps of Engineers built the present navigation system of locks and dams in this upper reach in the 1930s, huge areas of sediment accumulated behind the dams in the "navigation pools." The impoundments thus produced a huge increase in *Hexagenia* habitat. Mass emergences in the river towns of Minnesota, Wisconsin, Iowa, Illinois, and Missouri blanketed streets and bridges to the point of requiring snowplows for removal. The adults, attracted to lights, swarmed upon business establishments in these riverside towns.

Pollution from the Twin Cities effectively prevented large populations for many miles downstream. Much of the polluted sediment from the Twin Cities settled out in Lake Pepin, a large natural reservoir on the Mississippi. Thus, maximum populations of *H. bilineata* occurred only downstream from Lake Pepin, mainly from Lake Pepin to St. Louis, where pollution from St. Louis prevented mayfly existence farther downstream.

The other major species, *Hexagenia limbata*, occurs farther north and in small streams and lakes. To fly anglers *H. limbata* is the more important species. Nymphs are similar to those of *H. bilineata*: large in size, with prominent gills, and their characteristic burrowing habit. In small-to-medium trout streams, populations of *H. limbata* are not abundant in the swift, stony riffles that anglers love so well. Instead, they are found where stream currents are slow and the bottom is silty. Nymphs and adults of *H. limbata* tend to be lighter and more yellowish in color than *H. bilineata*, so a major emergence gives the impression of a "yellow blizzard."

This blizzard of a "Hex hatch" in late evening and into darkness is actually the mating swarm composed of both male and female adults, or spinners. Males create the swarm first; females enter the swarm for copulation and fertilization of their eggs and then drop to the water, releasing clusters of several thousand eggs from each female. The eggs disperse rapidly in the water and sink, lodging in the stream bottom. In southern regions of the Midwest, univoltinism is the rule, but the length of life cycle depends upon temperature. In more northern areas of the United States and in Canada, populations tend to be semivoltine. Incubation is rather short, only about two weeks, and the early instars' growth period leads through fall, winter, and the first half of the next year.

To the angler seeking *Hexagenia limbata* in a trout stream, common names tend to emphasize the large proportions of this mayfly, Giant, Grand, Great, and others. One puzzling appellation for *Hexagenia* years ago was the Michigan Caddis, a misnomer that persists in some quarters today. However, the term *Hex hatch* probably serves most of us quite well. The phrase, excitedly uttered over the telephone or posted on the walls of fly shops, is a clarion call to action.

◆   ◆   ◆

ANOTHER GROUP OF MAYFLIES that provides great excitement among fly-fishers is *Tricorythodes*, a genus in the family Leptohyphidae (formerly Tricorythidae). *Tricorythodes* includes 13 species that are distributed across the continent. Although important in many summercool trout streams, *Tricorythodes* is also common in streams we may classify as warmwater streams. Their habitat on the stream bottom is in small-particle substrates, such as sand, fine gravel, and plant debris. As scrapers, they are herbivorous, feeding on diatoms and other algae.

Perhaps the outstanding characteristic of *Tricorythodes* is their tiny size, with mature nymphs as small as one-eighth inch, and artificials in hook sizes 20 to 24, or even 26. Understandably, we tend to abbreviate this genus to "Trico" when on the water or in fly shops.

Tricorythodes occurs in bivoltine or trivoltine populations. Furthermore, emergences, oviposition, and egg hatching are not synchronous, so growth and emergence are spread out over long periods. The combination of multivoltinism and asynchronous emergence, like those of *Baetis*, is very fortunate for trout anglers because the emergence interval—midsummer to fall—provides a long period with superior fly-fishing opportunity. Occasional mass emergences create funnels of "smoke" over the water, but these large numbers cannot be sustained for long. With emergence and oviposition in the later part of the summer, eggs overwinter but do not hatch into first instars until spring. Growth during the spring and early summer provides mature mayflies again in late summer and autumn.

Another unique aspect of *Tricorythodes* is their propensity to emerge and oviposit in the early hours of the day. The exact times vary among streams and populations, but it is often before sunrise, or even in the semidarkness of first daylight. The dedicated Trico angler must arise early to meet this hatch.

On the other hand, meeting the sunrise on a cool morning can be a lovely way to start off an otherwise hot summer day!

◆   ◆   ◆

ANOTHER SMALL FAMILY IMPORTANT TO FLY FISHERS is the Polymitarcyidae, with its genus *Ephoron*. The genus is widespread across North America and worldwide in the northern hemisphere. Two species inhabit North America, *E. leukon* (eastern) and *E. album* (western); both species appear in the Midwest but may vary north to south. The Polymitarcyidae are burrowers, and they are similar in appearance and size to some of the Ephemeridae. There are some interesting differences.

These mayflies, rather than being typical trout stream insects, inhabit waters that in summer are warmer than summercool trout streams. However, this habitat does not mean that the insect is irrelevant to the trout angler.

On many trout streams, the summercool character changes slowly downstream into reaches where trout may not reproduce or occur in early year classes. But big brown trout may lurk in these transition zones. Such large trout can feed upon the abundant warmwater fishes that also inhabit these waters, and upon *Ephoron* adults when they emerge. Incidentally, emergence takes place after dark, which presents a special challenge to fly-fishers. The adult flights are very short, so fish rises may not last long, about an hour. Rare among mayflies, the female *Ephoron* does not reach the spinner stage at all—the female dun mates with male spinners and lays eggs as a subimago. Unlike *Hexagenia*, emergence and egg oviposition occur in late summer, but the eggs must pass through a cold period near freezing in winter and only hatch the following spring when water warms up early. These are conditions common in warmwater streams.

The flying subimagoes are milky white in color, lighter than any other mayfly, which may help while casting in the dark. So the most common name for these unusual insects is—of course—the White Fly.

◆   ◆   ◆

FINALLY, WE DISCUSS TWO OTHER MAYFLIES that although of little interest to anglers, still have such unusual life histories and behavior that we really should know about them.

One is a predator, a member of the family Siphlonuridae that feeds primarily on other mayflies. In some southern Adirondack Mountain streams, *Siphlonisca aerodromia*, the one species in its genus, emerges in the spring to lay its eggs in the stream channel.

Covered with fibers, the eggs are anchored to the streambed. Thus fixed in place, they incubate through a long summer and fall, and well into the winter. Small nymphs usually appear in January.

In March and April, banks overflow and floodwater inundates the surrounding floodplains, stimulating the nymphs to leave the stream and disperse into warm, sunlit floodplain waters. Here in these shallow, marshy habitats, many insects and other invertebrates grow by feeding on the abundant decaying detritus. But *S. aerodromia* nymphs, predaceous and hungry, now feed voraciously on these other invertebrates and grow rapidly. Interestingly, their principal prey consists of other members of the same family, Siphlonuridae, especially several species of the genus *Siphlonurus*. When floodplain waters begin to recede in late spring, *Siphlonisca aerodromia* matures, emerges, and lays its eggs back in the channel, to continue the next life cycle.

After it was first discovered and described in 1908, *Siphlonisca aerodromia* was left unstudied for many years. Its unusual life history was not understood, and entomologists were unable to find it; the species seemed to be extinct. However, in the late 1970s, Dr. Elizabeth Gibbs of the University of Maine found *Siphlonisca aerodromia* in the flooded waters of Tomah Stream, Maine, and unraveled the oddly different life history. Its specific habitat requirements undoubtedly restrict its distribution, as well as knowledge about its occurrence and ecology elsewhere.

Our last, most unusual mayfly belongs to the family Baetiscidae, with a single genus, *Baetisca*, comprising 12 species. It occurs almost entirely in eastern and north-central regions of North America. (*Baetisca* shares no special relationship to *Baetis* or the family Baetidae.) Members of this genus sprawl on the streambed, often on shifting sand where they feed on diatoms and detritus. The genus is univoltine, with emergence and oviposition over an extended period in spring; eggs incubate through much of summer and hatch in fall; nymphs grow during winter and early spring, to emerge again in spring.

Nothing about the life history of *Baetisca* is unusual. What makes these mayflies different is a wide, hard *carapace*, or shield, that covers most of the upper surface. Combined with forward projecting knobs and spines along the sides of its abdomen, the nymph appears ferocious, totally unlike other immature Ephemeroptera. Nymphs rest on the stream bottom in slow water, on sand or fine gravel, as if in ambush, although they are not at all predaceous. Adults differ from other mayflies, too. With very robust, high-arched bodies and broad abdomens tapering sharply to their short tails, they lack the fairy-like form of most other mayflies.

The emergence of *Baetisca* does not include swarming; only a few appear at a time over long periods. Anglers have paid little attention to imitating the flying subimago or adult for fishing, probably because emergence takes place away from the stream. Only the immature aquatic form has acquired a common name, Humpbacked Nymph, no doubt a reflection of its extremely robust body and broad carapace.

This nymph remains one of the great oddities of the insect world. It can easily be mistaken for a spiny beetle. *Baetisca* seems a freak—an ancient, lumbering hulk of a monster of mythology—downsized, of course, to about a half-inch long.

◆   ◆   ◆

A LONG AND COLORFUL LIST OF COMMON NAMES characterizes the mayflies. Among aquatic insect orders, only the Odonata (dragonflies and damselflies) have more common names than the Ephemeroptera, but these, unlike those for mayflies, do not typically refer to fishing imitations. Most mayfly common names have been created by the group of artisans who tie the artificials. In Patrick McCafferty's book on aquatic entomology, he characterizes this list as a "vast and unruly array," fanciful but descriptive common names for mayfly imitations.

Only a few decades ago many names were simply whimsical sobriquets that evoked visions of loveliness or grandeur: Pink Lady, Grizzly King, and, most enduring of all, the Royal Coachman. Namesakes and originators' names were also common: Adams, Cahill, Gordon, and Hendrickson (more recently, Wulff and Whitlock). Today, most common names have at least some connection to the color, size, or scientific name: Green Drake and Sulphur, Great Quill and Little Dun, Hex and Trico. Some flies suggest the time of day for the emergence: Pale Morning Dun and Pale Evening Spinner. As you should recognize, the winged stage appears frequently: Dun and Spinner for subimago and adult. The name Quill appears often, referring to an older material, porcupine quills, used for the mayfly's body.

Unruly array, indeed.

TECHNICAL REFERENCES:

Edmunds, George F., Jr., Steven L. Jensen, and Lewis Berner. 1976. *The Mayflies of North and Central America.* University of Minnesota Press, Minneapolis.
McCafferty, W. Patrick. 1983. *Aquatic Entomology: The fishermen's and ecologists' illustrated guide to insects and their relatives.* Jones and Bartlett Publishers, Boston.
Leonard, Justin W., and Fannie A. Leonard. 1962. *Mayflies of Michigan Trout Streams.* Cranbrook Institute of Science, Bloomfield Hills, Michigan.

RiverSketch

OLD MAN RIVER

NAMES OF THE MISSISSIPPI RIVER'S EARLIEST EXPLORERS ring through the history of North America like a mighty bell: De Soto, Jolliet and Father Marquette, Du Lhut, La Salle.

Spanish conquistador Hernando de Soto landed his ships on the Florida Peninsula in 1541 and, in search of treasure, drove west overland to the Mississippi, the first European to view the mighty river. More than a hundred years were to pass before

French explorers and fur traders entered North America, now by way of the St. Lawrence River and the Great Lakes, to leave their mark on the Mississippi.

An infant Mississippi River exits its source, Lake Itasca in northern Minnesota, through rocky riffles.

In 1673, Louis Jolliet and his Jesuit partner, Father Jules Marquette, made their way by paddle and portage from Lake Michigan to the Mississippi, by way of the Fox and Wisconsin rivers. They floated far downstream on the Mississippi, but not to the Gulf. To the north, fur trader Sieur du Lhut ventured westward in 1679 from the St. Louis River, headwater stream of Lake Superior and the Great Lakes. He also paddled and portaged to the Mississippi, opening up the river's upper valley, a vast, rich land teeming with beaver and other furbearers.

Three years later, Sieur de la Salle arrived at the Mississippi via the Great Lakes, and descended all the way to the Gulf of Mexico. There on a sandy strand in 1682, pennants flying in the ocean breeze, La Salle claimed for France the entire drainage of the Mississippi River—from the Rockies to the Alleghenies, Canada to the Gulf, source to mouth, it turned out. And then, in honor of his royal sovereign, Louis the Fourteenth, La Salle named this huge land *Louisiana.*

◆   ◆   ◆

THE MISSISSIPPI RIVER OF TODAY is not the same stream as in the days of De Soto and Du Lhut. Compared to its condition in pre-history, the Mississippi now is tamed and harnessed: straightened and narrowed, confined and diverted, dammed and dredged and polluted.

The Upper Mississippi lies under the navigation system of locks and dams, inundating shoals and creating wide reservoirs.
(Photo courtesy of the University of Minnesota Press.)

The United States Army Corps of Engineers divides the river, of about 2,300 miles, into three major segments: Headwaters, Upper, and Lower. The Headwaters reach extends from the river's source in Lake Itasca, Minnesota, to the Twin Cities of Minneapolis and St. Paul, a reach 500 miles long, dropping nearly 800 feet in elevation, from a northern wilderness to a spreading urban center. This segment, only about one-fifth of the

Mississippi's total length, includes a full half of the river's total drop in elevation.

The Upper Mississippi, 700 miles from St. Paul to St. Louis, drops another 400 feet in elevation. This middle segment has been the reach most modified by the engineers. With shallow rapids and shifting sandbars, the Upper Mississippi in the mid-1800s demanded extraordinary skills from Sam Clemens and other steamboat pilots. Today the rapids and shoals lie under 29 locks, dams, and reservoirs that facilitate navigation, the nine-foot channel, constructed mainly in the 1930s.

The Lower Mississippi, with no swiftwater shoals, requires no further locks and dams. Towboats and barges run freely between St. Louis and the Gulf of Mexico. This segment in its last 1,100 miles to the Gulf drops a final 400 feet. The engineers' main work in this lower segment consists of constructing levees, maintaining floodways, and straightening by cutting off bends.

◆   ◆   ◆

PRIOR TO THE RIVER-REGULATING ACTIVITIES of the Corps of Engineers, the Mississippi River no doubt hosted a huge, diverse benthos, unknown in its precise distribution. But the engineers changed all that. First was the construction of thousands of wing dikes, made of large fragments of rock, extending out from both banks. These were intended to narrow the main river current and keep it in place, facilitating navigation. Following the wing dikes came the nine-foot channel with locks and dams. Now the tailwaters below dams were covered with rock and the wing dikes covered with water. The resulting rocky substrate and swift currents—provided ideal habitat for caddisflies of the family Hydropsychidae. These caddis larvae build capture nets of silk to strain organic food, richly provided by the river's currents. Larval populations increased tremendously with the navigation system in place, reaching nuisance levels so great that winged adults covered surfaces of homes and businesses, caused allergic reactions in riverside residents, and obstructed river navigation.

At the same time that caddisflies were taking advantage of the swiftwater habitat in dikes and tailwaters, silt was settling out on the bottoms of the reservoirs upstream from the dams. The bottom accumulation of sediment and mud, as it turned out, created ideal habitat for burrowing mayflies, mainly *Hexagenia bilineata*.

Mass emergences of *Hexagenia bilineata* covered bridges over the Mississippi River and created traffic hazards. (Courtesy Calvin R. Fremling, Winona State University, Minnesota, and the University of Minnesota Press.)

Populations reached explosive proportions, all along the Upper Mississippi, creating nuisance problems that far exceeded the afflictions by the caddisflies. Accumulations of adult *Hexagenia* became so thick on river bridges that slippery surfaces created traffic hazards, and snowplows were called out to remove the offending piles of mayfly bodies and to sand the streets. Because both the caddisfly and mayfly adults are attracted to light, street lamps and lighted business windows further attracted the swarms. However, little mention is made in the scientific literature of a possible addition to fish-food resources.

◆   ◆   ◆

THE HUGE DRAINAGE BASIN OF THE MISSISSIPPI comprises an enormous variety of fish habitats—ranging from small, first-order creeks to the mighty stream where it flows past New Orleans and disperses through a host of distributaries in the Delta. We would expect a corresponding large assemblage of fishes, and such is indeed the case. In the mainstem river itself are found some 200 species; if we include all the tributaries throughout the watershed, about 260 species (compared with the total freshwater fishes found in North America, 600).

As in most streams, the number of fish species increases downstream in the Mississippi. In the Headwaters reach to Minneapolis and St. Anthony Falls, we find about 65 species. Below the falls (now a lock and dam), the number of species increases sharply, because many species had been blocked from further dispersal upstream by the falls. Throughout the Upper Mississippi reach (downstream to St. Louis), are about 130 species. In the Lower segment (St. Louis to the Gulf), a few more are added, for 150 species. Many of these are present throughout the river.

In the Headwaters segment, most notable for sport fishing, is the smallmouth bass, some of the best. Other game fishes include the rock bass and northern pike. Because this segment includes some large natural lakes as well as reservoirs, lake-living species such as walleye, largemouth bass, bluegill, and yellow perch are present. Several trout species can be found in a few cool tributaries. A dozen minnows are present in the river (more in tributaries), including the introduced carp, particularly common in the lower part. Several suckers, especially the white sucker and shorthead redhorse, often make up the greatest portion of fish biomass.

In assessing the fishery resource of the Upper Mississippi, we need to remember that the river is greatly changed from its condition prior to construction of the nine-foot channel, with its many dams and reservoirs. Consequently, the aquatic habitat has changed from a broad, braided, winding river to a narrower navigation channel, with many backwater lakes and interconnecting channels. The fish fauna now includes more typical lake-living species. The sunfishes, for example, have greatly increased, such as the largemouth bass, crappies, and small panfishes like the blue-gill, orangespotted sunfish, and pumpkinseed. The northern pike is also common as a large predator. Several species of the sucker family make up a big proportion of the fish biomass: white sucker, shorthead redhorse, the two buffalofish, and the quillback with its long, "quill-like" extensions of the first ray of its dorsal fin. The channel catfish is common, and, as in the past, it makes up a good portion of the anglers' catch; the flathead catfish, a larger and more southern species, is also common. The intro-duced common carp has reached high levels of population in this segment.

The Lower Mississippi has also been changed over the past century. More sinuous than the Upper Mississippi, it is much confined by the flood-control levee system. Significant differences exist between this and upstream segments. The sucker family is now largely represented by the river carpsucker, quillback, and buffalofish, and gone are the white sucker and redhorses. The large blue catfish is now in evidence, although the channel and flathead catfishes are still common. A relict fish from the dinosaur time, hundreds of millions of years ago, is the paddlefish, a spe-cies now listed as endangered. Abundant are the freshwater drum, white bass, several of the sunfish family, particularly the bluegill and largemouth bass, and of course the common carp. In the lower part of the segment, a number of marine species ascend from the ocean, especially below New Orleans in the Delta dis-tributaries.

Notable among the fish fauna of the Mississippi River are a few species that, despite significant differences in habitat, are common throughout the entire river. These include the emerald shiner and gizzard shad (which together provide a huge resource of forage for larger, predaceous species); for channel catfish (pro-viding sport and food for a host of anglers); for the bluegill and largemouth bass (mostly found in stillwaters everywhere); and the common carp. These ubiquitous species testify to the fact that some can prosper in a variety of environments, a circumstance that attests to the fascinating adaptability of our fish fauna.

◆   ◆   ◆

UNFORTUNATELY, THE MISSISSIPPI has served as the nation's sewer ditch for at least a couple of centuries. The river's condition worsened over a long period, reaching its nadir in the 1960s. Cities all along the river poured in sewage and industrial effluents; farmland chemicals, eroded sediment, and animal wastes have added to the witch's brew. Water below all major cities was unhealthy for body contact, and fish were too contaminated for consumption. The huge mayfly populations in the upper river declined almost to extirpation.

Conditions improved with the coming of an environmental conscience in the 1970s, and new federal laws, like the Clean Water Act, were implemented. Fish consumption became safer in Lake Pepin, and *Hexagenia* came back to the Upper Mississippi.

Throughout the Lower Mississippi, however, the job is far from done. Sewage disposal into the river has lessened but is still high; many fish advisories continue. Sediment, fertilizers, pesticides, and farm animal wastes continue to pour into the Mississippi, much of them from old deposits in small tributaries. High levels of toxic substances persist in riverbed sediments. The great volume of this deadly mix continues to empty into the Gulf of Mexico at the river's mouth, where it has created a "Dead Zone" of 8,000 square miles of ocean in which fish and invertebrate life hardly exists at all. The major problem is high fertilizer use on cultivated fields. Excess nitrates pour down the river to promote growth of marine algae that, when dead, uses up oxygen to create *hypoxic* conditions, concentrations of oxygen too low to support aquatic animal life.

Much research, stronger laws, national treasure—and a greater public sensitivity—will be needed to bring back some semblance of the Mississippi's past eminence.

◆   ◆   ◆

The Mississippi's longest tributary, the Missouri River, heads up in the Rocky Mountains to flow some 2,500 miles (now through some of the nation's largest reservoirs) to St. Louis, a distance equal to the total of the named Mississippi. If, through the vagaries of historical naming of rivers, the Mississippi name had followed up to the Rockies instead of to Lake Itasca, the "Mississippi" would have been over a thousand and a half miles longer!

It was Abraham Lincoln who first penned the appellation "Father of Rivers" for the mighty Mississippi. The "old man" must have come a little later.

SELECTED REFERENCES:

Fremling, Calvin R., J.L. Rasmussen, R.E. Sparks, S.P. Cobb, C.F. Bryan, and T.O. Claflin. 1989. Mississippi River fisheries: A case history. Pages 309-351 *in* Douglas P. Dodge, editor. Proceedings of the International Large River Symposium. *Canadian Special Publication of Fisheries and Aquatic Sciences* 106.
Hodding, Carter. 1970. *Man and the River: The Mississippi.* Rand McNally & Company. Chicago.

Chapter 15

CADDISFLIES

FEW ANIMAL ORDERS BOAST such great diversity in life histories as the Trichoptera. In both genera and species, caddisflies outnumber most of the other major aquatic insect orders, including Ephemeroptera and Plecoptera. Only the Diptera exceeds Trichoptera in number of species and abundance on the streambed. One of the major factors in this great diversity is the caddis larva's case, common to almost all species in the order. To the casual observer of the tops and bottoms of riffle stones, caddis larvae and their cases are almost always the most apparent of all insects. Clusters of cases sometimes cover almost entire stone surfaces. The larvae are truly the bread-and-butter of stream fish diets.

Another reason for this great success of caddisflies lies in the diversity of their behavior and habitat, particularly during the larval stage. The physical form of all caddisfly larvae—worm-like—is similar, but it is their dissimilarity in how they make their living that involves such a variety of both habit and niche. In the great variety of physical sites on stream bottoms, with gravel, cobble, sand, and boulders, they occupy and exploit every available kind of resource.

This diversity of life styles is dependent in turn upon varied ecological niches available in their habitat. And it is precisely this enormous heterogeneity of niches on the bed of a stream or river that has made possible this wonderful biodiversity among the caddisflies.

Like mayflies, caddisfly adults look much the same in all families, with wings folded back along the top of the abdomen, sloping tent-like along the sides. They vary mainly in size and color, and anglers' imitations of caddis dry flies differ but little. Unlike mayflies, anglers' names of caddisfly imitations are few; a half-dozen common names for caddis dry flies seem more than enough to describe most of them.

◆   ◆   ◆

ALTHOUGH THE ORDER TRICHOPTERA is not among the largest insect orders, it is nevertheless one of the most important aquatic groups we find in streams, with about 1,400 species in North America. All caddis families are represented in summercool, lotic waters, coldwater streams, but some have adapted to warmwater streams and lentic waters as well, even to seasonally temporary pools and streams that dry up in summer.

The typical life cycle throughout the order includes the egg, five larval instars in cases, a pupal stage also in a case, and one winged adult stage. The adults differ greatly from the larvae, so all species of the order are holometabolous.

Most Trichoptera are univoltine; a few are multivoltine and semivoltine. Voltinism is sometimes variable within a single species, and there is a tendency to multivoltinism in warmer waters. Univoltinism is the norm for headwater reaches with cooler water, with multivoltinism downstream.

Caddisflies are less synchronized than most mayflies with respect to times of egg hatching and emergence. Furthermore, the adult stage is long-living compared with the short life of adult mayflies. Consequently, adults of one species or another are present in the stream for almost all of spring and summer, to the greater benefit of rising trout and fly fishers!

In flight, the caddis adult resembles a moth, and both groups release a scatter of particles from their wing coverings when disturbed—caddisflies with hairs and moths with scales. (Take a close look sometime with a magnifying glass.) Both caddisflies and moths are attracted to lights around streamside cabins or lake cottages at night, but a close look for the tent-like slope of the caddis wings will usually distinguish between caddis and moth.

◆   ◆   ◆

ALTHOUGH ALL CADDIS LARVAE are wormlike, their life strategies of habitat selection, food acquisition, and mobility differ greatly. For example, most larvae can be classified as omnivores with a wide range of feeding strategies, some as shredders on leaves and other CPOM, some as scrapers of epilithon on stony surfaces, others as gatherers of detritus on the stream bottom. Still others are filterers of FPOM in water currents. Another family of free–ranging predators roams the streambed in search of prey.

The most important factor contributing to the order's great diversity is *silk*. Manufactured in the animal's body, this proteinaceous matter is secreted from organs in the mouthparts and used for many purposes. These uses include building meshed traps, *capture nets*, that filter FPOM from the water, lining burrows in which the larvae capture FPOM passing though the burrow, laying threads in streambed crevices to entangle small living prey, and making other constructions.

To the angler, researcher, or stream bottom observer, the most obvious use of silk is the larval case. Silk is the glue with which larvae build their cases. In a truly amazing variety, from vegetation or wood fragments to sand grains and small stones, or complex silken tubes and sacs, the variability in case types seems almost endless. Not all cases are obvious to the casual observer, however, for some are so tiny that they are nearly invisible, even to the trained investigator. The larva's compulsion to build a case is so strong that if one is removed from its case and returned to a sandy stream bottom, it will immediately begin to build another.

Some hobbyists place larvae into an artificial habitat contain n-ing flecks of rare gem or silver and gold, and the larva will build a very unusual case, indeed! Can you imagine ear rings constructed by a caddis larva with bits of diamonds and gold?

The highly diverse case-making contributes greatly to the Trichoptera's success in filling the many niches on the stream bottom and to its many ways of food gathering. Entomologists categorize caddisfly species into several ecological groups (like clingers and swimmers for mayflies) based on the kind of cases they construct. This classification includes:

• *tube-case makers*—builders of portable cases that are carried about on the stream bottom during their search for food; this is the predominant group in numbers of species;

• *retreat-makers* and *net-spinners*—sedentary modes for sheltering and food gathering, including filtering FPOM from passing currents; includes some of the most visible forms on the surfaces of stones;

• *turtle-shell* case makers—these make portable dome-shaped, oval cases of tiny stones, visible when larvae move slowly about on a stone surface scraping food; the pupae sometimes make large aggregations;

• *purse-case makers*—extremely small larvae (informally called *microcaddis*) that lack cases until the fifth instar, at which point a purse-shaped sac or case is made; within this case, the larva grows greatly in preparation for pupation;

• *free-ranging forms*—mostly predators, the larvae of which do not swim but move about slowly on the streambed, searching for prey.

◆   ◆   ◆

A HOST OF ENVIRONMENTAL FACTORS account for the variation in case making and feeding. Water current is one of the most important: heavy or firmly attached cases, or cases with "rudders" or "ballast stones," are used by some species in maneuvering or holding in swift waters. Current velocity also determines the kinds and sizes of FPOM and thus the kind, location, and mesh size of capture nets. Although the cases and filtering capture nets may be similar within a family or genus, each species is locked in to a type of case and its unique ecological niche.

The kinds of substrate on the streambed—boulders, cobbles, gravel and sand, and vegetation—often determine the location of case-building species that settles there. Whether a stony substrate is sunlit or shaded—that is, whether food found there consists of photosynthesizing diatoms or nonliving organic matter—determines not only the species with its unique case, but also its functional group and feeding guild.

Macrophytes, rooted plants on the stream bottom, constitute another important factor in caddisfly diversity. It's true that only a little feeding by invertebrates occurs on fresh plant material. But some species of caddis larvae use living plants as a substrate for attachment, especially in swift currents. Where plants are abundant, the surface area available for attachment is increased immensely. Because periphyton often accumulates and grows on macrophyte stem and leaf surfaces, additional food resources are available to caddisfly scrapers.

The availability of particular case-building materials helps determine the kind of case and thus the species that can exist in a particular location on the streambed. Silt beds can accommodate burrowers; sandy reaches, materials for fine-grained sand cases; cobble riffles, stone surfaces for retreat-makers and capture nets; vegetation and woody fragments, for shredding case-makers. All provide species-specific building materials.

The distribution of caddisfly species along the river continuum is partly due to the availability of case-making material. Vegetable and woody cases are made by shredders in upper reaches; heavy sand and stone cases for scrapers in sunlit middle reaches. Other materials are used for cases of many filterers in the lower reaches where FPOM is the major source of food. Again, silk is necessary to cement together all kinds of cases, and for some species, it is silk alone that is the case-making material.

Thus, environmental factors that create the mosaic of patches on the streambed—epilithon on stones and periphyton on leafy vegetation and woody CPOM, sunlight and shade, currents that range from stillwater to raging torrents—all influence the fascinating biodiversity in the order Trichoptera.

◆   ◆   ◆

SEDENTARY OR SLOWLY MOVING CADDIS LARVAE are easy to catch. Turn over almost any stone in almost any stream, and you will see a little collection of tiny stones cemented loosely to the larger stone. Soon the retreat-makers emerge from their retreats and begin to crawl all over the stone and your hand. These larvae are usually about a quarter- to a half-inch long. Then look on the stream bottom along a quiet stream bank and you will see the "stick caddis" crawling about on the sandy streambed in their cases of tiny stones or fragments of vegetation and sticks. These larvae are often about an inch long, and sometimes are used as bait for winter ice fishing. With experience, and some help from photographs in other publications and guides, you can soon identify some of the others, too.

The major factor responsible for the caddisflies' diversity is food acquisition. In turn, the many different means of feeding are closely attuned to the various cases, shelters, and food-catching filters we see when we turn over stones or peer closely at a sandy streambed in shallow water.

The feeding habit of filtering FPOM from stream currents is a major means of food acquisition for several families in Trichoptera. Filter-feeding is one of the most important means in the order. Capture nets are constructed in different forms, sometimes as silken sacs, sometimes as loosely woven traps in stream crevices. Most capture nets are attached to exposed stone surfaces. Contributing to the many niches available to caddisflies is the great variation in mesh size—from a half-micron to 500 microns, a thousand-fold difference! (A micron is one-millionth of a meter, or about 1/25, 000 of an inch.)

Filtering by caddisfly larvae has important relationships to downstream spiraling of nutrients and organic matter. Filtering "captures" both components and holds them in place for a while, tightening up spirals. As the larvae ingest and digest FPOM, fecal pellets are released to become part of the FPOM that continues downstream to serve as food for smaller organisms. Some streams originate in lakes where exiting water sometimes contains huge quantities of plankton, providing a large source of FPOM food for filterers.

Limnephilidae larva and "stick" case (top);
adult *Limnephilus* (bottom)

Fish feed on caddis larvae opportunistically. Many larvae drift free without cases, such as those in the families Glossosomatidae and Hydropsychidae, and are captured easily by fish, because of the larvae's poor swimming ability. For those species drifting in cases, fish seem to take the case along with the larva readily, even if the case is constructed of sand and small stones. The insect is digested and the sand and gravel are egested with feces. But many an angler has been puzzled when cleaning a trout to find the gut solidly packed with sand! Some caddis species drift with their cases in great numbers; some drift without cases after molting and while seeking new material to build larger cases.

So, let's look at some of the more common devices and cases typical of several families. Altogether, this hugely diverse order of stream insects exhibits a fascinating mosaic of life strategies.

◆   ◆   ◆

THE FAMILY LIMNEPHILIDAE is the largest in the order Trichoptera, with over 300 species in North America. They occupy a greater variety of habitats than any other family, and are particularly the dominant caddisfly group at higher elevations and in northern regions.

Limnephilids are tube-case makers, with a great variation in sizes of case. Materials used in cases include sand grains, small stones, fragments of vegetation, and small pieces or sticks of wood. The cases are portable, and larvae move slowly about on the streambed or other substrate in search of food. Limnephilidae are mostly shredders, chewing up decomposing leaves and fragments of wood and ingesting the associated microorganisms. Some members of the family are scrapers of periphyton.

Most species in the family are univoltine; some have life cycles of more than a year. Most overwinter as larvae, then pupate and emerge in spring or early summer. *Oviposition* times vary between individuals of the same species over a relatively long adult stage, up to several months, and eggs hatch in fall. This asynchronous life cycle ensures that some flying adults will be on the water through much of the summer period.

Limnephilids include some of the largest larvae with equally large tubular cases. A larva, pulled from its case, appears to offer a succulent mouthful for a hungry fish. Adults are large, too. An imitation of the largest of the adults may be up to a size 10, or even 8, hook size.

Because of their size, the cases of limnephilids can be readily observed in shallow areas. Often they are made of tiny stones combined with leaf and stick fragments. If you see a small stick or twig moving slowly along a sandy bottom, it will probably turn out to be a limnephilid larva and its case.

In some regions, limnephilid larvae are harvested (mostly from lakes) and sold as bait for ice fishing, labeled as "reedamites" (after their leaf-fragment cases) or (incorrectly) as "hellgrammites."

Two interesting genera in the Limnephilidae:

• *Limnephilus* is widespread across North America, but especially in the north and western mountains. The larvae are large and make many different kinds of tube-cases, from sand, gravel, vegetation, and wood. Larvae measure up to about 1 1/2 inches, the case up to two inches. These are the major shredders among caddisflies. They can be found in many kinds of habitat: streams, lakes, ponds, and temporary pools and spring seeps. *Limnephilus* species that occupy summer-dry habitats go into an inactive state, or *diapause*, during the summer that may last until late summer or fall. Because of their large size, *Limnephilus* often makes up a large proportion of the diet of fish.

• *Dicosmoecus*, a small genus of only a few species, is distributed in the mountain streams of North America. The larvae are robust and about 1 1/2 inches long, a good mouthful for stream fishes. Among the few species are both scrapers and shredders.

The family Uenoidae, about 50 species, contains two genera of special interest (formerly in the family Limnephilidae):

• *Neophylax* includes only a few species, but these are widespread across the continent, although restricted to swift streams. The larval case is constructed of sand and gravel and has larger stones along the sides for "ballast" to help the larva maintain its position and mobility in fast water. As scrapers, they feed on periphyton on stones in riffles and rapids.

• *Oligophlebodes* makes up another small genus, which is also restricted to swift streams in western mountains. These are small scrapers, with maximum larval length only about a quarter-inch, with a tiny, sand case. They have the unusual habit of grazing on the tops of stones during the day and retreating to the undersides at night, which probably accounts for their high drift in daytime and almost no drift by night. This is the opposite of most other drifting stream invertebrates. The cream colored adults make a notable upstream flight at dusk.

The large family Hydropsychidae contains only a few genera but about 145 species. They are some of the most common caddisflies and are often present in great abundance. Their widespread distribution and abundance mark this family as one of the most visible and influential among aquatic insects. The provision of food to higher trophic levels, the attraction for scientific study, and the potential nuisance, all combine to make the Hydropsychidae the best known, the most appreciated, and, occasionally, the most annoying of all stream Trichoptera.

Hydropsychid larvae most commonly build their stony retreats on riffle stones, top and bottom, in relatively swift water. Retreats are made of sand grains, small gravel particles, and vegetative debris, cemented loosely together with silk. This construction is the hydropsychid larva's "home," and it stays put. Alongside the retreat's front opening, the larva weaves a miniature net of silk, a capture net, to trap seston from water currents. Periodically the larva emerges from the retreat to glean food particles from its net. The mesh size in capture nets varies among species, and the mesh size increases as larvae grow through their five instars. Among different species, mesh sizes range from about 5 to 500 microns, a difference of a hundred-fold. The large variation in mesh size reflects the equally large diversity of kinds and sizes of food particles captured and consumed. The smallest meshes collect bacteria and algal cells; larger sizes catch small invertebrate animals, as well as detritus.

Hydropsychids are common in almost all streams. At times, they become extremely abundant below dams and lake outlets. Exiting from lakes and other stillwaters come large quantities of phytoplankton and zooplankton that are fed upon by filtering hydropsychids. And sometimes concentrations of caddis cases reach the point of creating a literal "carpet" of living larvae and their cases. Additionally, downstream from these outlets stony riffles and rapids create optimum substrates for the construction of hydropsychid retreats and capture nets. Some studies on the productivity of hydropsychids in stony stream reaches have recorded annual production rates five- to ten-fold higher than production rates upstream from the pond or impoundment. Emergences from these locations, especially in large rivers, often reach nuisance levels.

Most hydropsychids are classed as omnivores, taking whatever food enters their capture nets, whether plant, animal, or nonliving FPOM. Like all Trichoptera, hydropsychids are opportunistic in their feeding, so when large quantities become available, their populations increase in response.

Most Hydropsychidae are univoltine, with overwintering larvae, emergence and oviposition in spring and summer, and egg hatching in fall to produce the next cohort. Life cycle events are asynchronous, and flying adults may be on the stream for much of the summer.

However, some species in this family are flexible in their voltinism, and the development of a bivoltine life history may occur in warmer waters or when food abundance is greater, thus stimulating faster growth. A species may be univoltine in upper, cooler reaches but bivoltine downstream. In large, warmwater rivers, bivoltinism seems to be the rule.

Two genera, *Hydropsyche* and *Cheumatopsyche* together include most of the family's species. Species of these two genera occur all across North America, some restricted to the East, some to swift streams in the western mountains.

Adults of Hydropsychidae are smaller than those of Limnephilidae, most being less than one-half inch long. Nevertheless, when emergence occurs, "hatches" can be enormous in some localities. Mature *Hydropsyche* adults mate in dense swarms, which in some species appear like plumes of smoke; *Cheumatopsyche* does not swarm; instead males search out individual females on the ground where contact is made, apparently through sex attractant chemicals produced by the female.

Nuisance problems caused by these two genera along large rivers, particularly the Upper Mississippi River, has received major scientific attention from Dr. Fremling, along with his studies on *Hexagenia* mayflies in the same localities. Like the nuisance levels of *Hexagenia*, the great abundance of caddisflies is the result of navigation development in the Mississippi. Mayfly populations increased in the silted navigation pools, caddisfly populations exploded in the increased habitat on the stones, cobble-lined wing dikes, and channeled tailwaters below dams. Both the mayfly and caddisfly adults are attracted to lights, so riverside communities and businesses up and down the developed Mississippi River have been dealt a double dose of problem emergences from mankind's modification of these riverine habitats.

The family Brachycentridae is a group of caddisflies that can be easily observed in small streams. The family is relatively small, with 36 species in North America. All brachycentrids are tube-makers.

Rather than crawling about on the streambed, larvae of the genus *Brachycentrus* fasten their cases with silk to some solid substrate. In this sedentary mode, holding their rear two pairs of legs up into the water, they snatch passing particles of seston and other food items from water currents, mainly diatoms as they drift past. All inhabit streams only.

Brachycentrus are often the most visible of the family in their unique larval cases. Some larvae make the familiar "log cabin" cases, four-sided and square in cross-section, slightly tapered, made of plant and wood material cut smoothly and arranged transversely. Cases measure from about a quarter- to a half-inch long. Some move about on stones, scraping up diatoms from periphyton and are thus considered scrapers. Because they prefer diatoms, whether gleaned from the current or grazed from surfaces, they can be found mostly in unshaded stream reaches with enough sunlight for photosynthesis by algae.

In some localities, *Brachycentrus* larvae colonize the stems and leaves of rooted plants that grow in fast currents, often macrophytes like *Potamogeton*. The larvae, with their "log-cabin" or round cases form dense aggregations on the many surfaces provided by the plants. The noted "black caddis" of the Bighorn River, Montana tailwater fishery is an example of the prolific brachycentrid caddisflies.

While on your favorite stream sometime, peer down with a close look at some bottom structure. If you can find a sharp edge of a stone or small branch, you will probably be able to see a number of *Brachycentrus* larvae lined up in a row like birds on a power line, holding out their searching legs, no doubt hoping for a windfall of diatoms!

Brachycentrus in typical feeding mode. The hind two pairs of legs are held upright for seizing food particles in the current. (Photo by Dean C. Hansen of *WetBugs Press*, Stillwater, Minnesota.)

Another caddisfly in the family Brachycentridae common in summercool streams is *Micrasema*, similar to *Brachycentrus* except for its typically tapered, round cases made of plant fragments or sand, either straight or slightly curved. *Micrasema* are in the functional group of shredders, and are often found in and feeding upon moss patches.

A caddisfly family whose members scrape diatoms in sunlit streams is Glossosomatidae (80 species in North America). Their larval case is like a "turtle-shell" or dome made of tiny stones, with case lengths up to about one-half inch. Within this case, larvae move about on the surface of exposed stones, case and all, grazing on periphyton. Most species are univoltine, a few bivoltine.

With a unique life history among the caddisflies, glossosomatids cannot enlarge their cases as larvae grow. Instead, cases are abandoned and new cases built as growth necessitates larger homes for the larvae. The domed case has a hole in either end, so that the larva's head projects from one end and its rear out the other. Both holes are identical, so the larva can turn itself around at will, depending on its feeding requirements. Tiny openings all through the wall of the case allow water currents to penetrate the case, aiding respiration. When ready to pupate, the larva cuts away the ventral surface of the case and cements the edges to a stone surface all round with silk. Within this case, a cigar-shaped cocoon, brown and parchment-like, is constructed. Dense aggregations of pupal cases can be seen nestled tightly together on the tops of stones in shallow riffles. Most cases are empty after the pupae have emerged but can be found still stuck tightly to the stone.

Glossosoma is a good representative genus of this family. Most are restricted to western mountain streams, some in large, swift rivers. But one species, *G. intermedium*, is also very common in eastern and midwestern streams, both in the United States and Canada. It can be readily found and observed in small, sunlit trout streams almost everywhere.

The large family Hydroptilidae, with 220 North American species, comprises the "purse-case" makers, which construct small cases that look like a couple of tiny leaves stuck together with a slit at either end. Such cases are bivalved and appear clam-like, with each side a flattened dome joined at the base. They are frequently called "microcaddis," and they well deserve their diminutive name. Some larvae are only about 1/16 inch in length, maximum. These larvae are free-ranging through their first four instars; in the fifth instar, the larva builds its purse-shaped case, sometimes entirely of silk, sometimes with an exterior coating of fine sand grains. The mobile larvae move around a lot, but almost invisibly. Look for their tiny cases on the tops or sides of stones in almost any stream. The purse-shaped case will be standing on its ventral edge, appearing to be sharp on the dorsal edge. They may be located in some slight depression in the stone. After you get their image clear in your mind, you will probably see them all over.

The larvae of *Hydroptilidae* in their purse-like cases.
Because of their small size, they are known as "microcaddis."
(Photo by Dean C. Hansen of *WetBugs Press*, Stillwater, Minnesota.)

In the fifth instar's case, the larva feeds voraciously, scraping diatoms or piercing the cells of filamentous algae to suck out the cell contents. Feeding is so rapid in this last instar that the larva's abdomen grows to an enormous size (relatively, of course) in order to store food resources for its forthcoming pupation and adult metamorphosis. All hydroptilids are univoltine. Most species are common to lotic waters, particularly small, cold creeks, but some are common in lakes because their feeding mode does not necessarily require running water.

Hydroptila is the most common and widespread genus of caddisflies in North America, although he adult bodies of *Hydroptila* measure only about 1/8 inch long. Like other members of the family, *Hydroptila's* case is a flattened dome constructed of silk and covered on the exterior with fine sand grains, held vertically on the stream bottom. It is a large genus with about 60 species.

Did you ever experience a good trout rise but couldn't see a thing flying or on the surface? (Who hasn't?) Consider a hatch of microcaddis, maybe a size 28!

The family Rhyacophilidae, our last Trichoptera family for discussion, is perhaps the most unusual, especially with respect to its feeding, taxonomy, and distribution. Free-ranging and lacking cases, these are major predators in swift streams of both eastern and western North America, roaming the streambed in search of prey.

The caddisfly *Rhyacophila*, a predator that roams
the streambed for prey. The larvae of this group do not build cases.

North American species of *Rhyacophila* are widespread, inhabiting streams wherever topography includes surface relief sufficient to create swift water. The continental distribution includes *Rhyacophila* species across North America except for the midwestern plains.

Although most are carnivorous, a few species of *Rhyacophila* are omnivores or herbivores, feeding as scrapers of diatoms in the periphyton or as gatherers of organic detritus on the streambed.

And although the larvae are without a case, at the end of the fifth instar they build a crude shelter of small stones and gravel as a pupation chamber that resembles the "turtle case" of the family Glossosomatidae.

During your mountain sojourns in either eastern or western streams, look for free-ranging caddis larvae without cases. They are likely to be the predaceous *Rhyacophila,* but they are not likely to bite! And don't worry about their competition with fish for the same foods; trout like *Rhyacophila,* too, and furthermore they are bigger mouthfuls.

This large family includes only two genera, but one genus, *Rhyacophila,* is the largest in the order Trichoptera with over a hundred species in North America. Most of the other genus, *Himalopsyche,* inhabits swiftwater mountain streams in the Himalayan region of Asia.

◆   ◆   ◆

COMMON NAMES FOR FLY-FISHING IMITATIONS of caddisflies are not nearly as diverse and numerous as those for mayflies. The term *sedge* is common enough, probably from the vegetable-matter case of some species. Most anglers seem content with Elk-hair Caddis, although why elk hair, and not bucktail, deer body hair, caribou hair, or even polar bear hair, seems lost in fly-fishing legendry. The Henryville Special appears as one of the most accurate imitations of an adult caddisfly. But even if an Elk Hair Caddis looks more like cattail fluff than an actual caddisfly adult does, at least the trout seem to think it's something good to eat!

So here's another project: collect caddis cases! They occur in almost every stream in a dazzling array.

The tube-cases in the family Limnephilidae are a good place to start; they are large and easily visible in sandy-bottomed shallow stream margins. You can collect stick-cases, sand-and-gravel cases, "reedamites," and many other variations. The "log-cabin" cases of *Brachycentrus* are not difficult to find. Neither are the turtle-shell cases of the Glossosomatidae. Look for the purse-like cases of Hydroptilidae; they require careful visual searching to find and a magnifying glass to identify. Learn about other families and genera from some of the Technical References cited in this book and other books with pictures of caddis cases in your local libraries. The book by Glenn B. Wiggins, referenced below, has excellent pictures of cases for all North American caddisfly genera.

You can preserve the cases with larvae removed in small vials with 70 percent ethyl alcohol. (The case itself needs preservative, for without it the silk that holds the case together will decay and the case will fall apart!) You might wish to release the larva back into the stream; if unhurt, it will build a new case. In your collections, see if you can find the adults flying or resting nearby, and preserve them, too. Often the adult is necessary to identify accurately the genus and species, and you just might contribute to science by associating adults to unidentified larvae—or find a new species! At least create some new patterns, *and new names!* We need them.

TECHNICAL REFERENCES

Anderson, Norman H., and Margaret J. Anderson. 1974. Making a case for the caddisfly. *Insect World Digest.* November/December, pages 1-6.

Mackay, Rosemary J., and Glenn B. Wiggins. 1979. Ecological diversity in Trichoptera. *Annual Review of Entomology.* Volume 24, pages 185-208.

Wiggins, Glenn B. 1996. *Larvae of the North American Caddisfly Genera (Trichoptera).* Second edition. University of Toronto Press, Toronto, Ontario.

RiverSketch

A CHANGE IN THE WEATHER

A CARTOON IN A RECENT UPPER MIDWEST publication portrayed a highway sign posted just inside the border of Minnesota (which we all understand is located very near the Arctic Circle). It read: "Welcome to Minnesota, We Support Global Warming." No doubt, some Minnesota citizens would agree that a few degrees higher temperature, in mid-January, would indeed be welcome.

That the Earth is currently experiencing such an increase in atmospheric temperature has been well documented. "Global Warming," worldwide, is now accepted as a certainty. Those of us who spend much time out-of-doors may not worry too much about the one or two degrees that have already been recorded. "Warming, " however, is somewhat misleading. Warming is the *cause* of the troubles we face, not just the result. The result, that which the warming causes, has been more accurately termed "global climate change." The specter of such a profound event, around the entire Planet Earth, is worth our fear, as well as our immediate action.

Thousands of scientists and economists from prestigious institutions around the world now are convinced that global warming is the result of the "greenhouse effect" of recently increased carbon dioxide and other gases (methane, nitrous oxide) into the atmosphere. These layers of gases allow solar heat (infrared radiation) to pass through to Earth's surface, but do not permit all of it to be radiated back out, thus keeping Earth warm and habitable at an average 59° Fahrenheit, without which the earth would be too cold. Fortunately for the creation and sustenance of life on Earth, that average temperature has been constant for the past few millennia. However, with increased concentrations of the greenhouse gases, a lower proportion of solar heat escapes the Earth's atmosphere, and the Earth becomes warmer.

Considerable controversy has developed about the reasons for the increase of greenhouse gases, particularly carbon dioxide and nitrous oxide. Science is always conservative and slow to arrive at firm conclusions. But recently, scientists—physicists, ecologists, climatologists—have concluded with firm conviction that the increase in atmospheric carbon dioxide is the result of burning *fossil fuels*. Coal, oil, and natural gas, high-carbon minerals extracted from the Earth's crust after having been buried for many millions of years out of circulation in the planet's cycling of carbon, are being burned, pouring millions of tons of carbon into the atmosphere where such concentrations did not previously occur. When these fuels are burned for industrial manufacturing, electrical power generation, and the internal combustion engines that power our current modes of vehicular transportation, increases in their gaseous byproducts enter the atmosphere to raise concentrations worldwide.

The obvious and inevitable solution is to switch from fossil fuels to alternative energy sources. A number of such alternatives are under investigation, and several appear successful: wind energy, biomass (wood scraps, some crops and crop residues, animal and human waste, and others). One of the most promising is to incorporate the seasonal swings of water and air temperature (particularly in or over the ocean), into temperature-driven reservoirs of energy. Eventually, such a change will be an absolute. Eventually, we must cease burning fossil fuels.

The "controversy" over the greenhouse effect, however, is specious, manufactured by a coalition of coal and oil industries that fears loss of profits when alternative energy sources are developed. Massive propaganda has flooded the nation, including publications by "scientists" financially supported by the industry coalition and mass mailings to individuals requesting signatures on petitions (yes, I have received mine). Gross attempts to derail international agreements are underway, such as the Rio de Janeiro Earth Summit conference in 1992, and the 1997 global warming protocol in Kyoto, Japan. At meetings in Buenos Aires in November 1998, 160 nations met to sign the Kyoto Protocol. The United States administration joined the other nations in signing it, but it seems unlikely that an industry-dominated Senate will approve ratification of the treaty, for now.

Spokesmen for the coal and oil industry will tell you that other sources of carbon dioxide are equally important, such as wood burning and grassland fires. Burning of this biological matter (biomass) does indeed put large amounts of carbon dioxide into the atmosphere. But what the industry representatives fail to point out is that the carbon in biomass represents *recycling*: the carbon from burning organic material was recently *removed* from the atmosphere by photosynthesis that produced the biomass. Similarly, the industry claims that animal respiration (including our own) also emits carbon dioxide. True again, but again this carbon has also been recycled, having entered animal respiratory systems from digestion of food, which in turn had been recently synthesized from atmospheric carbon dioxide. On the other hand, carbon dioxide released in the burning of coal and oil, fossilized and stored deep in the Earth for hundreds of millions of years, represents a *net increase* in modern Earth's atmospheric carbon dioxide.

The known facts are these:

In the past 150 years (from about the time of the industrial revolution), the carbon dioxide content of Earth's atmosphere increased by 30 percent (highest in the past 160,000 years), methane (in trace amounts but more effective as a greenhouse gas) by 80 percent, and nitrous oxide by 100 percent. At the same time, surface air temperature has risen from an average of 59° (Fahrenheit) to over 60, and increasing more recently. These are worldwide averages, however, and variations among geographic locations are large. Temperature rise is greater, for example, in central North America. The rate of temperature rise is itself increasing; the 11 warmest years on record have been among those since 1980, with 1998 the hottest ever recorded in the United States. The year 1999 was also among the hottest, in spite of *el Niná*, which should have *cooled* the Earth.

Sea levels also have risen, due to polar glacier melting and thermal expansion of ocean waters, up to ten inches at present.

By the year 2100, at current rates of increase in emissions, atmospheric carbon dioxide will have increased (from 1850) by 200 percent, methane by 900 percent, and nitrous oxide by 400 percent. With similar "business-as-usual" emissions, average temperature will increase in the next hundred years by another two to six degrees, or to an Earth average up to 66 degrees. The calculated rate of temperature rise is higher than any other time in the past 10, 000 years.

Again, with emissions at "business-as-usual" levels, the projected increase in sea level is more than three inches per decade, or about three feet in the next 100 years, enough to flood populated areas around the world inhabited by hundreds of millions of persons.

With suggested tight controls on emissions, increases in greenhouse gases and elevated temperatures would be lessened, but not enough to prevent a global climate change.

◆   ◆   ◆

AND WHAT WILL HAPPEN with our streams and rivers? What should we fear most as the specter of Earth's climate change advances?

Worldwide changes in carbon dioxide, temperature, and sea levels, although bad enough, vary widely around the globe. Some regions will receive greater rates of change (and some less), but among those areas to receive greater than average temperature rises is central North America, where many of our most valued trout streams and canoe routes are located, roughly at latitudes from New Orleans to north of Lake Superior. Greatest temperature increases are likely to occur the farther north, like the upper Great Lakes states and provinces, including New England and the Canadian Atlantic provinces. With a projected rise of more than ten degrees in this region, during the next century, river ecologists estimate that streams will undergo changes that create annual temperature regimes similar to those *now characterizing streams 450 miles to the south!*

Accompanying the thermal changes will be a sharp reduction in precipitation, and thus stream flow, thereby contributing additionally to the warming of water. The resulting drop in watershed runoff and channel discharge will reduce groundwater supply, dissolved organic matter, nutrients from uplands and floodplains, and woody debris and autumn leaf production from riparian zones. Loss of productivity would be inevitable.

Does a dark cloud hover over
the future of our streams and rivers?

Drs. Penelope Firth and Stuart Fisher (see Selected References) prefaced their book with the possible effects of climate change on natural waters. These include alterations in "water temperatures, runoff, nutrient flux, discharge, flow regime, lake and aquifer levels, water quality, ice cover, suspended load, primary and secondary production, trophic dynamics, organism ranges, and migration patterns,"—a virtual litany of lake and river destruction. Even so, most authors in Firth and Fisher's symposium volume urge a cautious approach to the projections of our General Circulation Models (or GCMs). The models, however, even with their uncertainties, predict serious times in store, and so far, weather events are actually occurring in agreement with the GCM forecasts.

Resistance to American cooperation with the rest of the world is political, fueled by influential corporate interests, even though the United States emits 22 percent of Earth's total greenhouse gases, the highest in the world. But equally strong are the awareness and efforts of peoples and governments in the rest of the world, the vigorous action of scientists worldwide, activist environmental organizations in this country, and a growing awareness by American citizens, who, in the final judgment, can reverse the global threat with their votes.

SELECTED REFERENCES:

Firth, Penelope, and Stuart G. Fisher, editors. 1992. *Global Climate Change and Freshwater Ecosystems.* (Proceedings of a Symposium sponsored by the National Aeronautics and Space Administration, the United States Environmental Protection Agency, and the North American Benthological Society.) Springer-Verlag, New York.

Gelbspan, Ross. 1997. *The Heat is On: The high stakes battle over Earth's threatened climate.* Addison-Wesley Publishing Company, Reading, Massachusetts.

Schotterer, Ulrich. 1992. *Climate—Our Future?* University of Minnesota Press, Minneapolis.

Chapter **16**

CRUSTACEANS

C RUSTACEANS MAKE UP THE MOST WIDELY DISTRIBUTED and
diversely adapted group of animals on Earth. Fascinating in
their habits and habitats and in their greatly differing appearances, crustaceans include some of the most beautiful yet most
bizarre of Earth's small creatures. Common in all aquatic environments, they can be easily observed and collected alive in almost every body of water, fresh or salt. We can find some
whether we live by the ocean, a lake, a pond or marsh, or even
the tiniest, temporary woodland pool. And, of course, in virtually any stream, anywhere.

Crustaceans are crusty fellows. We know that especially
well when we pick apart a boiled lobster or extricate a tasty
shrimp from its shuck. This crunchy body covering is the
exoskeleton; it holds the body together from the outside, like
the interior skeleton of us mammals does from the inside.
Groups other than crustaceans have exoskeletons, too, like the
insects, but this outer husk of the crustaceans seems particularly crunchy when we bite into one, or pick one up at
streamside.

Although closely related, the life cycle of crustaceans differs
from that of insects in several distinct ways. Crustaceans do it
differently. Like insects they develop to maturity and produce
eggs, but then the adults do not die, but rather they live a while

longer and produce more. We call each batch of eggs a *brood*; among freshwater crustaceans, the females commonly produce a second brood, or more. For many species, this life cycle occurs within a single year, and for some species, it is repeated for several years. Does this make them univoltine or bivoltine? That's a difficult question, and we usually avoid answering it by not using the term *voltinism* with crustaceans!

Feeding habits of crustaceans can be simply stated: they are voracious omnivores and eat just about anything—algae, decaying organic matter with its microorganisms, dead animal bodies and sometimes live ones as well. Functionally, most are shredders and grazers, and some are active predators on other invertebrates and even fish.

Crustaceans form the stream's cleanup squad; for example, they'll make short order of dead fish. (And that's one reason why you don't see many dead fish around!)

Their crunchy shells do not discourage their being fed upon, in turn, by fish. In fact, crustaceans make up a huge food resource for fish in almost all waters worldwide. Crustaceans add tremendously to secondary production and energy flow in many waters, including streams.

The taxonomy of crustaceans, that is, the naming of family, genus, and species, is extensive and complex. We will not discuss more than a small proportion. But even these few groups are extremely important to the ecology of streams and rivers.

The class Crustacea includes orders, families, genera, and species, like the class Insecta. (Actually, Crustacea, as a class, was recently refigured into a larger category, a subphylum, which will not bother us much, because it still includes much the same major species.) Many crustaceans not covered here inhabit oceans and lakes, or odd habitats like burrows, caves and groundwater, thermal springs, and as parasites upon other animals.

Six crustacean orders are important in streams and rivers. Three of these are made up of very small individuals that are rarely seen by the casual observer of the benthos: Cladocera,

Copepoda, and Ostracoda. We will examine these three in the next chapter on *meiofauna* (very small animals).

The other three crustacean orders, Isopoda, Amphipoda, and Decapoda consist of larger individuals in the macroinvertebrate fauna which are familiar to all fly-fishers who use "nymphs," sow bugs, scuds, and crayfish, respectively, the subjects of this chapter. These three orders include many species that inhabit streams.

Most species in the groups we are considering here—isopods, amphipods, and crayfish—live for one or two years and produce one or two broods. Crayfish, however, often have life cycles of several years, and there are a few other exceptions.

Another very important difference between crustaceans and insects is the degree of parental care given the young. Insects abandon their eggs after either attaching them somewhere or just broadcasting them in the water. Female freshwater crusta-ceans produce a batch of eggs that are fertilized, but then she *retains* the eggs.

Isopods and amphipods keep their eggs in a brood pouch, or *marsupium*, until the eggs hatch into tiny larvae. After hatching, the larvae are also retained to complete their initial growth and development within the protection of the mother's marsupium. The full incubation period, from fertilized eggs to complete de-velopment of larvae, takes several weeks. Then the larvae are re-leased into the open stream environment to feed and fend for themselves.

Female crayfish also produce batches of eggs that they re-tain—not in a marsupium, but "glued" to their ventral sides. Upon hatching, the larvae are retained through several juvenile instars, and then released.

The number of eggs in a brood for these three crustacean groups ranges from about twenty to several hundred, depending on species.

Many species in these three groups are cave dwell-ers—*stygiobionts*, meaning "living in underground dark-ness"—that are blind and never see the light of day. Some sur-vived the Pleistocene glaciation in caves deep beneath the ice in north temperate zones. Many surface species from southern un-glaciated terrain have gradually recolonized northward and now inhabit permanent surface waters, adding to the biodiversity of our current stream fauna.

◆   ◆   ◆

THE ORDER ISOPODA comprises the aquatic sow bugs—small, flattened crustaceans that are inconspicuous and usually little noticed. Sizes range from only about one-quarter to one-half inch in length. However, sow bugs occur in great numbers in some streams, and when they do, it's "chow down" time for fish, including trout. As is the case with many other crustaceans, the largest populations of isopods are found in hard water rich in calcium—that is, in limestone streams.

Perhaps the outstanding concentration of sow bugs is in Pennsylvania's high-alkalinity Letort Spring Run, made fa-mous by Vincent C. Marinaro in his classic *A Modern Dry-fly Code* (1950). Favorite habitats for sow bugs are dense water-cress beds, which are common in the upper Letort. In fact, a small spring brook tributary to the Letort is used for the commercial production of watercress, so this crustacean's habitat has been thus greatly enhanced. Marinaro's preoccu-pation with dry flies perhaps caused him to downplay the sow bug!

Of the world's species of Isopoda, most inhabit oceans, caves and other subterranean waters, or are terrestrial. Only about five percent of all isopod species live in fresh water, and most of those in caves or other subsurface habitats. Terrestrial isopods known as pill bugs are those hard-shelled crustaceans you find under damp boards and boxes in basements.

The biology of sow bugs, like that of many crustaceans, sug-gests a univoltine life cycle. One brood per generation is the common reproductive strategy. Like other crustaceans, sow bug eggs are carried in the female's marsupium for incubation and subsequent protection of the tiny larvae.

◆   ◆   ◆

THE PRINCIPAL FAMILY OF THE CLASS ISOPODA is Asellidae, including the genera *Lirceus* and *Caecidotea*. In North America, we have only a bare handful of isopods—about 20 species in the two genera—in our surface streams and rivers.

Letort Spring Run, Pennsylvania, holds large populations of the sow bug, *Lirceus brachyurus*.

Lirceus, the smallest genus in terms of number of species, ranges in geographic distribution from the Midwest eastward. It is the most thoroughly studied genus among American isopods, but with only four species. *L. hoppinae* occurs in southern Midwest streams—for example, in the states of Missouri and Arkansas—where karst topography with many cave systems is common. *L. hoppinae* can be found in subterranean habitats as well as in surface streams. However, *L. fontinalis* is the most common isopod in streams of New England and other eastern states. And *L. brachyurus*, the watercress lover, has been studied most thoroughly in Virginia and Pennsylvania; it is the probable occupant of Letort Spring Run.

The other principal genus, *Caecidotea*, unlike *Lirceus*, is widely distributed across North America in springs, streams, caves, and groundwater habitats, where numerous species have evolved.

One stream species, *Caecidotea occidentatus*, occurs in the northwestern United States; another, *C. lineatus*, in the Great Lakes region. Several species occupy stream habitats in eastern states, including the most common, *C. communis*, in New England. Several occur in surface streams in the karst region of the southern Midwest, where most of the cave dwellers are also found in subterranean waters.

If you observe isopods in these areas, you will probably not detect differences between *Caecidotea* and *Lirceus*, which are distinguished only by minor anatomical points. So don't worry about tying your nymphs differently. Sizes do not range greatly, but you might take a close look at specimens from the stream you frequent and adjust your patterns. Hook sizes about 16 to 18 would be about right.

While sneaking up on a pool in a small spring brook, look for watercress beds, patches of aquatic moss, or other beds of macrophytes. Shake out a handful of vegetation onto a light surface, such as a white plastic wash basin, if you have one handy in your fly vest, or just a light-colored board. You'll probably see a maze of small animals—insects, worms, scuds, and, if you're lucky, some sow bugs. You may also find sow bugs hiding, like their cave-dwelling relations, in dark places under stones and leaves. They're small and flat, with seven pairs of legs often visibly stretched out sideways, and they wiggle a lot. Try putting a few into a bottle with fresh stream water, then look for a female carrying eggs or young larvae. When disturbed, the larvae may be seen leaving the marsupium and starting to swim about. Collect some in a vial of preservative—and then be sure to put the rest back into the stream!

The fly fisher's lexicon for sow bugs is pretty slim—just *sow bugs* (sometimes *cress bugs*). Or maybe isopods. But when you ever include Pennsylvania's legendary Letort among your destinations, better have some in your fly box.

◆　　　◆　　　◆

WHEREVER TROUT ANGLERS fish limestone streams, scuds (order Amphipoda) are among the most familiar crustaceans, imitated by the fly fisher's bright, pink-and-orange "nymph." There are only a few species, and most of these are distributed in central or northern North America. But in some streams—usually summercool woodland brooks and small creeks—they can be found in huge abundance in the benthos, as well as in the diet of trout.

Amphipods are laterally compressed and, when slightly curled up on their side, as they usually are at rest, they present a semicircular shape. They are also known as side-swimmers, but unlike sow bugs, scuds are excellent swimmers. They move a lot along the streambed, migrate upstream and down, and are common in drift.

Most amphipods have a one-year life cycle, so we can call them univoltine. But one species has a definite two-year cycle, and all species can produce two or more broods of young per year. Like female sow bugs, female scuds carry their eggs and newly hatched young in a marsupium.

About 200 genera and 1,200 species of amphipods occur worldwide, most in oceans. About 150 species occur in North America's fresh waters, but most of these are in subterranean habitats. We are left with only four families, three or four genera, and a half-dozen species in the surface fresh waters of North America.

Occasionally, cave dwellers leave the openings of their subterranean habitat and either swim or drift down into sunlit surface streams. At least one species makes regular migrations out of a cave at night—and back again by dawn.

Although some amphipods are obligate to streams and running water, their specific habitat on the streambed is in sheltered areas away from light, like most crustaceans. For example, you never find them on the tops of stones in swift riffles, like some mayfly nymphs and caddis larvae. Rather, look for them amid dense vegetation, like moss and watercress, and under stones. They are common also in shallow, silty-sandy runs close to the bank, where the silt is mixed with fine organic matter. Lightly run your fingertips through the silty surface, and you may see a cloud of side-swimmers suddenly scurrying about, swimming on their sides. Like most crustaceans, scuds are found only in high-alkalinity limestone streams.

◆   ◆   ◆

WE ARE MOST LIKELY TO ENCOUNTER two groups of amphipods in our rambles on streams, both summercool trout streams and some small, southern, warmwater streams: family Hyalellidae, genus *Hyalella* (one species) and family Gammaridae, genus *Gammarus* (four species).

The one species in the family Hyalellidae—*Hyalella azteca*—is sort of a generic amphipod. It is the most common freshwater amphipod, broadly distributed widely across the North American continent. It varies greatly in its preferred habitat: in size and form, in high and low water temperatures, common in streams, lakes, and ponds. This species is smaller than most other amphipods, attaining a maximum length of only about one-fourth inch. In some isolated populations, however, maximum length may be twice as long. Unlike other amphipods, *Hyalella azteca* is capable of producing many broods—up to fifteen—during its summer breeding period.

If you set out to look for it, your best bet is in the littoral of warmwater lakes. But we include *Hyalella azteca* here because we do find it in streams, usually in waters somewhat warmer than summercool trout streams.

Rather than a distinct species, *Hyalella azteca* may be a taxonomic complex that is still evolving in the direction of speciation. However, so far, taxonomists have not produced further divisions.

The family Gammaridae, with its one genus, *Gammarus,* is much more clearly divided into distinct species—four common species in North America, some occurring only in streams and some in lakes as well. These four stream species vary in size and distribution. They can be found in summercool trout streams as well as in warmwater streams of southern limestone regions.

Gammarus pseudolimnaeus is the common scud
of streams in the North Central region.
(Photograph by R. J. R. Johnson.)

Gammarus pseudolimnaeus is the principal species in cool trout streams in the upper Mississippi River drainage and eastward, including small tributaries of the Great Lakes and the St. Lawrence River. Its size ranges up to near three-quarters of an inch long, big enough to impale on a size 14 hook—and some have been used as bait in winter ice fishing. The life cycle is usually around one year to 15 months, but females can bring off several broods in that time. *Gammarus pseudolimnaeus* has been observed to drift at night in great numbers (more on this subject later). Very abundant in watercress beds and in leaf packs, it is a predator at times on other small invertebrates. Probably most scud imitations, hook size 14 or 16, are intended to simulate this species.

Gammarus lacustris is a bit larger than *G. pseudolimnaeus*, distributed throughout the northern United States and Canada up to the subarctic tree line. It is also circumpolar around the Northern Hemisphere, including Western Europe. It is common in Hudson Bay tributaries and in the mountain streams of western North America. In addition to cold streams, *G. lacustris* (as its name suggests) occurs in many northern lakes, where it takes on an open-water existence and feeds as a predator on zooplankton. The common life cycle for *G. lacustris* is two years, with four broods.

Gammarus minus—much smaller, with a maximum length only about a quarter-inch—is a species that inhabits warmwater streams and springs common in the karst regions of central United States and the southern Appalachian Mountains. It is more closely tied to a subterranean existence than the other gammarids. *Gammarus minus* is often found in streams that emit from caves; it probably spends much of its existence in cave habitats near surface openings. (Many other species of *Gammarus* are restricted to caves in these limestone regions.)

The fourth gammarid species, *Gammarus fasciatus*, while found occasionally in streams, occurs mainly in lakes. It has been found in the eastern Great Lakes and eastward through the St. Lawrence system. It also appears along the Atlantic coast in tributaries and some brackish waters, south as far as North Carolina. *G. fasciatus* is small, like *G. minus*. Unlike other gammarids, its life cycle is less than one year, and yet it produces two broods.

Some aspects of gammarid reproduction are easily observed. Collect some in spring or early summer, and you will see a few scuds in *precopula*, when the male (larger) carries the female (smaller) around, firmly grasping her by her back. After several days of this, when she approaches her first adult molt, the two separate—but not for long. The female undertakes a partial molt, during which her marsupium is formed. The male grasps her again, this time belly-to-belly, so to speak, and releases his sperm to her. She then quickly parts from her mate to undergo the final portion of her mature molt, releasing her eggs (25 to

50, depending on the size of the female) into the marsupium where they are fertilized; and incubation of the protected eggs begins.

Incubation time is fairly long, ranging from one to three weeks. When the eggs hatch into tiny young, they look much like the adults. The female continues to protect them in her marsupium for another week or so, after which they are released into a free world. You probably will have observed the pre-copula, the separated female with eggs, and some females still carrying their young, with only a quick collection of a few dozen specimens.

The color of fresh scuds found on the stream bottom is usually a rather dark brownish-olive, but it can range to a lighter hue of medium brown or even tan. Thus, it is somewhat of a puzzle that almost all angling imitations are tied in bright pink-to-orange hues, sometimes with shiny tinsel ribbing.

Actually, gammarids, like all crustaceans, have large quantities of the orange pigment *carotene* (a source of vitamin A) in their tissues. When they are placed in the researcher's preservative, digested in a predator's gut, or just plain cooked, the bright pink-orange-red color appears. Also, upon molting, crustaceans sometimes appear lighter in color, but then they hide in some secluded place for a time (to avoid predators?) until their new exoskeletons darken.

Perhaps most fly tiers have only seen preserved specimens as models. No matter: pink-and-orange nymphs seem to work well as stimulators to provoke a strike. The bright imitations are certainly more visible to predators (that is, to trout). Perhaps fish do see—and remember—newly molted individuals once in a while. In any case, if orange scuds work, use orange!

By the way, the bright red flesh of trout that have been eating amphipods has been attributed to their ingestion of carotene. Amphipods are good food for trout—and the red flesh of trout is reputed to be most tasty.

◆   ◆   ◆

ADULT CRAYFISH, MEMBERS OF THE ORDER Decapoda, cannot swim. At least, not in the usual sense. But they can move—backwards—and fast, actually sort of a *scoot*. These crustaceans have a wide, strong "tail fan," and when they flip it downward and forward beneath their abdomen, the animals virtually fly backward, *zip*, into safety under streambed stones. This velocity is known as "slip speed," and it can exceed a foot per second.

Did you ever wonder why crayfish imitations are tied backwards on the hook, with the giant front claws facing to the rear? Fish such a nymph, heavily weighted, on the bottom. A jerk with rod or line simulates a crayfish slipping backward under protective cover. Fish have learned to approach crayfish from the rear in order to avoid the claws!

The order Decapoda is large and comprises lobsters, shrimps, and crabs, in addition to crayfish; more than 10,000 species in the order have been described worldwide. Most of these—90 percent—are marine, living in the salty oceans. We find many crayfish and a few shrimps in North American fresh waters, but no true crabs or lobsters (although there are many in the tropics). In North America, we have about 350 freshwater crayfish species, and most of these are cave dwellers or restricted to ponds and lakes—and some only in moist ground! So the number of crayfish that can be considered regular inhabitants of surface streams comes down to only four genera and a couple dozen species.

Crayfish are much larger than isopods and amphipods (up to six inches long), and their life cycle is longer, one to two years for many species, up to nine years for some. Consequently, animals of all sizes are present at all times. Relationships to subterranean life are strong, so even strictly stream species are reclusive, always hiding. Young of the year, or juveniles, occupy shallow riffles among cobbles for protection, where they actively forage during the day. Adult crayfish, however, pretty much stay under larger stones or in deep pools during the day, then come out to forage at night. Decapods are omnivorous and feed on detritus, vegetation, and other animal tissue, dead or alive, wherever they can find it.

Crayfish serve as food for fish, wading birds, otters, and raccoons; several species are also valued as food by humans. They fill a menu much like marine shrimps. "Crawfish" are particularly coveted in some southern states—mainly Louisiana—where many tasty crayfish dishes are considered the epitome of hearty eating. In these regions, some crayfish are commercially raised for the market, but wild crayfish are also harvested in season for bait and food.

Part of the crayfish's reclusive life style is their custom of burrowing. Several burrowing strategies have been identified and classified. Some species live only in wet burrows under moist meadows, where they dig a tunnel an inch in diameter from the surface down into the water table. The animals form small pellets of mud, bring these up to the surface, and deposit them around the tunnel opening, where they form a mound up to a few inches high that we call a "chimney." Such species need no contact with open water, either lake, pond, or stream. They live out their life cycles foraging outside their burrows at night, needing only the water in their burrow's chamber near the water table for sufficient moisture. Crayfish will overwinter in their burrows safe below frost line.

A second group of burrowers build their tunnels near ponds or stream banks, sometimes with a chimney above ground, and foraging outside at night, often in the nearby water. Some of this group build their burrows with a lower opening in a streambed, under large stones, and make daily migrations up and into the open stream for feeding.

A third group, however, known as "rock crawlers," make no burrows at all, instead living out their life cycles in wholly aquatic stream environments. These have noticeably flattened bodies, which helps them occupy habitats underneath stones. This last group, and some of the second, are the crayfish that concern us most in this book.

Crayfish have some of the most interesting reproductive modes among the animal kingdom. Like both isopods and amphipods, female crayfish provide much parental care to their offspring.

The chimney of a crayfish can be found
along the edges of many small streams.

Copulation between the sexes takes place in spring, and the male's sperm is retained and stored by the female for several weeks or months until her eggs are ready. When the female produces her brood of 100 to 200 eggs for most species, but up to 600 or 700 for others—she also secretes a sticky substance on her ventral surface. Into this go the sperm and eggs, and it is there that fertilization takes place. The fertilized eggs are retained in this adhesive substance on small appendages on the female's abdomen. She is then known as being "in berry"—the clumps of small, round eggs having an appearance like a raspberry or blackberry. Incubation of the eggs takes several weeks or months in summer, and if you should catch an adult female crayfish from the stream bottom at this time, you will become immediately aware of the berrylike collection of eggs on her underside.

After hatching, young crayfish stay attached to the mother's abdominal appendages for several more weeks, molting twice (into the third instar) before finally leaving their mother and setting out into their natural world alone. The new generation matures by the following spring to produce another generation. Longer-lived species bring off several broods during their lifetime.

◆   ◆   ◆

TWO FAMILIES OF CRAYFISH are important in the streams and rivers of North America—Astacidae and Cambaridae.

The first of these, Astacidae, is small, with only one genus—*Pacifasticus*—and five species in North America. Almost all occur only in northwestern warmwater rivers tributary to the Pacific Ocean, but some can now be found in alpine lakes in mountains west of the Rockies, where they have been widely introduced into lakes and rivers. This group includes those with long life cycles—most of six to seven years, one species of up to nine years. The latter, *P. leniusculus*, has become important commercially and has been introduced widely among Pacific coast rivers as well as in Europe, where it is able to resist some diseases affecting native European crayfish.

The family Cambaridae is of greatest interest throughout much of the rest of North America; most of its species are found from the Great Plains eastward. Throughout the central and eastern United States and southeastern Canada, many species occur in both summercool and warmwater streams where stream inhabitants—especially the "rock-crawlers"—constitute major food supplies for trout and smallmouth bass. These stream crayfishes are most common from the Great Lakes region east to New England, as well as in the middle-southern areas of the Ozark and Appalachian mountains.

Cambarus and *Procambarus*, the largest genera of the Cambaridae, include a few stream species, but most inhabit lakes. *Cambarus hobbsi* occurs in sandy Ozark streams, *C. bartoni* in small, gravel-bottomed brooks and springs east and northeast from the Mississippi River, and *C. robustus* in the middle to southern Appalachians, where it burrows under stones in swift, clear streams. *Procambarus tenuis* occupies some clear, swift streams of Arkansas and Oklahoma. *Procambarus acutus* and *P. simulans* inhabit both lakes and streams throughout the eastern half of the United States, in small, swift streams where trout and smallmouth bass, their main predators, make up the main sport fisheries.

The genus *Orconectes*, with about 65 species, includes the crayfishes most commonly found in clear, swift, stony-bottomed streams in the eastern half of the United States and eastern Canada. In northern forested streams around the upper Great Lakes and eastward to Quebec and New England, three species of *Orconectes* are most common: *O. propinquus*, *O. immunis*, and *O. virilis*. In many streams of the "driftless area" of Wisconsin, Minnesota, Iowa, and Illinois, *Orconectes* supports a profusion of smallmouth bass streams that are tributary to the Mississippi River.

In the karst regions of the Ozark Plateau and associated areas, many *Orconectes* species occupy the many clear, productive, high-alkalinity streams that drain limestone uplands. Two species—*O. luteus* and *O. punctimanus*—are the most common in the Ozark streams of Missouri and Arkansas, including the Ozark National Scenic Riverways. There, the many streams tributary to the White River in Missouri and Arkansas run swift and clear, and hold abundant populations of crayfish. Their range extends also into nearby Kansas, Nebraska, and Oklahoma, and eastward into the southern Appalachians.

Orconectes rusticus—the "rusty crayfish"—originally found only in lakes and warmwater streams of New England has been inadvertently introduced farther west into the Great Lakes region where it has become a serious pest in lakes because of its aggressive feeding behavior. In some waters, the rusty crayfish has almost entirely consumed the aquatic vegetation. Attempts to eliminate populations or deter its spread have been largely unsuccessful.

In the many streams of central North America that have water temperatures a little too warm for trout but not quite what we usually term *warmwater*, the smallmouth bass predominates as the principal sport fish, with the rock bass (almost always a cohabitant with the smallmouth) a distant second. In streams where crayfish are abundant, they predominate in the diet of both smallmouth bass and rock bass. In fact, the diet for larger adult fish is almost exclusively crayfish.

Whether in streams of northern forests or southern mountains, the crayfish is the main supplier of energy to the smallmouth bass (and to rock bass, too). An angler enjoying the beauty of these special stream and river environments should carry an ample supply of imitations of these crustaceans.

Remember to tie them backwards.

TECHNICAL REFERENCES:

Pennak, Robert W. 1989. *Fresh-water Invertebrates of the United States: Protozoa to Mollusca.* Third edition.
Thorp, James H., and Alan P. Covich, editors. 1991. *Ecology and Classification of North American Freshwater Invertebrates.* Academic Press, Inc., San Diego, California.

RiverSketch

RIVERS IN DARKNESS

THE VISION OF A FREE-FLOWING RIVER deep underground has intrigued humans for centuries. No other feature of our natural landscape has elicited such fantasy and foreboding—and yet deadly attraction—as have the caves and streams that occur in the nether worlds beneath our surface footsteps. After all, it was the River Styx of Greek mythology, in the deepest darkness of Hades, that the souls of the dead had to cross on their journey from the living. But the adventure of caving, along with the science of *speleology*, today draw hosts of living, avid followers.

Many thousands of caves occur throughout the world, 12,000 in the United States alone. Most are "solution caves," formed by the dissolution of native rock, most often limestone, by surface water that contains carbonic acid from rain and soil.

Because strata of limestone underlie a great portion of the terrestrial surface of the earth, caves occur in profusion. The surface topography over limestone bedrock, with its abundance of caves and associated features, is *karst* terrain, a term that originated in a noted limestone region of Yugoslavia.

Surface features in a karst landscape include limestone outcroppings such as bluffs and ridges, cave openings with copious springs, and sinkholes, the latter being conspicuous surface depressions resulting from the collapse of underground galleries.

Millions of years ago, karst topography was initiated by calcium carbonate particles, byproducts of photosynthesis by ocean phytoplankton, forming in turn limestone layers on the ocean floor as the particles settled through the depths. But through geological time, the limestone strata were uplifted by tectonic forces to higher elevations hundreds or thousands of feet above sea level. With these earth movements, the limestone layers cracked into many fractures: fault joints (vertical) and bedding joints (horizontal), through which surface waters drained into the limestone mass, initiating the process of cave formation.

◆　　　　◆　　　　◆

MANY FEATURES OF CAVES attract scholarly attention, but one of the most fascinating is the underground river. Interdependent with the cave, the stream requires the cave's gradient, while the cave itself is the product of trickling and flowing water.

Underground rivers begin with the water of precipitation falling in a karst region, then percolating down to the limestone bedrock. Here water seeps downward through fault and bedding joints, literally wriggling its way through limestone, dissolving calcium carbonate as it goes. Thus does a miniature cave river begin its course through the blackness of the underground.

Canfield Creek flows out of a cave
in the karst topography of southeastern Minnesota.

Through eons of time and many miles of limestone fractures, the stream enlarges. Somewhere downslope through a lower outfall and spring, the cave river leaves its realm of darkness and enters the world of light as a surface stream. Eventually, the cave river returns its solution of calcium carbonate to the sea.

But deep beneath karst terrains around the world, the river of darkness has left its handiwork in huge caverns. In these rooms, percolating water continues to form grottoes, pits and domes; shafts and tunnels and ledges; and the limpid pools, cascades, and waterfalls of underground streams.

◆   ◆   ◆

THE STUDY OF CAVE LIFE is *biospeleology*, a special branch of ecology different from that at the surface. The most important environmental factor making that difference is light—actually the absence of it: total darkness.

We term underground habitats *hypogean* ("beneath earth's surface"), in contrast to above-ground habitats which are called *epigean* (open streams, plains, forests).

The trophic organization of cave communities, both terrestrial and aquatic, is relatively simple compared with epigean ecosystems. For one thing, green plants are missing. Without light, there can be no photosynthesis. Without photosynthesis, no energy-containing food is synthesized in the cave—no algae, no macrophytes, and of course no herbivorous animals. So the cave flora consists only of plant roots extending down from above, and only in shallow caves. The food and energy source for cave animals must be in the epigean surface—allochthonous organic matter—substituting for primary production.

Bacteria and fungi process the organic matter in much the same way as in shaded, headwater streams. Surface floods often bring in such inputs. But animals from outside—bats, birds, and insects—also bring in organic detritus and leave behind feces, sources of food for which cave animals have evolved feeding strategies.

The aquatic fauna of cave streams is sparse in both population abundance and number of species. Crustaceans predominate among the more visible aquatic invertebrates. This class includes the almost-microscopic ostracods and copepods, the more prominent amphipods (scuds), isopods (sow bugs), and crayfish. Also present, but less common, are a few insects, aquatic earthworms, and leeches. All of these are essentially omnivores—feeding on whatever happens by. Opportunism rules.

Lacking light and thus any need for vision, cave animals have lost the development of eyes through evolution. Because neither prey nor predator can see, pigmentation for both is absent, and the animals appear, when lighted, to be opaque but colorless. Other senses, however, become magnified—long, sensory antennae on crustaceans, highly developed lateral lines and other sensors on fishes.

Troglobites is the term applied to organisms that are permanent dwellers in the hypogean habitat. Troglobitic animals are true cave citizens, having no contact with the lighted world, eyeless and colorless, but highly sensitive to odor, touch, and the water vibrations of motion encountered in their stygian environment. Other animals are transitory, the *troglophiles* (cave lovers) alternately entering and exiting the cave; some, for example, reproduce in the cave but leave to forage for food.

The final trophic level, or top carnivore, is the fish. These are mostly members of the family Amblyopsidae (cavefishes) and the blind catfishes, relatives of surface catfish and bullheads (Ictaluridae). But even here there is no great specialization. Predatory cave fish consume every other living, moving prey that they can detect. So the whole rest of the troglobitic community serves as the fish's food source—copepods, amphipods and isopods, crayfish, and each other.

◆   ◆   ◆

RATES OF GROWTH AND PRODUCTION are low in cave waters. With the scant and uncertain input of allochthonous food and the lack of seasonal rhythms, life is slow-paced. Life cycles are long and reproduction limited.

Consequently, hypogean populations are especially susceptible to environmental disturbance. One catastrophe, such as a severe flood, especially if it carries with it toxic wastes, sewage, or a pulse of pesticide from a cultivated field, can eliminate many generations.

Sinkholes in rural areas present special problems in that they offer convenient places to dispose of trash. When such material includes hazardous wastes, such as unused pesticides, paints, and other volatile compounds, it not only pollutes groundwater and domestic water supplies, but also poisons the animals and other organisms of hypogean waters.

Our sensitivity to the fragility of these fascinating members of an unseen world has been slow to come about. General awareness of their presence and place among our fellow creatures is critically needed. For in addition to the surface streams and rivers we fish, paddle, and otherwise enjoy, rivers in the darkness of the underground also warrant our stewardship.

SELECTED REFERENCES:

Ford, T.D., and C.H.D. Cullingford, editors. 1976. *The Science of Speleology*. Academic Press, New York.
Jackson, Donald Dale, and The Editors of Time-Life Books. 1982. *Underground Worlds*. Time-Life Books, Alexandria, Virginia.

Chapter 17

MEIOFAUNA

IN TIMES PAST—A FEW DECADES AGO—biologists considered stream benthic invertebrates only as the small, swimming and crawling creatures readily seen by eye and found somewhere between the stream banks and among the stones and gravel of the stream bottom. They were visible. Fishery biologists studied only those invertebrates large enough and available enough to be eaten by fish, usually adult fish.

Today we know that these views were extremely limited perceptions of stream life. In fact, we now realize that a major proportion of energy inputs and transfers are accomplished by huge aggregations of very small, nearly invisible or microscopic animals—the *meiofauna*. The meiofauna has been known and studied in the oceans for many decades, but they have become appreciated in streams only recently. In fact, literally millions of individuals have been measured in one square foot of streambed. We have also come to realize that without this community of unseen, tiny animals inhabiting biofilms on streambed substrates or in subsurface *interstices*, stream systems as we know them today could not exist.

Earlier in this book, we made reference to microscopic life (such as algae, bacteria, and fungi) that thrives in the periphyton, epilithon, or "slime communities," on streambed stones and other surfaces. But we emphasized only those organisms that are photosynthesizing (like algae) or heterotrophic bacteria and fungi. It is in these same microhabitats that meiofauna also exist, literally unknown in streams until not long ago. A critical ecological function of the meiofauna is that they provide a major food resource for other, small invertebrate animals of many kinds which, in turn, are preyed upon by larger invertebrates. Besides, many animals in the meiofauna provide essential food for early-emergent fish fry.

These small animals are not at all restricted to the water between stream banks or on the streambed surface. Biologists have discovered many animals, small and large, occurring deep in streambed gravels. We find them even in subterranean sand and gravel through which stream water flows, sometimes miles away from the regular stream channel in the *hyporheic zone.*

You won't see any of these little fellows while stream fishing, paddling whitewater, or meditating at streamside. Nevertheless, they constitute such an important element in streams and rivers—especially in the benthos—that we should be aware of their presence under the water surface and underfoot—a great assemblage of stream life that went unappreciated only recently.

◆   ◆   ◆

MEIOFAUNA IS A TERM LOOSELY USED to describe the very small animals occurring everywhere on the bottoms of all aquatic habitats—freshwater or salt, lake, pond, or stream. The term is technically defined by size. Meiofauna derives from "meio-," or small in size (between "micro-" and "macro-"), and "fauna" (a collection of animals). Researchers do not agree on the numerical size of meiofauna, but typically dimensions range between 40 and 1,000 microns. A micron is one millionth of a meter, or about 1/25,000 of an inch; so, in the inches-and-feet system, the range in size of meiofauna is roughly from 1.5 to 40 thousandths of an inch—certainly visible to the eye in the upper portion of this range.

The meiofauna can be compared with two other size groups: one smaller, the *microfauna,* or microinvertebrates, in sizes less than 40 microns (about 1.5/1000 inch), and the other, macroin-vertebrates large enough to see. Thus, the most common ani-mals we see (for example, on the tops and undersides of riffle stones) are macroinvertebrates, including all the familiar, read-ily-visible animals—like immature mayflies, caddisflies, and scuds. But if you look closely, especially with a magnifier, you can see many members of the meiofauna. You will need a labo-ratory microscope to see the microfauna.

In practice, most of us ecologists are not so particular about these sizes; any of very small animals that we can just barely see—and many unseen—we usually term meiofauna.

By now, you are familiar with macroinvertebrates, partly from discussions in the last few chapters. If you are a fly fisher and a fly tier, you will have had hands-on familiarity in your attempts to tie various nymphs that imitate invertebrates that are common items of fish diets.

Most important of the meiofauna, however, are three groups of small crustaceans, not discussed in the previous chapter. These are so small that probably you have not tried to tie their imitation (how about a hook size 40?). These are: *copepods* (sub-class Copepoda, with several orders); *cladocerans* (formerly the order Cladocera, but now an informal name for several orders); and *ostracods* (subclass Ostracoda). These three groups are often lumped under the collective name, *microcrustaceans.* For sim-plicity, we will use just the three common names: copepods, cladocerans, and ostracods. We'll take up these three groups in order, and then consider some other non-crustaceans that fall into the meiofauna size range. As benthic animals, these small crustaceans feed primarily on organic items in the streambed, such as microorganisms, but they are also predators on even smaller animals.

A few decades ago, science had concluded that zooplank-ton—small animals occupying open water pretty much at the whim of lake and ocean currents—could not exist in swift cur-rents. For example, zooplankton originating in lake or reservoir outlets soon disappeared downstream.

But researchers examining more closely the material collected in fine-meshed nets from stream water—without lake or reservoir sources—found specimens of copepods, cladocerans, and ostracods and then concluded that zooplankton did indeed occur in streams. Then, it was later discovered that these little crustaceans found in streams were in fact *benthic* species, and not *planktonic*. They occupied stream sediments and, at times, rose up into currents where they were caught in biologists' drift nets.

So once again, we conclude that the small crustaceans of lake and ocean plankton do not, after all, occur in streams. But other species, typically stream microcrustaceans, live and thrive in streams—even in swift, stony headwaters. But they do not occur as *zooplankton*, but rather in their stream bottom habitat as part of the *benthos*.

◆　　　　◆　　　　◆

COPEPODS ARE AMONG THE MOST COMMON and abundant animal groups on earth, with probably around 10,000 species. They occupy virtually every kind of aquatic environment: oceans and fresh water, surface and subterranean habitats, benthic and open water, streams and lakes, and as parasites in or on other animals. Copepods make up the largest component of zooplankton in the oceans. Pick up a tumbler of water from a pond or lake or saltwater bay, look closely against the sky and you will probably see some tiny specks flitting about through the water—probably copepods. Almost all measure less than a millimeter in body length. Species differ, of course, between the plankton of lakes and the benthos of streams.

Free-living copepods—that is, those that are not parasites—are divided into three suborders. Two of these are planktonic in both lakes and oceans, but the third, Harpacticoida, is strictly benthic—copepods that attract our interest in stream ecology.

Harpacticoids are cylindrical in shape, tapering slightly. They have anterior antennae and caudal filaments, or tails. Adult females carry eggs in two external ovarian sacs, one on each side, each enclosing about a dozen eggs. The first instar after hatching from the egg—a *nauplius*—is small, round to oval, with a few bristly appendages, looking not at all like the adult. Length of life cycle varies among species from a couple of weeks to a year, depending on water temperature. Copepod females are very prolific, producing multiple broods after only one fertilization by a male.

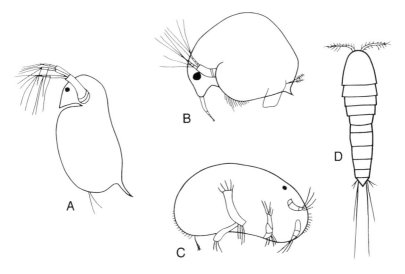

Microcrustaceans include: (A), (B) cladocerans, (C) ostracods, and (D) harpacticoid copepods.

Harpacticoid copepods often predominate among microcrustaceans in small streams. Under a microscope, all three stages can usually be seen at one time: nauplius, adult, and females with egg sacs. Densities on the stream bottom of several hundred per square foot are common, but occasionally they occur in much higher numbers.

Another suborder of copepods, Cyclopoida, is very common in streams; they resemble more closely the common copepods in lakes. Whereas harpacticoids are most prevalent within sand and gravel, the cyclopoids occupy the tops of streambed substrates, detritus particles, and leaves of macrophytes.

Copepods of all kinds are most abundant in high-alkalinity limestone streams. In view of the fact that they are readily eaten by small fish, their abundance in hard waters may contribute to the high rates of secondary production by fish.

◆   ◆   ◆

CLADOCERANS, ANOTHER IMPORTANT GROUP of microcrustaceans, swim about with hops and leaps, leading to the common name of "water fleas." Most cladocerans are inhabitants of fresh water, with only a few marine species. Almost all freshwater species occupy lakes and ponds, with only a few species in streams, which nevertheless can be individually abundant. Most stream species belong to the family Chydoridae, which are known for having especially heavy exoskeletons that adapt them for the rough-and-tumble life in the benthic habitat of rolling sand grains and gravel.

The shape and appearance of most cladocerans are among the most fascinating of the animal world. From the side, some resemble medieval warriors, with pointed, recurved, helmet-shaped heads—which, by the way, undergo marked variations in shape and form, changing during molting in a single season—a phenomenon known as *cyclomorphosis*. The sharp-pointed helmets, by the way, are thought to be an anti-predation device, protecting cladocerans against feeding fish.

Some lake-living cladocerans undertake a vertical migration that is tied to the daily photoperiod, rising at night and descending at the coming of dawn. The pattern is very similar to the well-known daily periodicities in drifting exhibited by many stream macroinvertebrates. In fact, benthic, stream-living cladocerans do exactly the same thing, rising from the streambed upon the fall of darkness and, caught in stream currents, they drift downstream during the night. (More on stream drift in a later chapter.)

Cladocerans are a bit larger than most copepods, with a maximum length up to 3 millimeters, or about 1/8 inch (most are smaller), and in lakes they constitute a major source of food for young fish of many species. However, less is known about the extent to which stream fish feed on cladocerans, but it is likely that they are readily preyed upon by fish, because of their larger size.

Reproduction includes some *parthenogenesis*: viable eggs produced by females without fertilization from males. Some cladocerans reproduce parthenogenetically during summer, but males appear in the fall for sexual reproduction, fertilizing eggs that then overwinter in special capsules.

◆   ◆   ◆

OSTRACODS CONSTITUTE THE THIRD GROUP of stream micro-crustaceans, and although they are generally smaller than cope-pods and cladocerans, they may predominate because of their much higher numbers, particularly in slow water rather than rif-fles. However, among the three groups of microcrustaceans, os-tracods have been the least studied, so we know little about their ecological significance to the rest of the stream animal commu-nity. Informally, the term "seed shrimp" is used to describe them, owing to their visual similarity to vegetable seeds.

The ostracods include the order Pedocopida, which includes some marine and all freshwater groups. Lotic species occur in several families. Over 400 species have been described in North America, but, because of the dearth of ostracod research, many more species probably remain to be discovered and described.

The form and appearance of ostracods are totally unlike those of copepods and cladocerans. They carry a pair of shells, or valves, one on each side, that enclose the animal within—much like clams. In fact, they resemble clams so much that they have often been mistaken for small clams and mussels by casual observers. The valves are hinged at the top and swing open for the animals' activities.

Ostracods occur in the oceans and all freshwater habitats, in caves, lakes and ponds, and streams. Some inhabit *interstices* in loose, sandy aquifers, where waters are well oxygenated and contain fine organic particles for food. In surface waters, all are benthic, living on lake and stream bottoms, or at least attached to some substrate like stones or macrophyte stems and leaves. When active, they move about on the substrate with their valves slightly agape, appendages extended for locomotion and feeding. However, a few actually swim, mostly briefly—for example, from one plant stem to another. Nonswimmers have a strictly benthic existence.

Ostracod activity is largely confined to the daytime, so drifting ostracods are captured in researchers' drift nets primarily during the day, unlike most invertebrates whose daily patterns show only nocturnal drift.

Most species produce only one generation per year, a few two or three generations. Nevertheless, ostracods occur in high numbers, often several thousand per square foot of stream bottom. Because they are smaller than copepods and cladocerans, they do not account for large quantities in terms of biomass or energy in calories, but in view of their abundance in high numbers, ostracods may make up the most available source of food in small sizes available to early-instar insects. Most ostracods measure less than one millimeter, or about 1/32 of an inch, in length.

For lack of study, we do not know the full significance of ostracods in stream benthic communities. Although they have been observed in the guts of a few species of fish, midge larvae, and predaceous copepods, we know very little about their overall contribution to trophic systems in streams. It seems probable that they are most important as food for macroinvertebrate predators. Time—and much more study—may tell.

◆   ◆   ◆

THE MEIOFAUNA OF A STREAM includes much more than microcrustaceans. If we stick closely to size definitions, many of these other groups would be classified in the microfauna, but they are still important as "very small animals" in stream systems.

We can start with the smallest—the Protozoa, animals of only a single cell. Do you remember experimenting with a hay culture in your early biology classes? Remember *Paramecium* (hairy and shaped like a foot print) and *Amoeba* (constantly changing form) in the hay culture? Protozoans have received a great amount of study in human medicine, but not nearly as much in aquatic ecology. It is remarkable that protozoans present so many of the basic biological systems—physiology, behavior, ecology—which can be studied in a single cell.

Most protozoans range from 30 microns (less than 1/1,000 inch) to 300 microns (about 1/100 inch), so they fall into both microfauna and meiofauna categories.

Some protozoans feed on solid particles, such as bacteria and algae, while others absorb dissolved organic matter (DOM) from their water environment. Reproduction is accomplished simply by splitting of the cell into two new individuals, although some unite in pairs to exchange genetic material in a primitive form of sexual reproduction.

Protozoans mostly thrive in habitats rich in decomposing organic matter and low in oxygen, but one group known as *katharobic* Protozoa commonly occupies freshwater springs and small streams and rivers that are oxygen-rich but low in dead organic matter. However, these populations are sparse compared to those found in still waters. We do not know much about the importance of these stream katharobes, except that they do provide food for other members of the meiofauna. Stream ecology could profit from protozoan research, including quantitative data on secondary production and use by other animals.

A common protozoan inhabitant of streams is *Giardia lamblia*, an intestinal parasite carried by beavers. Be careful—a drop of river water in your mouth may bring down the vengeance of the very devil on your sensitive intestinal system! (The author writes from personal experience.)

◆   ◆   ◆

THE PHYLUM ROTIFERA (SOMETIMES, ROTATORIA) is almost exclusively found in fresh water, but in this environment the number of special niches is enormous. Rotifers can be found in any kind of fresh water: lakes and ponds, streams and large rivers, temporary waters or permanent, deepwater and littoral, puddles and forest pools, water in treeholes. The number of rotifer species found in a single stream may be a hundred or more. They often make up, by far, the greatest proportion of stream meiofauna (over 90 percent), occurring in densities of several million individuals per square foot of streambed.

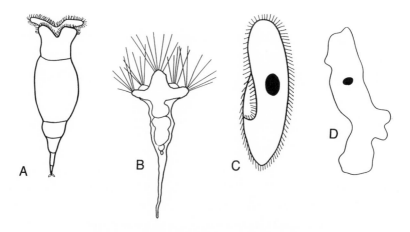

Examples of two kinds of rotifers (A, B)
and protozoans *Paramecium* (C) and *Amoeba* (D).

◆   ◆   ◆

Their name Rotifera (and Rotatoria) derive from an anterior pair of roundish openings, called a *corona*, through which the animals feed. This feeding behavior takes the form of whirling of the corona, two structures turning in the opposite direction of each other. The corona contains pulsating cilia, or hairs, which beat rhythmically in such a way that, from a head-on view, the corona resembles a pair of rotating machines. From the corona, the animal body tapers to the posterior end. The corona and body shape occur in many variations, depending on species.

Some of these, fairy-like and diaphanous, are regarded as the most beautiful forms in the animal world.

Almost all range in size from 100 to 500 microns (1/250 to 1/50 inch). It is notable that rotifers do not grow after hatching from eggs—they simply produce more eggs. Good observation requires a microscope. Most are planktonic and can readily be found swimming in samples of open water in any lake or pond. However, the class Bdelloidea is benthic in lakes and streams. Instead of swimming, these rotifers crawl about on substrates such as macrophytes, with the aid of a "foot" complete with two retractable "toes."

Like many of the meiofauna, rotifers are omnivorous, feeding on epilithic algae and bacteria, microfauna and other meiofauna, and organic detritus. Rotifers, in turn, are fed upon by larger invertebrates.

◆   ◆   ◆

NEMATODES, OR ROUNDWORMS—phylum Nematoda—often make up a significant portion of the meiofauna. Most members of this phylum are parasitic in higher animals (and often give humans trouble). Most free-living species are marine, and some of the freshwater forms are capable of occupying extreme habitats such as polar ice pools, cave streams, saline lakes, and hot springs.

Only a few species are free-living in the meiofauna of stream sediments. In shape, nematodes resemble earthworms, with circular cross-sections, but they are not segmented and are much smaller than earthworms.

Nematode adult length is most often only about 1/4 inch. It is their diameter that qualifies them to be included in the meiofauna group—less than 40 microns. Nematodes molt as they grow, with several instars, but the lengths of their life cycles are little known. Not good swimmers, their thrashing movements propel them about among vegetation and sediment particles on the bottom. The food of nematodes includes algae, bacteria, and many protozoans—omnivores, like many other members of the meiofauna. They are usually present in much lower abundance than other members of the meiofauna—typically only one to two percent of the total meiofauna. Interestingly, they are much more important in ocean sediments, often around 90 percent. Theory is that nematodes occupied their ecological niche earlier in the ocean, a niche largely filled in streams by small insects (which are not present in salt water).

◆   ◆   ◆

OLIGOCHAETA, A CLASS IN THE PHYLUM ANNELIDA, or segmented worms, includes the common earthworms with which most of us started our angling careers. In all probability these were terrestrial worms dug from the family garden or from a rotting garbage heap.

Most aquatic oligochaetes feed by ingesting sediment containing organic matter and digesting the associated bacteria and detritus. In streams, they may be found mostly in quiet pockets of organic sediment. Lotic and lentic species are not much different from each other in appearance or in the microhabitats they occupy.

Aquatic oligochaetes are small in length as well as in diameter, with length ranging from less than one millimeter (1/32 inch) to about 30 millimeters (1 1/4 inches). So it is likely that the occasional large worm you see in a stream is a terrestrial earthworm that has somehow entered the stream from the riparian zone, probably in runoff from a heavy rainfall.

The class Oligochaeta includes 10 families in which aquatic or semiaquatic species occur. Two of these families interest us most in streams: Naididae and Tubificidae. Both groups are *cosmopolitan*, with worldwide distributions. A few naidids (members of Naididae) are very small, have some swimming ability, and are not restricted to the sediment. Naidids of several species make up important proportions of the meiofauna.

The tubificids include the great majority of aquatic oligochaetes and are restricted to organic sediments. They often occur in huge colonial masses. They are pollution-tolerant and develop into colonies in sewage treatment facilities such as sewage lagoons.

The most common species is *Tubifex tubifex,* commonly called the "sludge worm," regarded as an "indicator species" of severe organic pollution. This species also has a great proclivity to thrive in the bottom habitat of polluted lakes and streams.

The same physiology that enables tubificids to survive and prosper where oxygen is low or absent promotes dense populations also in the bottoms of lakes and reservoirs where deposited organic matter accumulates. The angler's San Juan Worm, fished as a nymph, may very well imitate the tubificid worm. Low-level discharges from dams—such as the Navaho Dam on the San Juan River in New Mexico—are often intended to create cool water capable of holding trout and creating very productive tailwater trout fisheries—like that found in the San Juan River.

It seems likely that tubificid worms wash out with dam discharges into the streams below. So in these streams, the San Juan Worm is often the most effective producer of tailwater trout!

◆   ◆   ◆

FINALLY, WE SHOULD REMEMBER that all animals larger than meiofauna (macroinvertebrates, fish) start out as small ones. Thus, almost all stream macroinvertebrates begin life as tiny members of the meiofauna, even though they may soon reach a size that can be imitated with fur and feathers. But as small animals, they need food particles that are correspondingly small and smaller—other meiofauna, microfauna, and microorganisms like bacteria and fungi. Of course, as meiofauna, they in turn are preyed upon by larger animals, providing essential sustenance to macroinvertebrates and small fish. Virtually all newly hatched fish fry depend on meiofauna for their first foods after using up their yolk sacs.

Small larval insects constitute a high proportion of the stream bottom meiofauna, especially small species such as those in the mayfly genus *Tricorhythodes,* the microcaddis, and virtually all chironomid (midge) larvae. Many samples of stream meiofauna include huge numbers of very small larval chironomids.

So when we view the large animals that enrich our stream and river experiences—a rising trout or leaping smallmouth bass, a mating swarm of mayflies at dusk, or just a large caddisfly adult on a cabin window—it is important to appreciate the complex community of unseen life on the stream bottom that make these larger visions and experiences possible.

When disaster assaults a streambed—a pulse of pesticide, a flood from a channelized stream, or a massive sediment load from a carelessly cultivated field—it probably strikes first at the tiny forms of life in the meiofauna. Their loss reverberates up through higher trophic levels to impoverish the larger forms of stream life that so visibly support the quality of life for us river lovers.

TECHNICAL REFERENCES:

Palmer, Margaret A. 1990. Temporal and spatial dynamics of meiofauna within the hyporheic zone of Goose Creek, Virginia. *Journal of the North American Benthological Society.* Volume 9, pages 17-25.

Pennak, Robert W. 1988. Ecology of the freshwater meiofauna. Pages 39-60 *in* Robert P. Higgins and Hjalmar Thiel, editors. *Introduction to the Study of Meiofauna.* Smithsonian Institution Press, Washington, DC.

Shiozawa, Dennis K. 1991. Microcrustacea from the benthos of nine Minnesota streams. *Journal of the North American Benthological Society.* Volume 10, pages 286-299.

RiverSketch

GHOST OF THE RED RIVER VALLEY

T HE HAUNTING MELODY of Canada's classic cowboy song, "Red River Valley," is a prescient reminder of the watery ghost that revisits the valley each springtime—*flood.* Always unwelcome, the spreading waters bring trouble, sometimes disaster.

This ghost first materialized about 12,000 years ago with the melting of the miles-thick glaciers that had covered most of North America, on and off, for two million years. The glaciers' offspring was a contrary river that refused to follow the rules and flows from the bottom of the map to the top: the Red River of the North. It is said to be a river that runs amok while standing still.

Into a shallow but vast, spreading depression in a newly uncovered landscape, the decaying glaciers poured their icy meltwater. The inundated region was huge, almost beyond comprehension. It comprised parts of present-day Saskatchewan, Manitoba, Ontario, North Dakota, and Minnesota. This enormous area of land and the resulting water body, Glacial Lake Agassiz, is now estimated to have formed the most extensive freshwater lake ever to have existed on Earth. More than 200,000 square miles in extent, this greatest lake covered more area than all the present Great Lakes combined.

Of course, the shape and size of Lake Agassiz varied during its 3,000-year existence, enlarging as more ice melted northward, shrinking as outlets were gradually uncovered at lower and lower elevations. At the southern tip of the huge lake, Glacial River Warren drained some of it, creating the trench-like valley of the present-day Minnesota River and much of the Upper Mississippi. To the east, the huge lake eventually drained away through the Great Lakes basins and the St. Lawrence River to the Atlantic Ocean. At its extreme, meltwater extended from the lake's southern tip at the head of Glacial River Warren northward 700 miles to its northern shore of ice near Hudson Bay, where depths reached 600 to 700 feet.

Glacial Lake Agassiz, the largest lake ever,
and Lake Superior, the largest today.
(From Ojakangas and Matsch, 1982.)

Today's flood problem lies in the Red River's northerly flow. Because the advance of springtime also flows northward, the accumulated winter's snow and ice melts first in the river's headwaters in North Dakota and Minnesota—at a time when the Red's winter pack of ice still remains frozen in Canada. Meltwater rushes downstream (up the map), only to be blocked by the remaining winter ice to the north. Thus the perennial ghost—Glacial Lake Agassiz—returns annually to haunt the old valley.

As the glacial lake receded, water levels fell, not continuously and uniformly but in steps that remained in place at different levels, each step for hundreds or thousands of years. Beaches were formed whose existence today provides convenient time markers to help us ascertain the chronology of changes in lake levels. While the great lake existed, spreading wetlands and marshes extended behind the beaches to the horizons, where early settlers reported concentrations of waterfowl that, when flying, literally blotted out the sun.

The same settlers recognized the fertility of the lake bed sediments for farming, and these soils have become one of the richest agricultural areas in the world. Early settlers raised wheat, but diversity later became the rule; sugar beets and sunflowers predominate now.

The great marshes have been ditched and drained, and a myriad of small streams channelized. In 1971, scientists from the American Fisheries Society estimated that about 30,000 miles of streams had been channelized, mostly in Minnesota. And this was undoubtedly an underestimate, because channelized streams are shortened versions of the original. The spreading flatness of the valley remains the most intensively drained area for agriculture in the world. Instead of percolating into the soil, springtime meltwaters today rush to the Red River channel, exacerbating the flood.

The record-breaking flood of 1997, when the Red River spread literally from 30 to 40 miles wide and inundated farms, homes, and whole towns, bringing grief and dislocation of thousands of human lives. An outpouring of helpers provided shelter and food and everyday supplies to help clean up. Thousands of volunteers spontaneously appeared from hundreds of miles away and streamed into the stricken areas to help. All of which provided relief and some comfort, but not a cessation of the perennial return of springtime disaster.

Many minds now turn to devising methods of preventing, or at least lessening, the annual springtime calamity. The re-creation of wetlands and marshes behind the old beaches, which would allow snowmelt and spring rain to penetrate as groundwater instead of rushing to the river channel, could help.

The rich soil will continue to be cultivated for its valuable production, remaining a high priority. But perhaps new minds and perspectives can devise fresh approaches to land usage, and imaginative technology can keep more of the valley's water in place, instead of allowing it to rush downvalley and enlarge the problem.

But for now, as long as snow falls and melts, and the Red River of the North runs up the map, the ghost of Glacial Lake Agassiz will return. Perhaps someday mankind will know how to accommodate it and use it wisely, instead of doing battle with it each year. Perhaps someday springtime visitors will again include returning clouds of migrating ducks, geese, and shorebirds, perhaps to occupy their watery homes behind the old beaches—instead of the ghost of Glacial Lake Agassiz.

SELECTED REFERENCES:

Flint, Richard Foster. 1947. *Glacial Geology and the Pleistocene Epoch.* John Wiley & Sons, New York.
Ojakangas, Richard W., and Charles L. Matsch. 1982. *Minnesota's Geology.* University of Minnesota Press, Minneapolis.

Chapter 18

HYPORHEOS

PERHAPS IT WAS ONLY REASONABLE for fisheries biologists to assess the quantity of benthic invertebrates (the benthos) as the measure of productivity and fish-food availability. After all, the term *benthos* meant the assemblage of organisms on the streambed. And they had known for a century or more that animals in the stream's bottom fauna were the primary food source for fish.

Perhaps, too, we can be forgiven for not recognizing the possibility that some of these same benthic animals might occupy the sand, gravel, and stone matrix below—sometimes *deeply* below—the streambed surface.

But it was only a few decades ago that we came to appreciate this important ecological group—as we had the meiofauna. Again, it was Professor Hynes who mainly brought the concept of a deeper habitat to the attention of stream ecologists in North America. He emphasized the *hyporheic zone* (hypo- = below, or lower; -rheic = water currents). Soon the assemblage of animals occupying this ecological niche deep below the streambed became known as the *hyporheos.*

◆   ◆   ◆

AT FIRST, THE HYPORHEIC ZONE—dark, isolated, with only tiny living spaces—would seem to be an unfriendly place for life. Yet many forms prosper in this apparently hostile region. What is the living space like down there, and what are its dimensions and potential? At first, we knew almost nothing of the shape and borders of this underground region; as it turned out, the extent was at first grossly underestimated, and stream ecologists around the world were baffled in their attempts to probe the full reaches of the hyporheic zone. The biggest surprise came with the discovery of hyporheic organisms far removed from the regular channels of some rivers—miles away.

New results came rapidly with the efforts of many researchers who investigated the physical nature of the hyporheic zone. Depth varies according to the looseness of the gravel, but in small streams, at least, about one to two feet below the bed came to be an approximate average. Streambed particles tend to be smaller at greater depths, but where they remain loosely packed, many invertebrates can be found down to several feet in small streams and more than 30 feet in large rivers. Hyporheic zones tend to be smaller in limestone streams, where the cementing effect of finely ground calcium carbonate results in a heavily compacted matrix. Of course, where a stream flows directly on bedrock, there can be no hyporheic zone.

The hyporheic zone is not limited to the region immediately below the channel and between the banks. Rather, it often extends laterally beneath the channel's banks, particularly under extensive floodplains, where riverine water flow is connected to deep hyporheic water. Such connected water has been found under floodplains miles away from the river itself, and these distant regions contain benthic animals the same as in the river.

Hyporheic water under floodplain corridors runs parallel to river channels. It enters by downwelling at the upstream end of the floodplain, flows through, and returns to the surface by upwelling as springs and small brooks, eventually entering the open river at the lower end of the floodplain. Most river floodplains, especially along large rivers with gravel beds, have extensive hyporheic zones beneath their surfaces, complete with animal species originating in the river benthos.

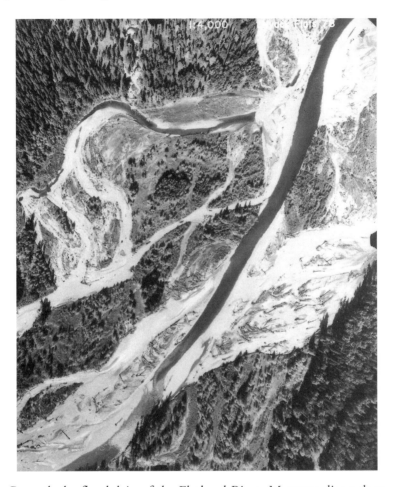

Beneath the floodplain of the Flathead River, Montana, lies a deep hyporheic zone, reaching laterally from the river for several miles. (Photo courtesy of Jack A. Stanford, University of Montana.)

The pore size of individual interstitial spaces and the total volume of space define the physical dimensions of the living space for animals. Pore sizes are microscopic in sand and silt, where meiofauna occurs, but nearer the surface, macroinvertebrates up to an inch or two in length may occupy larger pore spaces.

The fractional volume of interstitial space, or the porosity of an inhabited hyporheic zone, has been found in the neighborhood of 1/4 or 1/3. That is, a cubic foot of hyporheic gravel (close to 2,000 cubic inches) will have a total volume of habitable space of about 500 to 600 cubic inches. Porosity decreases with a heterogeneous mixture of gravel and sand sizes, in which small particles fill the spaces among larger particles.

Temperature and oxygen content are two physical factors critical to animals in the hyporheos. Water in the hyporheic zone tends to be more constant in temperature—cooler in summer and warmer in winter—than in the open stream above. The deeper in the hyporheic zone, the more consistent is water temperature.

Oxygen is essential in the habitat of all animals, but it is variable among the hyporheic zones of different streams. Although open stream water is usually well supplied with oxygen diffused from the atmosphere, hyporheic oxygen depends mainly on downwelling surface water. Although oxygen content may drop quickly to lower concentrations in the hyporheic zones of small streams, the more massive gravel deposits in large rivers usually contain sufficient oxygen for animal life many feet deeper.

The hyporheic zone is an *ecotone*, a transitional area between two ecologically different areas—in this case, the stream above and the groundwater below. Ecotones of all kinds are extremely dynamic environments. The environmental conditions of hyporheic zones change with weather, season, groundwater conditions, and other factors, and hyporheic water often becomes a mixture of surface water and deeper groundwater. The effects on invertebrate life vary accordingly. The hyporheic zone fluctuates with floods and drought, oxygen variations, mineral particle size, and animal populations above it.

With this additional perception of the hyporheic habitat, newly discovered and studied, we now enjoy a greatly expanded view of the natural stream, as well as an expanded concept of the stream ecosystem, a major advance in stream ecology.

◆   ◆   ◆

THE HYPORHEOS—THE FAUNA of the hyporheic zone—is a mixture of animals from different habitats. The hyporheic zone is sunless and dark, like caves and other subterranean habitats, but the fauna here does not necessarily comprise true cave animals. The hyporheic zone is really part of the *stream*: water currents flow, and animal inhabitants are relatively free to come and go between the upper hyporheic zone and the stream above.

This jaw-toothed cylinder, turned into a streambed,
is one technique to sample organisms in a shallow hyporheic zone.

In the absence of light, photosynthesizing plants cannot occur in these underground waters of the hyporheic zone. Consequently, strictly herbivorous animals cannot exist. Some algal cells may penetrate from the periphyton of the open streambed at the surface, but for the most part, the absence of light precludes primary production by green plants. On the other hand, detritivores feed on nonliving organic matter and heterotrophic microorganisms, such as bacteria and fungi. The hyporheic environment may even be more productive in its microbial, detritivorous, and carnivorous fauna than in surface waters.

In previous chapters, we discussed the various forms of life that make use of the energy in allochthonous organic matter. In the hyporheic zone, such food material produced externally and transported to deeper strata is essential. Fine particulate organic matter (FPOM), filtering downward or drifting with the water flow through the gravel, is one obvious source of energy. Another source is dissolved organic matter (DOM) contained not only in surface runoff and tributaries, but also in the groundwater itself.

In the dark of hyporheic zones, FPOM and DOM are processed by microorganisms in much the same way as allochthonous leaves and woody debris are processed in the open stream. Fungi require nitrate, as they do in the open stream, but here the source of nitrate is mainly water that has previously percolated downward from surface sources. Another source of nitrate for the hyporheic zone is nitrifying bacteria associated with certain plants that grow on gravel-based floodplains—like alders.

The result of all this microscopic activity is the production of *biofilms* on the surfaces of small gravel, sand grains, and other fine particles of organic matter. Periphyton (containing algae) does not occur in the hyporheic zone, but epilithon (on the surfaces of stones) is an example of biofilms in the hyporheic zone.

Hyporheic biofilms are the great generators of food for the animals of the hyporheos. Biofilms include not only the bacteria and fungi that absorb DOM and nutrients from the water but also the matrix of secreted matter and sugars—the "slime community"—that contain protozoans, rotifers, and other microscopic animal life. Animals of the meiofauna—small invertebrates and crustaceans—then scrape and glean the biofilms for their rich resources of food, nutrients, and energy. In turn, macroinvertebrates—like stoneflies and caddisflies from the open stream benthos above—feed upon these tiny animals, providing food for other predators, like stonefly nymphs.

The trophic pyramid of the hyporheic zone is remarkable in its function of energy transfer. It begins with dissolved substances and fine particulates in the interstitial flow among sand grains. Then bacteria and fungi process FPOM and absorb

DOM and nutrients, adding to the biofilms on sand grains and other tiny particles. Then microscopic animals, like rotifers and protozoans, feed on the matrix of organic matter and microbes in the biofilms, to eventually provide food for other, larger animals of the meiofauna, like microcrustaceans. Finally, the larger macroinvertebrates like carnivorous aquatic insects and other invertebrates feed on them. All of these groups can be found in the hyporheos, in shallow strata in small streams and deep down in the lower hyporheic layers of large rivers.

Does this dynamic but unseen system contribute to the production of flying, mating insects, predaceous stonefly nymphs and other predators, and crawling crustaceans like scuds, sow bugs, and crayfish—all so tasty to trout and smallmouth bass?

The answer is *probably*. But stream and river science has not fully answered these questions yet. We know generally *who* is down there, and what *functions* they perform, but so far we have little *quantitative* information, like feeding and growth rates and secondary production. We do not have the *numbers* yet that tell us the calories transferred from trophic level to trophic level, from prey to predator, from the darkness of the hyporheic zone to the sunlit stream overhead.

Yet, the mysteries of hyporheic zones have the attention of many scholars currently at work. No doubt, their intense involvement in research will give us these answers and numbers in the future.

◆   ◆   ◆

THEORETICALLY, THE FAUNA of the hyporheic zone should consist of many of the same kinds and species of invertebrates as those found in the open stream benthos. And to a large extent, this is true.

In the upper strata of the hyporheic zone, all kinds of benthic animals can be found, particularly shallow burrowers—like many midge larvae, scuds, and *Hexagenia* mayfly nymphs—which occupy loose sediments and gravel. This is their normal habitat; all benthic invertebrates need places or means to hide, and surface particles and their interstices provide just such cover and protection.

But down below these loose surface particles, the kinds of animals and habitats change. Oxygen, temperature, and food availability can change drastically, and the fauna must adapt in its composition.

Two major changes occur with increasing depth into the hyporheic: species change to smaller sized organisms, and feeding groups shift from mainly herbivores/detritivores at the surface, to detritivores/predators down below. Finally, the predominant group will be the microfauna that scrapes and gleans the biofilms for bacteria and fungi. Occasionally, large invertebrates—fishes such as darters and sculpins (normal benthic fishes), crayfish, and some large insect larvae—are found down deep, especially in large streams, but they are not permanent members of the hyporheos, requiring the surface habitat at least for reproduction.

In the top layer of streambed sediments, regular inhabitants probably come and go between the hyporheic zone and the open stream at will. Many insects must ascend to the open stream surface for emergence as flying adults. Some of these spend their entire aquatic life cycle in the hyporheos and migrate up to the surface *only* to emerge for reproduction. Newly hatched, early instars of the next generation may migrate back into the hyporheos.

Deeper, we find mostly the meiofauna. Great numbers of small midge larvae are often found several feet down into the hyporheic. These must later ascend to the surface for emergence, mating, and oviposition. These midge larvae are usually the only insects found at these depths, but permanent members of the meiofauna also occur here, particularly microcrustaceans.

Finally, at the greatest depths, individual spaces are tiny, oxygen may be low, and temperatures are constant year-round. All of these factors create niches for species that live permanently at these depths, including the microfauna that utilize microbial food in biofilms.

There are many exceptions, depending on the physical nature of the hyporheic particles. For example, large macroinvertebrates, such as some stonefly nymphs have been found in abundance both deep and far removed from rivers. Gravel strata, perhaps glacially deposited thousands of years ago, offer large interstitial spaces and good water flow. At the other end of the spectrum, some of the microfauna exist where hyporheic strata occur in close association with groundwater, which may have its own true subterranean microfauna.

Certain animal categories with typically elongated forms, such as nematodes and oligochaetes, can wriggle into small crevices much too small for other organisms of the same total length. Other species—mollusks, cased caddis larvae, and crustaceans—are robust enough to force their way through small spaces. And other tiny animals with swimming ability can move by swimming through small interstitial spaces. The dark hyporheic is a diverse and strange world.

◆   ◆   ◆

THE HYPORHEIC ZONE SERVES THE ANIMALS of the upper, open stream with a crucially important function: as a refuge in times of environmental disruptions. Floods, drought, and pollution can destroy communities of life in the open stream, but the hyporheic zone, isolated from surface stresses, protects many of the same animals during surface disturbance. Afterward, these members of the hyporheos are available to recolonize surface streambeds—restoring normal populations and productivity.

In the past, stream ecologists and fisheries biologists were often puzzled by such restorations. After viewing a stream that in drought appeared to be completely dry, insects reappeared, sometimes in advanced larval stages nearing adult emergence, indicating that these were *survivors*, rather than a new generation produced by flying adults. Even fish populations may return quickly to a normal fish fauna. Floods, too, can decimate or nearly destroy whole populations of invertebrates and fish, but normal communities of stream life return, provided by the reservoir of life in the hyporheic zone.

Of course, other mechanisms contribute to such recolonization: drift of invertebrates from upstream, upstream dispersal from downstream, eggs laid by migrating fish or flying adult insects in both directions. Even when circumstances make such mechanisms impossible—for example, when the same disturbance occurs in the headwaters or above waterfall barriers, still the puzzling recovery of populations often occurs.

Hyporheic zones serve as refuges through many other kinds of natural disasters. Sedimentation and even wild fires crossing a small stream may decimate streambed populations, but animals that seek refuge in the hyporheic zone survive. Some animal populations *increase* in the hyporheic zone during these disturbances, reappearing at the surface afterward—evidence that benthic animals in the open stream actively move *downward* when the stream environment approaches unfavorable conditions. The hyporheic zone thus serves as a resistant refuge, continuing to function even when weather-related calamities or human-caused disturbances, such as fire and pollution, decimate or eliminate open streambed communities.

◆   ◆   ◆

WHEN PROFESSOR HYNES'S DATA on invertebrates in the hyporheic zone were first published, a shock wave of uncertainty and despair swept through the stream and river scientific community. He reported finding 80 percent of a stream's benthos in the hyporheic zone and only 20 percent in traditional bottom fauna samplers. All of which meant—to our horror—that as much as *80 percent was being missed!* The finding cast doubt on virtually all previous sampling of streambed benthos.

Had all previous measurements of abundance, standing stock, and secondary production been grossly underestimated by such a huge proportion? Should all previous quantitative research on stream benthos now be cast in doubt—or corrected by multiplying by a factor of *five?* The mere thought was daunting, to say the least.

Later work revealed some qualifications, however. In the deep gravel beds of large rivers, numbers were indeed high, for small individuals and large, and some species not even present on the surface were found in the deep gravels. But in small streams flowing over bedrock and those with heavily compacted and cemented streambeds, no significant quantities of macroinvertebrates were found below top surfaces of streambeds. Furthermore, Hynes's initial figures were of *numbers,* not weight or *biomass,* so that the percentages first reported were not so devastating in terms of biomass and production, as the data on numbers alone would suggest. In data later reported from small streams, deeper-living organisms, if any, were tiny members of the meiofauna (discussed in the previous chapter), unlike the major macroinvertebrates commonly found in the deep gravels of large rivers.

The key element here is *variation:* all streams are different. Conditions in the hyporheic zone vary greatly among streams—with geology and hydrology, water chemistry, streambed sediments, and species of animals. The early results, alarming as they first seemed, alerted us to an extended view of the benthos, to the need to consider the hyporheos and potential errors in the design of future sampling programs.

Most important, discoveries of this invisible fauna have added a truly significant and fascinating component to our view of stream ecology. Early findings on the hyporheos, we now know, did not totally invalidate all previous studies. They did make us more aware of this vastly important element in our science and cause us to adjust our perspective, not only on the total benthos, but also of the greater stream ecosystem.

Early work on stream ecology, helpful and crucial as it was, concerned mainly small streams with headwater reaches in deciduous forests, mainly first- through third-order trout streams. Our view was restricted to narrow riparian zones and small hyporheic zones, if any. But later work on larger rivers revealed more extensive systems. We now view large rivers with much wider corridors, surface streams flowing over and through massive deposits of sand and gravel, downwelling water in the upper regions and upwelling farther downstream. Broad floodplains of river-sorted gravel, or *alluvium*, contain not only flowing, oxygenated water underground, rich in dissolved nutrients and organic matter, but also a host of aquatic invertebrates, small and large, that make special use of this subterranean habitat.

The new perspective has engaged the attention of stream ecologists worldwide. Our expanded view of the stream ecosystem is apparent now in three dimensions: vertically from surface waters to the deep hyporheic, laterally from the channel to surrounding floodplains and ancient gravel deposits miles away, and from upstream to down through a fascinating maze of hydrologic and biologic interactions.

It is true that studies on the hyporheic zone and the animals that inhabit it, the hyporheos, first both startled and enlightened us. Our view of the stream ecosystem has been greatly expanded, and new knowledge has enriched our appreciation of the great diversity of life at the bottom.

TECHNICAL REFERENCES:

Gibert, Janine, Dan L. Danielopol, and Jack A. Stanford, editors. 1994. *Groundwater Ecology*. Academic Press, San Diego, California.

North American Benthological Society. 1993. Perspectives on the hyporheic zone (a symposium of eight articles). *Journal of the North American Benthological Society*. Volume 12, pages 40-99.

Stanford, Jack A. 1998. Rivers in the landscape: Introduction to the special issue on riparian and groundwater ecology. *Freshwater Biology*. Volume 40, pages 402-406 (lead article of a special collection on hyporheic and riparian concerns).

RiverSketch

"RIVERS OF AMERICA"

IN 1937, PUBLISHERS FARRAR & RINEHART, INC., New York City, began a series of volumes about American rivers. The series became a classic publishing event lasting through 38 years: the *Rivers of America*.

The series was the brainstorm of Constance Lindsay Skinner, who sensed that it was the rhythm of flowing water that pulsed beneath the struggle and maturing of frontier life. Europeans changed to Americans along rivers, emerging with "the democratic ideal and American individuality." It was her intention to inculcate the reader with the intimate impact of the *river* on developing America. Artists and poets, who could sense and feel the river's rhythm were better at that job, she felt, than scientists and historians. Her initial plan was to develop the series into 24 volumes on rivers; the series blossomed, through nearly four decades, to 62.

These are not scientific tomes on natural history or hydrology, nor canoe or fishing guides. They are an interpretation of history—from the perspective of watersheds and the rivers within. It was a unique approach—unprecedented—and much more relevant to the colonizing of America than political boundaries. After all, early immigrants used rivers for getting where they wanted to go, for finding suitable land for homes and crops, for domestic water. The influence of a watershed on a growing nation made more sense to the cultural history of the country, as the nation grew and eventually became independent.

Most volumes include only a single, entire river or watershed. There are some interesting exceptions. For example, *Twin Rivers: The Raritan and the Passaic*, by Wildes, includes a pair of New Jersey streams whose waters together enter the ocean to surround Staten Island. Footner's *Rivers of the Eastern Shore* includes 17 streams emptying into the Chesapeake from the east side of the bay. *Salt Rivers of the Massachusetts Shore,* by Howe, traces the history of southeastern Massachusetts, with its many streams running into Buzzards Bay. Two rivers required two volumes each: *The Tennessee*—before and after the Civil War—by Davidson, and America's largest river split into two portions—*Upper Mississippi,* by Havighurst, and *Lower Mississippi,* by Carter. Some other unusual river volumes include *The Everglades,* a shallow stream flowing slowly through miles-wide plains of saw grass, by Douglas; *The Humboldt,* a stream of Nevada's arid lands that flows for many miles but ends by sinking into the desert sands, by Morgan; and *The Chagres,* by Minter, the river that traced part of the route of the Panama Canal, its natural flow into the Atlantic, but now emptying into both Atlantic and Pacific oceans. What must be the shortest river in the series is Braider's *The Niagara,* connecting Lakes Erie and Ontario, only 35 miles. As might be expected, most rivers are in the United States. However, several are in Canada: the Fraser, Mackenzie, Saskatchewan, parts of the Yukon and Columbia, and, as border river, the St. Lawrence.

Names of publishers changed as the series went on. Farrar & Rinehart continued until about the mid-1940s, then changed to Rinehart and Company, which in turn changed to Holt, Rinehart, and Winston in the early 1960s for the rest of the series.

Most volumes follow a formulary sequence: a chapter on geology, then aboriginal peoples, white explorers, the fur trade, timber harvest, the steamboat era, agriculture, political development, and finally some interesting human characters. Black and white drawings illustrate each book, varying in style. There is little on the ecology of the watershed, or environmentalism, although some mention of natural history enters the narrative in the last few volumes. The authors are not scientists, not biologists or hydrologists, nor historians. Rather they are novelists and poets, who, above all others, Ms. Skinner averred, could best fulfill the assignment of *interpretation.* This condition, of course, makes for easy and inspired reading. (And yes, I have all volumes and have read them all—honest!)

Each chapter starts out with a stylized, illustrated map, entertaining as well as informative, and ends with a bibliography and an index.

My favorites? A tough question. They vary in style, length, detail, and approach, but all make good reading. Among the ones I enjoyed especially were Carter's *Lower Mississippi*, Banta's *Ohio*, and Frank Waters's *Colorado* (no relation). I truly liked them all. It was a real treat to explore the history of America from this new view of rivers.

Here is the list, in order of date of publication:

Kennebec: Cradle of Americans. 1937. Robert P. Tristram Coffin.

Upper Mississippi: A Wilderness Saga. 1937. Walter Havighurst.

Powder River: Let 'er Buck. 1938. Struthers Burt.

Suwannee River: Strange Green Land. 1938. Cecile Hulse Matschat.

The Hudson. 1939. Carl Carmer.

The James. 1939. Blair Niles.

The Sacramento: River of Gold. 1939. Julian Dana.

The Arkansas. 1940. Clyde Brion Davis.

The Delaware. 1940. Henry Emerson Wildes.

The Illinois. 1940. James Gray.

The Wabash. 1940. William E. Wilson.

The Brandywine. 1941. Henry Seidel Canby.

The Charles. 1941. Arthur Bernon Tourtellot.

The Kaw: The Heart of a Nation. 1941, Floyd Benjamin Streeter.

The Allegheny. 1942. Frederick Way, Jr.

The Chicago. 1942. Harry Hansen.

The Kentucky. 1942. Thomas D. Clark.

Lower Mississippi. 1942. Hodding Carter.

The Sangamon. 1942. Edgar Lee Masters.

The St. Lawrence. 1942. Henry Beston.

The Wisconsin: River of a Thousand Isles. 1942. August Derleth.

The Humboldt: Highroad of the West. 1943. Dale L. Morgan.

The St. Johns: A Parade of Diversities. 1943. Branch Cabell and A.J. Hanna.

Twin Rivers: The Raritan and the Passaic. 1943. Henry Emerson Wildes.

Rivers of the Eastern Shore: Seventeen Maryland Rivers. 1944. Hulbert Footner.

The Missouri. 1945. Stanley Vestal.

The Salinas: Upside-down River. 1945. Anne B. Fisher.

The Shenandoah. 1945. Julia Davis

The Colorado. 1946. Frank Waters.

The Housatonic: Puritan River. 1946. Chard Powers Smith.

The Tennessee. Volume I: The Old River, Frontier to Secession. 1946. Donald Davidson.

The Connecticut. 1947. Walter Hard.

The Everglades: River of Grass. 1947. Marjory Stoneman Douglas.

The Chagres: River of Westward Passage. 1948. John Easter Minter.

The Mohawk. 1948. Codman Hislop.

The Tennessee. Volume II: The New River, Civil War to TVA. 1948. Donald Davidson.

The Mackenzie. 1949. Leslie Roberts.

The Monongahela. 1949. Richard Bissell.

The Ohio. 1949. R.E. Banta.

The Potomac. 1949. Frederick Gutheim.

The Winooski: Heartway of Vermont. 1949. Ralph Nading Hill.

The Fraser. 1950. Bruce Hutchison.

The Saskatchewan. 1950. Marjorie Wilkins Campbell.

Salt Rivers of the Massachusetts Shore. 1951. Henry F. Howe.

The Gila: River of the Southwest. 1951. Edwin Corle.

The Savannah. 1951. Thomas L. Stokes.

The Yazoo River. 1954. Frank E. Smith.

The French Broad. 1955. Wilma Dykeman.

The Susquehanna. 1955. Carl Carmer.

The Columbia. 1956. Stewart H. Holbrook.

River of the Carolinas: The Santee. 1956. Henry Savage, Jr.

The Merrimack. 1958. Raymond P. Holden.

The Minnesota: Forgotten River. 1962. Evan Jones.

The Genesee. 1963. Henry W. Clune.

The Cape Fear. 1965. Malcolm Ross.

The St. Croix: Midwest Border River. 1965. James Taylor Dunn.

The Cuyahoga. 1966. William Donahue Ellis.

The Allagash. 1968. Lew Dietz.

The Fraser, by Bruce Hutchison, documented the exploration
of British Columbia's Fraser River, one of North America's wildest.
(Photo courtesy of Thomas G. Northcote,
University of British Columbia.)

The Yukon. 1968. Richard Mathews.
The Niagara. 1972. Donald Braider.
The Cumberland. 1973. James McCague.
The American: River of el Dorado. 1974. Margaret Sanborn.

Supplement: *Songs of the Rivers of America,* 1942. Edited by Carl Carmer, music arrangements by Dr. Albert Sirmay. This is a treasure chest of folk songs about rivers. Nearly a hundred are included here, which is probably a small fraction of titles known elsewhere or lost in the mountains and prairies in the retelling (or resinging). There are plenty of old favorites, such as The Wide Missouri, Red River Valley, and Darling Nelly Gray. (Sadly, a couple of my favorites are not included—Old Man River and The Wabash Cannonball!)

Part Five

A Fine Kettle
of Fish

Introduction to Part Five

A FINE KETTLE OF FISH

TO ALMOST ANYONE first viewing a new stream, scientist or not, the first question that pops to mind is: What kind of fish are in here? Paddlers may wonder what there is to be seen at the bottom of a clear pool; anglers, upon noting the species, quickly crank out a mental list of tackle they will need and how to fish that certain riffle and pool. After all, fish are the most visible denizens of the water, and what kinds may determine the viewers' plans for the day.

In the birthing times of river and stream ecology, it was fish that first occupied biologists' attention. When river pollution first became a matter of concern in the late 1800s and early 1900s, the losses and reductions in fish populations were what mattered most. And note Professor Shelford's early work on the fish distribution of fish species through a stream's course, published in 1911. Furthermore, the first attempts to classify streams were based on the fish present—for example, Marcel Huet's fish *zones*.

Of all the biological components in a stream ecosystem, none have received as much human attention in the way of management—and mismanagement—as have fish. We have subjected them to unconscionable exploitation, regulated them with laws and rules based on ignorance, severely damaged or eliminated their natural habitats, overwhelmed and contaminated their populations with hatchery stock of poor quality, and introduced foreign species that resulted in the extirpation of native species. Now we are tinkering with genetic modifications that offer frightful potential for the future.

Only recently have a few folks—anglers, biologists, writers, outdoors users of several kinds—begun to point out the value and importance of Earth's *natural* ecosystems to the quality of our lives. Some of us now believe that evolutionary progress has produced natural communities, processes of energy flow, and plant and animal species that are far more stable and durable—and more productive of recreational quality—than all of our arrogant judgments of how to improve on nature.

Nowhere has the result of such presumptuous tamperings with natural systems been so apparent as in the recreational fisheries of our streams and rivers. Examples are legion: from the obliteration of a tiny trout stream by housing or industrial development, carried out by a boosterish small town eager to raise its tax base, to the gigantic dams on the Columbia River, which have eliminated forever naturally evolved genetic stocks of Pacific salmon.

A few voices, however, have raised the banner for conservation of natural systems and native fish species. For example, Robert H. Smith in his classic *Native Trout of North America*, and Robert J. Behnke in his books and columns for *Trout*, the magazine of Trout Unlimited. I predict there will be many more voices—rising in the future to a groundswell.

My major objective in preparing this volume was not simply to inform and entertain (although those are good objectives, too), but mainly to further my readers' deeper appreciation of *natural* river systems. I believe these new perceptions will lead not only to a stronger sense of stewardship, but also to a sharper satisfaction—not only in the joy of fishing, but in all other river uses as well.

◆　　　　　　◆　　　　　　◆

YOU WILL NOTICE THAT UP UNTIL NOW we have moved toward tip of the trophic pyramid: from bacteria and fungi, to algae, to microinvertebrates and meiofauna, to herbivorous invertebrates (and some carnivorous ones, too)—and now, finally, to fish.

Ironically, in spite of an early attention to fish, the relatively new field of stream ecology has not embraced fish ecology as part of its discipline. That is, most stream ecologists have been concerned with problems of invertebrates and their energy sources. In all fairness, however, it should be noted that our father of stream ecology, Professor H. B. Noel Hynes, devoted a full four chapters to fish in his 1970 classic, *The Ecology of Running Waters.* Nor is this to say that we know less about fish than we do about the rest of the stream community. But the two disciplines—benthology and fisheries—rarely have been connected in the broad discipline of *stream ecology,* and the two fields have advanced almost in isolation from each other. We will try to rectify this estrangement in the next few chapters.

In these chapters we must divide and classify—divide the stream fish community into an organized system of structure and function. That is, what kinds are there (structure) and what do they do (function)? It would be easiest to separate the whole array of stream fishes taxonomically—trout, bass, minnows, etc. However, because our approach is *ecological*—that is, how do we relate fish to their environment—and because the first, major environmental factor determining the kinds of fish present is *water temperature,* it makes sense to classify first by temperature. Thus, we will discuss *coldwater* species, *coolwater* species, and *warmwater* species. But as you will recall from earlier discussions, newer and more accurate terms (for example, *summercool*) better describe the environment.

In the next few chapters, we'll first take up the various coldwater species' needs, with emphasis on their ecological relationships to the rest of the stream community. A separate chapter will deal with non-salmonid stream fishes, including smallmouth bass, catfish, some small species we rarely see—and some new-style angling for heretofore-neglected sport fishes!

Chapter 19

SALVELINUS

B Y FAR THE MAJOR INTEREST IN STREAM FISHES has been
placed on coldwater species—those primitive, beautifully
colored, streamlined inhabitants of summercool streams, trout
and salmon. Great admiration has been bestowed upon them by
fisheries biologists and anglers alike.

The very words, *trout* and *trout stream*, evoke a sense of rarity and reverence. I still recall a popular panel in the Sunday
comics years ago: A middle-age father rowed his boat up to a
lake cottage dock, a huge northern pike draped across the boat
from gunwale to gunwale. "Quick," he shouted to his teen-aged
son, "get the camera!" "Can't, Pa," the boy yelled, running
down the shore toward a neighboring cottage where a hip-
booted fly-fisherman was displaying his seven-inch-long catch,
"somebody's got a *trout!*" We were left to imagine the sense of
disbelief on the father's face.

Today we know more about the biology and ecology of
trout and salmon than any other group of freshwater fish.
Across the continent, these species receive the most attention by
fishery scientists and managers. The scientific literature greatly
emphasizes salmonids in taxonomy, ecology, and management.
Angler-writers continue to pour out a high-volume stream of
books and articles filled with where-to-go and how-to-do-it information, tackle recommendations and fly dressings, and tales

of fighting huge coldwater fish. Modern angling literature includes trout and salmon from every known coldwater habitat in North America, as well as introduced populations throughout the world. All of these occupy the family Salmonidae, more specifically the subfamily Salmoninae. (Another subfamily of the Salmonidae is the Coregoninae, the whitefishes.)

The number of native trout and salmon species is remarkably small for such a high-profile group. Major inland stream species number only three: the brook, rainbow, and cutthroat trout. Three lesser species inhabit some waters in the far north. Salmon from the Pacific coast number five; salmon from the Atlantic coast, only one. A few minor species are located in the mountainous and desert Southwest. One inland lake species, the lake trout, enjoys a wide distribution in the Great Lakes, the large Canadian lakes, and many small, northern lakes, throughout northern North America. To these natives, we can add one highly successful naturalized species from the Old World, the brown trout.

All coldwater species require cool water in summer that is well oxygenated. Water temperature is critical in the environment of salmonids, especially in streams that may be thermally marginal—that is, where temperatures are near and sometimes exceed the upper limit. So an appropriate temperature is the factor most definitive in trout distribution—that is, whether a particular water is suitable for trout or not. Salmonids' apparent predilection for cold water is better described as a *stenothermic* trait—that is, as a preference for a narrow range in temperature. We have discussed previously the fact that trout streams are relatively cool in summer and relatively warm in winter—"summercool" streams. With their water supplies consisting mostly of groundwater that has a constant year-round temperature, trout streams vary little over both daily and annual periods. Warmwater streams, where daily and annual swings are greater (warmer in summer and colder in winter), hold *eurythermic* species, our common warmwater fishes such as many minnows, darters, suckers, and others.

Unlike temperature, oxygen is rarely a problem for trout. Although their oxygen requirement is high, cool and unpolluted streams have sufficient oxygen anyway. For one thing, cool water holds more dissolved oxygen than warm. For another, even the slight turbulence of freely flowing water ensures good diffusion of oxygen from the atmosphere. If oxygen does become critically low, something is wrong, and it should be fixed. Organic pollution of any kind—for example, pulp-mill waste, dairy waste, runoff from animal feedlots, domestic sewage—all can reduce oxygen to lethal levels. But barring any of these disasters, don't feel you must add falls and riffles to increase oxygen in your favorite stream. It's not a case of the more, the better; nature—if protected—provides just enough!

◆   ◆   ◆

NOW SEEMS AS GOOD A TIME AS ANY to introduce the concept of *stocks*. Until about the 1950s, a designated species of fish was thought to be a distinct entity, unlike all other species, but pretty much all alike throughout a species' range—sort of "a brook trout is a brook trout is a brook trout." Are all domestic dogs alike? Of course not, there are many breeds, but all the same species. All *Homo sapiens* alike? No again—there are many races scattered around the world. All brook trout alike?—or rainbows, browns? Well, no, not even these. A native brook trout from an ocean tributary in Newfoundland may look pretty much like one from a high mountain stream in the Smokies, but they clearly are genetically different.

The geneticist differentiates between two populations of the same species on the basis of the percentage of alleles (forms of genes) that the two share. If that percentage is high (close to 100 percent), they may be of the same *stock*. More likely, the percentage will be lower (say, 90 percent), and they may be of different genetic varieties. If the percentage shared is lower yet, the two may even be different species!

When two populations of brook trout have been isolated from each other for a long time (like those of Newfoundland

and the Smoky Mountains), evolution will have made its mark. Some traits that can be easily observed change—coloration, size of body parts, feeding behavior, kind of spawning stream. In the laboratory, the geneticist may find other and less visible changes—fewer alleles, for example, that are shared by the two populations, or different alleles representing differences in color, size, and others—even though an angler may still see just a brook trout while admiring its spots on a cool morning at streamside.

Millennia ago, humans practiced animal husbandry with domestic animals, and selective breeding with agricultural crops, to produce varieties that were more to their liking. Why not fish? Once we humans became aware of such different varieties—let's now call them *stocks*—some hatchery operations adopted the methods of animal husbandry. Their aim was not to create new varieties, but rather to ensure the continued existence of rare stocks—such as those in brook trout.

And so fisheries biologists found brook trout that were, well, different—the Aurora trout in an Ontario lake, for example, and the silver trout in New Hampshire. Through modern genetics, we identified different stocks in isolated locations—the southern Appalachian type, the Lake Nipigon form that grew faster and larger than brook trout elsewhere, and distinct strains from the Finger Lakes area in New York. We found differences between anadromous populations and stream residents, differences between fishes that spawned in different rivers, and variations between populations above and below waterfalls. All are (or were) brook trout—but all are a little different in some respect. Earlier taxonomists gave some of the different types formal species or subspecies names. Some stocks were recognized too late—after they had become extinct.

We will refer to the stock concept throughout the rest of this book. The practical definition of a stock is a population that is uniquely recognizable for *management purposes*. The distinction is important: It means that fishery managers should identify and treat different stocks differently. Increasingly, we take only those eggs that come from a known population to supplement that population with hatchery-reared fish. If we identify a remote stock of a dwindling species-form that has been affected by an environmental disaster, like a dam, we may be able to save the stock from extinction by hatching eggs from that small stock and introducing it into other suitable waters. In fact, the Endangered Species Act (ESA) applies to certain stocks of Pacific salmon in their separate natal streams. They are registered in the ESA list as threatened or endangered and managed by limitations on angling and on other activities that may affect their habitats, just as if they were full species.

The brook trout is held in high esteem, with praise lavishly laid upon its brilliant red-and-blue spots and shimmering golden flanks.

We'll find many stocks among salmonid species—rainbows, cutthroats, browns, as well as brook trout, and the salmons. We have not yet begun to find separate stocks for most warmwater fishes—smallmouth bass, channel catfish, creek chub. But we probably will.

◆   ◆   ◆

MODERN FRESHWATER FISHING IN NORTH AMERICA began with European settlement on the Atlantic seaboard. In the many lakes and streams, abundant in the dense forests, the single species of stream trout was smaller but more brilliant in color than what the English immigrants were used to. These fish were easy to catch, and perhaps tasted better, too: the eastern brook trout.

Salvelinus fontinalis has been praised as the most beautiful of all freshwater fishes. The appellation is well deserved. The object of young anglers armed with a "pole" of some kind and a rusty Prince Albert can of worms, especially along a small creek in northeastern United States or Canada a half-century ago, these sparkling jewels plucked from a cold brook on a spring day created memories that became lodged in the mental treasure chests of adult fly fishers for life—this author included.

The brook trout is evocative of the North Woods. To hold one in hand, resplendent with light and color and pulsing with life, brings up also the fragrance of pine and sweetfern and the early-morning sweet odor of a moist cedar swamp. In some quarters, the brookie is a "native," distinct from other trout, a true Yankee.

The brook trout's diminutive size—that is, relative to other stream salmonids—does not diminish the high respect it receives for its beauty. Smaller, on average, than rainbow, cutthroat, and brown trout, the brook trout prefers tiny headwater streams where it competes successfully against almost all other species by its ability to detect upwelling groundwater for spawning. In cold climates, relatively warm groundwater prevents its eggs from freezing in winter. Brown trout apparently lack this ability, and consequently the brown's eggs may not survive a cold winter. Another reason for the brook trout's success in small headwaters is that it attains maturity at younger, smaller sizes, enabling it to feed, grow, and spawn in smaller territories. The brookie's success is often thus assured in softwater, unproductive streams that cannot support the larger mature brown trout.

The record brook trout by hook-and-line is 14 1/2 pounds, taken from Ontario's Nipigon River by an angler in 1915. Lake

Nipigon and its outlet river to Lake Superior are noted for large brook trout, apparently a genetic trait that this stock has evolved through long isolation from other brook trout.

The original distribution of brook trout was eastern—in fact, the previously accepted common name was *eastern* brook trout. The native range was focused in three major regions: northeastern United States and Canada along the Atlantic coast, and west to include Hudson Bay and the Great Lakes; relict populations at high elevations of the Appalachians, south to Georgia; and tributaries of the upper Mississippi River north to the waterfalls at the present site of Minneapolis.

The Lake Nipigon stock of brook trout has the capability of growth to large size, a trait carefully preserved today.

The species still prospers in northern regions, holding out against others in large rivers as well as in cold, tiny Atlantic tributaries in the Canadian Maritime Provinces and Newfoundland. Much of Michigan's Lower Peninsula, however, used to be the realm of the grayling, which fell victim to logging drives, intensive angling, and the introduction of brook trout. Juvenile brook trout were stocked in virtually every suitable small stream in the region.

Brook trout populations in the Appalachian Mountains maintain a tenuous existence in small, high-elevation streams, but introductions of rainbow trout have pushed the brook trout farther and farther up the mountainsides to smaller, more remote streams. Brook trout were common in the North Shore streams of Lake Superior, in both Minnesota and Ontario, but originally only up to the first obstructing waterfall. The brook trout apparently did not arrive in the region until after glacial meltwater lakes had receded. Lake Nipigon is a remarkable exception, having received meltwaters from Glacial Lake Agassiz to the west that may have contained early brook trout colonists. Introductions above waterfalls have now distributed the brook trout throughout the headwaters of almost all suitable Lake Superior streams.

In the Mississippi River, St. Anthony Falls at Minneapolis obstructed early dispersal of the brook trout into northern reaches of the Mississippi drainage, but small populations still exist in tributaries of the Minnesota and St. Croix rivers, which enter below St. Anthony Falls. Introductions into Mississippi tributaries above the falls have distributed the brook trout widely into central and northern Minnesota. Farther south in the Mississippi basin, many native populations occurred in Driftless Area tributaries, mainly in Wisconsin and Minnesota, some in Iowa and Illinois. A few of these remain, although most have been displaced by brown trout. The brook trout has lost considerable ground throughout its native range because of brown trout replacements.

Today, naturalized, reproducing brook trout populations exist in many places around the world, but successful introductions were not always achieved. Experiments in introducing *Salvelinus fontinalis* to states other than those in its native range began in the late 1860s and were largely successful. No attempt to introduce the brook trout was made in about ten states of the Deep South and the arid Southwest; and attempts made in midwestern plains states were not successful. Nevertheless, about half of the United States today have naturalized populations where none existed initially. The brook (or speckled) trout is native to all eastern Canadian provinces, so only the western provinces received introductions, all successful, probably because of the cooler temperatures prevailing in mountainous areas.

Much of the success of brook trout introductions can probably be laid to its ability to prosper in small, headwater reaches and tributaries. At high latitudes and altitudes, such streams are often summercool, reasonably productive, and lacking in other, competing species. In many cases, such upper reaches occurred above waterfall barriers that had prevented previous colonizations. Much of the success of the brook trout in small tributaries in the western mountains can be attributed to the cooler environments of high mountain streams. In addition, the brook trout was almost always successful in competing against the cutthroat in such locations, to the detriment and frequent extirpation of the cutthroat.

The brook trout has been naturalized in virtually all European countries. Transatlantic shipments of fertile brook trout eggs from the United States began in the 1860s to the British Isles, Germany, and France. Later transfers from these three locations were made to other European nations, including all of Scandinavia and eastern Europe. Although most introductions were initially successful, many did not survive for long as reproducing populations.

Elsewhere in the world, brook trout were introduced with some successes in the Andes Mountains of South America. Introductions were attempted in South Africa, Kenya, and Tanzania, and in Australia and New Zealand, but few were successful. In some cases, brook trout naturalization, being difficult, was subsequently abandoned after brown and rainbow trout (both of which grew larger) became available. No doubt the stricter habitat requirements of the brook trout, combined with the larger sizes of the latter two, were factors resulting in fewer successful introductions for *Salvelinus fontinalis.*

One of the favorite habitats used for stocking is the small, clear ice-block or kettle lakes in northern Michigan, Wisconsin, and Minnesota. Most of these small lakes are darkly colored with bog stain, but some are clear. For the cold-loving brook trout, surface water must be clear in order that sunlight can penetrate into deep water and permit photosynthesis and thus the production of oxygenated water down deep.

The brook trout has been cultured widely, often stocked in small, clear bog lakes, such as this one in Michigan's Upper Peninsula.

Like all salmon and trout, some brook trout are migratory, abandoning their natal stream for the sea or freshwater lakes, to grow large and return later to spawn. When they migrate to the sea (from tributaries of the North Atlantic and Hudson Bay) and return to fresh water to spawn, they are known as *salters,* and the population is said to be *anadromous.* When they migrate to a freshwater lake (for example, Lake Superior) and then return to tributary streams to spawn, they are known as *coasters* and the population is said to be *adfluvial.*

As adults, the normal coloration of brook trout in lake or ocean is paler and more silvery than that of stream residents, when they may be mistaken for lake trout by anglers. In early historic times, angling for both salters in New England and coasters in Lake Superior streams produced boatloads of huge fish. Such overfishing caused declines to the point where today these large brook trout are rare.

Curiously, the Lake Superior brook trout is considered a unique stock, but the New England population is not. There, movement of stream resident brook trout to the ocean seems to be accidental. Restoration of the Lake Superior strain seems possible, and studies are underway in Ontario, Minnesota, and Wisconsin.

◆   ◆   ◆

THE GENUS *SALVELINUS* INCLUDES A NUMBER of closely related species in addition to the brook trout. All species of this genus are known as char (*charr* in Canada), the name being of Celtic origin, meaning "blood-red" in color, probably a reference to the spawning colors of the male brook trout. The lake trout (*S. namaycush)* is common in the same northern regions as brook trout, but inhabits lakes (although sometimes taken by anglers from inlet/outlet streams); a few migrate upstream from lakes to spawn. Other members of *Salvelinus* include the Arctic char (*S. alpinus*), including the stocks Sunapee, the Maine blueback, and the Quebec "red trout." Arctic char, similar in coloration to the brook trout, have a northern, circumpolar distribution, including northern Europe and Asia. The Dolly Varden (*S. malma*) is similar to the Arctic char in appearance but distributed only around the northern Pacific Rim in Arctic and Pacific drainages (North America and Asia). The bull trout (*S. confluentus*), similar to the Dolly Varden but less colorful, occurs only in western mountain streams, in both the United States and Canada.

Compared with that of its relatives, the brook trout's tail (or *caudal fin*) is decidedly square, especially in larger sizes (thus the nickname "squaretail"); the rest of the genus have notably forked tails. The forked tail is particularly visible in the lake trout, a feature that makes possible a clear distinction between a coaster brook trout and a "laker."

The Dolly Varden in times past has been the victim of much misunderstanding. Of the three species—Arctic char, bull trout, and Dolly Varden—the Dolly has had the worst press, being accused of serious predation on salmon fry and parr. In the 1920s and 1930s, a bounty was paid on the tails of Dolly Varden in Alaska, but about 75 percent of tails on which boun-ties were paid were later identified as coho salmon tails, another approximate 20 percent were rainbow trout, and less than 10 percent were from real Dolly Vardens! Actually, the Dolly Varden is the least piscivorous of the three species.

The Dolly Varden of some waters was separated out in 1978 as the bull trout. Now the previous record Dolly Varden of 32 pounds from Lake Pend Oreille, Idaho has been identified as a bull trout. On the other hand, the record *real* Dolly Varden, caught in Alaska in 1993, was smaller at 18 pounds, 9 ounces—a bit of a come-down for the Dolly, although most of us would consider anything over 18 pounds as quite respectable!

The brook trout, like most salmonids, is capable of hybrid-izing with other trout. Best known, perhaps, is the *splake*, a cross between brook and lake trout. (The name is a combination of "speckled" (a Canadian common name for brook trout) and "lake" (for the stillwater lake trout).

The combination was a compromise, invented by Canadian fisheries biologists who were trying to outwit the sea lamprey, the saltwater invader that had all but eliminated the lake trout from the Great Lakes. High hopes were once held for the resto-ration of *Salvelinus* in Lake Huron. The sea lamprey preys upon fish about two pounds or 18 inches in size, when the lake trout has not yet spawned. If it does evade the lamprey, it grows to a large size (maximum, a hundred pounds). But the brook trout matures at a much smaller size (as small as a quarter-pound) and does not grow nearly as large as the lake trout. The splake matures at less than two pounds, and thus spawns before the sea lamprey attacks.

It was hoped the splake would be big enough to be a commercial fish, as the lake trout had been. Unlike most hybrids, the splake is fertile, or mostly so, and so reproduced. Hybrids generated by the first cross of brook versus lake trout survived and grew well when stocked into Lake Huron. They matured, spawned, and to some extent reproduced. But success of these later generations has not lived up to expectations—at least to the point of adding significantly to the Lake Huron stocks of *Salvelinus.*

The "tiger trout," a hybrid between the brook and brown trout, occurs naturally but rarely where both species live together.

One hybrid occurs accidentally between brook and brown trout. Before the introduction of brown trout to North America, the two had not had a chance to try it out. In the wild, together at last, the two species brought forth the beautiful *tiger trout*—so-called because of the gold and black wavy markings on its flanks. It happens once in while when the two species occur together, especially when one species is abundant and the other one rare. This hybrid is sterile. Cultured in hatcheries, the tiger was stocked out for the catching, but it was only a novelty, and its popularity did not last long. However, keep an eye out for it in that little stream of yours that has many of one species and only a few of the other.

In the spawning of autumn, sometime in October in temperate zones, the male brook trout takes on its most dazzling coloration. The brook trout finds and selects areas of the streambed where groundwater is percolating upward, for digging its redd and depositing its eggs. The great advantage of this behavior is that the upwelling groundwater is free of silt. Another is that groundwater is respectably warm in winter for incubation of eggs, 45 to 50 degrees. Oxygenated water is essential, however, and the brook trout can sense it. This kind of spawning behavior often leads brook trout to spawning in lakes in sandy or gravel shoals where groundwater percolates upward. Such "lake spawning" at first confounded biologists, who were trained to believe that trout could spawn only in streams. It turns out that conditions of upwelling water in gravel shoals in Lake Nipigon and elsewhere were probably ideal for successful reproduction. At temperatures of 45 to 50 degrees, successful hatching of the eggs approaches 100 percent. Free-swimming fry are out of the gravel by December or January, although significant growth may not occur for another month or two.

Many years ago, in a remote Algoma lake, this author observed a prespawning feeding frenzy out from the mouth of a small creek, where a gravel delta had formed in shallow water. In an afternoon, my father and I caught about 25 to 30 fish. We caught most of them on dry-fly hoppers and squirrel-tail streamers, fished near the surface, and the fish seemed to strike by leaping up and down on the flies, their red bellies sparkling through a hazy afternoon sun. Most ranged from two to three pounds; a single, heavily laden female approached four pounds. All but one were males in brilliant color that matched the autumn hues of the maples on shore, the most beautiful fish I had ever seen. I didn't realize the significance of what was happening until many years later.

TECHNICAL REFERENCES:

Balon, Eugene K. 1980. *Charrs: Salmonid Fishes of the Genus Salvelinus.* Dr. W. Junk Publishers, The Hague, The Netherlands.
McFadden, James T. 1961. A population study of the brook trout *Salvelinus fontinalis. Wildlife Monographs,* No. 7. (The Wildlife Society.)

RiverSketch

CASTOR CANADENSIS

PRAISED AND MALIGNED, the beaver has had its ups and downs through human history in North America. In the northern wilds of forest and mountains, prehistoric beavers fed upon the fibrous bark of aspens, twigs of riparian shrubs, and aquatic plants. They added nutrients to their ponds and were hunted by gray wolves, their main predators. Estimates of beaver populations in North America ranged from sixty to four hundred million. But with arrival of French explorers and fur traders, future prospects for the beaver changed dramatically.

The North American trade in beaver pelts can be marked from the time Jacques Cartier, French explorer and navigator, sailed across the Atlantic Ocean and penetrated the St. Lawrence River, in 1535. His main hope was that the St. Lawrence would lead to the Northwest Passage and the riches of the Orient, but fur trading was also on his mind. Eighty years passed before another French explorer, Étienne Brulé, was to reach Lake Superior, in 1615. That water route opened the huge continental forests of the Northwest to exploration and fur trapping and, eventually, to a great empire of trading posts. The old Northwest was an immense land of a million square miles, fabulously rich with beaver and other furbearers.

For two centuries, the French and British, successively, traded with Indian trappers. Great quantities of beaver pelts—a half million annually—passed on to Europe. By the mid-1800s, the North American beaver population was near extirpation. Moreover, European hat fashions changed from beaver fur to silk. Currently, populations are estimated between about six and twelve million, still a fraction of presettlement numbers.

A beaver lodge and pond are surrounded by lofty mountains
in a Copper River wetland, Alaska.
(Photo courtesy of Robert J. Naiman, University of Washington.)

The beaver is unique in its ability to create its own habitat. It must have unfrozen water to survive northern winters, a house above water for protection from winter's severity and from predators, and an underwater food resource that will last through the winter. All of these needs are supplied by the beaver's own actions. It builds a dam to impound and provide water, constructs a lodge of small logs and sticks that can be entered from beneath the surface, and puts away its sunken food cache of limbs and branches, preferably aspen, near the lodge, which it has gathered from adjacent woodlands before ice-up.

Beavers can change a typical valley with upland forest and unimpeded stream to a topography of stair-step ponds, broad riparian zones, and clearings that extend into nearby forest. Ponds provide habitat for waterfowl and other aquatic furbearers, greater food resources such as aquatic plants for muskrats and moose, and an early-successional forest surrounding the pond, which benefits a variety of small mammals and birds.

Old beaver ponds, long ago abandoned, leave their legacy of spreading meadows in the forested Lake Superior region.

The mountain meadow that results from a long-abandoned pond now adds to the variety of habitats for other species and to our own enjoyment of landscape diversity. Impoundments promote storage of organic matter and nutrients, provide important reserves of these essential materials, and thus contribute to the system's stability against major disturbances like floods and droughts. In each of these circumstances, no other biological influence equals that of *Castor canadensis*.

Long ago an unresolvable controversy arose about the effects of beavers on stream trout habitat. It's true that in marginal trout streams impoundment by beaver dams can raise summer water temperatures. On the other hand, many tiny streams in northern regions, especially if they are continuously shaded, are too cold to permit good fish growth. In such situations, beaver ponds will warm the water slightly as well as increase water volume and invertebrate production. Woods-wise anglers locate these remote ponds and find extraordinary brook trout fishing.

Probably no trout stream angler has not been startled half out of his hip boots when, in the dusk of a late evening, a beaver slips up noiselessly from behind and slaps its tail—emitting an explosive splash. Why does a beaver slap its tail? Most biologists suggest it is a warning of danger for the benefit of the colony, which sounds logical. But sleep some quiet night alongside a beaver-inhabited trout stream and you will probably hear some beaver tail-slaps—for no apparent reason.

Many years ago one late evening on a small, remote lake in Michigan's Upper Peninsula, I watched fascinated as three beavers circled the lake's perimeter in a regular **V**-formation, periodically slapping their tails in perfect unison. I wondered why. Maybe they were showing off for the benefit of young females that might have been watching. Or maybe it was simply the beaver equivalent of—well—just plain fun.

SELECTED REFERENCES:

Longley, William H., and John B. Moyle. 1963. *The Beaver in Minnesota*. Technical bulletin No. 6. Minnesota Department of Conservation, Division of Game and Fish, St. Paul, Minnesota.

Naiman, Robert J., Carol A. Johnston, and James C. Kelley. 1988. Alteration of North American streams by beaver. *BioScience* Volume 38, pages 753-762.

Chapter **20**

TROUT OF DESERT AND MOUNTAIN

THE NATIVE TROUT FAUNA of western North America comprises only two major species, the rainbow and the cutthroat, each of which contains a dazzling variety of subspecies and races. This diversity reflects a broad spectrum of habitat: high mountains, arid deserts, and moist coastal plains. From remote mountain creeks to broad coastal rivers, from streams of the Pacific slope over the ridge to headwaters of the Missouri, rainbows and cutthroats long ago penetrated every suitable habitat. The rainbow spread far north and far south, Alaska to Mexico; cutthroats penetrated inland, to the Missouri and the Yellowstone, the Saskatchewan and Rio Grande.

Through a changing glacial topography, hundreds of thousands of years ago, these two species colonized closed basin lakes and streams and established self-sustaining populations. Distinctive external patterns and coloration created a bewildering diversity and confused ichthyologists and natural historians for 200 years. In the past, 15 separate species were described for the forms of rainbow that today we recognize as only one. This confusing variety of forms has recently been brought into a systematic organization by Professor Robert J. Behnke of Colorado State University, in his definitive work, *Native Trout of Western North America*. Using modern genetic tools as well as his long

407

experience as a field researcher and avid angler, Dr. Behnke brings the fascinating rainbow and cutthroat complexes into a welcome focus.

The glaciation of the Pleistocene Epoch, with its ever-changing distribution of meltwater lakes and rivers, created many dispersal routes. Over time, fish found a variety of habitats that, in turn, induced many variants of both rainbow and cutthroat trout.

Two million years ago, the rainbow and cutthroat shared a common ancestor, then diverged and went their (almost) separate ways. Actually, the rainbow and cutthroat today are not totally distinct, because both retain the capability to hybridize readily and produce fertile offspring. These circumstances have an unfortunate result when the two separated species come together: the original genetic character of one species or both may be forever lost. Rare, endemic strains of cutthroat trout have been extirpated by stocking rainbows on top, a practice fortunately no longer pursued by most fishery managers.

◆   ◆   ◆

THE RAINBOW TROUT *Oncorhynchus mykiss* (formerly *Salmo gairdneri*) comes closest of all stream salmonids to being a universal, generic trout. Today's trout hatchery product amounts to a genetic soup that today frustrates any investigation of its ancestral roots. Easily cultured and fast-growing in hatcheries, readily taking artificial food, exceedingly plastic through selective breeding, the domesticated rainbow is the delight of commercial aquaculturists. However, the foreign rainbow has caused great losses to indigenous species and stocks outside the rainbow's original range. The native may be replaced through competition for food and space, or by interbreeding that changes forever its genetic identity.

Yet, to the angler fishing either a native or naturalized rainbow population, whether stream resident or migratory, the rocket-like runs and high-leaping acrobatics of a large, healthy, wild rainbow must be the quintessence of angling thrills.

The original distribution of *Oncorhynchus mykiss* included Pacific drainages on both sides of the ocean, the species name, *mykiss,* being based on the native language in Russia's Kamchatka Peninsula.

In the American distribution of rainbows, the species separates readily into two subspecies, the coastal rainbow trout (*Oncorhynchus mykiss irideus*) and the interior redband trout (*O. mykiss gairdneri).* (A Russian subspecies is *O. mykiss mykiss.*) The coastal rainbow range extends from Alaska to Mexico. Interestingly, *both* subspecies include *both* stream resident and migratory forms, the latter being our familiar steelhead.

The redband trout's range includes interior streams from British Columbia south through Washington, Oregon, and California, plus parts of Montana, Idaho, and Nevada. The only exception to this distribution is in Alberta, where a small range extension projects into the Athabasca/Peace river system. Here, a few redbands must have made their way in some distant past across the catchment divide, from the Pacific drainage.

A number of variants of the rainbow like the Gila trout and Apache trout, for example, are thought to have branched off early from their rainbow ancestry. They now are together placed in a separate, single species, *Oncorhynchus gilae,* with two subspecies, *O. gilae gilae* and *O. gilae apache.* These occupy small basins in the lower Colorado River drainage, along with the Mexican golden trout, which is classified in a species distinct from either rainbow or cutthroat extraction, *O. chrysogaster.*

◆   ◆   ◆

THE PACIFIC STEELHEAD has generated a great deal of popular literature, from Rudyard Kipling to Zane Grey to Robert H. Smith and scores more. There exists more highly charged interest among both anglers and biologists, more excitement in the breathtaking, leaping fight when hooked, than any other inland freshwater trout (with no slight intended to the Atlantic salmon). The rainbow's introduction into the Great Lakes a century ago generated the first intense enthusiasm for fishing these midwestern waters, far inland from the fish's native rivers, for the steelhead.

Prehistoric steelhead ranged far afield. From southern California northward, many rivers saw great hosts of spawning adults. In the Columbia basin, steelhead migrated from the ocean all the way inland to Idaho's upper Snake River and its tributaries, a journey of over a thousand miles. Rivers flowing into the Gulf of Alaska still hold some of the best runs of steelhead. The Great Lakes introduction, which originated entirely of hatchery stock, was more successful than hatchery programs on Pacific streams, where failures were attributed to predaceous, aquatic mammals on the coast.

The history of wild steelhead trout management is a sad story. In great trouble all along the Pacific coast, steelhead are now blocked by dams and can no longer ascend many of their previous natal streams. Smolts migrating downstream more often than not are ground to bits in the dam's turbines or diverted to agricultural crop fields to desiccate and die. Stock after stock disappeared from rivers that once ran full with steelhead, and with Pacific salmon as well.

In the years prior to the Second World War, healthy steelhead populations along the Pacific coast could be found from southern California to the Alaska Peninsula. All were wild. Although some hatcheries produced and stocked steelhead fry of unknown or mixed origin, this stock did not survive wild environmental conditions and had no effect on the anglers' catch. Up until about 1960, the annual catch was about 250,000 fish from Washington, Oregon, and California rivers, all wild fish. Dams and hatcheries were constructed in profusion in the 1960s and 1970s, the hatcheries in part to mitigate losses from dam construction. But despite huge stockings of hatchery smolts, annual angler catches continued to decline.

What we didn't know then was that distinct races utilized specific streams, evolving unique life histories in each one—the stock concept. The hatchery system, however, whether state or federal, is deeply entrenched. The hatchery mentality was far more difficult to wind down than any of the steelhead stocks were to extinguish. Unaware of the validity of the stock concept, these massive fish hatcheries were built to "mitigate" losses, only to contribute to the extirpations and extinctions by interbreeding hatchery stocks with wild fish, destroying the genetic identity of the native.

The former runs of wild steelheads to the upper Columbia in Canada were exterminated by Grand Coulee Dam; runs to Idaho's Snake River and its two major steelhead rivers, the Salmon and Clearwater, were exterminated by Hell's Canyon Dam. Since "mitigation," the total angler catch dropped to only one-tenth of a percent of smolts stocked.

A recent American Fisheries Society report rated 26 native steelhead stocks as having a *high risk of extinction*, and 17 more at moderate risk. Twenty-three more stocks that once flourished in specific rivers are believed to have already become extinct. In almost all cases, dams were labeled as the major cause, but interbreeding with hatchery fish was partly responsible. Habitat damage in the spawning streams, owing to livestock grazing and logging-generated sediment, was also indicted.

◆   ◆   ◆

MIGRATORY POPULATIONS of coastal rainbows occur in Pacific tributaries along the entire North American coast. Steelhead populations occur also in the redband subspecies. Before dams, these fish were numerous in the upper Columbia River (British Columbia) and upper Snake River (Idaho).

Inland from Pacific shores, several redband subspecies currently occupy small interior ranges. These include the Columbia River redband *(Oncorhynchus mykiss gairdneri)* and the Sacramento redband (*O. mykiss stonei*), with populations of both stream resident and anadromous steelhead that migrate through their respective rivers to the sea. The Sacramento basin is also home to the striking, stream-resident California golden trout (*O. mykiss aguabonita*), the Kern River rainbow (*O. mykiss gilberti*), and the Little Kern River golden trout *O. mykiss whitei*, all redbands.

The rainbow trout of today can be found in all continents of the world except Antarctica. Even Hawaii claims rainbows in a single stream, supported by hatchery stocking. The rainbow is the darling of hatchery culture, "catchable" stocking programs, and tailwater fisheries. Adaptable, easy to spawn and rear in hatcheries, easy to catch by all angling methods, growing to large size with a wild fight on the end of a line, the rainbow in many quarters is almost synonymous with "trout" itself.

◆   ◆   ◆

NO OTHER FRESHWATER FISH shows such a variation in forms as does the cutthroat trout, *Oncorhynchus clarki*. Patterns and pigmentation of cutthroats vary over a kaleidoscopic range. The common name, *cutthroat,* derives from the bright red slash of color on skin of the lower jaw (the "throat"), although in some subspecies the red is replaced by orange or yellow, or sometimes is not visible at all.

The cutthroat has the widest distribution of all western trout: its waters empty into the Pacific Ocean, either directly or by way of Prince Edward Sound (Alaska) and the Gulf of California; the Atlantic Ocean by way of Hudson Bay, the Mississippi River, and the Rio Grande; and the Arctic Ocean by way of the Mackenzie River and the Beaufort Sea. The cutthroat also occurs in many closed basins, mainly in Utah and Nevada, isolated from all exits to the ocean. The cutthroat does not exist in Russia's Kamchatka Peninsula, as does the rainbow.

Historically, the cutthroat taxonomy was arranged in so many different species, subspecies, and common names that we cannot at this late date possibly sort them out. However, Robert Behnke places all cutthroats in the one species, *Oncorhynchus clarki*. In turn, he divides the species into 14 subspecies, two of which are now extinct.

The coastal cutthroat, *Oncorhynchus clarki clarki,* enjoys the greatest distribution, by far, of all the cutthroats. The one subspecies with the second greatest range is the westslope cutthroat, *O. clarki lewisi.* Obviously, these names honor Meriwether Lewis and William Clark who, in the journals of their famous expedition, in 1805 made the first scientific notation of cutthroat trout in the upper Missouri River.

Cutthroats have not been successfully introduced in very many places outside western North America, unlike almost all other trout species. A few were stocked in some eastern streams, but they were not naturalized, and the hatchery fish that were stocked briefly amounted to only some novelty fishing. In many western, high-mountain lakes, however, where no fish existed previously, introductions were highly successful. Such fisheries are usually maintained by regular stocking of juvenile fish, often by aircraft.

Lake-living, or *lacustrine*, populations of cutthroats are common, but to be self-sustaining they need tributaries or outlets for spawning. Like other lacustrine salmonid species, cutthroats feed more on other fish and grow larger.

Cutthroats select spawning sites in the tails of pools, apparently the same for all western mountain salmonids. Here, stream water is downwelling, and these redds receive *stream water*, unlike the eastern brook trout's redd in *upwelling groundwater*. Excess sediment in stream water presents severe problems to the reproductive success of western trout and salmon, often preventing successful reproduction. The fact that western rainbows and cutthroats spawn in the spring and some Pacific salmon in the fall may be a matter of evolutionary selection that provides the best possible spawning conditions for each species. So far, the exact mechanisms for these selections have not been worked out. In any event, anglers fishing for anadromous spawners during the rut, so to speak, have found that the best location to drift their gaudy flies is through the tails of pools!

◆   ◆   ◆

THE COASTAL SUBSPECIES occupies the largest distributional range of all cutthroats, from Alaska to northern California. Most stocks are strictly stream residents. Some run to the sea but stay for only two to three months and do not range far into the ocean, remaining near shore in shallow waters. The coastal subspecies has long been isolated from other subspecies, with no genetic mixing. Thus, it is readily distinguished from other cut-throats, in particular by many small, irregular, dark spots on the flanks. Most inland subspecies typically have larger and fewer spots, some so few that they seem to have none at all. Coastal cutthroats often coexist with the rainbow trout; cutthroats show a spawning preference for small tributary streams and the rain-bow trout for larger rivers. But when one species is stocked in another's native range, the results are much like those found in a laboratory experiment: hybridization occurs, often with devas-tating results for the cutthroat.

Two other major cutthroat subspecies are the westslope cut-throat, *Oncorhynchus clarki lewisi,* and the Yellowstone cut-throat, *O. clarki bouvieri.* These two occupy much of the upper Columbia, Snake, Missouri, and Yellowstone rivers, although typically their ranges do not overlap or occur in the same streams. The westslope cutthroat occupies the upper Columbia and Missouri rivers whose waters flow respectively into the Pa-cific and Atlantic oceans; the Yellowstone cutthroat occupies the upper Snake and Yellowstone rivers, which also flow respectively toward the Pacific and Atlantic oceans. The westslope is the cut-throat of the Clark Fork (Columbia) and the Yellowstone cut-throat in the Henry's Fork (Snake). Both subspecies have been widely stocked in other western waters and for supplementing populations in their native ranges as well.

The two subspecies are easily distinguished. The westslope cutthroat's spots are small and irregular (much like the coastal subspecies') and its flanks marked with brilliant colors of orange and red. The Yellowstone cutthroat's spots are few and large and rounded, but with much duller coloration. Both forms do well in lacustrine environments, where they grow to large sizes.

The westslope and Yellowstone subspecies are able to retain their genetic identity even when they occupy the same waters, partly because they diverged from each other so long ago (a million years), but also because their food habits differ. The Yellowstone cutthroat prospers in large lakes (like Yellowstone

Lake) by piscivorous feeding, whereas the westslope cutthroat rarely includes other fishes in its diet, perhaps only benthic fish like sculpins, which may be taken while they are foraging on benthic insects.

The westslope cutthroat, *Oncorhynchus clarki lewisi*, is distinguished from the Yellowstone cutthroat by the many small spots on its flanks. (Photo courtesy of George R. Spangler, University of Minnesota.)

In those places where cutthroats and rainbows come together, however, the outcome is different. The cutthroats lose out, both in direct competition and by genetic dilution. Rainbow trout have been introduced into much of the range of westslope and Yellowstone subspecies, and they are holding out well only in a few of their native streams, now only one to ten percent of their original distributions. The native westslope cutthroats in the Clark Fork now share their habitat with introduced rainbows, to the cutthroat's disadvantage. Heavily-fished Henry's Fork originally contained pure Yellowstone cutthroats, but now naturalized rainbows predominate, where only ten percent of the population is still cutthroat.

The Grand Canyon of the Yellowstone, with its high waterfalls and rapids, has been an obstacle to upstream dispersal of nonnative fish, helping to maintain the genetic integrity of the Yellowstone subspecies of cutthroat trout in the upper river and Yellowstone Lake.

Severely affecting cutthroats in lakes is the lake trout (*Salvelinus namaycush*), noted for its aggressive, piscivorous feeding habit. By this means, cutthroats were eliminated in Lake Tahoe (Nevada-California) and were seriously impacted in Flathead Lake (Montana). The lake trout's recent appearance in Yellowstone Lake, preying on cutthroats, is causing great concern.

One more form of cutthroat in the northern region is the subspecies known as the finespotted Snake River cutthroat, recently classified as *Oncorhynchus clarki behnkei*. The common name comes from the tiny, numerous dark spots on the flanks of the fish, the smallest of spots on all other western native trout, which are almost like pepper specks. Except for the small spots, all characteristics of this cutthroat subspecies appear identical to those of the Yellowstone subspecies. In fact, these two occur in the same drainage—the upper Snake River—but where they use different streams for spawning and thus maintain their distinction. The finespotted has been hugely successful in hatchery production and widely introduced into other waters, creating and maintaining heavily exploited fisheries. It adapts easily in many habitats—large lakes and reservoirs, tailwaters, and many small streams. The finespotted is the only cutthroat whose current distribution is larger than its native range.

◆   ◆   ◆

LATE IN THE LAST ICE AGE, ten to twelve thousand years ago, huge lakes of meltwater formed in the region of the arid West known today as the Great Basin. The lakes and streams in this region had no exit to the sea, and their waters either sank into desert sands or evaporated in the intense heat. These large glacial lakes formed mainly in the region of Utah, Nevada, and Oregon, less in parts of California. Two large sub-basins occur today within the Great Basin: Bonneville Basin (encompassing Great Salt Lake) and the Lahontan Basin (including the Humboldt River, Lake Tahoe, and Pyramid Lake). When these lakes were composed of fresh water, populations of cutthroat trout developed as piscivores, preying upon smaller fish. With this abundant food, some trout grew to great size. After the large glacial lakes receded or became too salty, cutthroats remained only in their small tributary streams. But these lacustrine fish had not evolved to prosper in streams and offered little resistance to introduced non-natives, primarily rainbow trout. Others, however, had adapted to streams long before the era of glacial lakes and persisted against the often-unstable conditions in this arid region. Stream-resident fish were better able to resist introduced species.

In historical time, six subspecies of cutthroat persisted in these closed basins. The most recent, arising only some tens of thousands of years ago, is the Bonneville subspecies, in the Bonneville Basin. The other five are all found in the Lanhontan Basin, the principal one being the Lahontan cutthroat, which, in smaller, separate subbasins, gave rise to the other four: Paiute, Alvord, Whitehorse, and Humboldt cutthroats. The Bonneville cutthroat, *Oncorhynchus clarki utah*, was the only subspecies in the huge Bonneville Basin when early settlers arrived. It occurred in three slightly differentiated groups: a lacustrine population in Bear Lake and the Bear River, which drain into Great Salt Lake from the north; streams in the Snake Valley region (not the Snake River of Idaho) on the western edge of the basin; and streams that enter the main part of the basin from eastern mountain ranges. Still, all three groups are lumped into the one subspecies.

The Bonneville cutthroat arose from the Yellowstone subspecies, having entered the Bonneville Basin from the upper Snake River to the north. It remains little differentiated from its ancestor. The ecology of the Bear Lake subgroup was different from the other two stream groups. The Bear Lake group was piscivorous and grew to large sizes. As such, they were more resistant to hybridization than other cutthroat subspecies. The Bonneville cutthroat, it was later discovered, was much more susceptible to angling and has been widely cultured and introduced. Stocking of the Bear Lake group is also continued in Bear Lake and some

Utah reservoirs (native spawning tributaries have been destroyed). Happily, management programs in both Utah and Wyoming now sustain and further protect the native Bonneville cutthroat subspecies.

The Lahontan cutthroat, *Oncorhynchus clarki henshawi*, is one of the four main cutthroat subspecies (along with the coastal, westslope, and Yellowstone subspecies). (By "main" is meant how closely a taxon is differentiated from other taxa, mostly a matter of how long it has been separated, rather than of how abundant it now may be.) *O. clarki henshawi* occupied the Lahontan Basin long before the last glaciation and evolved slowly and in isolation, giving it greater resistance to hybridization. The Lanhontan cutthroat has been a subject of much interest ever since early settlers found large individuals in Pyramid Lake. This subspecies originally occurred in several stream headwaters, principally those of the Truckee River, Nevada, which empties into Pyramid Lake, as well as several of their tributaries. The Pyramid Lake population, whose angler-caught fish averaged 20 pounds with a record of 40 pounds, was a genetically distinct stock capable of rapid growth to great size. It was piscivorous in its lake habitat and preyed upon an abundant food resource of other fishes.

Sadly, the Pyramid Lake cutthroat disappeared when siltation from agricultural diversions and irrigation projects prevented the Lahontan from entering the Truckee River to spawn. Although it became extinct in 1938 in Pyramid Lake, some small populations of the original genetic stock remain in small streams near the Utah-Nevada border, where they may be used in restoration efforts elsewhere. The Truckee River, much abused, now seems beyond restoration.

◆   ◆   ◆

OF THE FOUR OTHER SUBSPECIES of cutthroat present in the Great Basin catchments—the Paiute, Alvord, Whitehorse, and Humboldt subspecies—only one, the Paiute, *Oncorhynchus clarki seleniris*, has been officially described; the other three are designated by common names only and do not have formal subspecies descriptions. Another, the Alvord cutthroat, is now extinct. All four subspecies derived from the Lanhontan cutthroat.

Through long geologic time in the severe, arid conditions of small, closed basins, these four subspecies were successful. Since glaciation, the streams have been unstable in both water flow and temperature, and fish populations have had to deal with water temperatures into mid-80° ranges. And since human settlement, all four have been subjected to our two most debilitating acts affecting North American cutthroats: introductions of rainbow trout and unrestricted livestock grazing. Consequently, in addition to the loss of the Alvord subspecies, the others have suffered degradation of habitat or complete loss of native range. Some introductions of native stocks have been made into streams lacking other fishes, and a few hopeful cases of riparian protection have appeared on federal lands. In other areas, losses continue.

The Paiute, the one formally designated subspecies, has received the greatest amount of restoration effort and habitat protection. It occurred in only a single stream in the Lahontan Basin in California, Silver King Creek. The Paiute occupied the stream only below waterfalls, above which no fish at all existed. But in 1912, a sheepherder transplanted some Paiutes above the falls. Later, rainbow trout were introduced into the stream below the falls, resulting in the complete loss of the Paiute's original genetic identity through hybridization—below the falls. The sheepherder's introduction above the falls probably saved the Paiute from extinction or possibly from never having been discovered at all. Although a few rainbows were later released above the falls, and some hybridization occurred, intensive restoration efforts have managed to save this cutthroat from complete loss. Some pure stocks exist today in tiny headwater tributaries of Silver King Creek. Among all cutthroats, the Paiute is the only one totally without spots, although in all other respects it is identical to the Lahontan subspecies.

The Alvord and Whitehorse cutthroats inhabited streams that had experienced some of the most severe conditions in two small basins crossing the border of Nevada and Oregon. Streams containing Alvord cutthroats were stocked with rainbow trout in the 1920s-1930s, and in subsequent years only rainbow trout and obvious hybrids could be found.

The Whitehorse subspecies inhabits two small streams in Oregon, where it has been able to survive severe conditions of flow and temperature. Its current existence remains precarious, for both streams have been severely degraded by unrestricted livestock grazing. Some attempts to fence riparian areas against grazing have shown that such efforts benefit stream conditions and that would result in survival of the Whitehorse subspecies.

The Humboldt subspecies inhabits the drainage basin of the Humboldt River, Nevada, which, like other streams in closed catchments of the Great Basin, has only the desert sands as its final destination. These cutthroats were common and large in the Humboldt River in the early 1900s, but no trout live in the Humboldt in recent times. After being poisoned by extreme salt concentrations, the sun and desert-alkali mud consumes it in its final sink. Mark Twain cursed it and declared it "...unfit for drinking. The coffee we made of this water was the meanest compound man has yet invented." But down mountain slopes that surrounded and in some places penetrated the basin, flowed many streams that held the Humboldt cutthroat trout.

The Humboldt subspecies' history has been one of survival under the most extreme conditions, and consequently its evolution in the past has enabled it to resist the most serious hybridization with the rainbow. Other trouts, rainbow, brook, and brown now occupy streams managed for recreational fisheries in the Humboldt River basin. Livestock grazing, mining, and irrigation diversions have been the major factors reducing native habitat. Today, the Humboldt cutthroat exists in nearly a hundred other streams in which it has been introduced. As part of the Lahontan Basin, the Humboldt subspecies derived from the Lanhontan cutthroat with only slightly less spotting.

♦   ♦   ♦

FOUR OTHER CUTTHROAT SUBSPECIES REMAIN, all of them
native to streams and lakes in the southern Rockies. All of them
have been formally described: the Colorado River cutthroat,
greenback, Rio Grande, and yellowfin. One of the four, the
yellowfin, is now extinct.

The Colorado River subspecies, *Oncorhynchus clarki pleuriti-
cus,* of the upper Colorado, differs from the somber-colored
Yellowstone cutthroat in that it shines with bright colors of red,
orange, and gold. Its native range includes the two main tributaries of the Colorado above the Grand Canyon, the Green and
San Juan rivers. Partly bordering the Great Basin to the west, its
range also includes parts of the west slope of the Rocky Mountains. The Green River's cutthroat habitat is the headwaters region in Wyoming, but downstream in Utah, Flaming Gorge
dam has greatly changed the river. The Colorado River subspecies is extremely susceptible to hybridization with the rainbow.
Consequently, cutthroats rapidly disappeared from mainstream
reaches of their native rivers and from most of the smaller
streams as well. It is present now only in isolated headwater
reaches of its original distribution. Some introductions of the
pure-strain Colorado River cutthroat have been made in new
waters to assist in preserving some populations of the native
stock.

To the east of the Colorado drainage and on the east slope of
the Rockies, the greenback cutthroat subspecies, *Oncorhynchus
clarki stomias,* occupied the Colorado headwaters of the South
Platte and Arkansas rivers, which drain toward the Mississippi
and the Gulf of Mexico. The greenback is similar to the Colorado River subspecies, from which it is derived by headwater
transfers. It is colorful and has larger, much more notable spots.

The greenback's common name originated with Dr. David
Starr Jordan, an early ichthyologist; but interestingly, this subspecies is no "greener" on its back than any other cutthroat! Like
its ancestor the Colorado, the greenback is very susceptible to
hybridization, and it came extremely close to extinction. At one

point, only five small populations existed. Recent culture of this subspecies and introductions into other, fishless waters have successfully recovered this native from the brink of extinction.

The Pecos River, New Mexico, an original home of *Oncorhynchus clarki virginalis*, the Rio Grande cutthroat subspecies.

The Rio Grande cutthroat, *Oncorhynchus clarki virginalis*, exists in two forms in separate geographical locations, the upper headwaters of the Rio Grande in New Mexico and southern

Colorado, and upper reaches of the Pecos River, just to the east of the Rio Grande range.

A tributary of the Rio Grande in southwestern New Mexico is the southernmost extension of the Rio Grande cutthroat's range, as well as the most southern occurrence of any cutthroat trout. The Rio Grande cutthroat is now rare throughout its native range. The subspecies has been severely reduced both by habitat destruction from livestock grazing and by its susceptibility to replacement by other species, by brown trout particularly in its southern range. Several restoration efforts are underway by New Mexico and Colorado state agencies and by the U.S. Fish and Wildlife Service. The two forms differ in spotting: the Pecos form has the larger spots, but both have the rich red and orange coloration like the previous two Rocky Mountain subspecies.

Although it is now extinct, the yellowfin cutthroat, *Oncorhynchus clarki macdonaldi*, has been an enigma throughout its short but almost mythic history. In the late 1800s, some unusually large cutthroat trout were caught by anglers in Twin Lakes, a pair of glacial lakes in the heart of greenback cutthroat country near Leadville, Colorado. Twin Lakes at that time held a large population of small greenbacks, so the catch of something really different and large—cutthroats up to 10 pounds—created much excitement. Ichthyologist David Starr Jordan visited the lakes at the invitation of an angler and caught both kinds—small greenbacks and the new trout that was totally unlike the greenback. This strange fish had small, irregular spots (unlike the greenback's large round spots), and it was silvery in color (unlike the colorful greenback). It had no red at all, but definite yellow-gold fins. This became the yellowfin cutthroat, with its subspecific name of *macdonaldi* after Marshall MacDonald, United States Fish Commissioner at the time.

The yellowfin's preferred feeding behavior was piscivorous and its flesh pale; the greenback, which fed on invertebrates including abundant scuds, or *Gammarus*, had the fiery red flesh typically deriving from such foods. Obviously two distinct and ecologically separated forms of cutthroat inhabited Twin Lakes.

But where had the yellowfin come from—this large stranger among the small greenback natives? Some clues were forthcoming, but nothing seemed certain. Using hatchery culture operations, introductions were attempted to establish the yellowfin in other waters, but eventually the identity of its source of eggs—and the hatchery product itself—became uncertain. The question arose because, eventually, introductions of rainbow trout and other salmonids were made in Twin Lakes. And by the early 1900s, rainbows were dominant and yellowfins gone.

Since then, odd reports have turned up here and there, like ghosts and visions. Some have seemed fruitful, others simply imaginary, but all inevitably turned out to be other cutthroats. In *Native Trout of Western North America*, Robert Behnke poses the intriguing question: "May any offspring of those early introductions be lurking in some remote water...?" The finding of yellowfins, perhaps in a lake in some high, rocky valley, would be a treasure recovered.

◆   ◆   ◆

THE CUTTHROAT IS OUR NATIVE TROUT of western arid lands. As such, it has been subjected to one of the most degrading of environmental offenses, the streambank trampling by cattle. In dry range, cattle and other livestock are attracted to streams and their riparian zones for water and the lush vegetation that grows there—often the only green forage in sight. The result is a transformation from cool, productive streams to warm, wide, shallow trickles, often braided and filled with sediment. Riparian zones become completely destroyed. Warmer water, lack of invertebrate food, and absence of cover have brought about great losses in trout abundance, including extinctions of unique genetic stocks. Although some improved means of protecting streams and riparian zones have been implemented on public lands, such restoration is far from complete, on public lands as well as private. Improvements are often resisted continuously and strenuously.

Other factors have also brought about severe declines in cutthroat populations. We have discussed the problem created by
cutthroat-rainbow hybridization. But cutthroats also competed
poorly against all other trout species—rainbow, brook, and
brown trout—that were naturalized in native cutthroat waters.
This, too, brought about drastic reductions. The brook trout,
especially, although noted for its own susceptibility to exotic
species competition in its eastern, native range, has competed so
successfully against cutthroat trout that it now dominates most
of the mountain headwater streams in which the cutthroat
evolved alone. Most pure-strain cutthroat stocks now live only in
some cold, high-elevation headwaters above waterfall barriers.

The introduction of alien species into the habitats of native
species has always been fraught with trouble. The effects of
competition and interbreeding may be the most harmful, but
changes in management operations and angling habits (the latter
also resulting from alien introductions) can also reduce the
quality of native fisheries, particularly of the cutthroat. Susceptibility to angling varies greatly among the four major inland
trout species. The brown trout, particularly, is much more resistant under most angling conditions than any other. When it is
stocked on top of brook, rainbow, or cutthroat trout in their
native range, the native invariably loses out. The series goes like
this: brown, least susceptible; rainbow, more susceptible; brook
trout, much more susceptible; and cutthroat, the most susceptible of all.

Different effects of angling have little effect when fishing
pressure is light, as it was decades ago. But today pressure
mounts. Greater numbers of anglers create the need for more
protective rules, like catch-and-release, which under conditions
of the heaviest pressure can do wonders in maintaining or restoring normal size-distributions in wild populations. But unrestricted harvest by angling in a mixed-species fishery removes
the greatest proportion from the most susceptible species, like
brook trout when brown trout are stocked on top, or cutthroat
when rainbows are stocked on top. Especially when large numbers of hatchery fish (for example, rainbows) are stocked on top

of a wild cutthroat population, the effect is likely to be an increase in fishing pressure stimulated by the stocking. The added fishing is then followed by a fall in cutthroat population, because the most susceptible fish is taken in higher proportions. In all probability, declines of cutthroat in the American West can be at least partly attributed to this differential in their susceptibility to angling.

Our perspectives on angling are slowly changing. Protective regulations are used increasingly to ameliorate the selective effects of hook-and-line fishing. Management programs in some states are shifting away from hatchery fish and stocking. Some of us now more highly value the angling experience for native species in natural habitats. Best of all, our perspectives on wild or tame trout, natural or created habitat, is also shifting, thanks to the efforts of a host of new fisheries biologists. Greater value is being placed by anglers and fishery managers alike on healthy, diverse systems. Some enlightened anglers are finding heightened appreciation on entering a wild, self-sustaining fishery, not as exploiters and consumers now, but as participants in the workings of a natural ecosystem.

TECHNICAL REFERENCES:

Behnke, Robert J. 1992. Native trout of western North America. *American Fisheries Society Monograph* 6.
Smith, Robert H. 1984. *Native trout of North America.* Frank Amato Publications, Portland, Oregon.
Trotter, Patrick C. 1987. *Cutthroat: Native trout of the West.* Colorado Associated University Press, Boulder, Colorado.

RiverSketch

FISH OUT OF WATER

F ISH ASEMBLAGES IN THE DESERT SOUTHWEST are probably less appreciated than any other group of fishes in North
America. In fact, the phrase "desert fish" seems almost a con-
tradiction in terms, an oxymoron. Fish need water; deserts are
dry. How can fish survive?

That question has been the focus of intensive research for
only the past 25 years. But among these desert ecosystems are
ideal opportunities for research in fish ecology. Fish prospering
in harsh desert conditions provide rare opportunities for scientific study. Results can help us to better forecast their future,
which, sadly, is in peril, and to make plans for their betterment.

Among Earth's aquatic ecosystems, those in the low desert
with its arid environment are the least habitable by fish. Two
main factors determine the limits of livability: scarcity of water
and, where there *is* some, its temporary occurrence. Temperature of water in deserts is another important factor, although
deserts as such are defined by the scarcity of water, not by their
temperature, and cold deserts do occur.

Many waters holding fish are remote and isolated. Some
small streams, flowing down from a source at higher elevations,
sink into the desert sands; some originate from springs, from
groundwater (also from distant mountains), forming pools but
going nowhere. In these aquatic habitats, rich in salts and nutrients, receiving almost continuous, direct sunlight, primary production is high. Some species of herbivorous fish, prospering in
water as warm as 110°, use the superabundance of algal food.

Most fishes of the deserts fall into two families: the minnows
(Cyprinidae) and the suckers (Catostomidae). Human perceptions of these two groups have been largely derogatory, contributing to the public opinion as either just "little fish" and "bottom ooze feeders." Nor do these hostile environments attract

the tourist interest that might otherwise engender concern for their conservation.

The common names of desert fishes are strange to those of us familiar with fishes of eastern North America and the Pacific Northwest. Common names that include Colorado, Gila, Sonoran, Yaqui, Opata, and Rio Grande readily suggest a southwestern origin. Descriptive names like humpback, bluehead, spikefin, bonytail, and woundfin are unknown in wetter regions, ichthyological strangers to our more common sport fish fauna.

The Southwest is a region deprived of moist winds blowing inland from the ocean. East of the mountains, winds are dry, and in these rain shadows little or no water remains. So the stage was set long ago for development of four major desert regions: the Great Basin, Chihuahuan, Sonoran, and Mohave deserts.

The four deserts present a basin and range environment, vast areas of arid plains and desert separated by isolated mountain ranges and plateaus. The Great Basin, the largest of the four, includes much of Utah and Nevada and smaller parts of California, Oregon, and Idaho, a region where streams and rivers find no outlet to the sea. The Chihuahuan Desert, next in size, lies mostly in the State of Chihuahua in northern Mexico but includes some of southern New Mexico and western Texas. The Sonoran Desert, mostly in the Mexican State of Sonora, includes parts of southern California and Arizona, and surrounds the lower Colorado River and the Gulf of California. The Mojave Desert, the smallest, lies east of the Sierra Nevada mountains in southeastern California and extreme southern Nevada; it includes Death Valley and the Salton Sea.

These are lands where evaporation exceeds precipitation, so theoretically there should be *no water*. But small water bodies exist, scattered within these huge arid regions, and it is their *isolation* that has created their diversity of fishes. Even in the hottest deserts, embedded oases occur with rich, moist riparian corridors. Before human intervention, highly evolved fish species lived in their isolation through thousands of years.

Almost all water abundant enough in the desert to provide for fish drains down seasonally from the mountains in streams or underground. A little flows on to the sea in the Gulf of California (by the Colorado River) and the Gulf of Mexico (by the Rio Grande), but much more evaporates, sinks into the desert sands or is consumed through human use.

Desert waters can be fairly divided into three types:

• medium to large rivers that have originated in mountains and flow into desert regions;

• small streams at intermediate elevations that result from seasonal spring rains and groundwater but often shrink to only a series of isolated pools in dry seasons;

• springs in the low desert that remain isolated with little or no outlet.

Major streams include the Colorado River and its desert tributaries, the Green, San Juan, Virgin, Little Colorado, Bill Williams, and Gila rivers. These waters flow through parts of the Great Basin, Mojave, and Sonoran deserts, emptying into the Gulf of California where the Colorado channel (typically with no remaining water) meets salt water. The Rio Grande, heading in Colorado and New Mexico, flows south and eastward through a northern part of the Chihuahuan Desert to form the international boundary between Texas and the Mexican State of Chihuahua. The Rio Yaqui originates in southeastern Arizona and northern Mexico and flows southwestward through Mexico to empty into the Gulf of California through the Sonoran Desert. Other important streams flow through Mexico to the Gulf. All of the river basins originate in tributaries in their upper watersheds, some with cutthroat trout, but at lower elevations they become home to a desert fish fauna.

Fishes in these streams of swift currents are fusiform with sharp fins and forked tails. Some are relatively large fish:

• bonytail, a minnow that attains two feet in length;

•Colorado squawfish (recently renamed pikeminnow), North America's largest minnow that used to be caught up to six feet in length, now rarely;

Many species of suckers also are resident in these larger streams; a sampling includes:

• razorback sucker, the most unusual, which has a prominent hump, or *keel*, in its back that helps the fish maneuver in swift currents; its original presence throughout the Colorado River has been greatly reduced, and it is now seriously endangered;

• flannelmouth sucker, historically common in the Colorado basin, much reduced now;

• desert sucker in the lower Colorado, Gila, Bill Williams, and Virgin rivers;

• Sonora sucker in the Gila and Bill Williams rivers, closely resembling the white sucker of northern regions;

• Yaqui sucker in the Rio Yaqui and formerly in extreme southeastern Arizona but now extirpated;

• bluehead sucker in the Great Basin, Snake River, and the Colorado system above Grand Canyon.

The razorback sucker, a fish of swift rapids in large rivers like the Colorado, is now listed as endangered.
(Photo courtesy of Paul C. Marsh, Arizona State University.)

Small streams in deserts of intermediate elevations flow intermittently through arroyos. Seasonal conditions are extremely unstable, ranging from flash floods to almost complete dryness. Winter rains and summer thunderstorms produce high flows, but these are temporary. Food supply varies greatly, as does reproductive activity, which takes advantage of suitable conditions existing for only short periods.

Nevertheless, some species of fish, almost all of them small minnows, survived and prospered in these harsh conditions. These include:

- roundtail chub and the beautiful shiner (actually highly colored) in the Rio Yaqui and other large to medium-sized rivers;
- Mexican stoneroller in the Rio Grande and other Mexican streams;
- virgin spinedace in the Virgin River;
- woundfin, a fish with no scales, rare and now found only in the Virgin River;
- spikedace and longfin dace in the Gila River basin.

With such precarious habitats that depend upon infrequent rains or rare outlets of groundwater, the desert group of fishes has probably suffered the most of any fish assemblage in North America. Some have already become extinct. Of the some 40 species remaining in the United States deserts, two-thirds are listed as either endangered, threatened, or of special concern. On the other hand, the speckled dace, resident throughout the Colorado basin and elsewhere, is the most common fish species in the western United States.

Found in the oases of small springs and pools is another small family of rare species, including the pupfish (family Cyprinodontidae). Most only an inch or two long, these tiny, chubby fish with unusually broad tails feed on abundant algae in the warm pools, where the pupfish production reaches into hundreds of pounds per acre (although one acre of water is rare). Another uncommon group of cyprinodontids, the springfishes, is characterized by the absence of pelvic fins. Few species of this small group reside in the United States, all in warm springs in small ranges located in the Sonoran Desert of southern Nevada. A few minnows also inhabit warm springs, but most pupfishes, springfishes, and minnows are listed as endangered or threatened and still face uncertain futures.

Life for desert fish is precarious. Because species in these isolated environments have in the past adapted to such small, specific bits of water, their existence in the face of human technology becomes even more uncertain. When the water in a small, isolated stream is impounded, withdrawn for irrigation, or confined in straightened channels for residential and industrial use, the inevitable result is extinction. Almost two-thirds of all fish species listed in the federal Endangered Species Act are those from the southwestern deserts.

Prior to white settlement and its dams and diversions, native Americans lived along rivers that flowed year-round and by desert springs with predictable flows, despite the heat and scarce distribution of water. But the needs and desires of new colonists changed all that.

To these new inhabitants, the extremes of heat and shortage of water seemed insupportable of life. Then it was discovered that desert soils were rich in nutrients, lacking only water; after all, the rare spring rains made the desert bloom.

The water-scarcity problem was soon solved by two means: damming the mountain rivers and pumping the deep groundwater. Today no mountain river practicable for damming is left undammed. With the hydropower produced in the mountains, electric pumps elsewhere reached deep into the desert's groundwater. Water for irrigation became plentiful, and from the dams more electricity was amply available. The desert bloomed, not only with lettuce and strawberries, but also with cities that attracted increasing human populations. It was this paradise of mild winters (and air-conditioned summers, requiring huge amounts of electrical power) that spelled doom for the fishes of aquatic habitats that lost their water. Water tables in most low desert valleys have been lowered by more than 150 feet, in some areas over 650 feet, drying up streams and springs.

And the native fish? In the heady craze of development, bumper stickers once read "Kill the pupfish." Native fishes prospered no more in their familiar small desert streams and pools, nor in the alien waters of stilled reservoirs, cold tailwaters, irrigation ditches, or concrete canals, nor in the empty springs that had nurtured the pupfish and springfish for hundreds of thousands of years. The bumper stickers prevailed.

Some conservation measures have been planned or implemented, but for the many species now extinct these measures came too late. And more extinctions appear imminent.

The metaphor "like fish out of water" refers to the condition of any animal taken out of its normal, life-sustaining habitat. But among the shrinking fish fauna of our southwestern deserts are many species that are running—or have run—literally out of water.

SELECTED REFERENCES:

Rinne, John N., and Wendell L. Minckley. 1991. *Native Fishes of Arid Lands: A dwindling resource of the desert Southwest.* United States Forest Service, General Technical Report RM-206.

Sigler, William F., and John W. Sigler. 1996. *Fishes of Utah: A natural history.* University of Utah Press, Salt Lake City.

Chapter **21**

SALMO

ONLY A FEW YEARS AGO, fish taxonomists decided that the genus name of rainbow and cutthroat trout should be *Oncorhynchus,* and not *Salmo.* Now there remain only two species of *Salmo* in North America: the brown trout and the Atlantic salmon). So, here we take up these two species in the same chapter. Besides sharing the same genus name, the brown and Atlantic share some other traits, including a few striking look-alikes in certain life history stages.

The two species diverged from a common ancestor about 20 million years ago, and no major form has diverged from these species since. However, each exhibits some differences between isolated populations, expressions of the stock concept. Atlantics vary among spawning rivers; browns vary over a host of inland locations. Atlantics are mostly anadromous, although a number of stream-resident and landlocked forms exist; the brown, although primarily a stream resident, also occurs in anadromous populations. The migratory brown can be found as a native in Europe where it is known as "sea-trout," as well as in some successful naturalized populations around the Great Lakes and along the coasts of the North Atlantic, especially in the Maritime provinces and Newfoundland. Both species build redds, like other trout and salmon, and both require a tributary stream (or at least partly upwelling water in lake shoals) for spawning.

The two species may be easily confused in some circumstances. For example, juvenile Atlantic salmon during their parr stage, in small streams, look like stream brown trout at the same age, complete with golden color and red spots. During the parr stage (a sort of adolescence), both species display definite *parr marks*. These appear much like thumb prints on the fish's flanks, and they disappear as fish approach maturity. Folks familiar with the two species in the same stream recognize several distinct traits in the Atlantic salmon:

- larger eye;
- more of a forked tail;
- slimmer appearance;
- thinner, longer pectoral fins;
- shorter *maxilla* (upper jaw), which does not extend beyond the eye, giving the fish the appearance of a smaller mouth.

Another look-alike example is the external appearance of landlocked salmon and lake-run brown trout. Both are duller or tannish in color, not yellow or golden, and both lack red spots. Both have cross-shaped black spots unlike the round spots of the stream brown and the sea-run Atlantic.

The native range of the salmon includes both sides of the Atlantic Ocean, but the brown trout is indigenous only on the European side. Of course, the brown has been widely introduced into North America, although not very much within the native range of Atlantics in North America.

One of the most interesting questions is how these two related species have remained as distinct species in the same waters of Europe over such a long time. Twenty million years is a long time to be living together and still maintain species independence! There are some marked differences in the life histories of the two species—feeding, spawning, seasonality—and these may be responsible. We'll explore some of these differences and how both species have attained such enormous popularity and respect in the streams and rivers of North America.

◆   ◆   ◆

WE HAVE DISCUSSED MANY ASPECTS of genetic diversity, the stock concept, and original distributions of species in previous chapters. These were all related to native species whose populations were isolated over long periods of time, during which evolutionary processes created distinct forms. In many cases, several discrete races of European brown trout lived together in sympatric populations.

Atlantic salmon parr (top) and brown trout parr (bottom)
look much alike, with a few differences described above.
Note parr marks in both species.

The brown trout (*Salmo trutta*) is a foreigner to North America, and its introduction has been with hatchery stock of unknown genetic origins. Various forms that existed in Europe have been thoroughly mixed in North American hatcheries. Distinct stocks undoubtedly still exist in Europe, reflecting such concepts that apply to native stocks in their native habitat. But with brown trout in North America, all bets are off. The genetic character of brown trout here, like that of hatchery rainbows around the world, has become a homogeneous soup.

The brown trout's introduction into North America began in 1883, when fertilized eggs from Germany were shipped across the ocean to a New York hatchery, kept cool with large quantities of ice in ship cabins. The eggs were from two sources: a stream resident population and a large, lake-living type. From the Long Island Cold Spring Hatchery, the eggs were divided and sent to hatcheries in Caledonia, New York, and Northville, Michigan. In these two locations, the first brown trout were born in North America.

In the next year, 1884, more eggs, these from Scotland's Loch Leven, were brought across in a similar fashion to be hatched and stocked in Newfoundland. In the next few years, transfers were made to streams in other states and provinces. The colonization of North America by brown trout had begun.

The first shipment of eggs had been collected from a German stream that flowed through the estate of a Baron von Behr as well as from a lake. The combination was therefore known as the "German brown." Later, all offspring from this shipment were called the Von Behr strain. The offspring from eggs collected in Scotland became known as Loch Levens. Apparently existing as distinct stocks, the fish from these two sources were quite different in appearance. The Von Behr form was the more colorful, with a golden belly and red spots. In contrast, the Loch Leven was duller and without the bright spotting.

For some time, the two groups were separated in different hatcheries, but they were soon mixed in various other hatcheries. The following decades saw fisheries management worldwide emphasizing the introduction of exotic species, including brown trout, to all waters that seemed suitable (and many waters that were not). It was a shotgun approach to colonizing the Earth with brown trout.

Brown trout became naturalized in many, far-distant streams and lakes. Today, the species is broadly acclimated to many localities—35 of the United States, most Canadian provinces, South America, South Africa and Kenya, India, Australia and New Zealand, and various other areas—anywhere that summer-cool streams occur. Successful introductions have been mainly in northern (and southern "down-under") regions and high elevations of mountain ranges in the tropics.

Next to the rainbow, the brown trout is the hatcheryman's second choice. It is easy to raise and transport. More likely to be successful in marginal waters, the brown tends to persist longer and grow larger than other species, especially when stocked in small streams. Although less susceptible to capture by hook and line than other species, the brown usually plays by the rules during distinctive insect hatches, readily rising to artificials as well as naturals if the imitations are tied to a precise match. More often than not, matching the hatch is a challenge, and far from always successful.

Particularly in view of its popularity among anglers, the brown trout is here to stay in a big way. In the world's experience with transporting and introducing many exotic fish species, the brown trout stands out as perhaps the most successful of all—from both the brown trout's and the angler's point of view.

Such success has not always been greeted with enthusiasm. Browns have become *personae non grata* in much of New England. There they are perceived as serious competitors to native brook trout and Atlantic salmon, both much loved in that part of the country. The brown, in fact, has been partly blamed for the catastrophic decline of salmon in Maine and other northern Atlantic coastal states. Elsewhere in the United States, the brown is unwelcome in national parks, where regulations allow taking of browns but protect native trout such as brook trout and cutthroats in their native ranges. Then, too, Canada has increasingly emphasized its native species and has essentially ceased all hatchery stocking of brown trout.

Before modern fisheries management began the introduction of foreign species around the globe, the brown trout existed in many forms and races in its Old World dwelling places. It was known as a *polytypic* species, occurring in a multitude of forms. The Von Behr and Loch Leven strains are only two examples. Included in the native range of brown trout—all of Europe, western Asia, and scattered spots around the Mediterranean—exists an enormous diversity of habitats. For example, a recent report described a brown trout population in an isolated mountain range in northern Spain where water temperatures were recorded into the $80°$ range Fahrenheit.

Many millions of years ago, the European brown trout had colonized all suitable habitats until stopped by desert, arid plains, or ice. The different forms described by past natural historians, commercial fishermen, and anglers are legion. As many as 30 different common names were once in vogue, reflecting different external appearances, seasons of migration, and locations. Early ichthyologists listed 50 or more described species—and one especially enthusiastic taxonomist described 83!

Not too long ago, the long lists were reduced to only three species: stream-resident (German brown, *Salmo fario*), lake-resident (Loch Leven, *S. lacustris*), and sea-trout (*S. trutta*), migrating to the ocean. Now, however, fish taxonomists around the world agree on just one species—*Salmo trutta*—which exists in many different forms—or stocks—in appearance, coloration, and habit.

Lake-living brown trout, like other salmonids in lacustrine habitats, generally are larger fish. With the greater room for foraging, especially feeding on other lake fish, lake-living browns were able to attain larger sizes than stream fish, sometimes huge. Of course, spawning must take place in the flowing water of the lake's tributaries or in outflow streams. In times past, such was especially true in some large alpine lakes of central Europe as well as in the Caspian Sea of eastern Europe. Dr. Robert Behnke gives an account of a 68-pound brown from an Alpine lake and a 72-pound specimen from a Caspian Sea tributary around 1900—neither taken with rod and reel tackle, though. It is from distant naturalized populations, however, that modern angling records have been taken. For some years, a brown trout caught in Argentina in 1951 of 35 pounds, 15 ounces, held the rod and reel record. More recently, a specimen of 40 pounds, 4 ounces was taken in 1992 from the Little Red River, a tailwater of the White River system in Arkansas.

The brown trout has made an enormous impact upon the angling community, for several reasons. It can prosper in habitats of lower quality—lower oxygen, higher temperatures, greater sediment loads and other pollutants—than those required by native species in North America. In marginal waters, the brown can use small, warmwater species, such as some minnows, for food and then grow to large sizes. The brown readily takes to lakes, reservoirs, and tailwaters, and with periodic stocking, it thrives in marginal waters where suitable spawning gravels are absent.

To the growing army of fly fishers, the brown is the quintessence of a surface-feeding predator, rising easily to emerging insects. Such surface feeding frenzies, however, seem to contradict an extremely important reason for its success—its strong resistance to being caught by angling. Even in the wildest hatches, all of us have been sometimes frustrated by the brown trout's ability to select *against* our best imitations!

The downside of the brown trout's success is its ability to outcompete other stream salmonids in many river systems. As such a successful competitor, the brown has been responsible for the loss or reduction of many native populations, such as cutthroats in western waters and brook trout throughout the East. Of course, its resistance to capture by angling, compared with the relative susceptibility of the brook and cutthroat trout, is partly responsible. In many former brook trout streams, the brown predominates except in the tiniest headwater reaches.

This author had the good fortune to document such a change in a small stream in Minnesota. From a population composed almost entirely of brook trout, the brown trout nearly replaced the native brooks in only 15 years—even though no fishing or hatchery stocking occurred.

Many other reasons have been put forth to explain the brown's mastery over other species. Faster growth and larger sizes give it advantage in claiming food, space, and spawning gravels, as major factors. Brown trout juveniles appear to frequent faster water in riffles, while brook trout favor slower recesses along banks or in aquatic vegetation like watercress. While electrofishing the Minnesota stream mentioned above, fingerling brown trout were always found in the fast water of riffles and cobbles, brook trout along slower edges. And when a major flood ripped out all the watercress from the stream, brook trout numbers took a nosedive.

Another important factor lies in the different spawning behaviors of the two species when they occupy the same stream: brown trout spawn a little later in the fall than do brook trout. The result is that the brook trout's redds may be *superimposed*—dug up and destroyed—by the brown's later redd construction, giving the browns a greater likelihood of reproductive success over the brook trout's.

Although some anglers mourn the loss of native species, the brown trout is popularly viewed as the salvation of American trout fishing. Providing high-quality angling in heavily fished streams, the brown survives where native brook trout would be quickly overexploited. However, modern-day protective regulations, such as lure restrictions and catch-and-release, can do wonders to restore and maintain rare or threatened species—a popular and successful approach to trout management.

◆   ◆   ◆

ALTHOUGH THE ATLANTIC SALMON was once abundant in the ocean tributaries of New England and eastern Canada, it now has to struggle for survival. A profusion of dams, sediment, sawdust, and other pollutants have for a century and a half brought declines and extirpations of salmon to this part of its range, especially in the rivers of the United States.

The Atlantic salmon has been called the King of Fish. No other freshwater fish has enjoyed as much admiration as has this sovereign of swift and tumultuous rivers around the shores of the North Atlantic.

The salmon's high esteem is most appropriately credited in its return from the sea. In the fecund ocean it feeds well, reaching large sizes in short periods of time. Most returnees are one-year fish who come back to the river weighing in at three to eight pounds. The 10- to 15-pounders we most often hear about are either two- or three-year fish, whereas the four- and five-year fish (repeat spawners) provide the really big ones—40 pounds and larger.

Maine's Narraguagus River is one of the few important Atlantic salmon streams remaining in the United States.

The world angling record is near 80 pounds, from Norway. In North America, 55 pounds, from Quebec's Grand Cascapedia River. In the United States, historical records of 40 to 50 pounds are listed from the state of Maine, the country's major salmon producer. Obviously, the cold waters of the North Atlantic's upwelling, nutrient-laden water, mixing with the Gulf Stream, are one of the most productive ocean regions of Earth.

Unlike Pacific salmon, all of which die after spawning, the Atlantic can repeat, although only one in twenty lives to spawn again. Atlantic salmon continue to live and grow in the ocean between spawnings and put on their considerable weight.

◆   ◆   ◆

THE RIVER LIFE OF JUVENILE ATLANTIC SALMON is much like that of other anadromous species, such as the migratory rainbow (steelhead) and the European sea-trout (brown trout). From its humble beginnings as a tiny fry in the streambed gravel, the fry advances to a fingerling or parr that is barely distinguishable from the brown trout. In a couple of years in the stream, it changes to a silvery smolt ready for its ocean adventure.

Like other salmonids, the Atlantic's life history varies with location and quality of its natal river. Infancy is a critical time of life. Upon it depends the successful return of the adult, so strong and large after its growth in the ocean, so prized upon its spawning run. But unless the river nurtures the fish from helpless infant to healthy adolescent, the enormous productivity of the ocean cannot be garnered.

Good spawning redds require coarse gravel that can be excavated by the adult female and clean, oxygenated water that flows through and sustains the eggs and embryos. Turbid water with suspended sediment can clog the redd and suffocate eggs and fry.

Fertilized eggs are laid in the autumn, buried beneath several inches to a foot of coarse gravel, safe from most predators and environmental calamities. The redd, constructed by the female parent, is the only form of parental protection the little offspring receive. For two to three months, the eggs develop into tiny embryos. Upon hatching, a minuscule Atlantic salmon, with eyes, musculature, and newly forming fins, pops into life as an *alevin*, or *sac fry*. Within the darkness of its stony chamber, the alevin carries its bulky yolk sac, which must serve as its food and energy source for the next three or four weeks.

When the last of the yolk has been used up, this newborn becomes an independent *fry* able to swim and wriggle through the interstices of the gravel above. The struggle upward is another dangerous stage of its new life. The objective now is *emergence*—leaving the protection of its redd—a struggle through dark and torturous passageways toward the lighted river overhead.

Not always is the struggle successful. If the stream water coursing through the redd becomes heavy with sediment, oxygen may be reduced to such low levels that suffocation results. If a flood lays down a compact layer of sediment and gravel overhead, forming an *armor* over the streambed, the fry may become entombed.

And for those new fry that make it, their new world is now a matter of seeking food and energy for themselves. They must also avoid many predators, dashing back into the stony crevices of a gravel riffle when threatened. In this new challenge of the open stream, the fry face another critical stage in their life history. It is in this river phase that the strength of their year class—and the size of their eventual spawning run—is set.

After one year, in most cases, an Atlantic salmon juvenile has grown to become a *parr*—like the brown trout—about three to four inches long. The parr marks on its flanks are distinctive, numbering ten to twelve from its head to just in front of its tail. The lateral line runs through each one, with a red spot between each adjoining parr mark. These will be retained until smoltification, just before migration out of the river.

The quality of river habitat forecasts the number and size of smolts that eventually migrate to the ocean. The river quality is, in turn, equally important to adults returning on their spawning run—and to sport fishing.

Three principal habitat factors are essential for juveniles:
- suitable gravel for spawning and incubation of eggs;
- summer productivity of benthic invertebrates for food;
- the proper streambed structure to provide winter protection to fry and parr.

In summer, the fry and parr need the right streambed to establish feeding territories: small pebbly riffles with shallow water for fry and coarse gravel and cobble bottoms with deeper water for parr. In winter, both fry and parr move to coarser substrates or pools, the larger parr at greater depths, which afford them added protection from predators. They continue to feed in winter, parr more actively than fry, mainly at night.

Success through the Atlantic salmon's river life depends greatly upon the production rate of the juvenile salmon, which, in turn, depends upon the productivity of available invertebrate foods. Growth rates of fry and parr, and number and size of smolts reaching the ocean, depend upon the basic productivity of the natal stream system. Ultimately, the number of returning adults is contingent upon the number of juveniles—and so also will be the fishing.

The food of the fry, parr, and smolts has been studied but little, especially fry still in the gravel. The main points that we can make are that juveniles are carnivorous and opportunistic. In the laboratory, direct observations have led to the conclusion that their first foods after exhausting the yolk sac must be moving, either in the current or swimming. A good guess about food in the wild stream at this infant stage includes microscopic components of the meiofauna, possibly some protozoans and rotifers that inhabit the hyporheic zone. On the streambed, benthic microcrustaceans and first-instar midge larvae may fill the bill. Their choices, as well as the size of their prey, increase with the size of fry and parr and the gape of their mouths.

In the second year of life, parr from about four to seven inches are able to take advantage of a more diverse host of aquatic invertebrates, feeding on the drift of benthic mayfly nymphs, caddis larvae, and other macroinvertebrates. The parr become familiar to us fly fishers when they strike our nymph imitations. And if we do not already know what's coming, we might think them just tiddler brown trout!

For most of their river life, Atlantic salmon fry and parr stay close to home, with a strong territoriality confining them to small areas. Some instream migration may occur in late fall and winter to more suitable wintering sites. Territories must provide proper streambed structure and sufficient foraging space. The size of territory varies with the size of fish (larger territory for larger fish) and with food availability (smaller territory when more food is available).

Eventually the time arrives for the Atlantic salmon's next life cycle stage—migration to the sea, where it will roam widely in the open ocean. Preparation for smolting comes in the autumn before seaward migration, which occurs in spring. Larger parr, mostly one-and-a-half years old, begin a slow drift downstream from former stream reaches, to overwinter in lower sections of the river.

With spring, they undergo a marked change in coloration and appearance. Parr lose their parr marks, red spots, and golden bellies. They take on a shimmering silver and no longer resemble brown trout. Physiological changes also take place that allows the fish to survive and prosper in salt water. (The density of fish blood is between the density of fresh water [dilute] and the density of salty ocean water [concentrated], so all osmotic processes must be reversed.) The change into *smolts* is termed *smoltification*. And then, perhaps in the first spate of spring meltwater, the new smolts start to drift downstream, tail first in the swiftest waters.

◆   ◆   ◆

EONS AGO, MANY LANDLOCKED POPULATIONS developed in the Atlantic salmon's range. Some were locked into large lakes that had once been connected by river to the sea but were cut off by long-ago geological events, creating falls or impassable rapids. Landslides occurring as the result of earthquakes, even in recorded history, block headwaters reaches of a river to migrating fish and isolate upstream populations.

Other stocks, however, for whatever reason, have adapted to lakes that still connect to the ocean and remain "landlocked" rather than migrating to the sea, spawning in tributary streams. Some landlocked populations also developed in streams above impassable waterfalls, over which returnees from the ocean could not ascend.

A few dwarf populations of Atlantics occur in isolated streams where parr never grow larger than four or five inches but mature and reproduce. Two such stocks have been described, one in Norway and one in Newfoundland.

The Little River, Newfoundland, is one of many excellent Atlantic salmon streams along eastern Canadian coasts.

This author had the opportunity of observing a dwarf population in Newfoundland a few years ago. While fly fishing for brook trout in a small stream on a foggy, spring day, I began catching some Atlantic salmon parr perhaps four to five inches long. A figure appeared behind me on the stream bank, a local biologist, and asked me how I was doing. When I replied that I was catching and examining some young salmon, he told me that these were probably adults several years old. He pointed downstream where, through the fog, I could barely discern what seemed to be a high bank, almost a small mountain. It was an enormous gravel bar, deposited across the stream at the edge of the sea, by some long-ago, huge storm. Now the stream just trickles through the gravel to the ocean—and the salmon cannot access salt water. He told me that the mature parr spawn over riffles by depositing eggs the same size as those from ocean-run fish, but in greatly reduced numbers. The eggs fall into stony crevices on the streambed, for the fish are too small to dig normal redds.

The native distribution of Atlantic salmon extends over a wide latitudinal range—from the Temperate Zone to the Arctic. The productivity level of most of its streams is typically low, as in most freestone streams with low alkalinity, but productivity also varies with latitude. In southern portions of their range, one year may be the norm before smolting; in higher latitudes, longer. In northern Labrador and northern Scandinavia, the length of parr life can be seven to eight years before migration to the sea. The length of river life, then, depends not so much on a set schedule of years as on the size reached, about six or seven inches. That size depends in turn on a number of environmental factors, water temperature and productivity of invertebrate foods being the most important.

The problem of competition between different species has long occupied the concern of fishery biologists and managers. Unwise introductions of alien species have brought about most of this concern, particularly when the introductions have extirpated native species. The brown trout, although it is highly regarded in many regions as a worthy addition to our sport fish fauna, has caused perhaps the greatest trouble. For example, it is responsible for the reduction or loss of brook trout in the latter's native range in eastern North America. In the Appalachian Mountains, the stocking of rainbows in native brook trout streams has greatly diminished brook trout populations. In the West, the cutthroat's many stocks have been reduced or extirpated by introductions of the other trout species.

On the other hand, a few cases of *sympatry*, in which two species coexist successfully, are well known. Brown trout and Atlantic salmon coexist in Europe, and Atlantics and brook trout in ocean tributaries of eastern Canada. It is clear, however, that in both of these cases the two species have existed together over long geological periods, obviously partitioning their habitat between the two. For example, we know that when brown and Atlantics are managed together in North America by brown trout stocking, the two species tend to separate the physical habitat, with Atlantics in shallow riffles and browns in deeper water and pools.

◆   ◆   ◆

THE EXPLOSIVE FIGHT OF AN ATLANTIC SALMON fresh from the salt on the end of a fly line, including repeated leaps into spray-filled air, may be thought responsible for the species name, *salar*, which means the *leaper*. More likely, however, the name comes from the fish's ability to leap up and over high waterfalls—up to 12 feet, vertically—in its struggle to gain its natal spawning gravel. His Royal Highness of angling legendry genuinely earns his appellation of high jumper—whether over river obstacles or on a fly line.

Take your choice—*salar*, indeed.

TECHNICAL REFERENCES:

Gibson, R.J. 1993. The Atlantic salmon in fresh water: Spawning, rearing and production. *Reviews in Fish Biology and Fisheries.* Volume 3, pages 39-73.

Waters, Thomas F. 1983. Replacement of brook trout by brown trout over 15 years in a Minnesota stream: Production and abundance. *Transactions of the American Fisheries Society.* Volume 112, pages 137-146.

RiverSketch

THE AVIAN LINKAGE

HARDLY A RIVER TRAVELER, whether with camera, paddle, or fly rod, has gone far without being surprised by the sudden rattle of a kingfisher, disturbed during its river patrol by the human intruder. Kingfishers are strongly territorial. And they don't take kindly to intruders, human or otherwise. Beautifully colored, stubby-bodied, large-headed and big-eyed, and notably crested, this natural fish predator may be the most common of river birds that we notice along our favorite streams. But few of us, perhaps, have seen its plummeting dive into shallow water, with open beak aimed at an unsuspecting small fish.

The most common and abundant in North America is the Belted Kingfisher, named after a rust-colored "belt" across the female's undersides. The Belted Kingfisher is distributed across the continent, from coast to coast. Migrating seasonally, north and south, it may stay farther north when a mild winter allows more open water on rivers. The kingfisher provides great parental care to its young—in a cavity deeply-tunneled into a high, overhanging stream bank, preferably well above river floods. The floor of the nesting room even slopes outward, so soil moisture that may percolate downward into the nest will run out.

Another river denizen—the Harlequin Duck—is not so familiar to most of us, preferring remote, rushing mountain rivers. Like its namesake, the comic dancer of European Middle Ages, this most dapper member of the diving ducks is similarly dressed in gaudy colors and quilt-work designs, disporting with seeming abandon in the wildest rapids.

The "harlie" is also migratory, but in an unusual way—east and west. Known commonly as a sea duck, harlequins migrate from the ocean coast inland to the mountains for breeding. Like salmon, they follow river courses from the sea to the mountains and their natal streams. Although nesting takes place along quiet reaches, ducklings later drift downstream to play in cascading rapids, feeding on benthic aquatic invertebrates to satisfy their ravenous juvenile need for protein.

Excellent swimmers, buoyant like corks, harlequins can ride either river haystacks or pounding ocean surf, power dive into turbulent depths, or speed with strong legs like motorboats in a rough sea. An ocean's rocky lee shore, disaster to ancient sailing mariners, and the roaring river rapids of classes III and up, are home and hearth to the Harlequin Duck.

The Belted Kingfisher, a common inhabitant
of riparian zones along streams and rivers.
(Carving in basswood, by Paul and Tracey
Lambrecht, Lanesboro, Minnesota.)

Akin to harlequins in their ecological relationship to streams are a few other species of waterfowl. Two ducks of the Southern Hemisphere, tied closely to torrential streams as their regular habitat, are the Torrent Duck of South America and the Blue Duck of New Zealand. Both species are residents in swift, high-gradient mountain streams, feeding on aquatic insects in rocky rapids, and strongly defending territories of river reaches that are defined by their aquatic invertebrate food supply. Other species of fish-eating raptors, waterfowl, and shore birds, are also common but temporary occupants of rivers. Mergansers, cormorants, herons, gulls, eagles and ospreys are often present but not obligate to flowing-water environments.

Two small shore birds are particularly fascinating and frequently observed by river users—the American Dipper (or Water Ouzel) and the Spotted Sandpiper. Both are capable of skilled underwater behavior. Limited in distribution to southwestern North American streams, the dipper can be seen along edges of swift streams walking with a "teetering" motion, almost appearing to be unstable and about to fall over. But it is an excellent swimmer and can actually walk on the stream bottom underwater. The Spotted Sandpiper is also common along small, swift streams but is not so limited to flowing water. It displays similar teetering movements and literally "flies" underwater. Both species feed on stream invertebrates or small fish, picking over stones and organic detritus along the water's edge. Furthermore, many other wading and shore birds—other sandpipers, plovers, rails, snipes, and herons—can often be seen along streams, but these are not limited to a riverine habitat.

The Louisiana Waterthrush, a small, inconspicuous warbler that inhabits small, swift streams, makes up for its drab color with ringing song and clear whistles. Breeding along streams in deciduous woods of eastern United States and southern Ontario, it builds a hidden nest in cavities under stream banks, root masses, and small brush collections. It is one of the earliest of spring migrants.

The Louisiana Waterthrush is a "tail-wagger." It can be distinguished by the early trout angler by its bobbing behavior while patrolling stream edges or perched on exposed stones in a riffle. Like other avian stream associates, it feeds mainly on aquatic invertebrates and, during insect emergences, on flying adults of mayflies, caddisflies, and other stream insects. This species is noted for its feeding behavior of pulling out and flipping over leaves from leaf-pack collections in stony riffles and edges, searching for invertebrate prey. Like other riparian birds, the Louisiana Waterthrush is territorial, defending a reach of stream of perhaps five hundred yards or more for nest building, rearing of young, and feeding. It is strongly dependent upon clean water and a healthy riparian zone, free from human disturbance.

We always see and hear many birds along streams, although only a few are truly obligated to a riverine habitat. Some of these occupy other watery edges—along lakes, ponds, and oceans—as well as stream banks. Some we see are essentially riparian—living in the moist terrestrial strip along streams—and these may also inhabit wetlands elsewhere. But several seem drawn to specific stream elements—like rushing rapids for play or feeding, and eroding stream banks for nesting.

An avian stream complement adds greatly to the colorful and fascinating diversity of life along our rivers and streams. A love of this rich variety of color, music, and sport should also lead us to a tenacious stewardship. Our river wealth can be easily lost—in polluted water or by unwise river manipulations such as dams and misplaced bridges. There is little avian diversity on the flat water of a dammed-up reservoir.

SELECTED REFERENCES:

Chadwick, Douglas H. 1993. The Harlequin Duck: Bird of white waters. *National Geographi.* Volume 184, number 5 (November), pages 116-132.

Line, Les. 1996. The Fisher King. *National Wildlife.* Volume 34, number 5 (June/July), pages 28-35.

Chapter **22**

PACIFIC SALMON

F IVE SPECIES OF PACIFIC SALMON (genus *Oncorhynchus*) inhabit the North American waters of the Pacific Ocean. As anadromous fishes, they also occupy the myriad streams and rivers tributary to the sea in their early life and, later, as spawning adults.

For millennia, salmon were the literal mainstay of a host of native American tribes and populations, and later—for the past century and a half—these five fishes have enriched the culture of the European immigrants who fished for them commercially.

The five species are: the pink (or humpback) *Oncorhynchus gorbuscha*; the sockeye (or red) *O. nerka*; the chum (or dog) *O. keta*; the coho (or silver) *O. kisutch*; and the chinook (or king) *O. tshawytscha*. Differences in natural histories among these five fishes, ecological contrasts that distinguish the species, illustrate some of the most striking examples of evolutionary divergence.

Two of these fishes provide spectacular sport fishing when, as adults, they approach or enter coastal streams. Two other inland fishes that used to be included in the genus *Salmo*—the rainbow trout and cutthroat—are now classified in the genus *Oncorhynchus*. The basic behavior of the anadromous rainbow, the steelhead, is much like the salmon's and is mentioned here as well.

Drs. W. B. Scott and E. J. Crossman, in their classic *Freshwater Fishes of Canada*, state: "Few fish...have had as large an impact on man, and *of man on them,* as have the Pacific salmon—" (emphasis added).

The scientific literature on Pacific salmons is enormous. Although it concerns both the ocean phase (main growth period) and stream stages (juvenile and returning adult), we will be concerned here with the two freshwater periods. The basic life cycle common to all species includes:

• incubation and hatching of eggs in a salmonid redd in an inland stream;

• juvenile life in the stream ranging from a few days to four years;

• migration downstream to the ocean for one to four years, where most growth occurs;

• return of the adults to spawn and die in their natal streams.

We'll take up each species in turn, emphasizing the stream, or freshwater phases of its life cycle, especially the differences between species.

◆   ◆   ◆

PINK, OR HUMPBACK, SALMON travel the shortest distance upstream on their spawning run, live a short time as juveniles in fresh water, grow in the ocean for the shortest time and, of the five species, grow as adults to the smallest size.

Pink salmon were originally distributed from central California northward, but they no longer occur in California or Oregon. Currently, they are distributed in Pacific tributaries from Puget Sound, Washington, north along the coasts of British Columbia and Alaska to the Arctic Ocean and the mouth of the Mackenzie River. They return to spawn upstream only short distances, from estuaries to a distance of 40 miles, and some spawn only in the estuaries. Spawning occurs in autumn in Washington, but in midsummer in Alaska. Incubation of eggs is about four to five months, and free-swimming fry, about 1 1/2 inches long, migrate immediately downstream toward the ocean in early spring, after which their ocean phase is about 18 months.

The pink salmon's life history is on an almost strict two-year cycle. This pattern means that the species is divided into even- and odd-year populations that remain almost completely separated. A rare three-year old may interbreed with a two-year old, an event that probably keeps the entire population from evolving into two separate species. Some streams have only an even- or an odd-year spawning run. The average size of spawning adults is about four pounds in weight and the length about 18 inches. Pink salmon adults may already be largely deteriorated at the time of spawning and die soon after. Because spawning is undertaken so close to the ocean, neither the young nor the adult feed to an appreciable extent during these two life stages.

In contrast to some of the other salmon's bright red flesh, the pink salmon's flesh is lighter, pinker. Spawning males bear a distinctive "hump" of fatty tissue just ahead of their dorsal fins, accounting for their common name "humpback salmon" or "humpies."

Few intentional introductions of pink salmon into non-native waters have been successful or long lasting. One *accidental* introduction into Lake Superior was remarkably successful. In 1956, hatchery-reared juveniles from the fall 1955 spawning were accidentally released into Ontario's Current River, a tributary of Lake Superior. Nothing was heard or seen of them until several migrating adults were captured by puzzled anglers in Minnesota's North Shore streams in the fall of 1959, the second generation after their release into the big lake. In a few years, this odd-year population exploded into huge runs of adults that created nuisance problems along the Minnesota shore. Adult bodies deteriorated into nothing much more than fungused skin and fins after only a short time in flowing water, and dead carcasses littered streams in great numbers.

Thus disdained at first, the runs gradually declined. Eventually a few enterprising anglers discovered means of taking these fish (mostly with yarn-flies), bright from their large-lake life, at the mouths of streams just as the salmon enter flowing water.

Anglers also discovered that these fresh, silvery fish were delicious eating; with minute scales, thin skin, and pink flesh, they resembled brook trout in the frying pan.

Pink salmon adults from a Lake Superior tributary exhibit severe fungus infections, yet still respond to electrofishing. (Photo by Stanley L. Smith, U.S. Fish and Wildlife Service.)

For several years in September of odd-numbered years, anglers gleefully awaited the Lake Superior runs of these small but tasty pink salmon, about 14 inches in length and weighing about one pound. Eventually a few fish of larger size were taken, 18 to 20 inches and two to three pounds. These were adults that had stayed in the big lake one year longer—that is, they were three-year-olds. Soon an even-year population developed. Eventually, the three-year-olds became more common, the result of retarded growth in the cold waters of Superior. Today, autumn runs of pink salmon are common in all years. Successful spawning runs of pink salmon now have spread around the lake and into the other Great Lakes, and even downstream into the St. Lawrence River. Some concern has been expressed about possible ecological effects of dispersal into the Atlantic Ocean.

◆   ◆   ◆

TRADITIONALLY, THE CHUM, OR DOG, SALMON has been at the bottom of the list of Pacific salmon. Disdained even by native tribes, legend has it that the fish were useful only to feed the dogs—thus their common name. For long, chum salmon were not sought by sport anglers, but soon they were found to readily take a surface fly and to put up a determined fight. Their inclusion in the commercial catch, especially in the Far North, is increasing, and it is not difficult to find canned chum salmon in the market today throughout much of the United States. Chum salmon are also pen-reared commercially and sold on the market as "silver bright" salmon. Sounds better!

The chum salmon's native distribution extends along the Pacific coast from northern California around the Alaskan Peninsula to the Arctic Ocean and the Mackenzie River, much like the pink's distribution. Alone among the five salmons, however, the chum occupies distant river reaches as far up the Mackenzie as Great Bear Lake. The chum has been little introduced outside its native streams, and where it has been attempted (Hudson Bay), it has not been successful. The seasonal migrations of chum salmon are extremely variable. Most adults ascend rivers short distances (like the pink salmon) and spawn in tidal waters. Others enter larger streams and ascend for extremely long distances, such as in the Mackenzie and Yukon rivers, where upstream migration extends to about 1,500 miles.

Free-swimming fry of chum salmon descend to the sea through short distances in only a few days; from larger, longer streams, several months are required, during which fry feed on their downstream journey and reach lengths of about two to three inches. Adults return at age three to five years. In commercial catches, they average about 25 inches in length and seven to eight pounds in weight. Chum and pink salmon appear to be closely related, as indicated by genetic evidence, similar spawning behavior, and some hybridization between the two species.

◆   ◆   ◆

AMONG THE FIVE NORTH AMERICAN SPECIES of Pacific salmon, the sockeye, or red, has the most unusual life history. The growth period of this anadromous fish in the ocean is similar to that of the others, but life history characteristics in its two freshwater phases are markedly different. The native range of the sockeye in North America extends from the Columbia/Snake rivers basin, north along the Pacific coast and around to the northern tip of Alaska. The major areas of sockeye production are the Gulf of Alaska and Bristol Bay.

Autumn-maturing sockeyes in the ocean prepare for their upstream journey to spawn, not in all kinds of streams, but rather in a river that has a lake in the headwaters—a lake that itself has an inlet tributary. After reaching the lake, sockeye continue up the inlet, their natal stream, and here the adults leave their fertilized eggs in redds built of the same gravels from which they themselves hatched as free-swimming fry perhaps five years previously. In some stocks, spawning takes place in a lake outlet, or even in a tributary of the outlet, in which cases the fry make their way upstream to the nursery lake. Thus the adaptations of sockeye to lake environments require a more precise homing instinct than those of other salmon. The following spring, a new generation of free-swimming fry descends to its nursery lake—where they stay for one or two years. There, the young fish feed primarily on zooplankton and grow well, reaching five to six inches in their first summer. After this initial growth period in fresh water, smoltification takes place, and the smolts then descend to the sea and, as in their nursery lake, feed largely on zooplankton.

After one to four years in the ocean, sockeye adults return to their rivers at about five pounds and 26 inches long, to seek their own natal nursery lake and its associated streams.

The sockeye has long been prized as table fare, the best of all the Pacific salmons. The flesh is deep red and highly flavored. This author's first taste of Pacific salmon—fresh, broiled sockeye eaten in the British Columbia city of Vancouver many years ago—remains the most memorable gustatory experience among my fish-eating encounters. The sockeye has supported a huge commercial fishery, particularly in Alaska; it is the favorite for canning and the dinner table, enjoying the highest price in the market. In some quarters, *salmon* means *sockeye salmon.*

At some time in the distant past, some lake-living juvenile sockeyes evolved a permanent existence in their nursery lake. These entirely freshwater populations, now known as *kokanee*, occur naturally, but only where anadromous populations once had access to the sea. Perhaps landslides blocked their migrations. However, some kokanee populations also developed in lakes that remain open to the ocean and, in the lake, co-occur with anadromous stocks. Furthermore, some progeny of anadromous parents take up permanent life in these lakes, where they are known as "residuals."

Adult kokanee ascend an inlet of the lake to spawn, and their fry descend to spend the rest of their lives in the lake. Interestingly, kokanee adults are known to spawn along lakeshores, apparently where upwelling groundwater provides currents through the redds. In other cases, adult kokanee spawn in the outlet stream or a tributary of the outlet (like some anadromous sockeye adults). These different behaviors are expressions of distinct stocks.

Food for kokanee in the lake remains predominantly zooplankton throughout life. Because of their obvious adaptability to fresh water, kokanee have been introduced widely to other fresh waters in North America as exotics to add new angling opportunities.

Sport fishing for sockeye and kokanee is on the increase, and some introduced kokanee populations have been successful in acquiring a large angling clientele; the greatest success has been in northern Lake Huron (Ontario), Lake Pend Oreille (Idaho), Flathead Lake (Montana), and Lake Tahoe (California/Nevada), and many reservoirs in California. Their habit of feeding on plankton at first frustrated aspiring anglers, but inventive techniques and lures later were successful. Typical size in the sport catch is about 16 inches and two pounds.

Introduction of the opossum shrimp (a lake-living, predaceous crustacean) to Lake Pend Oreille and Flathead Lake was responsible for disastrous declines of kokanee. The opossum shrimp was expected to provide an additional food resource for the kokanee, but as it turned out, the opossum shrimp preyed so heavily on the lakes' zooplankton that the kokanee's food supply was nearly destroyed. And the kokanee, contrary to expectations, did not feed upon the opossum shrimp. This is an outstanding example of the perils of making an exotic introduction without sufficient knowledge of probable consequences.

◆   ◆   ◆

THE COHO AND CHINOOK have long been noted for sport fishing in ocean tributaries, especially as adult spawners that remain silvery and fresh under river conditions Even far upstream, both present strong, leaping fights on a fly line.

The life history of the coho, or silver, salmon is most like that of the anadromous rainbow trout, or steelhead, with which it cohabits many Pacific streams. Spending one or two years in fresh water (three or four in colder northern waters), juveniles feed on benthic invertebrates, as do young steelhead. Usually at the end of 1½ years in fresh water, coho smolts descend to the sea. There they grow rapidly, spending only another 1½ years in the ocean before reaching adult sizes of about 26 inches in length and a weight of six pounds. When coho and chinook occur together in the same river system, the coho will prefer the smaller streams and tributaries.

In cases where coho juveniles have access to lakes, some individuals remain inland and do not descend to the sea. In the lake, they feed voraciously and grow to adult size. Although they do not spawn, they provide important sport fisheries in the lakes. The persistence of these "residual" populations thus depends on continued migration and spawning of adults from the ocean.

The native distribution of the coho, much like that of other Pacific salmons, extends from central California north to and around Alaska, although not as far as other species. For some reason, their previous native range coincided with the historic distribution of California's redwood forests. Before dams, the coho's native range also extended up the Columbia and Snake rivers. Current stocks can move only moderate distances to spawn. Several coho salmon stocks are listed as endangered or threatened in California and Oregon, the result of habitat degradation caused by improper logging.

Introductions of coho salmon have been common into other waters of the Pacific states and provinces, mainly where they have become established as sport fisheries in inland lakes. Early attempts in the Great Lakes were unsuccessful. However, after the sea lamprey nearly extirpated the lake trout in the Great Lakes; introductions of coho were immensely successful, with spectacular survival and growth of hatchery juveniles. The coho was stocked in both Canadian and United States waters, first by the state of Michigan in the three upper lakes—Lakes Michigan, Superior, and Huron—in 1966. Especially in Lake Michigan, food in the form of the exotic alewife, which had entered the Great Lakes from the ocean after the sea lamprey, became superabundant. The coho population in Lake Michigan, however, has since declined, due apparently to a decrease of forage fish. The coho does not provide an important stream fishery in Great Lakes tributaries because of its rapid deterioration in fresh water; most angling is by open-water trolling or from shore.

◆   ◆   ◆

THE CHINOOK, OR KING, SALMON certainly is the king of the salmons. It grows to the largest size, fights the strongest, attracts the greatest angling following, and has always made up a large proportion of the commercial catch. The literary works of Canadian fly fisher and author Roderick Haig-Brown, writing from his streamside home along British Columbia's famed Campbell River, have created a circle of admirers with almost mythic devotion to the chinook salmon.

The chinook's native distribution ranged from central California (San Joaquin and Sacramento rivers, Central Valley) north along the Pacific coast and around the Alaskan Peninsula.

Like the coho and sockeye, the chinook did not extend its range eastward to the Mackenzie River, as did the chum and pink. Like the coho, the chinook's range extended up the Columbia and Snake rivers. Introductions into freshwater systems have been attempted throughout the United States, Canada's eastern provinces, and elsewhere around the world (more so than any of the other Pacific salmon). The only successful reproducing population of chinook established outside the Western Hemisphere is in New Zealand.

The most successful chinook introduction of all, however, has been in the Great Lakes. Along with coho stocking by the state of Michigan in 1966, chinook stockings in Lake Michigan turned out to be explosive. Not all the angling fraternity—or all fishery biologists—welcomed these new exotic fishes. But the increase in new salmon anglers in mid-central United States became a groundswell. Introductions into the other Great Lakes followed, in which the chinook was moderately successful. At first, fishery managers thought it was necessary to stock hatchery-produced juveniles to maintain populations in the lakes, but eventually some fish began to reproduce in tributary streams. The chinook remains the most common salmon stocked in the Great Lakes today. Most angling is in open water, where fish exceeding 30 pounds have been taken. Fish that migrate up tributaries, although occasionally taken by anglers, deteriorate rapidly.

From the Pacific Ocean, chinook adults move up coastal rivers at different seasons, depending on the distance they must travel to reach their natal spawning grounds at the appropriate season. Consequently, spawning runs occur at most times of the year. A common adult length is 36 inches and weight 30 pounds. Some rivers have several distinct runs at different seasons. Most adults proceed upriver to points just above tidal reaches, but some, for example in the Yukon River, travel 1,500 miles. Chinooks use the largest rivers, they build the largest redds in deeper water than do the other Pacific species, using the biggest gravel particles. But after all, they are the largest fish!

After emerging from the redd, free-swimming fry begin feeding immediately. Many start their downstream journey to the sea as fry; the amount of time that juveniles spend in fresh water varies greatly, a reflection of the many different stocks in this one species. Some in the Yukon spend two years.

An adult chinook salmon taken in a Lake Michigan tributary on a tiny yarn fly.

The size of adult chinook salmon has produced angling records in the neighborhood of 100 pounds in Alaska, and considerably greater in commercial catches. Before the age of dams on the Columbia and Snake rivers, the chinook accounted for the greatest commercial catch of its time, now reduced to a minor element among all salmon in the North Pacific catch.

At first, anglers believed that migratory adult chinooks in Great Lakes streams could not be taken by angling because they were not feeding. However, imaginative fishers soon developed innovative techniques that prompted adult chinooks to strike lures.

Crouched on the bank of a small Lake Michigan tributary, I watched as my fishing companion cast a small yarn fly to a large chinook salmon resting on the bottom of a shallow pool. Twenty, thirty, or more times he dropped the fly just upstream from the fish and let it drift past its snout. I watched fascinated as, eventually, the fish rose slightly, mouth agape, and slowly engulfed the fly. "He's got it!" I shouted. My friend struck, and there then ensued a 20-minute period of high excitement while a 15-to-20 pound chinook plowed its way up this relatively tiny stream, bulldozed its way though debris dams, through riffles and pools, charged through brush piles and rocky rapids, and finally succumbed to our efforts to direct it into a large landing net. Darkly colored and deteriorated, the fish was released, still able to exert its great strength and swim away toward its reproductive destiny.

◆   ◆   ◆

THE GROUP OF PACIFIC SALMON is one of those great assemblages of fish species that comprise a whole host of distinct genetic identities, or stocks. In the early 1900s, it was recognized that different runs produced different kinds of fish. At the time, we chose not to believe it. Instead, common thought was that a chinook was a chinook was chinook. No more. Modern knowledge of dissociation of one species into separate stocks was hard to come by, and full appreciation is still not complete.

Neither steelhead nor salmon species are homogeneous. Each species, we now know through technologies of modern genetics, includes many different stocks (known as races, or demes, or strains, or breeds, or varieties, occasionally subspecies), each a little different from its cousins. Sometimes, different stocks can be recognized by their form, coloration, or the number of their scales, fin rays, or gill rakers. Actually, commercial and sport fishermen recognize many stocks by size and coloration, timing of the runs, and location of spawning grounds.

The articulation of so many wild stocks has presented us with problems. For example, when the population of a species in a particular river (for example, chinook salmon) took a nosedive, we did not worry too much about extinction of the *species* so long as ample numbers existed somewhere else. Fishermen simply moved on from one stream or season or spawning run to another, always believing there were plenty of chinooks left. Because the total number of a species in commercial catches might not decline at all, the actual decline or extinction of a stock would not be detected until too late.

A similar situation occurred with the lake trout in the Great Lakes. When commercial fishing overexploited the trout of one breed (as the commercial fishermen called them), the gillnetters moved to another location, shoal, or embayment to take a yield equal to a previous catch, and the overall statistics remained the same. The impending disaster, of course, was not predicted.

Another problem has been mitigation. Dam builders and managers believed that if a natural population of fish (for example, steelhead) became reduced because of blockage by a dam, they merely needed to build hatcheries, produce huge numbers of steelhead smolts to stock in the river, and replace those lost to electric turbines. The theory had two flaws: Number one, the hatchery stock did not perform well, did not grow or survive like the wild stock—and sometimes hardly survived at all. Number two, the domestic hatchery fish, through predation, interbreeding, and competition for food, further decreased the wild stock. Mitigation, in most of its variations and after all its initial promise, has been a lose-lose situation.

In California's Central Valley, the historic abundance of chinook salmon was prodigious, with immense numbers of fish migrating to the San Joaquin and Sacramento rivers, distributed in several seasonal runs. Chinook was the only species of salmon of consequence in the region, but the fishery was one of the richest producers in the world.

Commercial fishing began about 1850 in the Delta region to support early settlements, and it expanded around 1900 to broad-scale ocean fishing. Declines of the huge runs followed. Other factors—loss of spawning habitat by dams and irrigation diversions—added to the losses by overfishing. Currently, only a single seasonal migration remains, and that one has undergone substantial reduction.

Within the native ranges of Pacific salmon and steelhead, the stocks in the Columbia River basin have also taken a particularly hard hit—by dams. It has been written that the greatest insult that can be laid on a river is a dam. That's obvious—when a dam converts a flowing river into a reservoir, the river disappears. The Columbia, once a raging stream, is very close to no longer being a river at all. The obstruction that any dam places in the way of migrating fish is absolute. Fish-passage facilities have been installed at some dams, but like mitigation, fish passage has failed in its total objective.

The Columbia River system has the dubious distinction of owning so many dams that they cannot reasonably be counted. Sixty major dams and about 3,000 lesser ones impede stream and river currents. The Columbia is virtually a "lost" river—just back-to-back reservoirs almost throughout its length. At the lower end of the river, Bonneville Dam can block spawning runs to every tributary in the Columbia. Even with various provisions for passing spawners upstream (like fish ladders, which are notorious for not functioning), over a third of the Columbia's salmon are permanently blocked by Grand Coulee Dam (upper Columbia) and Hells Canyon Dam (upper Snake), neither of which was built with fish passage installations. These two high dams are responsible for the loss of half of the salmon and trout-rearing habitat in the entire basin.

Furthermore, electric turbines within the high dams, as might be expected, take a terrible toll on downstream-migrating smolts, which somehow have to survive the whirling blades in order to reach the ocean. Mortality of smolts during their downstream journey can reach up to 20 percent at single dams. From the upper Snake River, eight large dams stand in their way of reaching the ocean.

The combined Columbia and Snake river systems once claimed the most productive salmon and trout community in the world. No more. The Columbia/Snake river salmon and steelhead runs have been reduced to only two percent of historic runs that occurred before the dams.

◆   ◆   ◆

ASSOCIATED WITH PACIFIC SALMON, both in geographic distribution and angling interest, is the Arctic grayling. The grayling probably dispersed from Asia to northwestern North America during the last glaciation, when the Bering Strait was exposed above ocean salt water and freshwater lakes and rivers existed. From the Yukon (parts of which were spared glaciation), this ancestral grayling spread eastward across the northern rim of North America in streams and lakes mostly within the Arctic Circle, including the Hudson Bay drainage. In these ancient times, Missouri River waters flowed through the region of Montana and north toward Hudson Bay. Thus did the grayling colonize some upper Missouri streams—and later become the Montana grayling. When glacial ice pushed southward over much of North America, the Missouri changed direction, flowing eastward to empty into the Mississippi, as it does now. The Montana grayling thus became isolated from Arctic populations. At the same time, glacial meltwater lakes connected the Missouri with the Great Lakes region, by which route the grayling colonized some streams in Michigan. (At the same time, and by the same route, the lake trout of the Great Lakes found its way westward to the upper Missouri basin.)

Today, the Arctic grayling (*Thymallus arcticus*) persists in abundance in the Far North of Canada, while the Montana grayling (also *T. arcticus)* occurs as a native only in Red Rock Lake (Montana). The Michigan grayling (same species) is gone.

As a boy fishing with my father, who began trout fishing with *his* father in the early 1900s, I was fascinated by his reminiscences of grayling in Michigan streams like the Manistee, Pine, and Au Sable, and their demise due to logging and overfishing. Brook trout followed into their "empty" niche, and later rainbows, for both of which Dad and I fished beginning in the 1930s.

At one time, the brilliant spotting on grayling was thought to result from their eating gold—possibly because the species was common in Alaskan streams heavily mined for gold. Today, the grayling in Alaska is still taking blows from the gold mining that continues to put massive amounts of sediment into streams.

Arctic grayling today are widespread, with native populations in Arctic Ocean drainages from Alaska to Hudson Bay, Pacific Ocean drainages in Alaska as well as in central Alberta and British Columbia, plus the small population in Montana. Hatchery-generated populations occur in both lakes and larger rivers of Montana, which now have more grayling than in the historic past. These spawn in springtime in small tributary streams.

In Alaska, many otherwise-suitable spawning streams no longer function as such because the spawning adults will not enter stream waters carrying heavy suspended silt loads from active gold-mining operations.

Adult size at maximum is about two to three pounds, although larger specimens are possible. The world record is near six pounds, caught in Canada in 1967. Grayling are known to strike bait and artificials readily, making cutthroat trout by comparison seem difficult to catch—a behavior that contributed to their overfishing in Michigan. Three other species of grayling occur in northern Europe and Asia, in all probability arising from ancestors of those that dispersed across the Bering Land Bridge.

◆   ◆   ◆

IN 1991, THE AMERICAN FISHERIES SOCIETY published an account of the status of Pacific salmon and steelhead (reprinted in the Winter 1992 issue of Trout Unlimited's magazine, *Trout*). The report emphasized, above all, the significance of the *stock*—the product of long-term evolution, not merely the adaptation to a particular habitat condition. A stock constitutes a heritable, unique pattern of genetic material. Once destroyed, it can never be restored or recreated. The authors of the published account emphasized further that the current deplorable status of Pacific salmonids is the result of mismanagement that neither realized the presence or significance of distinct stocks, nor managed for individual stock conservation. For successful restoration of *species*, rehabilitation and conservation have to occur at the *stock* level. In other words, the stock concept has to be incorporated into management of the species.

The report listed anadromous salmonid stocks according to their risk of extinction. The report included the five species of salmon, steelhead, and sea-run cutthroat trout in the states of California, Idaho, Oregon, and Washington. The stocks were placed at one of three levels of risk:
• high risk of extinction, functionally equivalent to an endangered listing;
• moderate risk of extinction, equivalent to a threatened status;
• of special concern, a category indicating that population numbers are so low that intensive and continuous monitoring is required.

Two hundred and fourteen individual stocks from all species were listed. Most were among the coho and chinook salmon and steelhead species: coho—35, chinook—64, chum—17, pink—4, sockeye—6, steelhead—75, and sea-run cutthroat—13. Thirty-nine stocks are listed in California, 58 in Oregon, 41 in Washington, and—as might be expected—a whopping 76 stocks in the Columbia River basin.

Nearly half (101) were rated at *high risk of extinction*, about one-fourth (59) at moderate risk, and another one-fourth (54) of special concern. At this writing, the federal Endangered Species Act lists the Sacramento River chinook run and the Snake River sockeye as endangered, and three different stocks of Snake River chinooks as threatened. State listings include the coho as threatened in California and southern Oregon; spring-run chinooks as threatened in California; and steelhead as threatened in California's Central Valley.

These lists were made possible only after we became knowledgeable about the identity of stocks. What stock extinctions had already taken place? In another list, the American Fisheries Society reported that *106 major stocks were already known to be extinct*, and this compilation is only *partial*. Given the known richness of different populations by river and spawning season, and our only recently acquired ability to identify stocks, it is fairly certain that losses of stocks in the past were much higher.

The long line of declines, extirpations, and extinctions includes a short list of well-known causes: dams, destruction of spawning gravels mainly due to overgrazing and logging, and interbreeding with introduced non-native stocks.

First, the number of dams, especially in the Columbia basin, is huge. An enormous percentage of riverbed area previously available to spawning salmon and steelhead has now been destroyed by the stilled waters behind dams. One of the worst cases is the Clearwater River, dammed and inundated for most of its length by Dworshak dam, which exterminated most of the river's salmon and steelhead stocks. Some efforts are afoot to breach some dams to allow passage of adults upstream and smolts down, but some of the dams are enormous, hundreds of concrete feet high.

Secondly, damage to salmonid spawning habitat in the uplands, by livestock grazing, row-crop cultivation, logging, and mining, has contributed immensely to the loss of many stocks, mainly through sedimentation of spawning gravels. Ironically, measures for reducing sediment production are well advanced through scientific research done by a number of state and fed eral agencies, but implementation is far behind or woefully lacking.

The third major cause of stock declines is hatcheries. These have not only failed to mitigate losses but have also imposed hatchery fish of mixed genetic ancestry on wild stocks. The resulting interbreeding with native fish has diluted wild stocks' original genetic character. The domestic hatchery strain—those that do "best" in the hatchery environment—do not prosper in the wild environment of natural rivers. Nearly half of the stocks in trouble are known to have a high probability of interbreeding with hatchery stocks of unknown genetic identity. Stocking the wrong fish on top of a native stock is certain to result in the native's extinction.

The beauty of Idaho's Clearwater River belies its tragic loss of Pacific salmonid stocks because of dams.

Solutions? Many have been tried, and most have been found lacking. Chief among the most effective solutions to the decline and extinctions of Pacific salmon stocks must be new approaches to the chief destructive agents. The most widespread problem is that dams have been operated solely for purposes of hydropower, navigation, irrigation, and flood control—but not for fish. This misdirected approach, of course, failed to prevent damage to fish and other river resources. If wild Pacific salmon and trout are to survive, solutions must be sought that benefit fish, too.

Management throughout the entire system can change its mixed-stock approach and emphasize the presence and specific needs of distinct stocks. We now know that recognizing the stock concept is essential for further success—even for just survival—of wild salmon and trout. Operations can be formulated around stocks that currently remain viable, with long-term programs for those stocks in specific natal streams. The American Fisheries Society authors pointed out that hatcheries can be a major means of restoration if they are used to restore specific, identified stocks. Some hatcheries have already made some progress toward this objective, but not enough.

◆　　　◆　　　◆

ALTHOUGH THE FUTURE OF PACIFIC SALMONIDS is clouded, the means to recovery has been pointed out to us. If we want a better future for these species, we must become serious enough about this resource to get tough enough—with money, effort, and votes enough—to demand reform of the frontier mentality and behavior in both the West and in Washington, DC, that have been so destructive of Pacific salmonid fishes in the past.

Recovery and enhancement of stocks that have survived *are* possible. Enough *are* left to provide a return of an overall, productive fishery that will return the ancient richness of abundance and diversity, if nurtured properly—*and managed as if fish mattered.*

SELECTED REFERENCES:

Groot, C., and L. Margolis, editors. 1991. *Pacific Salmon Life Histories.* University of British Columbia Press, Vancouver.

Moyle, Peter B. 1993. Saving California's salmon: The legacy of Ishi. *Trout* (Trout Unlimited). Summer issue, pages 14-17.

Nehlsen, Willa, Jack E. Williams, and James A. Lichatowich. 1991. Pacific salmon at the crossroads: Stocks at risk from California, Oregon, Idaho, and Washington. *Fisheries* (American Fisheries Society). Volume 16, number 2 (March/April 1991), pages 4-21.

Scott, W.B., and E.J. Crossman. 1973. *Freshwater Fishes of Canada* Bulletin 184, Fisheries Research Board of Canada, Ottawa.

Simon, Raymond C., and Peter A. Larkin, editors. 1972, *The Stock Concept in Pacific Salmon.* H.R. MacMillan Lectures in Fisheries, University of British Columbia, Vancouver.

RiverSketch

THE BLESSED AND THE DAMMED

MANY PROBLEMS NEED TO BE RESOLVED in order to restore and preserve the natural values of our free-flowing rivers. Pollution, channelization, sedimentation, dewatering, thermal changes—all are too common across the nation. All have degraded the great majority of United States streams.

Technically, these damages can all be corrected. Pollution can be halted and the stream will cleanse itself. A channelized stream can be realigned to its original course. A sediment source of erosion can be healed. Dewatering, through groundwater withdrawal for irrigation, can be reduced. High temperatures resulting from a deforested watershed can be lowered with afforestation. The physical and biological solutions are easy. Political obstacles can change with the next election.

But a *dam*—especially one of the huge concrete monuments common to the American West—as long as the concrete remains in place, is forever. In the impoundment upstream from a dam, the river ceases to exist. And it will never exist again for foreseeable future generations—and possibly for continuation of the human species. The large dam is the greatest degrader, the ultimate destroyer, of rivers because it cannot be undone. Dr. Kenneth Cummins, one of the nation's foremost river scientists, bemoaned the fact that because of the near entirety of rivers dammed, we may never know, even through the most sophisticated scientific study, the pristine condition of our streams and rivers. The effect of dams is the least reversible among all forms of river degradation.

The number of dams on American rivers is staggering. The number of dams over five feet in height was estimated by the U.S. Army Corps of Engineers at 75,000. Smaller dams run into about two million; we don't know exactly. What is clear, however, is that the number of medium-to-large rivers, still free of dams, is dangerously low, and that these few streams can be perceived today only as remnants, "museums of natural history disasters."

◆　　　　◆　　　　◆

WHEN TODAY A NEW DAM IS PROPOSED, river advocates may first feel their rage against the loss of the river section that will be inundated. A reach of a beloved river will be lost—a river no more. But much more than the inundated reach is lost—upstream, downstream, laterally. In the first place, the dam—a *discontinuity*—creates a break in a line, an obstacle not only to water, but also to plants and animals that evolved to benefit from the river's original *continuity*.

Laterally, the destruction of a wide, spreading still water destroys immense riparian habitats. Plant succession is changed in its rate and quality. Terrestrial animal migrations across or along the riverway may be blocked. Human use of the valley—what's left of it—may increase greatly, resulting in overuse. Downstream, the river is a new stream for a long way. All aquatic plants are changed. Water temperature may be lowered or elevated drastically, completely altering the thermal habitats of fish and invertebrates. Endemic species may be extirpated or brought to extinction. Tailwater trout fisheries created in the

desert may be considered a boon, but the new angling experience may be bought at a terrible ecological cost. The food supply to fish and invertebrates in the downstream reach is converted to a resource totally different. Food available to fish then
becomes dependent upon the output of zooplankton and sludge
worms from the reservoir, rather than an undammed community of mayflies and caddisflies. Furthermore, all streambed
organisms become subject to unpredictable flows from the dam.

When sediment is deposited in the reservoir, clear water is
released through the dam. In a river that used to carry a suspended sediment load, the clear water may be just as much a
detriment to the stream as it may seem an improvement to our
own eyes. Ironically, clear water has a greater capability to
erode, pick up, and carry off new sediment from the river bed
and banks (and deposit it farther downstream!). It is called
"hungry water," and the result is an increased erosion of the
river's natural floodplain and riparian zones. Streambeds are
eroded to lower elevations, dropping local water tables. Even
upstream, streambed erosion is increased due to upstream migration of the "head cut" (the point where river flow "falls" into
the reservoir)—destroying riffles, pools, and other streambed
and bank covers. Biodiversity—upstream, downstream, and
alongside—is lost. Quite apart from the drowned streams beneath stilled water, dams are losers.

◆   ◆   ◆

IN THE HEYDAY OF BIG DAM CONSTRUCTION—beginning in the
1930s, slowing slightly in the war years, accelerating in the
1950s and 1960s—a great economic euphoria gripped the nation. Objectors were few and ignored. The benefits were unlimited, so it seemed—cheap electricity, new lands irrigated for
food production, "barren" arid lands to be "reclaimed." The
desert will bloom, prosperity for all. Dam building took on the
aura of an extension of "God's work." It was big dam foolish-
ness at its zenith.

What American civilization failed to recognize was that the benefits were illusory, short-term at best, at worst ecologically disastrous. The cheap electricity turned out to be paid for by taxpayers elsewhere who, with no choice in the matter, paid the overrun costs of construction and maintenance. The desert soils, at first blooming with new food production, later became dried up and poisonous. In short, the great boom became an enormous, expensive failure, a white elephant, maintained by deal-wheeling government agencies and utility commissions defending their personal stakes and ill-conceived positions.

A true assessment of environmental damage to America's streams by dams—more accurately to watersheds or catchments—would require many books. A list of degraded rivers in the United States probably cannot ever be completed. We are familiar with a few of the worst. While entire books have been written on some of these—on the Columbia and the Colorado dams in particular—thousands of dams go virtually unnoticed by the nation's citizens.

The number of dams in the Columbia basin is incredible: 14 huge edifices on the mainstem, including Grand Coulee, the biggest in North America, and *thousands* more, large and small, in the watershed. The loss of anadromous fisheries, all five Pacific salmon and steelhead, is now described as the worst case of a natural resources disaster—created through human folly—in civilization's history. Only one 50-mile stretch of the Columbia—the Hanford Reach, located between the fourth and fifth mainstem dams—remains free-flowing. The Hanford Reach in its unobstructed condition of good spawning habitat today holds the only successful population of salmon in the entire river, small as it is.

The Colorado is dammed and diverted to the point where it enters the Gulf of California only as a series of stagnant, toxic pools; the scenic loss of Glen Canyon must go as mankind's greatest blunder, destroying forever a portion of Earth's beauty unparalleled anywhere in the world. Proponents claimed that impounding the canyon's flow would "raise boaters and water-skiers 90 feet closer to heaven," while detractors retorted,

"Should we flood the Sistine Chapel so tourists could more closely view Michelangelo's masterpiece?" (Of course, the water skiers, in their celestial ambitions, won out.)

The listing of other damages to some of our most elegant and productive rivers is a litany of shame.

• The Dworshak Dam on the North Fork Clearwater River—by itself—eliminated over half of the anadromous fish production in the entire Clearwater system, and a large steelhead hatchery for mitigation has completely failed to bring back any simulation of native stocks. The river's waters downstream from the dam, 50 miles to its mouth in the Snake River, now abound in hatchery fish that do nothing to enhance the population of wild stock. For over a hundred miles upstream, and many more miles in tributaries, choice spawning gravels previously used by coho, chinook, and steelhead now lie deep beneath the reservoir.

• Flaming Gorge Dam on Utah's Green River reduced temperatures for nearly a hundred miles downstream, extirpating native species now classified as endangered. Clearer waters badly eroded stream banks, increasing sediment farther down, and the annual spring floods (now "controlled" by Flaming Gorge) no longer flush the sediment out.

• The Snake River is the most intensively impounded river in the West, with 25 large dams. Something like 5 percent to 15 percent of the salmon attempting to reach their spawning grounds were blocked at *each* of eight dams. In places, the Snake has become a waterless river.

• Elephant Butte Dam on the Rio Grande was designed to use the entire river for irrigation. With occasional releases due to high runoff, however, sediment has accumulated in the riverbed downstream from the dam, decreasing the size of the channel. When floods now occur, the channel cannot hold their waters as they did before—and even relatively minor floods now cause extreme agricultural damage in the downstream region.

The list could continue almost indefinitely. There exists in this country hardly a single major river that has not been degraded by dams. The greatest future threat is hydropower.

With energy shortage crises popping out continuously, the cry goes up for inexpensive sources that do not pollute or contribute to acid rain and global climate change. Yet hydropower is a tiny proportion of national energy usage and can never be otherwise. This continual threat of dams is real. Opposition will be tough.

◆   ◆   ◆

Dworshak dam on Idaho's Clearwater River brought
the river's wild steelhead to the brink of extinction.

A FEW BRIGHT SPOTS HAVE EMERGED from these scenes of destruction. For one thing, the development of citizens groups interested in protecting rivers has accelerated greatly.

In the early 1930s, it must have seemed to John Muir that he was the only one who cared, in his unsuccessful fight to prevent Hetch Hetchy Dam on California's Tuolumne River in Yosemite National Park. But today's river organizations in the United States, large and small, number around two thousand. American Rivers, the country's leading river advocate, has been notably successful in preventing dams, as well as promoting other river protection issues, for 30 years. The venerable and activist Sierra

Club increasingly drags river offenders into court. Trout Unlimited, vastly broadened from its initial group of Michigan fly-fishers only four decades ago, has fought many battles for the protection of salmonid streams across the country. It is evident that the numbers of users of rivers—fishers, paddlers, campers, hikers, and all who love flowing water—have increased enormously.

With passage of environmental laws, beginning in the 1970s (and Earth Day), federal legislation such as the National Environmental Protection Act, Clean Water Act, the National Wild and Scenic Rivers Act, and many others, powerful tools were created to force better treatment of our streams and rivers. Recent federal budget cuts have also contributed to a lessening of new dam approvals, which at the same time have become more expensive. A significant movement is afoot to actually remove dams, and already a few on some of our smaller rivers have been dismantled. The removal of Edwards Dam on Maine's Kennebec River—to restore Atlantic salmon runs—was accomplished in July, 1999, a notable example. Smaller dams have been removed from rivers elsewhere: California, Minnesota, North Carolina, Ohio, Oregon, Pennsylvania, Tennessee, Vermont, Washington, Wisconsin, and other dams in Maine, to name a few. Nationwide, 269 dams have been removed since 1980. The four major dams on the Snake River, chiefly responsible for blocking salmon and steelhead spawning runs, are under consideration for at least breaching, to pass migrating fish. Even the Glen Canyon Dam on the Colorado is under assault by the Sierra Club and the newly-founded Glen Canyon Institute. American Rivers has initiated a new campaign to remove dams called *Rivers Unplugged*, nationwide.

It may not be premature to conclude that the big dam era is over. And some big dams themselves may be due for extinction.

◆   ◆   ◆

WHEN WE FULLY ADOPT THE CONCEPT of ecosystem management—the holistic view of the watershed—the full, degrading impact of a river dam will be more thoroughly realized.

Only when we stop computing cost/benefit ratios that include only how many dollars it takes to build vs. the kilowatt-hours produced, can we make a judgment of the full cost of hydropower projects. Only when we start stacking up the total influence of a river dam—biological losses, scenic degradation, riparian alterations—*throughout the watershed,* against temporary, overstated, economic "benefits" of tax-subsidized irrigation schemes and "cheap" electricity, will we be able to comprehend what a dam really does for—and to—us. It will be necessary to stop trying to *conquer* and *tame* rivers, but rather to adapt our needs and desires to the natural stream. Under this expanded appreciation, no new dams should ever be built on our few remaining, free-flowing streams and rivers.

SELECTED REFERENCES:

Benke, Arthur C. 1990. A perspective on America's vanishing streams. *Journal of the North American Benthological Society.* Volume 9, Pages 77-88.
McCully, Patrick. 1996. *Silenced Rivers: The ecology and politics of large dams.* Zed Books, Atlantic Highlands, New Jersey, and International Rivers Network. Berkeley, California.

Chapter **23**

SMALLIES, MINNIES, AND CATS

M UCH CONTROVERSY SURROUNDS THE QUESTION of which species of freshwater fish deserves the highest respect for its fighting ability. The debate will never reach a unanimous conclusion, of course. Nevertheless, a small but growing portion of the angling fraternity holds out vehemently for the small-mouth bass. No one on any side of the dispute will deny that the strength of the smallie at the end of a line is extraordinary.

The native distribution of this member of the sunfish family, Centrarchidae, covers roughly the northeastern quarter of the United States. Bounded on the east by the Appalachian chain from Maine to Georgia, and on the west by the upper Missis-sippi River, the native distribution of *Micropterus dolomieu* is essentially northern in character. Its range includes much of the Great Lakes region, southern Ontario, and—separated from the rest of the smallmouth's range—the Ozark Plateau in Missouri and Arkansas. Introduced and naturalized populations have been established in Pacific Coast states, northern Atlantic states east of the Appalachians, Hawaii, and various locations world-wide.

The smallmouth is basically a stream and river fish, although it has been successfully established in many northern lakes and midwestern reservoirs as well. The species achieves its greatest productivity in the high-alkalinity streams of northern midcontinent and the Ozark Plateau.

Unlike the spawning habit of salmonids, which build redds, the male smallmouth builds an open nest of clean gravel. After fertilization, the adhesive eggs fall into the cracks and crevices of the stony nest. The male guards the nest against predators with aggressive behavior while the eggs incubate and even after hatching. The tiny sac-fry, at first less than a quarter inch long, remain in the nest until their supply of yolk is exhausted. Upon reaching the free-swimming stage, the fry form concentrations above the nest, a dense, black cloud that will last for only a few days or even hours. During all this time the male parent stands guard. Later, the black fry leave the protection of the male and scatter out into the stream's currents, where they suspend above the streambed, visible to a sharp eye in clear water.

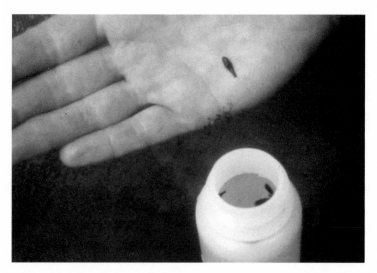

The "black fry" of smallmouth bass, a few days old, suspend off the stream bottom to feed on tiny, drifting meiofauna.

Try to find them some day of good weather and clear water in your favorite smallmouth stream in early June in northern states, or mid-May in more southerly locations. They can be easily captured with close observation and a fine-meshed net.

(But be careful that you release them or follow all your local regulations!) After a few days suspended above the bottom, fry change to their normal greenish coloration and look more like smallmouth bass. This black color of the fry, by the way, is the source of the name "black bass," and is similar for the largemouth bass, whose early fry collect in dense, black concentrations in ponds and lakes.

Eggs of smallmouths are much smaller than those of salmonids, but with numbers ranging up to 20,000 eggs per female, depending on age and size. With such numbers of eggs, fry and juvenile mortalities are very high: only about one-half of one percent may live through the first year. Compared with salmonids, growth of smallmouth bass is slow. Juveniles reach about three inches at one year, maybe six inches at two years. Five years are required to reach 12 to 13 inches, and a trophy of 20 inches will be nine or ten years old.

Although smallmouth bass are frequently considered a warmwater species, a classification of *coolwater* would be more accurate. In many northern streams, the upper reaches may be trout water, but downstream, at a slightly higher temperature, smallmouths may predominate as the principal game fish. Farther downstream yet, in larger and warmer waters, more truly warmwater species—such as largemouth bass—prevail as the principal game species.

Although smallmouth bass are most successful and productive in highly alkaline streams, their annual production never is as high as that of trout in streams of the same alkalinity (but cooler) streams. For example, annual production by trout may be more than 100 pounds per acre in alkaline streams, but the smallmouth's annual production may be only 10 pounds per acre or less—only about one-tenth of that for trout. The reason lies in the greater numbers of other fishes that inhabit these warmer streams, with which the smallmouth must share resources. Accounts of 50 fish species or more are common in streams that are still rated as good smallmouth waters. The smallmouth bass is particularly noted for its susceptibility to hook and line, so among all the other species, the smallmouth often predominates on the angler's hook.

The combination of slow growth, high annual mortality, and great susceptibility to angling creates an important risk: excessive exploitation. Most fisheries biologists agree that fishing pressure aimed specifically at smallmouth bass is generally light across much of its range. But that is changing, evidenced by angling censuses, increased coverage in fishing magazines, a new generation of how-to-do-it books, and new angler organizations like The Smallmouth Alliance, which urges good stewardship in smallmouth management.

Many fishery managers forecast problems of overuse in the future. Some special regulations have been implemented where pressure is heavy. Like the beneficial experience with special regulations on trout, these regulations have also shown some remarkable successes with smallmouth bass. Certainly the future of smallmouth management must include these protective regulations, such as catch-and-release and lure restrictions, in order to retain high-quality angling for smallmouth bass.

In Dr. James A. Henshall's classic 1881 treatise *Book of the Black Bass*, he considered them "inch for inch and pound for pound, the gamest fish that swims." Actually, Henshall was referring to the *black bass*, which included both the smallmouth and largemouth. Since then, many writers and anglers have interpreted his statement to apply to only the smallmouth—obviously an inaccuracy. Small matter. This author agrees with the more recent interpretation.

Almost always associated with the smallmouth bass is the rock bass (*Ambloplites rupestris*), a smaller cousin in the family Centrarchidae. The rock bass occurs in a large range of north-central and mid-south states, almost the same range as that of the smallmouth, but the rock bass is strangely absent in the Driftless Area, where there are good smallmouth populations. Also in the genus *Ambloplites* are the Ozark bass and the shadow bass, present in small ranges in southern Midwestern states. Like the rock bass, these two species are also associated with the smallmouth bass.

Habitat of the rock bass, or goggle-eye, is slightly different from the smallmouth's, preferring a rocky bank or boulders, which leads of course to its common name. But it also likes the cool, clear, swift water demanded by the smallmouth. Shaped more like the bluegill and other "sunnies," the rock bass grows to a little larger size, averaging up to 10 inches. It rises to a fly or popper and takes a crayfish imitation, and if you fish these waters for smallmouth, you'll probably hook a few rock bass, too.

The rock bass has the interesting capability to change its external coloration quickly, in accordance with its immediate streambed background. When you catch one, try placing it alternately in water in a white bucket, in a dark one, and in a speckled one (just in case you're carrying these three buckets along with you on the stream).

As a small boy fishing in a rocky pasture creek, I was fascinated by the rock bass's habit of changing its appearance with its background. I caught rock bass by dangling a worm beside a dark, submerged boulder. The almost black-hued fish would dart out, grab the bait, and then return to its underwater retreat. But when I brought the hooked fish out over a bright, sunny sand bar, it lightened up before my wondering eyes.

Similar to the smallmouth bass as a stream fish is the spotted bass (*Micropterus punctulatus*), in a range to the south of the smallmouth, although overlapping in their ranges. Its appearance, however, is more like that of the largemouth bass, and although its habitat is similar to the smallmouth's, it better tolerates waters a bit warmer and more turbid in larger streams. The spotted bass also adapts to reservoirs better than the smallmouth. The spotted bass has been stocked widely in streams of the southern Midwest, where it was thought to survive better than the smallmouth in streams degraded by poor land use.

In contrast to both the smallmouth and largemouth, spotted bass fry do not show the black color of the other two; so technically, they are not *black bass*. Fry remain translucent until their normal green coloration comes on later. Although still a desirable sport fish for anglers, the spotted bass is outnumbered by

Wildstream

the largemouth in large, slow rivers and reservoirs, and by the smallmouth in small, clear, swift-running streams.

◆   ◆   ◆

COMMON SMALL FISH IN SUMMERCOOL headwater streams—and therefore familiar to trout fishers—are sculpins, family Cottidae (26 freshwater species). Lacking a gas bladder, sculpins closely associate with the streambed, and thus are truly benthic. Most species are denizens of streams and rivers, some of very deep, cold lakes. The two most widely distributed species in streams, especially in the Midwest and East, are the mottled sculpin *(Cottus bairdi)* and the slimy sculpin *(C. cognatus)*, which look much alike. Several other sculpins are common in Pacific drainages, such as the coastrange, prickly, reticulate, and torrent sculpins.

Sculpins are common inhabitants of cold, headwater stream reaches, and often are the only companions to trout.
(Photo by Dean C. Hansen of *WetBugs Press*, Stillwater, Minnesota.)

In summercool streams, sculpins (or muddlers) usually occur with trout in north central and Great Lakes regions, as well as with smallmouth bass in southern small streams. Like the brook trout, creek chub, and cutthroat, sculpins also prefer first-order streams and often are the only fish that occur with trout in small headwaters. Sculpins are commonly fed upon by trout and provide a large food resource, and so are often used as bait. Nymphing anglers will catch the occasional sculpin, up to about five inches long. But to correctly imitate a sculpin, use a heavily weighted muddler "fly." The sculpin spawns by attaching a glob of pink eggs to the bottom of a stone; turn over some stones on a day in spring, and you'll find them.

The mountain whitefish rises readily to a dry fly, and thus is no stranger to fly anglers in western mountain trout streams. (Bitch Creek, Idaho.)

Trout anglers in western mountain streams frequently encounter the mountain whitefish (*Prosopium williamsoni*). This member of the family Salmonidae and the lake whitefish subfamily inhabits rushing mountain streams and, like trout, readily takes to nymphs and dry flies. It occurs in streams of the Pacific Northwest and north through western Canada. The mountain whitefish may be annoying to anglers seeking cutthroat and rainbows, but it is highly regarded by some and managed as a sport fish in many regions, with regulations on open and closed seasons. Moreover, this fish, like other whitefishes, is delicious eating, especially when broiled over an open bed of coals. Many anglers smoke these fish for some delicious eating.

Similar to the mountain whitefish is the round whitefish (*Prosopium cylindraceum*), sometimes caught in streams and rivers of the Great Lakes region and the Far North of Canada. Its name derives from the round cross-section of its body. The round whitefish, like the mountain species, also takes a fly and is also excellent eating. If you catch-and-release trout, but still desire some fish to eat, try either of these two small whitefishes, very fresh, filleted, and then broiled. You will not be disappointed.

◆   ◆   ◆

IF YOU EVER HAVE THE CHANCE to accompany a fisheries crew electrofishing a smallmouth stream or a marginal trout stream, you may be surprised at the almost overwhelming abundance of suckers that keep bobbing to the surface, attracted by the positive electrode. The family, Catostomidae, with 63 species in North America, is one of our largest. Several species of catostomids might better be termed coolwater fishes that predominate in some trout or smallmouth streams, often making up over 90 percent of the fish biomass. The most common and widespread is the white sucker (*Catostomus commersoni*), with a range that covers most of North America, one of the most common freshwater fish on the continent. Only the Deep South, Pacific Coast, and Arctic Canada are without it. With a range almost as great, the shorthead redhorse (*Moxostoma macrolepidotum*) is a large sucker often found in company with the white sucker. Many a trouter, fishing in early spring when the redhorse runs upstream for spawning, has had a heavy fish of several pounds hit hard, make a spectacular, strong run, setting off a rush of adrenaline in the angler with rod in hand—and then quit. Such behavior is typical of a redhorse, not a trophy brown trout. On the other hand, all catostomids are perfectly palatable, mostly suckers and redhorses, especially smoked.

No doubt about it—sport angling for warmwater "rough" fish is catching on. In addition to white suckers and redhorses, other members of the sucker family are entering the angler's lexicon, tackle arrangements, and dinner menus—a new breed of angler. New books, articles in many fishing periodicals, a new specialty magazine, *Warmwater Fly Fishing*, and a new organization, North American Roughfish Institute, all attest to a new appreciation of some of these big, hard-fighting, previously disdained but now esteemed warmwater fishes. Most are in the sucker family, Catostomidae. Some of the largest are the buffalofish—more precisely, the smallmouth buffalo and the bigmouth buffalo. The bigmouth is the more common and grows the larger, reaching 40 inches in length and around 50 pounds. It occurs throughout the Mississippi drainage and into Canada via the Red River of the North. Its preferred habitat is large rivers, often in clearer water than that preferred by many other large, warmwater fishes. Differing from all other members of the sucker family, the mouth of the bigmouth buffalo is terminal, or to the front, rather than subterminal, or under the snout. A favorite food fish among all suckers, the bigmouth is also harvested commercially from wild populations in lakes. The smallmouth buffalo is not nearly as abundant as the bigmouth, but it occurs almost as widely. Growing to about 30 inches and 40 pounds, common weights taken by anglers range up to about five pounds. Like the bigmouth, it inhabits mostly medium to large rivers in the Mississippi drainage. As bottom-feeding fish, the buffaloes can best be caught with bait or, newly appreciated by fly anglers, with nymphs and weighted streamers.

◆   ◆   ◆

FOUND IN WARMWATER RIVERS IN MANY AREAS of the central United States is the white bass (*Morone chrysops*), much sought after as a sport and food fish. The white bass is native to the Mississippi River and its many tributaries, from Minnesota south to Texas, in the southern Great Lakes, and northeast through the St. Lawrence River drainage. White bass congregate in schools in their springtime spawning season, when they make upstream runs from large rivers to tributaries. They are hard fighting and excellent eating and grow to a usual adult size of two to three pounds. White bass are members of the "temperate" or "sea" basses, family Moronidae, many of which are marine in habitat. Only four species occur in fresh water.

A close relative to the white bass is the striped bass (*Morone saxatilis*), a marine species anadromous in its spawning migration up tributary rivers. It spawns by broadcasting its eggs in large, long rivers. Because the eggs are buoyant, they drift downstream while the eggs incubate. Fry hatch after only a few days and then continue their downstream journey to the sea. The "striper" is a popular game fish in eastern rivers tributary to the ocean, as well as in many western and midwestern rivers and reservoirs, where it has been introduced. The striper grows to large sizes; most freshwater-angled fish are of five to 20 pounds, but individuals of over 100 pounds have been recorded from the ocean. Naturalized striped bass have been greatly successful in large reservoirs across the country, due to their spawning behavior and the buoyant eggs. The striper does not depend upon littoral areas of reservoirs, which may alternately dry and become inundated due to severe water level fluctuations common in large reservoirs.

Managers have developed the white bass/striped bass hybrid, or *whiper* (or *wiper*), popular in many western and midwestern rivers and reservoirs. These hybrids exhibit several favored traits of both parent species, such as rapid growth to large sizes and strong fighting qualities when hooked. Foods of both species consist of smaller fish; they readily take baitfish, spinning lures, and white streamer flies.

◆   ◆   ◆

AROUND THE WORLD, THE MOST COMMON and abundant fishes in streams and rivers are the *minnows*. Although we often refer to any small fish as minnows—like "bass minnows" or "pike minnows"—this assemblage of mostly small fishes is a distinct family, the Cyprinidae. With about 2,100 cyprinid species worldwide, it is the largest of all freshwater fish families. The greatest diversity of species occurs in southeastern Asia, with 600 species. In North America, we have about 230 native species and a half-dozen exotics, mostly carps and goldfish. Most of our native minnow species are ecologically adapted to streams and rivers. Many species of minnows are used as bait for fishing, and what with anglers using these in different streams, "minnie-bucket introductions" have spread some species into distant waters.

We anglers are prone to lump all of the minnows that annoy us by rising to our trout flies as "chubs." Actually, the true chubs occur in several genera, and other common names—dace, shiners, minnows—are less known. With so many genera and species of minnows, however, we'll just hit a few high points.

The cyprinids comprise mostly small fishes, but some are large. Most notable are the large squawfishes (genus *Ptychocheilus,* several species) in the West, some growing to lengths of nearly six feet. With so much dam building and fishery bias against nonsalmonid fish, the squawfishes have been greatly reduced in abundance. Even so, when trout and salmon aren't biting, some California anglers fish for squawfish just for sport—they are big! The Colorado squawfish, for example, is the largest but is now listed as an endangered species. However, the northern squawfish is smaller, maximum of about 24 inches and common in the mountainous, northern Pacific drainage.

The genus *Gila* (14 species) is a western group of chubs that also grow to large sizes—some species 15 to over 20 inches. Some have been greatly reduced because of damming, water diversions, withdrawals for irrigation, and exotic introductions, and are listed in a threatened or endangered status. The native ranges of these *Gila* chubs are in rivers draining either to the Pacific Ocean, into Mexico, or into the Great Basin.

The tui chub, native to the Columbia River drainage, is large, growing to about 18 inches; this species is divided into several subspecies, two of which are included as endangered sub-species on the federal list. The large humpback chub, also native to the Columbia drainage, has also become scarce and is listed as endangered. Another endangered species is the bonytail, the biggest of the genus *Gila* (up to 24 inches). It was originally abundant in large, swift river rapids of the Colorado and Green rivers, but it has been brought to near extinction by high dams on these rivers.

The northern squawfish is a large minnow common in streams and rivers of the Pacific Northwest. (Clark Fork, Montana.)

The roundtail chub has also been divided into several subspecies, two of which are listed as endangered; the roundtail is also a large river-rapids dweller, greatly reduced by dams in the Colorado River. A small, abundant species is the leatherside chub, native to the upper Snake River drainage in Wyoming and Idaho; a small species, it grows to only six inches in length and occupies creeks with pools and riffles and small rivers. Several small chubs (five to ten inches) occur in streams in Arizona and New Mexico that flow into Mexico: Yaqui, Rio Grande, Sonora, and Chihuahua chubs. The Yaqui chub is listed as endangered and the Sonora chub as threatened. The small Alvord chub (five inches) inhabits small streams and springs that flow into the closed Alvord basin in Oregon. A lake-living species, the Borax Lake chub exists only in this small lake in the Alvord Basin and is listed as endangered.

Most species of minnows, however, are distributed east of the Rocky Mountains and are much smaller than many of the western species. Even so, a few of these eastern species inhabiting trout and smallmouth streams, grow to fairly large sizes—10 to 12 inches—and are well known to stream anglers, such as the creek chub and the golden shiner.

Chubs in the genus *Semotilus* (four species) are abundant in the eastern United States; the most widespread is the creek chub, *S. atromaculatus,* whose range covers most of eastern United States and parts of Canada. This is the same fish that was a prominent subject of Professor Victor Shelford's classic studies of fish distribution in streams. The male of this species grows noticeable hornlike tubercles on its head during spring spawning season, with which it defends the spawning nest against intruders. After fertilization of the eggs, the male covers the nest with additional gravel and small stones, much as salmonids cover their redds. (My trout-fishing father used to call these tubercled male creek chubs "horned dace," believing they were a separate fish—an inaccuracy, of course, that I innocently perpetuated for many years.)

The pearl dace (*Margariscus margarita*) closely resembles the creek chub in that the breeding males have tubercles on their heads. Unlike the creek chub, however, it is smaller, and the breeding male takes on a bright, orange-red color on its flanks. The pearl dace's native range is large, extending from all of Alberta eastward through the northern Great Lakes region and all eastern provinces to the Maritimes.

Some other eastern minnows also carry the common name of chub. Included in the genus *Nocomis* are six species that occur around the Great Lakes and in the Southeast. In the genus *Hybopsis* are seven chub species, varying from other minnows in that they are almost strictly bottom-living fish. They have upward-directed eyes (to watch for predators?) and a long snout with a subterminal mouth (down-turned, like that of suckers). *Barbels* at the corners of the mouth assist in bottom feeding. Most of the species' ranges are in southeastern states, but this genus also includes the pallid shiner (*H. amnis*), which ranges throughout the Mississippi River, from Minnesota to Louisiana, and is rare. The pallid shiner is well named from its coloration—silvery on its sides with no noticeable pigmentation.

Campostoma (four species) includes the stonerollers, herbivorous fish that feed almost entirely on algae. The most common and widespread species is the central stoneroller, *C. anomalum*, occurring throughout most of the Central Plains and east almost to the Atlantic Ocean. This species, as an herbivore feeding on abundant algae in a warmwater stream, often reaches extremely high abundance, sometimes greater than all other species in a stream, which are mostly carnivores, combined.

One of the most common genera to be encountered in trout and coolwater streams is *Rhinichthys* (nine species of dace). Any electrofishing census in a small, cool stream turns up good numbers of the blacknose dace and longnose dace. The blacknose, especially common in trout streams, is distributed throughout the northeastern quarter of the United States and part of eastern Canada. However, the longnose dace is the most widespread of all North American minnows, ranging coast-to-coast across the northern United States and mid-Canada, and from the Yukon south to the Rio Grande drainage. Another species, the speckled dace, is present in an unusually large western range, throughout all states west of the Rocky Mountains.

Another group of dace is the genus *Phoxinus* (six species), distributed mostly around and east of the Great Lakes. The northern redbelly dace is widely distributed across the United States from Montana to New England, and in Canada from northern Alberta east to the Maritimes. In spawning season, the male of this species is a particularly beautiful fish, commonly turned up in electrofishing sporting a striking red belly. *Phoxinus* is the only genus of minnows native to both North America and Eurasia.

Several genera of dace occur in the Southwest, mainly in desert springs and small streams. Some can tolerate temperatures up to 120°, and live in temporary streams that dry up in daytime; these fish survive in moist sand, becoming active during the night when flowing water returns.

A largely herbivorous group of cyprinids is the genus *Hybognathus*, with the common name of *minnow* (six species). These algae-eating small fish are common denizens of larger streams, backwaters in slow rivers, and deep pools. One species, the brassy minnow, is a popular baitfish and has been introduced widely outside its native range, which extended across most of the north-central and northeastern United States from the Rocky Mountains to New England. Another widespread species in this genus is the plains minnow; as its common name suggests, it is familiar in creeks and small rivers in the Great Plains states, from eastern Montana south to Texas. Members of the genus *Pimephales* (four species) are also known as *minnows*. Included is the fathead minnow (*P. promelas*), the most common baitfish of all cyprinids. Its ability to tolerate poor-quality water conditions—low oxygen, turbidity, and high temperatures—much more than other fish, makes it the first choice as a baitfish, long lasting in anglers' minnow buckets. The fathead is often the only fish species to survive northern winterkills in shallow ponds, owing to its ability to tolerate low oxygen. It is widespread in its native range (almost all of the United States and south central Canada) and has been introduced widely.

The common name carried by the most species in the Cyprinidae—117—is *shiner*. Many of these have a bright, silvery or golden appearance; others have red or pink fins and flanks, especially when in spawning colors. Most shiners are distributed in North America east of the Rockies. Different genera occupy small ranges throughout the southeastern states and larger distributions around the Great Lakes, into the Great Plains, and a few range northwestwards to the Yukon. Strangely, the shiners almost totally avoid the Atlantic coastal areas. As a group, the shiners are not well known—to many fishery biologists as well as anglers. A few are known to stream fishers, however, because they are caught commonly with either bait or flies, especially the common shiner and golden shiner, which are commonly sold for bait.

Shiners include the genera *Luxilus* (9 species), *Lythrurus* (9 species), *Pteronotropis* (5 species), and *Cyprinella* (22 species), mostly found in states around the Great Lakes and in the Southeast. *Notropis*, with 71 species, is the largest genus of shiners, and the second largest genus of freshwater fish in North America. (The largest is *Etheostoma*, a genus of darters.)

The common shiner, *Luxilis cornutus*, is a species greatly deserving of its name. It is shiny like a new silver dollar and even more common. Although it is small—six to seven inches—its range includes the northern Great Plains, Great Lakes region, and eastward into southern Ontario and Quebec. It may be taken frequently by trout fishers, especially with dry flies.

The most abundant shiner in North America is the emerald shiner, *Notropis atherinoides*, found especially throughout the entire Mississippi River drainage, including both the Missouri and Ohio rivers and their tributaries. Its native range also includes the Great Lakes region and across Canada from western Alberta east to the Maritimes. A favorite baitfish, sold widely, it is a small shiner of up to four or five inches and is a favorite bait for crappies. Not common in small streams, it primarily inhabits large rivers and lakes.

The golden shiner is the best known and the most widely distributed of all shiners, commonly used as bait by anglers. It is the single species in its genus, *Notemigonus crysoleucas*. The large native range of the golden shiner extends from Montana east of the Rocky Mountains south to Texas and the entire rest of the United States, plus small southern parts of all Canadian provinces from Manitoba east to the Maritimes. Its popularity as a baitfish has extended its naturalized range into many lakes and streams where it did not originally occur, no doubt by "minnie-bucket" introductions. Most trout fishers have caught this species on dry flies. Unique among all minnows, the golden shiner has a body that is extremely compressed laterally and a deep belly with a thin, fleshy *keel* running from between its pelvic fins backward towards the vent. And the keel has no scales! Take a close look next time you catch one. An unusual upturned mouth correctly suggests that it feeds easily on the surface, taking terrestrials, emerging mayflies—and dry flies. Its common name derives from a beautiful golden sheen on its flanks. It grows to good size, up to 12 inches. It is common in trout streams that are on the thermally marginal side. (One time while popping for bluegills I hooked a golden shiner about a foot long—it leaped high into the air like a rainbow trout, an astonishing experience.)

Members of the family Cyprinidae are like the mice and hares of the prairies—they form a large forage base for the predaceous animals in higher trophic levels. By feeding on primary producers like algae and some of the smallest invertebrates, minnows constitute trophic links to other, larger fish (including other minnows), creating one of the most efficient transfers of energy from lower to higher trophic levels, an essential ecological function in almost all freshwater communities.

◆   ◆   ◆

THE *DARTERS* MUST TAKE SECOND PLACE in terms of numbers of stream species—147. They are small and, yes, they dart about, on the stream bottom. Many are brilliant in hue, especially the males in spring spawning colors. They are present only east of the Rockies, except that some introductions have been made into western waters. Most widely distributed and common are the Johnny darter, Iowa darter, and the rainbow darter.

Darters are members of the perch family, Percidae, all of which have two separate dorsal fins, a useful characteristic for identification. Except for the walleye, sauger, and yellow perch, all other native North American percids are darters. They are divided into only two genera—*Percina* and *Etheostoma.*

Members of *Percina* (33 species) run a little larger than the other genus, *Etheostoma*—up to six or seven inches—and they have gas bladders like most fishes that enable them to swim about above the streambed. Six *Percina* species are known as *logperch,* and with several vertical bars on their flanks and greenish-to-yellow coloration, they do look a bit like yellow perch. Most of the logperch are rare and have very limited ranges. The exception is the species simply called "logperch," *Percina caprodes*. This darter is common over a broad range: from northern North Dakota northeast to Hudson Bay, all around the Great Lakes, and south to the Gulf Coast. With some searching, you should be able to catch one by sweeping with a net around stream edges (not in a trout stream, however). If you do net one, note that it has a tough, bulbous projection on the end of its snout, which is used for turning over stones to forage for insects!

Another *Percina* (not logperch) that became famous (or notorious) is the snail darter, *P. tanasi*, once an endangered species, now downgraded to a threatened status. The snail darter gained fame by almost stopping the Tellico Dam on the Little Tennessee River, a trout stream, back in the 1970s. At the time, the snail darters in the Little Tennessee were thought to be the only existing population. Then others were found elsewhere, Tellico was built, and the trout stream was extinguished.

The genus *Etheostoma* includes a whopping 114 species, the largest genus of freshwater fish in North America. These are smaller (two to three inches) and, unlike *Percina*, have no gas bladders. Consequently, like sculpins, they are truly benthic fishes. Species of *Etheostoma* are widely distributed over much of eastern North America, most in or east of the Mississippi River. The most common darter of all is the Johnny darter, *E. nigrum*, which ranges through most of the eastern half of the continent, from Hudson Bay to the Deep South. You can find it in almost any warmwater stream, and it can easily be identified by the distinctive **W**-shaped marks on its sides.

A half-dozen species of *Etheostoma* are known as sand darters. They have clear or translucent bodies, no scales, and long, slender, wiggly bodies—all of which enable them to dig themselves into sand, or near wood debris half-buried in sand, thus making themselves virtually invisible to predators. The sand darters' habitat has been degraded in much of eastern and midwestern streams as the result of human civilization, resulting in excessive siltation over previously clean, sandy streambeds.

Common in many small streams is the bottom-living Johnny darter, easily recognized by the **W**-shaped marks on its flanks. (Photo by Dean C. Hansen of *WetBugs Press*, Stillwater, Minnesota.)

◆   ◆   ◆

The *Etheostoma* are noted for their bright, sometimes very intense, coloration. The most beautifully colored, in this author's opinion, is the rainbow darter, *E. caeruleum*. Many other darters are brightly colored, too, as their names suggest: tangerine, cherry, gilt, firebelly, bluebreast, redband, orangefin, and many others. The males are particularly colorful in their springtime breeding hues. Incidentally, these make excellent freshwater aquarium fishes. You can easily catch a few by rapidly dragging a net along the stream bottom in a riffle; be sure to drag your net in a downstream direction. You can distinguish darters from all other small fish by their double dorsal fins. Seven species of *Etheostoma* are listed as either threatened or endangered.

ALTHOUGH THE BULLHEAD-CATFISH FAMILY, Ictaluridae, comprises about 40 species, one among all of these is an extremely common, popular, and basically stream and river fish: the channel catfish (*Ictalurus punctatus*). All ictalurids sport four pairs of barbels around their mouths, which resemble the "whiskers" of cats—and hence *cat*fish. What with their habit of feeding at night or in muddy water, their sensitive barbels assist in identifying food items. They also have taste buds located all along their flanks.

The channel catfish, long a favorite in middle and southern states, is increasing in widespread popularity as a warmwater sport fish. (Photo courtesy of the University of Minnesota Press.)

The channel cat enjoys a particularly wide distribution—the entire eastern half of the United States, plus bits of Manitoba and southeastern Ontario. Introductions of channel catfish into western regions have extended its distribution greatly, especially into the warmwater streams of the Southwest. The channel cat inhabits water clearer than other family members, usually with good current, but it can also thrive in turbid water in medium-to-large rivers. The channel cat also occupies some small streams and creeks and can be fished for much like trout. It can grow to lengths of four feet, but most angling catches will be on the order of 14 to 18 inches.

The channel catfish, more than any other freshwater fish, has been cultured commercially; they can be found as frozen fillets in almost any food market as well as on the menus of many restaurants as deep-fried catfish with hush puppies. Farm ponds throughout the southern United States are commonly stocked with channel cats for sport and food.

In all probability, the channel catfish occupies the number one position in terms of numbers of fish caught by sport anglers in the United States. Long favored in warmwater streams in the South, catfish are increasing in popularity in northern states as well, where traditionally they were disdained by stream anglers seeking trout and smallmouth bass. The wide variety of foods eaten by these carnivorous fish means that they can be taken with a similar variety of lures and baits. Live bait of all kinds—especially worms, crayfish, and other small fish—are always effective. Home-brewed or commercial "stinkbaits" are popular, too—which, after a day on the river spent baiting and rebaiting hooks, assures you of a quiet night's sleep undisturbed by the rest of your family!

Two other catfishes grow much larger than the channel cat: the blue catfish (over 100 pounds) and the flathead catfish (to 90 pounds), both to more than five feet in length. They are increasing in popularity for recreational fishing. Both inhabit large rivers, mostly the Mississippi and its major tributaries, but never in upland creeks and streams, where the channel cat thrives.

Smallmouth bass anglers are occasionally surprised to find a catfish on their spinners or baits, and an increasingly enthusiastic group of fly fishers are devoted to the pursuit of catfish. Some variant of the Woolly Bugger, weighted and fished just off the bottom, seems to be the most effective. The channel cat is well prepared for feeding actively at night, in muddy water, or on dark days, so angling is believed to be most effective between sunset and midnight.

Fishing methods vary from single-hook, rod-and-reel angling to multiple-hook rigs (where legal) with several droppers, trot lines with many droppers, and "jugging" (setting out many lines and baited hooks below floating jugs, then setting them adrift).

Channel catfish have adipose fins, forked tails, and spots on their flanks—all of which are common to trout, too. You wouldn't really have trouble telling them apart, now would you?

SELECTED REFERENCES:

Buffler, Rob, and Tom Dickson. 1990. *Fishing for Buffalo: A guide to the pursuit, lore & cuisine of buffalo, carp, mooneye, gar and other "rough" fish.* Culpepper Press, Minneapolis.
Stroud, Richard H., and Henry Clepper, editors. 1975. *Black Bass Biology and Management.* Sport Fishing Institute, Washington DC.

RiverSketch

OZARK RIVERS

THE OZARK PLATEAU IN MIDDLE NORTH AMERICA has been long recognized as a region of extraordinary qualities. Remarkable in its geologic history, this uplifted tabletop of ancient limestone and dolomite remains as our continent's outstanding example of karst topography, encompassing most of southern Missouri and northern Arkansas. The Ozarks, diminutive "mountains" though they may be, comprise highland scenes of timbered hills and craggy cliffs—and remote valleys where hill folk used to make a little 'shine and still play some rollicking string music.

Through this rugged landscape of ridge and valley flow myriad streams and rivers with special features. Along with the deeply dissected streams, surrounding lands of the Ozark Mountains make up a wilderness of gentle beauty.

The karst topography has produced an extensive system of caverns and underground rivers, leading to huge springs of crystalline water. These springs are the genesis of the clearest of streams, vibrant with pools of brilliant blue and emerald. Amply supplied by these many springs, streams run lucid and clear, with high chemical alkalinity. Such clear alkaline water absorbs the red end of the light spectrum, leaving blues and greens in the deep pools.

A typical aspect of all Ozark rivers is the profusion of gravel bars, alternating from one stream side to the other. The bars make convenient stopping places for river floaters and anglers, for lunch and overnight camping. The bars, as well as the beds shallow riffles, are composed of *chert* fragments, a flintlike, fine-grained form of quartz, hard and exceptionally resistant to weathering. Chert strata are embedded in the native bedrock, so when dolomite and limestone are dissolved away, abundant chert pieces remain.

Many Ozark streams are noted for their fishing. Although nearly 100 species of fish inhabit these streams, one principal species is favored above all by anglers—the smallmouth bass. Along with the smallmouth are its constant companions, the rock bass and Ozark bass. The smallmouth is highly productive in these waters, feeding on an abundance of crayfish, typical of Ozark streams. The most common large fish in the rivers, however, are the redhorses, golden and black, in the sucker family.

Of the many Ozark rivers, a number have been selected as streams of unusual quality and designated for protection in national river systems. All were early recognized as something special, but at the same time, they were targeted for dams. These include: the Current River and its main tributary, the Jacks Fork River, in Missouri; the Eleven Point River, arising nearby and flowing into Arkansas; and the Buffalo River, across much of northern Arkansas. All waters flow to Arkansas's White River and eventually the Mississippi.

Since designation, all four rivers have become popular for recreation, mainly canoeing. Fishing runs a far second. River-running difficulty is mild, rarely more than class I. The Buffalo is an exception, with more class II water, notably in the ten miles above the usual "head of navigation," where class III and IV rapids are present. All streams are particularly susceptible to flash-flooding, and extreme caution is required in the spring and summer stormy season. Fallen trees, debris dams, and tree root wads present the more common hazards, especially in the smaller Jacks Fork and Eleven Point. With all that, all streams provide generally a leisurely float, with just enough twists and riffles to require some occasional close attention.

The Jacks Fork River, one of several federally protected Ozark streams, is a favorite for paddlers and anglers after smallmouth bass.

The Current and Jacks Fork were the first to be protected as exceptional, free-flowing rivers—designated together in 1964 by the U.S. Congress as the Ozark National Scenic Riverways, within the National Park Service.

The Current begins as a series of small springs in the east-central part of the Ozarks, and flows southeastward for 140 unimpeded miles. Ninety-four stream miles were placed in the designated system. The Jacks Fork also begins with springs, flows northeastward for about 50 miles, and meets the Current at their junction known as Two Rivers. Most of the Jacks Fork is designated for protection.

The Current is the larger of the two rivers, and a float with canoe or johnboat is relaxed; the Jacks Fork is more intimate, smaller and narrower. Frequent stops allow the exploration of springs, caves, and hollows, and searches for fossils among the cherty gravel bars.

Enacted in 1968, the National Wild and Scenic Rivers System was created with eight "instant wild rivers," the beautiful Eleven Point as one. Administered by the U.S. Forest Service, the designated reach includes 44 stream miles. By comparison, the Eleven Point may be no wilder than hundreds of other worthy eastern streams, but its special loveliness won out in congressional hearings, and a proposed dam was stopped. Smaller than the other Ozark rivers, with fewer gravel bars, the Eleven Point is greatly supported by two dozen major springs. The largest is Greer Spring, which creates a deep, forested gorge over a mile long. It adds enough water to double the size of the main river. Owing to the copious, cool groundwater of this large spring, the river supports trout for about 18 miles downstream.

Five streams in the Boston Mountains, part of the Ozark Plateau in western Arkansas, are included in the National Wild and Scenic Rivers System: Big Piney Creek, Hurricane Creek, Mulberry River, North Sycamore Creek, and Richland Creek. In sum, these streams comprise nearly 165 river miles in the national system. They are a bit warmer in summer than the other Ozark streams and include largely warmwater fish species, including the spotted, smallmouth, and Ozark bass, some small sunfishes, and a host of minnows and darters.

The Buffalo River, all of it in Arkansas, is the Ozarks' longest undammed river at over 150 miles. In 1972, a federal act established the Buffalo National River, administered by the National Park Service; it is a long, narrow national park, with a river running through it. The Buffalo shares many qualities with the other Ozark streams, but some traits are different. Springs, for example, are not common on the Buffalo. In low, clear water, however, the Buffalo's pools are still bright with rich blues and greens. Bluffs are higher and gravel bars fewer. However, there are many more side excursions available—to hidden canyons, tributary waterfalls, and old historic buildings. Many more hiking and horse trails are maintained along the Buffalo.

Much attention is paid by the National Park Service to keep the Buffalo wild; many tracts of riparian land were acquired to complement the river and to keep intrusive development away from the river. Several designated wilderness areas are also nearby in the Buffalo's watershed, in national forests.

Understandably, not all longtime residents were enthusiastic about the government's wilderness concept. One elderly lady, definitely unenthusiastic, was heard to remark "...they're going to let it all go wild again!"

Yes, indeedy.

SELECTED REFERENCES:

Schuchard, Oliver, and Steve Kohler. 1984. *Two Ozark Rivers: The Current and the Jacks Fork.* University of Missouri Press, Columbia.

Smith, Kenneth L. 1970. *The Buffalo River Country.* Second edition. The Ozark Society, Fayetteville, Arkansas.

Part Six

By Clock and Calendar

Introduction to Part Six

BY CLOCK AND CALENDAR

A LMOST ALL ANIMALS MIGRATE. They do so for several reasons: to escape from severe weather, to reach better feeding areas, to reach suitable, safe areas for reproduction.

Strictly speaking, a "migration" involves a two-way trip: a movement in one direction followed by a later return. Waterfowl migrate south in autumn and return in spring; western elk move down from the mountains for the winter and back up in spring; young salmon leave their natal stream for a year or more in the ocean and return as adults. Some migrations involve the movement of adults in one direction and a later "return" of juveniles, such as the monarch butterfly's trip south in fall and the return of the next cohort of juvenile monarchs the following spring.

Migrations are almost always tied to seasons—that is, to the calendar—with spring and fall movements being the most common. The approximate time of onset is inherent in the animals' genetic makeup; a more precise time may depend on weather—that is, temperature and meteorological events.

Other kinds of population movement involve only a one-way trip, such as the sea lamprey invasion of the Great Lakes, or the movement of animal populations to colonize new areas. These movements are sometimes termed "migrations" but are more correctly termed *dispersals*—that is, expansions of the animals' range. In this sense, the colonization of North America by *Homo sapiens* by movement across the Bering Land Bridge was a dispersal, not a migration as it is frequently called.

Many animals undertake specific movements during a day's time—that is, by the clock. These may be true migrations if we hold to the strict definition—out and back—although these daily excursions are not usually termed migrations. The same species may undertake both kinds of movement—waterfowl, for example, move to feeding grounds and back to roosting areas in the same day, but they also undertake seasonal migrations during a year's time.

In streams, we most often think of migrations in an upstream direction. (Of course, there is a downstream element, too.) These are essentially movements on a horizontal plane, between two geographical locations. In other cases, the distances covered sometimes are so extensive that they inspire our greatest awe and wonderment—near 2,000 miles for some salmon—but for some aquatic invertebrates a daily migrational movement may be only a few feet.

In other habitats, movements may be vertical. Western elk, mentioned earlier, undertake movements between different altitudes, mountain to valley, where the purpose is based on weather conditions at different elevations, which in turn affect the availability of their food. In many lakes, some planktonic and benthic invertebrates make daily migrations from lake depths to near-surface strata, to seek better oxygen conditions or denser phytoplankton concentrations of food.

An exceptional example is the phantom midge, a separate family in the order Diptera, and so-called because of its appearance. (Its black eyes are about all that's visible in its otherwise transparent body.) This aquatic larva lives a benthic existence in lake sediments often devoid of oxygen, and consequently it makes nocturnal excursions to the oxygenated surface water to renew its supply. Many zooplankters, mainly microcrustaceans, also make nightly ascents in lakes for feeding. Such nocturnal movement appears to be an evolved behavior that provides protection against predators (sight-feeding fish, for example). We will see some analogies in the nocturnal movements of stream insects, scuds, and microcrustaceans in the chapter on invertebrate drift.

Migrations of any kind often create large concentrations. A superabundance of potential prey thus attracts predators, and migration becomes a dangerous time for the migrants. Protective behavior, such as movement at night, is often employed. Even so, the concentrations may provide a feeding bonanza for the predator, like Alaskan grizzly bears that feast upon migrating salmon, food resources that have become essential in the predators' annual cycle of nutrition. In prehistory, native Americans also came to depend upon the concentrations of fish, bird, and mammal migrations. In today's sport fishing and hunting, regulations are often devised to protect the animals during their migratory concentrations.

The genetic force to migrate is not always as certain as we might believe. Species we most usually think of as migratory, having a strong urge to migrate, we term "obligate;" we can think of their migration as obligatory, that is, they *have to*. At the other end of the migratory scale are those that sometimes do, sometimes don't—an "optional" category—subject to severity of environmental conditions, such as weather. Some populations do, other populations of the same species don't. Or it's just that some may show some tendency to migrate, but really don't go all the way. Some inland trout and salmon, and also some warmwater species, fall into these latter categories.

Let's take a look.

Chapter **24**

RETURN TO THE RIVER

A MONG ALL MAJOR GROUPS OF FISHES receiving admiration from both anglers and scholars, the migratory, anadromous species have received the most. Shrouded in the mystery of their navigation, spectacular in their concentrations, favored for food and sport, the several species of salmon share top honors.

All juveniles undertake migrations from their river spawning redds downstream to the ocean, a sea life of one or more years to feed and grow, and an upstream return journey of the adults to spawn in their natal streams. The ability of the adults to find their way around the broad oceans and back to the river of their youth, and then to locate the exact tributary—and often even the same gravel bed—of their birth, is legendary.

In addition to the salmons, however, most all other salmonids with access to the ocean have developed anadromous stocks. Various populations of rainbow, cutthroat, brook trout, and the introduced European brown trout have long ago evolved the migratory behavior to some extent. (However, it is still debated as to which came first—freshwater or saltwater life.)

The spawning migrations of these salmonids that spawn in freshwater streams and grow in the ocean are the most common forms of *anadromy*; we term the species that practice it *anadromous*. Some salmonids, mostly those that are anadromous, include distinct stocks that spawn in freshwater streams but migrate to a freshwater lake to grow; these stocks we term *adfluvial*. The kokanee—the totally freshwater form of the sockeye salmon—is the outstanding example of an adfluvial life history, but other species introduced into the Great Lakes have also developed adfluvial populations: the rainbow, brown trout, and several Pacific salmons. The singular example of the reverse migration is that of the American eel, spawning in the Atlantic Ocean and migrating to inland rivers to feed and grow. This is *catadromy*, and thus its life history is termed *catadromous*. Another variant type of migration is *potamodromy*, migrating upstream or downstream entirely within a freshwater stream system. An example is the *potamodromous* grayling, which moves from small spawning streams to large rivers and backwaters for feeding and growth.

Many warmwater species undertake shorter migrations, to escape the rigors of winter and to search for food, or to reach suitable reproductive habitat. Several marine species undertake anadromous migrations into streams, for example, the striped bass. Inland, stream-resident trout that travel to better spawning gravel, usually upstream to headwater reaches, are other examples of potamodromy. Many migratory movements of other fishes undoubtedly occur but have not been researched. Still, the long, complex journeys of the Pacific salmon have received the most attention.

◆　　　　　◆　　　　　◆

THE FIVE EASTERN PACIFIC OCEAN SALMONS—pink, chum, chinook, coho, and sockeye—have migration patterns that, in broad outline, are much the same. Common to all are egg hatching in upstream gravels, downstream (sometimes upstream) migration of fry, juveniles, and smolts, one or more years in the ocean, and upstream migration of adults to spawn. At a finer scale, however, differences in this general pattern distinguish all five species.

The downstream migration of salmonid fry begins in the redd, when the newly formed larvae, having exhausted their yolk sac, begin to struggle upward, to free themselves of the enclosing gravel. Often the fry begin to feed during this struggle, preying upon meiofaunal animals such as midge larvae, usually present in these hyporheic habitats.

The pink and chum salmon are most similar. The new fry, arriving in the open stream after their upward struggle through the redd's gravel, immediately begin their downstream journey to the ocean, reaching salt water quickly. The major difference between the two species is that most pink salmon fry begin only a short way upstream from the ocean, often in the estuary (with some important exceptions). On the other hand, the chum adult traverses a much longer distance upstream and consequently the downstream migration is also longer. The pink is not adept at leaping waterfalls (with one major exception); most of its spawning rivers lack falls and turbulent cascades. Both pink and chum fry usually move downstream by night, actively feeding on small stream insect larvae by day, although the pink fry reach the sea at the smaller size. In turbid water fry will move by day as well as by night.

The great exception to the usual short river run of pink salmon is in the Fraser River, British Columbia. Prior to the infamous Hell's Gate slide of cut rock material, from railway construction in 1913, pink salmon migrated far upstream to spawn. Upriver runs included as many as forty million spawners, making the Fraser the world's largest producer of salmonids. The 1913 slide, however, completely blocked the pink salmon's migration, and the upstream runs were essentially destroyed. Some runs are being restored by fishways at Hell's Gate, and although turbulence and high velocities still occur, the pink salmon appear capable of adapting.

The chinook, the largest of the five species and the most noted as a sport fish, travels the farthest upstream. The most sought-after of the Pacific salmon group, the chinook is detailed in Roderick Haig-Brown's classic, *Return to the River*, his celebration of the chinook's incredible migratory journey.

The chinook has a renowned capability for leaping high falls. Consequently, the fry have the farthest to travel downstream—up to about 2,000 miles from the ocean. The downstream migration of chinook fry varies in distance, need for food, and the size at smolting. Upon emergence from the redd, some fry start immediately downstream, others will take up stream residence for several weeks, months, or a year. If the spawning redd is near the ocean, all will migrate immediately, but if the redd location is in middle reaches, they may stay longer before their run to the sea. Other fry will take up residence in the estuary as a nursery area. For those spawned at extreme distances, the trip downriver becomes a nursery excursion, the fry feeding voraciously on the way, arriving in the ocean at a size large enough to ensure better survival in the sea.

The fishway at Hell's Gate on the Fraser River allows pink salmon to resume migrations after they were blocked by a landslide in 1913. (Photo by Thomas G. Northcote, University of British Columbia.)

The aggressive nature of the chinook is manifested not only by its angling quality as an adult, but also by its feeding behavior while still a fry in the stream. While fly fishing for brook trout in a Lake Superior tributary, I once began having a series of aggressive strikes by small fish barely a couple of inches in size, often several fish attacking the fly at one time. They were actually too small to ingest the fly (a size 14 Adams, as I recall). Eventually a fish was foul-hooked, and to my surprise, I held a small, parr-marked salmonid—which I later determined to be a juvenile chinook. Obviously, their foods included surface-drifting invertebrates and probably many terrestrials. They had been stocked as fry far upstream in a river that held an enormous array of wild cascades and high waterfalls, with hopes of their growth to smolts on their way down and eventually supplementing the catch of sport fish and the spawning run of adults. I wished them well on their wild adventure toward the cold waters of Superior.

An aggressive chinook fingerling stocked
in a Great Lakes tributary and caught on a dry fly.

Coho salmon juveniles make the greatest use of freshwater streams on their eventual trip to the ocean, mostly a feeding and growth period of two years (some one or three). Taking up stream residence almost upon emergence in spring, much like stream-dwelling trout, the fry feed and grow rapidly in their stream life through two summers (surviving one or two winters). Juvenile coho arrive at salt water in a spring freshet as silvery, fully developed smolts. Some populations, however, migrate to freshwater lakes attaining a larger weight.

Migrations of sockeye salmon to their nursery lake differ greatly from the other four species. This migratory pattern has been studied more intensively by salmon researchers than all other salmon life histories. As a result, the migrations of sockeyes have been found to be much more sensitive than other species, necessitating a more precise timing at all stages. The onset of emergence, upstream or downstream orientation, and arrival time at the lake, all require precise coordination.

The growth from fry to smolt in the nursery lake, feeding heavily upon abundant zooplankton, assists greatly in the success of young sockeye during their later downstream migration and survival in the ocean. The rapid descent of smolts precludes the necessity of further feeding and growth in the stream. By the time they arrive at the river's mouth, sockeye smolts are amply fit for the next important stage of their life cycle—ranging the open ocean where they will accrue by far the greater part of their adult body mass.

◆   ◆   ◆

MOST OTHER SALMONID SPECIES UNDERTAKE anadromous migrations between stream and ocean. The steelhead, or migratory rainbow trout, the Atlantic salmon, and some populations of those we usually think of as being strictly stream-resident, such as the cutthroat, brook trout, and brown trout, include stocks that migrate to the ocean to grow and later return to spawn.

The Pacific steelhead and the Atlantic salmon are native to their respective ocean coasts. They are not closely related, but their migrational patterns are similar in broad outline. Both are also native to coastal streams on the other side of their respective oceans—the steelhead in Russian Pacific tributaries and the Atlantic salmon in European tributaries of the North Atlantic.

Both follow the migration routes that connect spawning sites with the ocean, with fry that will spend two years feeding and growing in the stream until smolting, then migrate downstream to the ocean to spend one or more years to feed and grow much larger. The return of adults to their respective natal streams completes their migration cycle.

The steelhead migration and other life history features are highly variable. Distances to spawning sites vary greatly, from near salt water to 1,000 miles upstream. Accordingly, timing of entry to the natal streams also varies. Mature adults must arrive at their stock-specific spawning grounds in time for swimming fry to emerge into the open stream when weather conditions and food supplies are favorable, in late spring. Steelhead adults do not necessarily die after spawning and may return to the ocean, spawning later in subsequent years.

Arrival times at the river mouths from the ocean designate the "runs" of different stocks. Summer-run steelhead enter streams from June to September; at this time, they are sexually immature and so overwinter in stream pools, arriving at the spawning ground by the following spring. Winter-run fish enter streams layer, from December through March, sexually mature, also arriving at their spawning grounds in spring. The new fry take up residence in streams, feeding and growing until time for smolting, usually in two years at a length of about six to eight inches. Growth history is variable, however, depending on pro-ductivity characteristics of the stream. Some adfluvial rainbow trout populations live their entire life in freshwater lake systems, spawning in inlet or outlet streams, migrating between stream and lake.

◆   ◆   ◆

THE MIGRATION PATTERN OF THE ATLANTIC SALMON is roughly similar to that of the steelhead: spawning in gravelly headwaters, juveniles feeding and growing in the river for two years, smolting in spring and entering the Atlantic Ocean to spend one or more years, and adults returning to the natal stream. In contrast to the steelhead's array of numerous streams and rivers, Atlantic salmon spawning streams are fewer and much shorter.

After the spawning in late fall, Atlantic salmon eggs incubate through the winter, and new fry emerge from the redds in time for a springtime abundance of small food items in May or June. The young fry and parr live in rocky, gravelly headwaters for two or three years. Parr are territorial throughout most of their stream life, remaining in a given area for the summer, where they feed mainly on benthic insects. The parr in their second year move downstream in the autumn—through tumultuous rapids and waterfalls—before smoltification and entry to the ocean the following spring.

Some variation occurs in the time of adult entry into rivers for spawning, depending on river location and distance to be traveled upstream. Like the Pacific steelhead, however, each spawning run of the Atlantic salmon is timed to achieve the spring emergence of fry at an opportune season for early feeding. The ability of the adult to surmount waterfalls is legion, making headwaters reaches of streams with falls available to the salmon, but inaccessible to other anadromous species.

Like steelhead, Atlantic salmon do not necessarily die after spawning, although the spawning effort takes its toll in mortality. Those that successfully move back to the ocean continue to feed and grow, and it is these multiple-spawners that provide the large trophy salmon to the angler. Returning adults do not feed, although they take the angler's fly, providing one of the world's most admired and prestigious sport fisheries.

Anadromous brook trout occurred in large, native populations in Atlantic coast streams and in the Great Lakes, although they have declined greatly. Adults in ocean or lake, known as salters or coasters, attained larger sizes but were duller in coloration than their stream resident cousins.

Although usually considered strictly a lake-resident fish, some migratory stocks of lake trout were native in a few Canadian tributaries of Lake Superior. These ascended the tributary streams for spawning, and the fry descended to the lake for growth. Sawdust from lumber mills and pollution from paper industries are blamed for the extirpation of these stocks.

Contributing to the decline of the lake trout in the Great Lakes was the exotic, predaceous sea lamprey, *Petromyzon marinus*. This primitive fish, which lacks true bones, is anadromous in Atlantic Ocean populations but adfluvial in the freshwater Great Lakes, running up tributary streams to spawn.

Naturalized brown trout populations in the Great Lakes developed fall runs of large adults into many small inland streams. (Nemadji River, Minnesota.)

◆   ◆   ◆

THE OUTSTANDING EXAMPLE OF POTAMODROMY is the migration of the Arctic grayling, *Thymallus arcticus*. The grayling is taxonomically located in the family Salmonidae, but in a group different from trout and salmon. Its North American distribution is in large rivers and tributaries, mainly in Alaska and British Columbia, with some smaller populations in the Rocky Mountains of Montana.

The potamodromous migrations of the Arctic grayling have been categorized into four types:

  • movements within a single river that provides separated areas for spawning, feeding, and winter refuge;
  • movements between large river and tributaries, with spawning in the smaller tributaries;
  • movement into lake inlets for spawning, with much of their life cycle in lakes;
  • movement into lake outlets for spawning, with much of their life in lakes.

Grayling populations exhibiting these variations represent different stocks. In all four examples, however, relatively short migrations lead to sites suitable for spawning, feeding, and winter refuge. Spawning takes place in early spring in small streams and tributaries, which provide fine to coarse gravel, where the male selects the territory and the female joins him for egg fertilization. No redd is constructed, only a shallow depression in the streambed. Sexual maturity is variable between about four to eight years in most locations. Feeding and growth of juveniles requires rearing habitat in slower water at stream margins, in backwaters, and in lower reaches of large rivers. Feeding in summer may be chiefly at the surface on terrestrials, which probably accounts for the grayling's well-known susceptibility to dry flies. The severe winters of the Far North require a refuge habitat, mainly in lakes, springs that do not freeze, or downstream to slower, deeper reaches of mainstem rivers.

Distances traveled by grayling in seasonal changes are short, compared to those of salmon and steelhead, but they may vary from a mile or so to a hundred miles in some stocks and rivers. The summer/winter cycles for juvenile rearing are repeated through several years, leading up to sexual maturity and movement to spawning sites.

◆   ◆   ◆

MANY WARMWATER SPECIES OF FISH also make regular migrations, for a variety of reasons; reproduction is the most common. The striped bass (*Morone saxatilis),* highly prized for angling during its spawning run, is native to the East Coast and has been introduced into many large reservoirs in the South. It migrates from the Atlantic Ocean and Gulf drainage upstream in large, long rivers to spawn. The "striper" spawns by broadcasting its eggs, and because the eggs are buoyant, they drift downstream during incubation. Thus it is the eggs that make a downstream "migration." Fry hatch after only a few days and then continue their downstream journey to the sea.

Anadromous striped bass ascend Atlantic coastal rivers for spawning, among America's best-loved sport fish. Roanoke River, Virginia.

The striper grows to large sizes. Most freshwater-angled fish are of five to 20 pounds, but individuals of over 100 pounds have been recorded from the ocean. Naturalized striped bass have been greatly successful in large reservoirs across the country, due to their spawning behavior and the buoyant eggs. Successful reproduction does not depend upon the reservoir bottom in littoral areas, which may be alternately dried and inundated with severe water level fluctuations, common in large reservoirs.

The northern pike (*Esox lucius*) migrates upstream through small creeks in early spring to spawn in connecting ponds and marshes; adults, after broadcasting the fertilized eggs on pond vegetation, return immediately to its lake, and in the warm, sunlit waters of the pond the eggs soon hatch. Fry grow rapidly, feeding on zooplankton and aquatic insects, then leave in summer as fingerlings before the pond or marsh dries up. Before this migration was well known, many northern pike populations were severely reduced by filling in marshy shorelines for cottage development.

Adult smallmouth bass descend their rivers in autumn and overwinter in larger pools downstream, then return upstream in the spring, a migration that appears to be for the purpose of avoiding the severe winter conditions that can develop in warmwater streams. Many other examples are known.

◆   ◆   ◆

THE AMERICAN EEL (*ANGUILLA ROSTRATA*) is one of our most unusual fish. Although it migrates between the Atlantic Ocean and freshwater streams, its routes are the reverse of more familiar anadromous fishes. The eel is *catadromous*—running down rivers to spawn in the ocean, with juveniles migrating back into rivers to feed and mature.

Spawning takes place in an area of the North Atlantic known as the Sargasso Sea southwest of Bermuda, but few details of its spawning behavior are known. (The Sargasso Sea is not really a seaweed-choked oceanic swamp that traps unwary exploring ships; rather, it is a biologically rich area with calm seas and an abundance of floating macrophytes.) The female eel is greatly fecund, producing ten to twenty million eggs. The new hatchlings or larvae are tiny and transparent; from mid-ocean, they move toward the North American coast, taking about one year and reaching a length of about 21/2 inches (analogous to the downstream migration of salmonid fry.) At this stage, it is known as a *glass eel*, still transparent.

Nearing land, the juvenile eels become pigmented and resemble the adults, at about three inches in length. Then commences the long upstream migration into North American rivers (analogous to the ocean phase of salmonids.) But here an unusual difference appears between the catadromous eel and the anadromous salmonids—only the females ascend freshwater streams to feed and grow. Males remain at a smaller size near the river mouths to await the females' return. When females reappear after several years (nine-year-olds have been observed in fresh water), both sexes return together to the Sargasso Sea to spawn (analogous to the upstream spawning run of adult salmonids.)

The head of an American eel with jaws like other bony fish.
It hatched in the Sargasso Sea, traveled across much of the Atlantic, and then migrated deep into the North American continent.

Distribution of female eels in North America includes many tributary streams along the coasts of the North Atlantic and the Gulf of Mexico, the St. Lawrence River and Great Lakes, and the Mississippi River and tributaries upstream to Minnesota. The eels' presence in the Great Lakes does not usually extend into Lake Superior, but several years ago while electrofishing for a trout study in a Lake Superior tributary in northern Minnesota, we captured a small eel, about six or seven inches long. This young lady had apparently traveled a long way from her natal waters in the Sargasso Sea—a long ocean trip, up the St. Lawrence River, through all the Great Lakes, to a small trout stream at the far western end of the largest and longest of the Great Lakes.

Eels are sometimes confused with lampreys, and vice versa. When in hand, however, the two may be easily distinguished. The lamprey has a round sucker mouth; the eel has jaws and teeth like other bony fishes. The lamprey should never be called a "lamprey-eel" (as it commonly is in newspaper articles!).

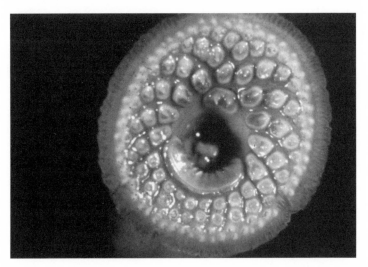

The mouth of the sea lamprey, showing its round, tooth-lined oral cavity with which it rasps an open wound in the flank of its prey. (Photo by Lawrence D. Jacobson, Southwest Fisheries Science Center, La Jolla, California.)

SO FAR AS WE KNOW, very few aquatic insects or other inverte- brates undertake long migrations. Common stream insects, such as mayflies, caddisflies, and stoneflies, are weak fliers. But even in severe winter conditions in the North, many streams do not freeze, and the larvae of these insects survive well. Dragonflies, however, are more common in shallow ponds and marshes, many of which freeze solid in winter. Dragonfly adults are no- tably good fliers, and some have been observed to make speeds of 20 to 30 miles per hour. It should not be surprising therefore, that some species of dragonflies undertake continental migrations, north to south. In the spring, adults in southern, subtropical regions fly north, aided by southerly early spring winds, ovipositing in newly thawed marsh habitat. Progeny hatch, grow, and emerge in summer, and in the fall, these adult dragonflies return to southern swamps for the winter.

In early spring one year, this author observed apparently fully-grown damselfly nymphs (adults of which are not good fliers) in a thawing, shallow pond. During the winter, the entire pond had been frozen solid, and the bottom was still frozen, leading me to wonder where the nymphs had come from. Was it a puzzle in winter survival—or an unknown type of migration?

◆   ◆   ◆

TO THE HUMAN CONSUMER, one of the most significant results of migration, particularly in anadromous fishes, is that the dense concentrations often serve as natural mechanisms for harvesting the rich nutrient resources of the sea. Bringing back from the vast ocean expanses huge volumes of nutritious protein in fish flesh is like passing the bounty of the sea through a river conduit, depositing it in front of our waiting eyes. Spawning in small, headwater streams that often are relatively unproductive, resident fish could never produce the same volume of fish tissue as their ocean-going relatives.

The steady return of adults, especially of the large Pacific salmon that die after spawning, provides another beneficial gift to freshwater-bound stream organisms—a huge supply of nutrients released to infertile stream waters when the fish die and their carcasses decompose. Nutrients from the fish's remains, especially nitrogen and phosphorus, stimulate growth of algae and other food for benthic invertebrates, providing prey for the new cohort of salmon fry. It's a healthy spiral—young salmon leave their natal stream for the ocean and return to fertilize the headwater streams for the next generations.

◆   ◆   ◆

THE MYSTERY OF "HOMING" among anadromous fishes has long stirred intense curiosity among scholars of natural history. Many fishes exhibit homing—the migrational return of the adult to the spawning grounds of its parents—and although most intense research effort has been expended upon salmonids, probably many more species are involved. Even on a microscale, like that of a small lake, perhaps all species have at least some latent instinct to return "home."

The mystery, manifested most visibly by those species that travel long distances, lies in how these so-called primitive animals find their way. Anadromous salmonids must successfully traverse three long segments:

• downstream to the ocean from their natal spawning redds, often for hundreds of miles;

• wandering in the open ocean, often for thousands of miles, then back to the mouth of the river of their birth;

• back upstream, now as large mature adults, over the same hundreds of miles to the same small, headwater tributary, and often to the same gravel bed.

The mystery, of course, lies in the physiological mechanisms used to find their way with such precision. A number of tools have been postulated, and researchers have accumulated some good evidence. In this book on streams, we emphasize the two river journeys, but the ocean segment is equally intriguing.

The downstream movement of fry, parr, and smolts is fairly simple: a passive drift with the currents—or so it seems. But modifications of the simple drift strategy are evident: some fish actively swim to supplement the current; some move temporarily upstream (for example, the sockeye); some pause in interconnected lakes.

Possible cues the juvenile fish must remember include visual contacts with the stream bottom and perhaps the landscape appearance along the banks and horizon. However, because most movements during the juvenile migration occur during the night, sole dependence upon these visual cues does not seem likely. Another possible visual cue is the sky overhead—celestial bodies visible to the small fish like the sun, stars, planets, and moon. Again, these could not be effective on cloudy days and nights.

The Earth's magnetic field is another possibility, and some good evidence has been obtained about the fish's travels in the open expanses of ocean. Magnetic-compass cues combined with visible celestial bodies seem to be the main mechanisms for navigation in the sea.

But such simple plans at first hide the most important factor of all migrational mechanisms: the imprinting that the juvenile fish receive during their initial journey downstream—the precise recollection of the way back. It almost seems too much to ask of such a small creature, barely an inch or two long.

The most important cue during upriver runs, however, is the distinct, unique *odor* of the water in a given stream. (It's OK to call it an odor, even under water, because fish detect it through their *nares*, a pair of openings in their snout that have sensory capability analogous to our own nose.)

The odor of a stream can have several sources: the chemical nature of the catchment's soil, rock, and vegetation; chemical leachings from other fish, probably the same species and stock; from skin, surface mucous, fluids and excretions; and perhaps leachings from aquatic insects and other organisms. (Remember what we once said about no two streams being exactly alike?)

Much evidence exists for the presence of specific odors in each small tributary, which can lead the adult through a maze of odors from other tributaries, remembered from years ago, to its home ground. But probably in the final few miles or yards, visual cues obtained from streambed configurations assist or take over from the evidence of odors.

The odor of a specific stream must be first apparent at the river mouth, thereby aiding the adult returning from the ocean. At this point on the river, the water is a chemical soup of compounds originating from many tributaries, springs, marshes, and lakes. Yet the adult salmon seeking one specific odor is capable of detecting its home smell and unerringly ascending that river to its own tributary.

Even so, some straying does occur, and a few adults may ascend the "wrong" river—even to spawn successfully. It has been hypothesized that such a "mistake" does not really indicate a failure of the genetic code. Rather, it seems that strayed fish perform useful functions—for example, extending the range of a species, beginning a brand new stock that will henceforth be faithful to its adopted stream, replacing a stock that for some reason has been destroyed in its natal stream, or that has lost suitable habitat. This characteristic of occasional straying may even have been selected in the fish's genetic evolution. But for most adults, although the return migration is fraught with the danger of unremembered cues and wrong turns, the homing is most often successful.

The return trip of the adult salmon has been termed a miracle of migration. It requires a sequence of a thousand choices, directed by the memorizing ability of the tiny brain in a one-inch fish years previously, retained by the huge adult a thousand-fold greater in mass, years later, seeking consummation of its reproductive instincts on its long journey home.

TECHNICAL REFERENCES:

Groot, C., and L. Margolis, editors. 1991. *Pacific Salmon Life Histories.* University of British Columbia Press, Vancouver.
Northcote, Thomas Gordon. 1984. Mechanisms of Fish migration in rivers. Pages 317-355 *in* James D. McCleave, Geoffrey P. Arnold, Julian J. Dodson, and William H. Neill, editors. *Mechanisms of Migration in Fishes.* Plenum Press, New York.

RiverSketch

ALDO LEOPOLD
and the
RIVER OF THE MOTHER OF GOD

A Spanish conquistador, exploring high on the western rim of the Amazonian basin, probably in the late 1500s, reported the discovery of a rushing river that fell in thundering cascades into an unseen, impenetrable forest. No doubt in a seizure of faith and maternal respect, he christened it *el Rio Madre de Dios*. No one has seen it since.

Aldo Leopold wrote of the River of the Mother of God in 1924, in an essay that reflected the early evolution of his wilderness doctrine, a philosophy that continues today in our appreciation of the importance of natural ecosystems. Unpublished, the essay lay yellowing and unread in his desk through the years. Today it is included in a new collection of his essays.

In 1924, Aldo Leopold was 37 years of age. Raised in the Midwest, educated in the East (Yale Forest School), he moved to the desert Southwest to begin his career with the U. S. Forest Service. In the wilds of Arizona and New Mexico, he saw and wrote of government mistreatment of fragile lands. The experience resulted in a maturing of his incubating doctrine of land conservation. Also in 1924, he moved from the southwest desert back to the Midwest, as assistant director of the Service's Forest Products Laboratory in Madison, Wisconsin.

Leopold continued to write further articles and essays based on the Southwest, but his evangelism for the natural land broadened. Now came an awe, but also an anxiety, for wild lands everywhere, for the forests and lakes of the upper Great Lakes region and the Quetico-Superior wilderness, for free-flowing streams and rivers across the nation, for abuse of wildlife and its habitats. He reached for a heightened concept of the human-land relationship. It was the beginning of our current and still evolving perception of the linkage between land and mankind.

His professional *Game Management* (1933) became a standard text in wildlife curriculums across the country. His writing was prolific. Even as a former member of the Forest Service, he preached and belabored the need for incorporation of wildlife habitat conservation within the Service's programs, decrying those timber management operations that caused erosion, habitat destruction, and cutting of special old-growth forests. Outrage showed through routinely. He pleaded and begged for the preservation of the "bits of wilderness" still left, railing against the continual encroachment of roads built into the few intact forest wildernesses—the demon that he repeatedly and derisively called the "Great God Motor." He enshrined the "Unknown Places" of the world and grieved when they fell—including his unseen South American river.

Many years after the Spanish officer's discovery, maps of the South American forests contained a "short heavy line," without beginning or end, as Leopold saw it, labelled the "River of the Mother of God." Just as the officer saw it disappear into the green Amazonian depths, Leopold later noted the absence of the short, heavy line from the maps of South America. He saw its disappearance as a symbol of the loss of wilderness itself, a vanishment of the wild lands that had in the past so profoundly uplifted his own spirit. In the river's loss, as illusory as was the stream, he saw a terrible vision of our own losses to come.

In a lecture given on the campus of the University of Wisconsin in 1935, Leopold introduced the term "land ethic." In this paper, he emphasized the interdependence between humans and land, and the need for a combination of private and government stewardship of land. The principle came to grips with the potential loss of the Unknown Places on Earth's dynamic surface.

In 1939, Leopold became chairman of the Department of Wildlife Management and began teaching, acquiring a new forum for his conservation evangelism. His messages in writing and speaking continued into 1948, the year of his death at the age of 61. At that time, he had been working on a book manuscript, a series of essays on wilderness and the importance of natural lands, with the working title of *Great Possessions.*

Aldo Leopold tending tamarack seedlings
near his family shack in rural Wisconsin, 1947.
(Photo: Fred McCabe, permission of The University of Wisconsin.)

On April 14, 1948, Leopold was notified by the Oxford University Press of their acceptance of his manuscript for book publication. One week later he succumbed to a fatal heart attack while helping a neighbor extinguish an errant grass fire. Oxford Press published the book in the fall of 1949, retitled *A Sand County Almanac and Sketches Here and There*. Influence of the book, republished and reprinted over and over, echoed around the world.

The point of the missing river in South America was not whether *el Rio Madre de Dios* was really a gift from God's mom—or just the product of a careless riographer. Most significantly, the mythic stream that disappeared into the Amazon forest helped inspire Aldo Leopold in the formulation of his land ethic, the concept that is prerequisite to humankind's continued, successful dependence upon the land.

Leopold, in turn, inspired an entire civilization.

SELECTED REFERENCES:

Flader, Susan L., and J. Baird Callicott, editors. 1991. *The River of the Mother of God, and Other Essays by Aldo Leopold*. University of Wisconsin Press, Madison.

Meine, Curt. 1988. *Aldo Leopold: His life and work*. University of Wisconsin Press, Madison.

Chapter 25

INVERTEBRATE DRIFT

N IGHT FALLS ON THE RIVER.
With fading of the western sky, afternoon winds drop to
an eerie silence, and a chill creeps slowly down the valley. By an
hour past sunset, complete darkness envelops the encircling forest and hovering landscape. Except for the rustle of the river and
a distant whip-poor-will's haunting whistle, all is quiet. The
creatures of forest and stream have retired for the night.

Or have they?

On the darkened stream bottom, *biological clocks* tick on to a
critical moment, and a sudden flurry of movement begins.
From under the riffle's stones and the hidden crevices of the
streambed, hundreds, thousands, hundreds of thousands of
small, bottom-living creatures emerge from their daytime hiding places to commence a nightly ritual.

Mayfly and stonefly nymphs appear from their hideaways, a
few caddis larvae crawl from their cases, immature black flies
release their silky holdfasts. Tiny members of the meiofauna—copepods and cladocerans—wriggle up from the bottom sediments. Predators—some stonefly nymphs, carnivorous
caddisfly larvae, dragonfly nymphs—soon follow. Almost the
entire benthic community is in an agitated state of swimming,
darting and ducking, and excited bustle. In the swiftness of the
riffle's current, many are swept away—and soon a literal storm
of invertebrates drifts with the rushing current, to establish new

territories and continue life in new locations farther down-stream.

Most—perhaps all—indulge in feeding, relatively safe from predators in the darkness. Perhaps many individuals actually seek out the current, taking advantage of its swiftness to move to new feeding sites—patches of periphyton and biofilms rich with the carbohydrates and protein synthesized on the previous day's sunlit streambeds. Although most survive this apparent riot and revelry, some succumb to the rushing currents and the abrasion of the inevitable collisions.

At dawn the frenzy is checked. The soft light of a cool day-break filters through overhanging canopies of cedar, willow, or alder. The clocks tick on to another critical moment, and the downstream drifting ceases.

◆   ◆   ◆

SCIENTISTS CONCERNED WITH BIOLOGICAL CLOCKS, or *bio-rhythms*, often use the term *diel*, meaning 24 hours, or *circadian*, meaning approximately 24 hours, to express the behavioral pat-tern of a plant or animal during its day-length pattern of activ-ity. A circadian rhythm is set in genetic code, but a more precise pattern emerges when this approximate pattern is synchronized with changing light and temperature or other environmental triggers that result in a *diel periodicity*. This has been a subject of intense study and experimentation over about the last four dec-ades.

When diel periodicities in drift were first documented, the high numbers involved at night appeared incredible. It seemed impossible that any stream could sustain such huge "losses" and still maintain viable populations upstream. Science was conserva-tive, and many scholars remained unconvinced that such quanti-ties of invertebrate animals really moved downstream. Never-theless, the subject of drift as a research object soon attracted great interest, and similar results soon appeared in virtually all aquatic and ecological journals, worldwide. The diel drift phe-nomenon was quickly documented as a universal happening in almost any stream, anywhere. Throughout the United States and Canada, in all of Europe, Asia, the tropics, in New Zealand and Australia—wherever benthologists explored the mysteries of stream ecology—similar drift periodicities were found.

Even so, the question remained: Why *doesn't* a stream run out of invertebrates? What keeps the population of mayflies, scuds, and others from disappearing downstream and leaving the headwater streambed barren? This question became a para-dox—and some ecologists feel it has not been resolved even yet.

◆   ◆   ◆

NOT ALL SPECIES OF INVERTEBRATES participate equally in this nightly frenzy. A wide variation, in fact, exists in the likeli-hood of any given species drifting in quantities anywhere near those that might deplete upstream populations. Some do not join in a drift periodicity at all.

But most species share in the nocturnal excursion, every night, to some extent. A few exhibit an exceptional propensity to drift. Two of these are old friends—the crustacean *Gamma-rus* and the mayfly *Baetis*—the scud and the nymph of our Bluewinged Olive. When diel periodicities were first reported in the early 1960s—in Japan, Minnesota, and Germany—*Baetis* was featured in all three locations, different species but ecologi-cal counterparts within the same genus. *Gammarus* was also im-portant in two of the three places—Minnesota and Germany. Since those early times of investigation into drift, *Baetis* and *Gammarus* have been reported more often in diel periodicities than any other taxa. Although many taxa exhibit diel peri-odicities, usually their patterns are not as spectacular as are those for *Baetis* and *Gammarus.* Caddisfly larvae make up one group that drifts regularly, but usually not in large quantities; the fact that they live in cases, some of them heavy, probably inhibits much activity. Stonefly nymphs commonly occur in diel drift periodicities, but not in great numbers; nymphs of the small stonefly *Hastaperla* (adult: Yellow Sally) were once observed by the author in great abundance in a stream but totally absent in the drift. As with many other aspects of stream ecology, biodiversity is the rule.

◆   ◆   ◆

WHEN LARGE QUANTITIES OF AQUATIC INSECTS and other invertebrates were first reported in diel drift periodicities, a new and increased scientific interest was expressed for the possible influence these drift events might have on fish feeding. Was this huge increase in invertebrate availability at night beneficial to fish? Did fish, following the abundance of food, also exhibit a diel periodicity in feeding? What might be important to fly-rodders: Will angling success be better at times of greatest drift?

It's true that a drifting organism may be more visible and accessible to predation by fish, and a few reports in the scientific literature reported greater feeding during high drifting. Brown trout especially, which are noted for night feeding, have been reported feeding intensively at times of high drift. By and large, however, most stream fishes are sight feeders and do their feeding in daytime, or at least at dawn and dusk. After all, night drifting is probably a selected behavior that protects the invertebrates from fish predators in the dark.

Considerable drifting occurs during the daytime, but it may not be synchronized with the invertebrates' biological clocks. All invertebrates are somewhat active during the day anyway, and it is to be expected that some of them will lose their hold on a bottom substrate and get caught up by passing currents. There seems to be an ample supply of active invertebrates, especially in high-alkalinity limestone streams, to satisfy fish feeding on drifters during the day—and occasionally to be fooled by your drifting Prince or Pheasant Tail.

Long before diel periodicities were known, New York trout biologist Dr. Paul R. Needham, who did some early drift research (but only during daytime), proposed a novel idea: Perhaps many invertebrates drift down from a riffle, where they have been produced, to a pool downstream where fish feed on them as they drift into the pool. All trout anglers know about this anyway. Needham did not know about the larger quantities in a diel periodicity, but probably a similar system of events happens when large quantities drift into a pool during the night, settle out, and become available to feeding fish during the following day. All of which seems like a very neat system indeed.

◆   ◆   ◆

The basic sampling device used by researchers is the *drift net*, fastened firmly in the streambed to collect invertebrates drifting in the current.

SAMPLING AND COLLECTING DATA are accomplished with *drift nets*. These are made of a fine-meshed fabric fastened to a rectangular or circular frame, the meshed material extending in a bag downstream from the frame. Usually the bottom edge of the frame rests on the stream bottom and is held in place by rods pounded into the streambed or by other means. Most often, a full 24-hour set of samples is collected; the drift net is replaced every hour, after a sample of invertebrates is washed out of the bag and into a sample container each hour. (My graduate students and I missed some sleep doing this, which is probably why drift periodicities were not discovered long ago.) The ma-

terial in the net bag is preserved and later analyzed in the laboratory, where it is counted, weighed, and separated into species or
other taxa.

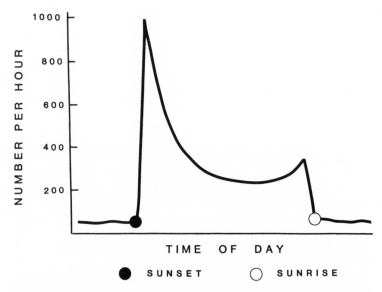

When darkness arrives in the streambed, many invertebrates begin
drifting downstream, ceasing at dawn the next morning.

The resulting set of numbers are plotted as a graph with time
of day along the bottom horizontal axis, and numbers or weight
per hour on the left, or vertical axis. The resulting curves almost
always show a low drift during the daytime, a sharp, high rise at
dark, and a sharp drop at dawn with a return to low drift during
the next day. Often the sharp rise at first dark results in the high
point of the 24-hour day, and sometimes a lower peak occurs
just before dawn. Sometimes the shape of the curve is a mirror
image, with the minor peak at first dark and the maximum just
before daylight.

German scholar Karl Müller, an early researcher of drift,
named the first of these shapes *bigeminus* (having two points)
and the second curve *alternans* (the alternative, or mirror image). For some, the shape of the diel curve is indicative of the
species. The genus *Baetis*, for example, exhibits both bigeminus

and alternans curves (although in different species). *Gammarus* always produces the bigeminus form. Many organisms simply show an undistinguished "hump" at night.

Most stream invertebrates undertake a diel drift pattern that is night-active—that is, with high drift at night. Some species, however, are day-active, with high drift during the day. These are mostly caddisflies, black flies, and midge larvae. Some years ago, I had the rare opportunity of documenting a day-active diel drift by a tiny caddisfly in a small Utah mountain stream. Water temperature, rather than light, controlled the pattern, and the quantities, estimated at several hundreds of thousands per day in the total stream, rose and fell with warm days and cool nights.

Another periodicity was soon discovered: seasonal. Not unexpected, drift is higher in summer, low in winter. In all probability, drift is correlated with biomass levels, growth rates, and rates of production, all of which are higher in the warmer, sunlit waters of spring and summer.

Sometimes the quantity in a drift net, even if collected only for one hour, is large, and a quick peek into the net may reveal a great mass of crawling, struggling animals. These are *macro*invertebrates, plenty large enough to see with the unaided eye.

But the *micro*invertebrates, the meiofauna—those tiny larvae, microcrustaceans, and other invisible organisms hidden in the sediments—drift, too, and exhibit diel periodicities. For a decade or so after diel periodicities were first observed, most researchers concentrated on the more visible macroinvertebrates—scuds, mayflies, caddisflies, stoneflies, and others. Soon it became obvious that cladocerans, copepods, and ostracods were also involved in drift periodicities. Although small enough to slip through the relatively coarse mesh of the usual drift net, a few of them would become entrapped in the meshes and then might be visible during the sorting and counting.

Observations of material collected with much finer nets revealed that tiny organisms, some visible only under a microscope, lived in the soft sediments along stream edges during the day. Then, coming out at night they appeared to swim into the upper water—perhaps only an inch or two deep—and got swept away in even the mildest current. Like that of macroinverte-brates, the drift of microcrustaceans is generally higher in summer and low in winter. Diel periodicities for the meiofauna vary greatly, and their patterns during the 24-hour periods are not as clear as for macroinvertebrates. Some show night-active drift, some day-active, some with no periodicity at all. It would be helpful to increase our study of drift in all meiofauna groups.

◆   ◆   ◆

THE QUESTION POSED EARLIER—what keeps the upstream reaches from becoming depleted?—fascinated scores of ben-thologists. There was no doubt about the large quantities of in-vertebrates drifting—and there was no letup day after day (or night after night). So, again, why did upstream reaches not be-come depleted?

Two major theories surfaced:

• somehow, the drifters (or their progeny) manage to re-turn upstream, recolonizing the upper reaches;

• the rate of production in the upstream reaches remains high enough to supply the downstream drift and still to main-tain normal abundances.

Even before the discovery of diel periodicities and the large quantities involved, Professor Karl Müller proposed an intrigu-ing theory that he termed a *colonization cycle*. In this scheme, the drifting animals, having reached downstream areas and ma-tured, take wing and fly back upstream to lay their eggs. When hatched, the new generations begin to drift downstream, colo-nizing all suitable habitats, completing the cycle. This proposal was immensely attractive. The discovery of diel periodicities sparked a further profusion of research aimed to test the idea of the colonization cycle. The upstream flight of winged aquatic insects was abundantly confirmed for some species—caddisflies in particular—with females carrying eggs. Although *Gammarus*, or scuds, don't fly, some researchers reported scuds *swimming* upstream. Winter stoneflies were observed on snow-covered banks, *walking* upstream.

Some years ago, this author was fortunate to be in the right place and time to observe a truly dramatic upstream flight of the adults of an aquatic insect. In the high mountain stream in Utah mentioned previously, a graduate assistant and I were collecting samples containing small caddisfly larvae, drifting in exceptional abundance, in the *daytime* in step with water temperature. On an evening just beginning to darken, adults began to appear, apparently from the willows lining the stream. Their creamy coloration stood out clearly in the gathering dusk. Assembling over the water, they formed a long line, and then slowly, in the awkward flight common to caddisflies, they flew upstream following the current's course. Their upstream progression was almost at the same speed as that of a person walking, so I picked one out of the crowd and walked along beside it, mentally holding hands, for a ways. It was one of nature's spectacular phenomena that largely go unseen—a migration in miniature. I thrilled to watch it, until darkness closed it down.

Downstream drift and upstream flight—these were two essential, fully proven elements of the colonization cycle. Did these behaviors prove the hypothesis? Again, many researchers sought a further truth—the critical experiment. This was needed to answer the question: Did the downstream drift really deplete the population upstream? That is, was the upstream flight (or swim, or walk) really necessary?

This question has been tested scores of times, in many streams and at scattered points of the world. In virtually all cases, depletion in upstream reaches severe enough to require a return of some kind was not detected. Furthermore, many studies concluded that drift continues to occur, in immense quantities, even without either depletion or upstream migration. So the question remains: what *does* keep upstream populations from being depleted? And that brings us to the second hypothesis.

The paradox of drift/depletion greatly stimulated this second theory. We know that as individuals of a given cohort grow, each individual requires more space. And we know that mortality occurs along with growth. A given stone on the streambed holds many small individuals, but when they grow larger, there must be fewer of them. What happens to the missing? Do they get pushed off the stone because of crowding—and then drift downstream?

Karl Müller, in the same paper in which he proposed his colonization cycle, suggested just that—namely, with the concentration of newly hatched insects in the upstream reaches, crowding occurs as the young larvae grow, and some drift away to colonize other suitable habitats throughout the stream's course.

It thus seems to make sense that with growth of juvenile insects on the streambed, crowding occurs and so, consequently, will drift. With more adult females, more eggs to hatch, and highly suitable conditions (the features we find in productive streams), biomass may also be high—high enough to exceed the available space on stones. Something must give, and that something may be more drift. This explanation—when production rate exceeds the carrying capacity—became known as the "excess production" theory. Much later evidence supported the hypothesis, but it is not universally accepted.

The best conclusion about drift that we can make at this time is that diversity exists in drift processes as well as in much else. We have discussed biodiversity many times in this volume, most commonly with respect to the size, shape, and function of stream organisms. But diversity appears also in systems and processes; animals do not behave the same way in all streams. The only absolute constant is that diversity applies to all streams: no two are exactly alike. Many differences exist in water chemistry, riparian vegetation, supply of allochthonous materials, size and kind of streambed particles, and a host of other factors.

The grip that the drift paradox exercises over many stream ecologists' research efforts exemplifies the lack of attention paid to biodiversity. An investigator can prove, beyond doubt, what happened in a study stream, but the extrapolation of one result should not be made to apply to all streams.

It is worthy—and exciting—to search for unifying concepts, like the river continuum concept (RCC), the constancy of production:biomass (P:B) ratios, or a certain drift theory. But we must be careful not to deliberately avoid diversity when we construct such broad concepts. As we have seen in earlier chapters, diversity does occur within the RCC and P:B ratios. Certainly, the drift behavior of stream invertebrates varies, too.

We must contemplate again the warning of English stream ecologist T. T. Macan, who cautioned us about making a narrow conclusion or classification (like a colonization cycle or an excess production theory!) into a *cage* from which we may not be able to escape and search for further truths.

The very diversity that sometimes frustrates us may be like the variation we find in angling success, the varying levels of whitewater canoe runs, or the diverse scenery that attracts us to streamside in the first place. That diversity continues to draw us to explore these splendid natural resources we know as free-flowing rivers.

TECHNICAL REFERENCES:

Allan, J. David. 1995. *Stream Ecology: Structure and function of running waters.* Chapman & Hall, New York. (*see* Chapter 10, on Drift.)

Waters, Thomas F. 1972. The drift of stream insects. *Annual Review of Entomology,* Volume 17, pages 253-272.

RiverSketch

WILD AND SCENIC

THE EXTRAORDINARY SYSTEM of river protection established by the United States Congress—the National Wild and Scenic Rivers System—is unique in the world. No other nation has enacted the quality of natural resource safeguards or the breadth of its coverage. Well over three hundred rivers or selected reaches and tributaries are now included. The list grows continually, albeit irregularly.

The fundamental element of the act is contained in a single phrase: the preservation of selected rivers in *free-flowing condition*. Selected rivers that possess "outstandingly remarkable scenic, recreational, geologic, fish and wildlife, historic, cultural, or other similar values" shall be protected. In many cases, the courts have ruled against development proposals that threatened the basic protection contained in this language.

President Lyndon Johnson called for a rivers bill in his State of the Union message in 1965; the act was passed by Congress in 1968 and signed by the president. In its initial form, the system included eight "instant wild rivers" (actually twelve named streams, including four tributaries). Three categories of "wildness" were established, depending upon the initial condition of access, impoundment, and development on riparian lands: Wild, Scenic, and Recreational.

In addition to the twelve initially named streams, a category of "study streams" was established, including 27 more named rivers, temporarily protected while Congress and several agencies were directed to review the rivers for possible inclusion later. Most of the study streams met with ignominious rejection; a few graduated into full inclusion in the Wild and Scenic system. Over the years, a host of other streams were placed into the study category, but only a few of these made it into the big league.

Two methods for later inclusion were spelled out:
* passage by act of Congress;
* administrative designation by the Secretary of the Interior.
Both methods have been employed, largely depending on the politics of the time. Several agencies were named to administer the rivers: the National Park Service, United States Fish and Wildlife Service, the Bureau of Land Management, and the United States Forest Service, either singly or in combination for a particular river. In a few cases, the state natural resources agency participates.

Border between the states of Wisconsin and Minnesota,
the St. Croix River was included in the eight "instant wild rivers."

Growth of the national system has not been accomplished without struggle. Dam building has been the major opponent. Beginning with high dams on major rivers in the 1930s, construction reached boom levels in the post-Second World War years, characterized as the big-dam-building era. Current totals have reached about 75,000 large dams on United States rivers. As a result, the struggles for most additions to the wild and scenic system were fought to prevent an impending dam construction. Powerful federal agencies—the U. S. Army Corps of Engineers and the U. S. Bureau of Reclamation—were always formidable adversaries. Nevertheless, some equally forceful members of Congress, state governors, presidents, and citizens have championed the cause of river protection. Citizen organizations such as the Sierra Club and the Izaak Walton League often initiated and carried through the battles for specific, outstanding rivers threatened by dams or other development. The principal national citizens group for river protection, American Rivers, played critical roles in obtaining designation for most of the rivers now in the national system. Literally hundreds of smaller citizen groups, as a whole, added to the success of crucial struggles. President Jimmy Carter, by far, tops the list of American presidents as the most significant river protector.

Some single additions to the national system have increased the system materially. For example, 25 river systems (a total of 61 named streams, including tributaries) were included in the large Alaska Lands Act. This single act passed after a tough contest in Congress and was signed into law by President Carter in his last remaining months. In 1980, a major group of California rivers, requested by Governor Jerry Brown and administratively designated by Interior Secretary Cecil Andrus, was added, literally in the closing hours of President Carter's term, in early 1981. With other important designations, the total additions under President Carter increased the national system by 5,000 river miles, or 300 percent. With great force and dedication, the Oregon congressional delegation in 1988 pushed a bill past attempted blocking by a conservative administration, adding forty-four Oregon rivers (plus nine tributaries) to the Wild and Scenic System.

The total in 1992 reached 325 named rivers and tributaries in 37 states. About a dozen more river systems were added in the following years under President Clinton, up through 1999, for a total of about 350. Late additions (at time of this writing) include the Lumber River, a blackwater stream in North Carolina, and three rivers in Massachusetts. And yet, despite the objectors' shrill cries for "balance" amid charges that the river environmentalists wanted *everything*, the Wild and Scenic System includes—among all United States rivers over five miles in length—less than one percent.

Streams in the National Wild and Scenic Rivers System vary greatly by geographic location. Leading the list is Oregon with 58 rivers and tributaries. California boasts 38 rivers, including the longest combination of connecting mainstem and branches, the Eel River system, at 346 miles. Alaska, with 33 streams, benefited with almost all of these from the Alaska Lands Act of 1980. Michigan, with its many beloved trout streams, claims 26, including the shortest river in the system, the Yellow Dog in the Upper Peninsula, at four miles.

The majority of rivers in the system are in the Pacific Northwest. Particularly lacking are many eligible streams and rivers in the eastern half of the country, especially in the south Atlantic and Coastal Plain regions. The Lumber River is the only one in the southeastern Coastal Plain. Emphasis so far has been placed on salmonid streams, mountain streams, and streams already in public ownership, such as in national forests.

Nevertheless, many more streams and rivers throughout the United States are recognized as having exceptional attributes, possible candidates for the national system. The American Rivers' Outstanding Rivers List includes some 15,000 streams and rivers, a compilation of lists assembled from federal, state, and private citizen sources.

Although not in the National Wild and Scenic System, a host of streams and rivers across the United States has received protection of some other kind. Hundreds are included in the National Wilderness System, National Parks, Refuges, and Recreational Areas. A few, specially designated "national rivers," such as some in the Ozark Mountains and a half-dozen others, were set into a national category prior to establishment of the Wild and Scenic System, or through other channels. Making up another group are those included in state wild and scenic systems in over 30 states that have established river programs.

Among all national resource protection systems, objectives of the National Wild and Scenic River system is the most eclectic. River inclusion is not selective for trout streams, canoeing rivers, warmwater or cold rivers, north or south. The criteria are few but they are precise. The principal criterion is quality. The attributes to which quality standards are applied are clearly specified. The included rivers are all open to public enjoyment—virtually no recreational activity is precluded except when contrary to the system's objectives. Fishing, hunting, hiking, floating, painting, birding, photography, and camping—all are available and in many cases provided for with access and assistance.

The three categories of wildness provided in the national act make sure that all levels of user density and difficulty of use can be found, including the degree of solitude and quiet for which a person is willing to walk or paddle, or train for necessary skill development. No other public recreation system is so equitable to all as is the National Wild and Scenic Rivers System.

SELECTED REFERENCES:

Huntington, Matthew H., and John D. Echeverria. 1991. *The American Rivers Outstanding Rivers List.* Second Edition. American Rivers, Inc. Washington DC.
Palmer, Tim. 1993. *The Wild and Scenic Rivers of America.* Island Press, Washington DC.

AROUND THE BEND

WHAT LIES AHEAD for our streams and rivers? What's in their future? We hear much from all sides about the disasters that impinge upon our rivers.

Here, there is one more local creek transformed into a ditch to make way for a sprawling housing development. There, a world-famous trout stream is certain to be destroyed by a proposed gold mine. An ongoing battle continues against pollution of the Mississippi River, which has created an 8,000-square-mile Dead Zone in the Gulf of Mexico, no longer supporting healthy aquatic life.

So, does only disaster lie in the future, around the next bend?

I don't think so, but in a very real sense, we are already around the bend. In the early 1900s, acts of natural resource desecration were commonplace, unreported, and not even recognized. Today the same acts are more widespread, permitted and abetted by larger government agencies, and inflicted upon more people. So, am I going to toll the death knell for our environment, for streams and rivers? Am I discouraged, burned out, mad and angry and about to give up? At times, temporarily. *Pessimistic?* Not on your life.

Am I *optimistic?* Better believe it.

It would be easy to feel discouraged, and to list all the perpetrators and their transgressions. But what do we do with them? Turn the other cheek? No. Try to talk them out of it? Forget it. Pass some new laws and send them all to prison? A pleasant thought, but it wouldn't happen. Not now, anyway.

So what will work? A tough question, and answers that will be both effective and feasible are hard to come by.

Who stands in the way? Let's first make a list. Know thine enemy.

• Agriculture: sediment, fertilizer, and pesticides from cultivated fields; runoff of animal waste from feedlots; excessive withdrawal of groundwater for irrigation; unrestricted grazing of livestock in riparian zones and on stream banks, particularly in the West.

• Forest management: clear-cut logging that strips the land and promotes erosion and sediment deposition in streams; excessive construction of logging roads; off-road vehicles of all kinds that break up forest soils and leave deep scars on the land.

• Mining: creation of massive sediment piles; leaching of toxic metals from tailings; groundwater contamination from ore processing operations; broad-scale destruction of landscape features.

• Urban development (read: *sprawl*): sediment from construction; threat of leaching and runoff from overfertilized and over herbicided lawns; soil and salt pollution from streets; air and water pollution from industrial operations; loss of unique natural features.

• Fossil fuels: Aldo Leopold warned us long ago about the Great God Motor—gasoline-burning vehicles—that stimulated so much irresponsible road-building into the wild places of the nation. If the destructive effect of burning fossil fuels had been known in Leopold's day, he would have railed against that, too. Now huge conglomerates of oil and coal corporations mail out millions of pieces of propaganda urging American citizens to disbelieve the harmful effects from fossil fuel emission of greenhouse gases, agents responsible for global warming. They claim climate change is a hoax and distribute their "petitions" to individual American citizens, urging us to persuade our government to refrain from joining the rest of the world in the control of destructive emissions. All the while the polar ice caps continue their pervasive melting, and unprecedented severe weather patterns bombard the Earth with meteorological regularity.

Global warming is the most subtle and yet the most profound of all environmental omens. Global climate change (the direct result of warming) is already with us, affecting all aspects of our life and living conditions. But subtly, so that we may not recognize or even believe it. For streams and rivers, global climate change will mean more frequent floods and droughts, as well as warmer stream waters almost everywhere.

However, it is one of the greatest ironies that within each of the above threats *technological solutions have already been developed.* In both laboratory and field, scientists and engineers have found solutions—even those working within the very agencies and companies that are responsible for damage in the first place.

Many technical and operational answers are known and have been for a long time. So, the problem is *implementation.* And whether the threat of further damage is abolished depends, first, upon public perception and then, following, *political action.*

With the environmental revolution of the 1970s, public perception of natural resources improved dramatically. But politics changed in the 1980s, resulting in the most environmentally abusive decade in modern times.

There remains no fundamental reason why all the above listed threats to rivers cannot be eliminated or greatly reduced with vigorous implementation of already developed technology.

Let's take a look.

Agriculture—the greatest threat to good natural resource management, as well as the strongest opposition. Crop cultivation operations provide the most serious problems, namely, land surface disturbance in ways that permit downslope erosion. But losses of sediment and added amendments can be controlled, agricultural scientists have found out, through the use of techniques developed under the overall term of "conservation tillage." Feedlot operations could receive manure treatment much like municipal sewage, with bacterial decomposition onsite, instead of disposal into nearby streams; there is no excuse for "accidental" breaching of holding ponds. Fencing of streams, such as small salmon-spawning tributaries and their immediate riparian zones, especially in the West, has been shown to provide complete protection of riparian zones against livestock trampling. It's easy to provide drinking water to livestock through special fencing techniques. Irrigation water can be obtained through means other than mining unconfined aquifers—those that most commonly serve as sources of cool water for trout streams. Limitations on the quantities withdrawn must be based on sound scientific analysis.

Clear-cut logging is pure overkill. To obtain high-quality timber for lumber and other wood products, it is not necessary to strip the mountain hillsides to the bare earth. More profitable, of course, but not essential. Scientists in the U.S. Forest Service (within the Department of Agriculture) have developed techniques to remove selected logs without construction of logging roads and skid trails—by overhead cable and helicopter—reducing logging roads and thus sediment erosion *to near zero*. More costly, they say. But not if the environmental costs of current clear-cutting operations are figured into the budget.

Solutions to the destruction of wild lands by four-wheeling trucks and off-road vehicles should be easy to figure out. Stiff regulations, *confining all such vehicles to designated trails* and total bans in sensitive areas such as parks, wildlife lands, refuges, scientific and natural areas, and designated protected rivers and their catchments, are essential. It will take some strong action by legislators, congresspersons, enforcement officers—and judges.

The solution to global warming and climate change is technically short and simple, but politically difficult. Eventually, we *must find sources of energy other than oil and coal.* We must learn to be skeptical toward television ads about how the big oil companies are doing us a favor by searching for more oil.

Effects of mining can be eliminated by pre-planning for leaving the landscape in its original condition and properly treating toxic tailings and overburden onsite—*read*: zero-tolerance for any removal of wastes off the site of its generation.

The polluting effects of sediment and strong toxics can be reduced or eliminated by a host of techniques under the heading of BMPs (Best Management Practices), which are coming into increasing use in *some* residential development, forestry practices, and highway constructions. Unfortunately, the continued use of more and more land, especially in uses that eliminate valuable forests, prairies, and streams and rivers—urban, suburban, *and* rural sprawl—remains as a large unsolved problem. However, the latest studies have indicated that, when business and industry are deliberately attracted into a community, the financial result is not a net increase in municipal income from business and industrial taxes. Instead, a net *loss* is incurred, resulting from added infrastructure—utilities, fire and police, schools, street maintenance, water and sewage treatment, etc.—necessary to serve additional residents attracted by the businesses and industries!

With technologic solutions at hand, why so little implementation, why so slow?

There are many specific answers: corporate profit-above-responsibility, ultra-right radio and television personalities, mendacious government agency heads, fallacious propaganda by purveyors of fossil fuels, citizen apathy, and more.

Basic to all is a large proportion of American citizens that are still ignorant of the facts, overly impressed by politicians' good looks, charming smiles, and promises of tax cuts.

So why am I optimistic?

It is simply this: The proportion of American citizens belonging to the ranks of informed advocates—although still small—*is on the increase.* An outstanding example: The latest estimate of citizen conservation organizations and agencies concerned with river protection, for the nation as whole, is over *three thousand.* These range from the national American Rivers and the federal Environmental Protection Agency to a small association of a few dozen neighbors, joining together to protect a local creek. And most states now have a *major* river protection/advocacy group, plus many smaller associations.

Increasingly, court actions are brought by citizen groups to forestall or eliminate development threats to streams, frequently carried out by volunteer lawyers or financed by citizen dollars—*and won.* Lawsuits brought by large advocacy groups such as the Sierra Club, Trout Unlimited, Izaak Walton League, and the Audubon Society are on the increase, and smaller groups are assisting with vocal support and volunteer efforts.

What can a citizen do for rivers? Here's some suggestions:

Join a citizen environmental group; organize a new one. Support your selected organization, specifically a river group, financially (yes, with dollars). Join and support a nationally strong advocacy group, like the League of Conservation Voters (LCV); their success rate in defeating anti-conservation politicians in their "Dirty Dozen" campaigns and electing environment-friendly candidates has been phenomenal.

And finally, VOTE—vote to *turn the rascals out* and elect informed, responsible persons who have come to value our natural environment above the profiteers.

I look forward to the day when an environmental bloc of voters will be large enough in America to be a force to be reckoned with—to be feared by the anti-conservation politicians—even to be a major voting group influencing the composition of the U.S. Congress, the credo of the President and Governors, and the ideological makeup of the Supreme Court.

When that happens we can bring about the reforms needed to restore and maintain healthy streams and rivers in the United States. As well, perhaps, elsewhere in the world.

I believe the American dream is changing. Gradually evolving from the rags-to-riches-Horatio-Alger model, aspirations of informed citizens are turning toward a higher quality of life—most importantly with a sustaining, symbiotic relationship with our natural world—where we will be integrated into Earth's ecosystems, not as exploiters and destroyers but as participants. We are changing, albeit slowly, from a worship of profit and the Great God Motor to reverence for the natural systems we have entered with such arrogance in the past.

I hear a river singing. Across the country, I hear a murmur rising toward floodtide in a song of river advocacy, like the rising of a rapid's roar after a downpour. When we reach its crescendo, we will have arrived at a higher plateau of culture, a new level of responsibility for the nurture of Earth.

And a new vision of our clear waters running free.

GLOSSARY OF TECHNICAL TERMS

Note: definitions given here apply to their use with streams and rivers in this book. Many words have a broader meaning elsewhere.

A

acid neutralizing capacity: ANC; the property of water that reacts with an acid; recently replacing *alkalinity*.

adfluvial: descriptive of migration pattern of fish species that spawn in a freshwater stream then migrate to a freshwater lake for growth.

alkalinity: property of water containing alkaline substances, mainly bicarbonate in natural water, expressed as parts per million (ppm); *see* acid neutralizing capacity.

Allen paradox: the observation that the quantity of benthic invertebrates in a stream is not sufficient to provide food for the observed fish population; named for K. Radway Allen, New Zealand fisheries biologist.

allochthonous: describing organic matter that is produced on land and then is moved to the stream; *compare* autochthonous.

allochthony: study of production, transport, and use of allochthonous matter in a stream.

allopatric: not existing in the same stream; *compare* sympatric.

alternans: daily pattern of stream invertebrate drift with a minor peak early in the night and a major one just before dawn; mirror image of *bigeminus*.

anadromous: descriptive of fish that spawn in a stream and migrate to the ocean for major growth; *compare* adfluvial.

anadromy: form of fish life history with spawning in a stream and major growth in the ocean.

ancestral: relating to ancestors; ancient streams that led to modern rivers.

ANC: acid neutralizing capacity; *see* alkalinity.

annual production: the total elaboration of fish or invertebrate tissue in a defined area of stream in one year; expressed in units of pounds per acre per year.

anthropogenic: caused through human activity; usually applied to sediment or other pollutant.

aquifer: layer of groundwater beneath the land surface.

artesian: spring or well arising from pressure in deep aquifer.

autochthonous: term applied to organic matter produced by aquatic plants within the stream; *compare* allochthonous.

autochthony: study of organic matter production within a stream; *compare* photosynthesis, primary production.

autotroph: green plant, "self-feeding;" *compare* heterotroph.

autotrophy: study of production by green plants; *compare* heterotrophy.

B

barbel: fleshy, sensory protuberance near the mouth of some fishes, such as catfish and bullheads, used to detect food on the streambed.

bark mark: brand stamped on the side of a log to identify ownership among different owners of logs in a river log drive; *compare* end mark.

base flow: flow of a stream when it is composed entirely of groundwater from springs.

baseline discharge: base flow.

benthic: referring to the bottom of streams, lakes, and oceans; *see* benthos.

benthologist: scientist who studies the benthos.

benthos: assemblage of organisms inhabiting the bottoms of streams, lakes, and oceans.

bigeminus: daily pattern of stream invertebrate drift with two peaks, a major one at full darkness and a lesser one before dawn; *compare* alternans.

biodiversity: property of a community of organisms varying in number of species, in their relative abundance, and life histories.

bioenergetics: study of energy flow through the biological community.

biofilm: accumulation of biological matter on the surface of stones and wood, consisting mainly of algae, bacteria, and fungi; *see* periphyton, epilithon.

biomass: total weight of organisms occurring at a point in time, expressed in units of pounds per acre; *see* standing stock.

biome: major subdivision of Earth's surface based upon type of vegetation, such as desert, rainforest, tundra, etc.

biospeleology: study of biological communities in caves.

biota: assemblages of living organisms.

bivoltine: having two generations, or cohorts, per year.

borer: a functional group of organisms that feed by boring into wood.

brood: group of young that are hatched or born at a single time, the issue from a female parent.

buffering capacity: ability of water to resist change in its chemical property when receiving a toxicant.

C

calorie: amount of heat energy required to raise one cubic centimeter of pure water one degree Celsius.

capture net: fine-meshed net made of silk by some caddisfly species to filter fine particles of organic matter from water currents for food.

carapace: hard covering of the head and thorax of some aquatic insects and crustaceans.

carnivore: animal whose food is the flesh of other animals.

carnivorous: descriptive term for carnivores.

carotene: orange-colored hydrocarbon produced by plants and transformed to vitamin A in animal liver.

carrying capacity: maximum level to which the biomass of an animal population can reach in accordance with the quality of its environment.

catadromous: descriptive of fish species that spawn in the ocean and migrate to fresh water for growth; the eel is the best known species; *compare* anadromous.

catadromy: the type of life history exhibited by catadromous species; *compare* anadromy.

catchment: total area drained by a stream or river; older usage: watershed.

catch net: net made by some species of caddisfly larvae to filter food particles from water currents; *see* capture net.

cave: opening in land surface leading to interior.

cavern: space in interior of Earth surface.

caudal filament: tail fiber of insects and other invertebrates.

caudal fin: tail fin of fish.

char: fish of the genus *Salvelinus*; primarily Canadian usage as charr.

chert: fine-grained form of quartz, pieces making up stream channel bars in Ozark Mountain streams.

chimney: build-up of soil around surface opening of crayfish burrow.

circadian: approximately 24 hours, descriptive of some rhythmic animal behaviors.

coarse particulate organic matter: CPOM; particles of organic matter ranging from about 1/32 inch (one millimeter) up to a fallen tree; *compare* FPOM.

coaster: brook trout exhibiting an adfluvial life history, mainly in Lake Superior.

cohort: group of animals hatched or born at the same time; a generation.

cohort production interval: CPI; period of time that a cohort is alive and growing; not in egg, pupa, or other quiescent stage.

coldwater: descriptive of salmonid fishes; implies they need cold water.

collector: functional group of invertebrates that either filters or gathers fine particulate organic matter.

conditioning (of organic matter): transforming fresh organic matter into form more palatable to invertebrate consumers; accomplished primarily by bacteria and fungi.

conduit spring: freshwater spring where water has flowed through large subsurface openings; *compare* diffuse spring.

confined aquifer: subsurface layer of water under pressure from impermeable rock strata above and below the aquifer; *compare* unconfined aquifer.

conservation tillage: suite of agricultural practices aimed at reducing erosion and retaining precipitation on land.

continuum: predictable downstream changes in river conditions.

coolwater: descriptive of some fish species that prefer cool summer water temperatures; example: smallmouth bass.

corona: pair of round openings at the anterior of rotifers, through which the animal feeds.

cosmopolitan: found throughout the world.

CPI: *see* cohort production interval.

CPOM: *see* coarse particulate organic matter.

crenon: area of headwater springs.

cyanobacteria: blue-green algae; believed to be the first oxygen-producing organisms with fossils estimated at 2.3 billion years old.

cyclomorphosis: life history feature involving a regular, annual change in animal form; characteristic of some cladocerans.

D

desert: arid region of little or no water; may be hot or cold.

detritivore: animal that feeds primarily on detritus, or nonliving organic matter.

decapitated: river that does not conform to the original RCC in that it does not begin in a wooded area.

decomposers: organisms that accomplish the decomposition of organic matter, such as bacteria and fungi.

denitrification: process of transforming nitrate in stream water back into atmospheric nitrogen.

denitrifying bacteria: organisms responsible for denitrification.

detritus pool: total accumulation of nonliving organic matter in streams.

dextral: rightward spiral of the shell of some species of snails; *compare* sinistral.

diapause: temporary cessation of metabolism in some insects, usually to survive severe environmental conditions.

diatom: group of algae with cells containing large quantities of silicon; important component of periphyton.

dichotomous: stream tributary pattern, branching by twos.

diel periodicity: 24-hour pattern of behavior in plants and animals; involved with many species of stream invertebrates subject to drift.

diffuse spring: freshwater spring fed by groundwater that arrives at the spring through many small interstices in rock and soil.

dioecious: possessing male and female flowers on separate, unisexual plants; *compare* monoecious.

discharge: flow of water in a stream, measured in units of cubic feet per second (cfs).

discharge area: that part of a catchment where groundwater exits the surface as springs; *compare* recharge area.

discontinuity: obstacle to the stream continuum; *see* reset.

dissolved organic matter: DOM; organic matter in dimension smaller than 0.45 micron (about 1/50,000 inch).

DOM: dissolved organic matter.

drainage basin: watershed, catchment.

duckweed: floating plants with tiny leaves and roots; genus *Lemna*.

dynamics: processes and functions expressed as rates.

E

ecological niche: functional position of an organism in a community.

ecology: scientific discipline treating the relationships among living organisms and their environment.

ecosystem: spatial area inhabited by organisms living together in an orderly manner, interdependent among their cohabitants and with their environment.

ecosystem management: practice of applying operations that affect fisheries to the entire catchment.

ecotone: transition zone between different biological communities; example is riparian zone.

effluent stream: stream flowing below the water table and receiving water from the groundwater; *compare* influent stream.

elver: juvenile life history stage of eels when they approach the North American continent, resembling adults; *compare* glass eel.

emergence: metamorphosis of immature insects into flying adults; the hatch!

end mark: brand hammered into the end of a log in a river drive to establish ownership; *compare* bark mark.

energy: calories needed by a biological system to function or do work.

engulfer: functional group of predators who take in the whole prey animal in their feeding; compare *piercer.*

epigean: above ground habitats; open streams, forests; compare *hypogean.*

epilithon: surface film on stones, consisting of algae, bacteria, fungi, and other organisms and organic matter.

eurythermic: preferring a wide range of temperature; characteristic of warmwater fish species.

eutrophic: overly rich and productive; descriptive of a water body that is overfertilized, as with organic pollution.

eutrophication: the state of being eutrophic; generally a pejorative term.

evapotranspiration: water loss from a plant or tree; combination of evaporation and transpiration.

exoskeleton: hard exterior covering of insects and crustaceans, giving support to the body.

F

fauna: assemblage of animals.

feeding guild: group of animals using a common type of food.

ferric oxide: insoluble compound of iron and oxygen, found where ferrous compounds in groundwater reach an oxygen-containing atmosphere.

ferrous: descriptive of iron compounds in dissolved form.

filterer: functional group that filters fine particles of organic matter from stream currents; many caddisfly and black fly larvae; a subdivision of *collectors*.

fine particulate organic matter: FPOM; nonliving organic matter ranging from 1/50,000 inch (0.45 micron) to 1/32 inch (one millimeter); *compare* CPOM.

floodplain: relatively flat riparian area consisting of soil particles deposited by river water in flood.

food chain: progression of feeding from prey to predators; *compare* food web.

food web: feeding pattern of predators and prey in a complex web of different forms.

FPOM: fine particulate organic matter.

freestone stream: softwater stream usually with igneous rock and cobble substrate.

fry: early life history stage of fish after complete absorption of the yolk sac.

function: role of an organism in an ecosystem.

functional group: a group of organisms having the same function.

furcula: spring-like organ possessed by springtails (Collembola) that enables them to hop about on land surface or snow.

G

gallery forest: woodlands along the sides of a stream, often referring to forest downstream from headwaters.

gatherer: functional group that forages for food particles on the streambed; a subdivision of *collectors*.

glass eel: juvenile eel that is transparent migrating from the area of its hatch in the ocean toward continental streams.

glochidia: bivalved larvae of a certain family of clams, parasitic on fish.

gouger: functional group that feeds on woody debris by gouging the conditioned wood surface.

gradient: drop in elevation of stream surface per unit of stream length.

grazer: functional group that forages on periphyton, especially algae.

groundwater: water existing below the land surface.

groundwater outcrop: where groundwater exits the land surface as a spring.

H

hardness: property of water rich in calcium and magnesium and that is difficult to make suds with soap.

hemimetabolous: life history trait where change in form from immature insect to adult is incomplete, or "half-changed"; *compare* holometabolous.

hemoglobin: red colored matter in blood, conveying oxygen.

herbivore: animal feeding on plants.

herbivorous: descriptive of feeding behavior on plants.

hermaphroditic: descriptive of animal having both male and female reproductive organs.

heterotroph: organism that depends on tissue produced by other organisms; animals, fungi, bacteria.

heterotrophy: process of feeding on food produced by other organisms.

holistic: treating a subject in its entirety.

holometabolous: life history trait of immature insects that change to adults with complete transformation of form; *compare* hemimetabolous.

home range: area used by an animal for all its needs, such as feeding, reproduction, refuge from predators.

hydrologic cycle: cycle of major events involving water of precipitation, runoff to the ocean, evaporation, and again to precipitation over land.

hydrologic sequence: similar to hydrologic cycle except it emphasizes a more detailed sequence of many minor events.

hydrology: science of natural water, its form, transport, and transformations on land and in the atmosphere.

hypogean: below ground habitats, such as caves, hyporheic zone; *compare* epigean.

hyporheic: habitat of gravel and other sediments below the streambed with water flowing through.

hyporheos: assemblage of animals in the hyporheic zone.

hypoxic: condition of extraordinarily low oxygen.

I

influent stream: stream flowing above the water table and losing water into it.

instantaneous growth method: method of estimating secondary production, usually for fish.

instar: life cycle stage between two molts.

interstices: tiny spaces within streambed sediments.

interflow: subsurface flow of groundwater between catchments.

iteroparous: descriptive of an animal that reproduces more than once annually, or having more than one brood in its lifetime.

J

jassid: common name for members of Jassidae, an older family name of terrestrial leaf hoppers, now Cicadellidae.

K

karst topography: landscape resulting from erosion of limestone bedrock, such as caves, springs, sink holes, and underground rivers.

katharobic: descriptive of a group of protozoans found in springs and small streams with oxygen-rich water.

keel (golden shiner): hard, fibrous ridge of tissue on the ventral surface of the male golden shiner.

keel (razorback sucker): large hump on the dorsal surface of the razorback sucker, enabling the fish to better maneuver in large, turbulent rivers.

kilocalorie: 1,000 calories; "calories" on food packaging and in diet books are actually kilocalories.

kingdom: major category of all life on Earth; examples are *plants* and *animals*.

L

labium: hinged, prehensile organ of a dragonfly nymph, which the nymph can extend rapidly to snatch swimming prey.

lacustrine: referring to lakes.

landscape ecology: new branch of ecology that entails the broader aspects of a landscape, rather than parts such as forests, rivers, lakes, etc.

leachate: solution of dissolved organic matter from material such as leaves, wood, and other nonliving matter.

leaf pack: accumulation of leaves on streambed structures.

lentic: pertaining to still water, lakes and ponds; *compare* lotic.

life cycle: sequence of life stages in an animal's existence.

life history: series of ecological events during major stages of life cycle.

limestone stream: hardwater stream with streambed particles of sedimentary origin; productive of invertebrates and fish; *compare* freestone stream.

limnocrene: spring pool.

lithologic: referring to sedimentary rock.

logmark: brand stamped on a log in a river drive identifying owner; *see* bark mark, end mark.

longitudinal profile: graphical representation of stream decrease in elevation.

lotic: pertaining to streams and rivers; flowing water; *compare* lentic.

M

macroinvertebrate: stream invertebrate large enough to be seen easily.

macrophyte: large plant usually rooted in the streambed.

mandible: lower jaw; *compare* maxilla.

marine: pertaining to the ocean.

marsupium: protected space formed by the appendages of some crustaceans to hold newly hatched young.

maxilla: upper jaw; *compare* mandible.

meiofauna: small animals of the streambed, ranging from 1.5 to 40 thousandths of an inch.

mesotrophic: middle range of productivity; between oligotrophic and eutrophic.

metamorphosis: change is size or form at molting of an insect or crustacean.

microcrustaceans: small crustaceans, consisting of ostracods, copepods, and cladocerans.

microfauna: assemblage of very small animals.

microinvertebrate: very small invertebrate too tiny to see without magnification.

micron: one-millionth of a meter, about 1/25,000 of an inch

mineralization: breakdown of a chemical compound into lesser compounds or elements.

monoecious: term applied to a plant having both male and female reproductive organs; *see* hermaphroditic.

multivoltine: having several generations per year.

MYBP: million years before present.

N

naiad: older use for the immature stage in certain insect orders; now: nymph.

nare: nose opening in fish.

natural history: science of distribution, behavior, and taxonomy of organisms; *see* ecology.

nauplius: juvenile form of copepods.

nekton: group of aquatic organisms capable of swimming; *compare* plankton.

neuston: group of aquatic animals occurring in the surface film of water; *see* nekton, plankton.

nitrification: process of transforming ammonium nitrogen into nitrate.

nitrogen-fixation: process of transforming atmospheric nitrogen into ammonium.

nutrient spiraling: pattern of nutrient movement downstream, into and out of various forms.

nymph: immature stage of hemimetabolous insects.

O

oligotrophic: referring to low level of productivity.

omnivore: animal with feeding habit including all forms of food.

omnivorous: descriptive of varied feeding by an omnivore.

oviposition: act of laying eggs, usually referring to insects.

ovoviviparous: term applied to animals wherein the females produce eggs, retain them until hatching, and then release the living young; *compare* viviparous.

P

parr: juvenile stage of salmonid fish between fry and adult, usually reached at the end of the first year of life.

parr marks: prints on the side of the parr stage of fish resembling thumb prints.

parthenogenesis: giving birth or developing eggs by females without fertilization by male.

P:B: production/biomass ratio.

periphyton: film of algae and other organisms on stones and other substrates on the streambed, the principal food of many benthic insects and other invertebrates.

photosynthesis: process of transforming water and carbon dioxide, with the energy of sunlight, into new organic matter; base of all plant and animal life.

phytoplankton: assemblage of free-floating algal cells common to lentic waters.

piercer: functional group whose members are equipped with a piercing organ used to penetrate the tissues of other organisms for feeding; some are herbivorous, some predaceous.

plankton: free-floating small organisms, plants and animals, in lakes.

plastron: envelope of air that some air-breathing insects use for respiration under water.

polytypic species: species of animals with many genetic types or stocks, known for many salmonids.

potamodromous: referring to fish species that migrate solely between portions of streams.

potamodromy: life history feature of migrating for spawning only in rivers.

potamon: lower section of rivers where currents are slow, water temperatures high, and the fish fauna of warmwater species; *compare* rhithron.

precopula: reproductive stage in *Gammarus* in which the male grasps the female from behind and carries her about, prior to copulation.

predator: animal feeding on other animals.

primary producer: green plant.

primary production: process of elaborating plant tissue; *see* photosynthesis.

processing (of organic matter): conditioning nonliving organic matter by bacteria and fungi, making it more palatable for invertebrates.

production: elaboration of organic tissue.

production:biomass ratio: P:B; the relationship between production rate and biomass; turnover ratio.

pupa: life history stage of holometabolous insects during which larvae are transformed into adults.

R

radula: chitinous organ with which mollusks rasp the surfaces of stones, grazing on algae.

RCC: River Continuum Concept.

recharge area: part of a catchment where precipitation filters into the ground; *compare* discharge area.

redd: spawning nest of trout and salmon.

refractory: resistant to decomposition.

reset: return to downstream succession below a dam.

retreat: chamber constructed of small stones and sand by members of the caddisfly family Hydropsychidae, in which the larva lives and gleans food particles from its capture net.

rheogenesis: origin of a stream or river.

rhithron: upper portion of a stream where currents are swift, water temperatures are low, streambeds are composed of stones and gravel, and the fish fauna often includes salmonids; *compare* potamon.

riparian zone: corridor of land along either side of a stream, wetter and richer in species; *see* ecotone.

River Continuum Concept: RCC; theory that describes the physical and biological succession in a stream through its course.

rostrum: nose of a fish.

runoff: water from precipitation as it flows over land toward a stream.

S

salter: anadromous brook trout that spawns in freshwater streams and migrates to the ocean for growth.

scraper: functional group equipped with an organ to scrape surfaces for periphyton or biofilm; *see* grazer.

secondary producer: animal feeding on primary producer (plant), commonly applied to any animal; *see* heterotroph.

secondary production: process of elaborating animal tissue.

sediment: inorganic particles deposited on the streambed, ranging in size from clay to boulders.

semelparous: reproducing only once during a life cycle.

semivoltine: one generation living for two or three years.

seston: small particles of drifting organic matter.

shredder: functional group of invertebrates that chew up pieces of CPOM.

sinistral: leftward spiraling of the shell of some species of snails; compare dextral.

size-frequency method: method of estimating secondary production, usually for invertebrates.

smolt: life cycle stage of migratory fish, particularly salmonids, when they approach leaving their natal stream for the ocean.

smoltification: process of metabolic and physical changes into a smolt.

snag habitat: twigs, branches, and trunks of trees and bushes that fall into a stream, providing habitat for insects that cling to the structures.

speleology: the science of caves.

spiraling: term describing the movement of chemical elements downstream, changing from elements to compounds to organic matter, and around again.

splake: hybrid between lake trout and brook (speckled) trout.

standing stock: see biomass.

stenothermic: term applied to fish and other animals that prefer a narrow range of temperatures, often salmonids; compare eurythermic.

stock: distinct genetic identity within a single species.

stock concept: theory of the presence of distinct stocks within a species.

stream order: Horton system of classifying stream reaches by order, involving progression of tributaries downstream.

structure: objects on the streambed that support periphyton and biofilms, cover, and attachment sites for invertebrates, such as stones, woody debris, and macrophytes.

stygiobiont: cave dweller.

subimago: life cycle stage of mayflies, a flying, immature form preceding the flying adult.

succession: sequential changes in vegetation, invertebrates, and fish downstream through the course of a stream.

summercool: quality of a stream whose temperature is cooler than air temperature in summer, usually holding salmonid fishes; replacing coldwater.

sympatry: when populations of two species occur together.

synchrony: referring to the occurrence of each of a species' life cycle events occurring over a short period of time.

T

taxa: plural of taxon.

taxon: unit of taxonomy, such as phylum, order, species, etc.

taxonomy: system of naming plants and animals with internationally accepted terms.

template: model theory that can be used to test a unifying concept in ecology.

tiger trout: hybrid between brown and brook trout, naturally occurring where the two species are sympatric, but offspring are not fertile.

trivoltine: with three generations, or cohorts, per year.

troglodyte: permanent dweller in caves.

troglophile: animal that alternately enters and leaves caves.

trophic: referring to food and feeding.

trophic level: group of organisms with common feeding behavior.

trophic pyramid: graphic representation of pyramid-shaped structure of successive trophic levels.

U

unconfined aquifer: aquifer located only above an impermeable rock stratum.

underfit river: small river flowing through a large valley.

univoltine: with one cohort per year.

V

valley: catchment, but often connoting a scenic view.

viviparous: giving birth to living young; *compare* ovoviviparous.

voltinism: expressing number of cohorts per year.

W

warmwater: term roughly defining stream with warmwater fish species.

watershed: older term often used for valley, drainage basin, or (currently) catchment.

X

xylophage: organism feeding on wood.

Y

year class: cohort of fish, named by year of hatching.

Z

Zero Order: headwater region of stream consisting of small spring seeps; that is, above First Order.

zooplankton: free-floating small animals in lakes, ponds, and oceans.

INDEX

(Boldfaced numbers refer
to illustrations.)

A

acid neutralizing capacity
(ANC), *see* alkalinity
acid rain, 98, 115, 157-162
Acroneuria (stonefly), as carnivore, 208, 261
adfluvial fish spawning, 398,
514
Adirondack region, 160, 161
Agassiz, Glacial Lake, 87,
212, 363-366, 396
map of, **364**
aging of rivers, 33
agriculture
chemicals used in, 90
effects on streams, 83, 84
in Everglades, 181
in Lahontan Basin, 421
in Red River valley, 364
row-crop cultivation in,
89, 473
in southwest deserts, 433
and Truckee River, 418-
419
Alaska
Arctic grayling in, 470,
521
cutthroat trout in, 414
Dolly Varden trout in,
400
pink salmon in, 456
sockeye salmon in, 461
trout in, 409
Alaska, Gulf of, 410
Alaskan Peninsula, 410, 464
Alberta,
trout in, 409
alders, **118**
alevin, 445
algae
in benthos

of blackwater rivers, 199
in desert waters, 429
diatoms, group of, 151,
166
drifting of, 150, 167, 207,
538
in epilithon, 167
filamentous, 159, 166
as food for clams, 265
as food for herbivores, 204
as food for meiofauna,
349
in limestone streams, 189
in Minnesota streams,
175-176, 230
in periphyton, 196
in photosynthesis, 105,
126
primary production by,
104
and productivity, 128,
174, 176, 232
in seasons, 250
in streams, 51, 62
of stream water, 83, 115
Algoma, Ontario, 402
alkalinity
as ANC, 115
buffer effect of, 158
cause of hard water, 115
concentration of, 159,
176, 231
in coniferous forests, 175,
230, 231
from dissolved calcium,
158
in freestone streams, 135
in hardwater streams, 131-
132
in limestone streams, 115,
132
in Minnesota streams, 230
and mosses, 160
and nitrate, 230
in Ozark streams, 504
in plains streams, 231

and productivity, 174,
176, 227, 231-232
Allagash River, Maine, 235
Allegheny River, Pennsylvania, 235
Allen, K. Radway, fisheries
biologist, 221, 225
Allen paradox, 225-226
alligator, in Everglades, **178**
allochthonous
primary production, 198,
230, 231
terrestrial invertebrates,
126
allochthonous material, 126,
184, 187, 191, 192,
217, 234, 346, 347
allochthony, 125-137, 165,
170, 176
aluminum, 159
Amblyopsidae, family of
cave fishes, 347
American Dipper, 453
American Fisheries Society,
364, 411, 471, 474
American history, along rivers,
379-384
American Rivers, 481, 482,
548, 551
ammonium, 150, 151
Amphipoda, order of
crustaceans, 115, 170,
206, 211, 329, 333-337
see also Gammarus,
scuds
Amundsen, Roald, Norwegian
explorer, 70
anadromous fish spawning,
398, 455, 513, 514
anadromy, 513-514
Andes Mountains, 397
Andrus, Cecil, Secretary of the
Interior, 548
Anisoptera, suborder of dragonflies, 257
annual production
by fishes, 201, 220

by invertebrates, 201, 250
by smallmouth bass, 485
units of, 218
Apache trout, 409
Appalachian Mountains
acid deposition in, 159,
160
brook trout in, 396, 449
crayfish in, 341, 342
fishes in, 51
Gammarus in, 336
leaf types in, 132
logging in, 54
rainbow trout in, 395 449
and steamboats, 235
streams in, 34, 37, 98
aquifers
confined, 81
unconfined, 80
Arachnoidea, class of water
mites, 268
Arctic char, 399
Arctic Ocean
and search for Northwest
Passage, 66, 69, 70
Argentina, brown trout in, 441
Aristotle, Greek philospher, 75
Arkansas, 342, 441, 483, 594
Arkansas River, trout in, 423
Armistice Day storm, 215-
216
blizzard in, 216
deaths in, 216
Army Corps of Engineers,
U.S., 288, 296, 297,
549
artesian spring, 81
Asellidae, family of sow bugs
331,
Asian clam, *Corbicula*, 266
aspen, 403, 404
Astacidae, family of crayfish,
341
Atchafalaya River, Louisiana,
109
Athabasca River, Alberta, **113**,
409

A tlantic Ocean, 397, 435, 443,
      459, 514, 520-521, 522
Atlantic salmon, 443-450
   distribution of, 436
   dwarf populations, 448
   in Europe, 518
   food of, 446, 519
   fry of, 444, 519
   interaction with brook trout,
      139
   interaction with brown
      trout, 439-440, 450
   in Kennebec River, Maine,
      481
   life history of, 436, 443-
      447, 519
   migrations of, 444, 445,
      447, 519-520
   naming of, 435
   in New England, 443, 450
   parr, **437**, 444, 520
   spawning of, 435-436,
      444, 519-520
   territoriality in, 447
Aurora trout, 392
Australia, 397
autochthony, 170, 217, 231
autotrophy, 163-177,
      183, 201, 217

B

Babbitt, Bruce, Secretary of
      the Interior, 202
bacteria
   affected by acid rain, 159
   in caves, 346
   in conditioning of wood,
      196
   in cycling of nutrients, 148
   in epilithon, 167
   as food of meiofauna, 349
   as food of scrapers, 205
   in hyporheic zone, 371,
      374

importance of, in streams,
      133, 185-196
   in periphyton, 166
   in spiraling, 150
Baetidae, family of mayflies,
      245, 246, 278
   as scrapers and gatherers,
      279
   in stream drift, 278
Baetis, 98, 211, 218, 246, 269,
      276, **277**
   bicaudatus, 275
   drift of, 279, 538
   emergence of, 279
   as food for predators, 279
   synchronous life cycle of,
      279
   tricaudatus, 245, 246, 249,
      250, 275, 279, 280
   vagans, 245
   voltinism of, 279
Baetisca, life history of, 293
Baetiscidae, famiy of mayflies,
      278, 293
barbel
   European, 48
   zones, 48
Bardach, John, professor and
      author, 126, 184
base flow in streams, 79, 100
Bdelloidea, class of rotifers,
      359
Beaufort Sea, 70
Bear Lake, Idaho/Utah, 417-
      418
Bear River, Idaho, 417
beaver, 403-406
   aspens as food of, 403
   gray wolves as predators
      on
      403
   tail slap of, 405-406
   and trout, 405
beaver dams and ponds, **45**,
      63, 64, 194, **194**, **404**,
      405

Beaverkill, dry fly imitation of mayfly, 283
bedrock
  and ancestral rivers, 40
  beneath glacial drift, 37, 96
  control of stream morphology by, 37, 63
  and groundwater, 97
  limestone, 82, 345
  sedimentary, 230
  valleys in preglaciation, 40
beetles, as borers into wood, 206
Behnke, Robert J., fisheries scientist, 387, 407-408, 412-413, 424, 441
Belostomatidae, family of true bugs, 253
  as predators, 208, 209
  holometabolous, 251
benthos
  derivation of term, 240
  in hyporheos, 367
  invertebrates in, 242, 254
  and stream bottom type, 37
Bering Strait, 469, 471
Bermuda, 524
Bighorn River, Montana, 314
Big Piney Creek, Arkansas, 507
binomial system, of naming organisms, 28, 246
biodiversity
  in benthos, 242, 243-269
  in crustaceans, 330
  effect of dams on, 477
  among fish, 301, 407, 430
  in hyporheic zone, 375
  in invertebrate drift, 544
  in life history, 250
  among mayflies, 275
  among minnows, 493
  among streams and rivers, 29, 250

bioenergetics, in estimation of production, 218
biofilms, 167, 192, 200, 205, 349, 372, 374, 536
biological clocks, 535-536
biomass, 218, 248
biorhythms, 536
biospeleology, 346
birds, riparian, 155
Bitterroot Mountains, 69
Bivalvia, class of clams, 262, 264-266
black flies (Simuliidae), 193
  emergence of, 252
  filtering FPOM, 193, 200, 207
Black Hills, South Dakota, 98
blacknose dace, 48
blackwater rivers, 198-202
Blue Duck (New Zealand), 452
Blue Dun, dry fly imitation of mayfly, 249, 280, 286
Bluegill, 299, 300, 301
Blue Quill, dry fly imitation of mayfly, 286
Blue-winged Olive, dry fly imitation of mayfly, 98, 248, 280, 538
bog lakes, with trout, **398**
Bonneville basin, 417
Bonneville Dam, 468
boreal forest, **160**, 161, 174
borers, 206
Boston Mountains, in Ozark Plateau, Arkansas, 507
bounty, on Dolly Varden trout, 400
Bow River, Alberta, **95**
Brachycentridae, family of caddisflies, 314, 315
Brachycentrus, 229, 314, 315, **315**
  americanus, 246
  "black caddis" of Bighorn River, Montana, 314
  food of, 314

"log cabin" cases of, 314, **315**, 319
Bristol Bay, Alaska, 460
British Columbia
    Arctic grayling in, 470, 521
    and pink salmon, 456
    and sockeye salmon, 461
    trout in, 409
brook trout, **50**, 168, **393**, 394-399,
    affected by acid rain, 160, 160-161, 161
    anadromous populations, 392, 398
    angling for, 406, 397
    coasters, 398, 522
    competition with other trout, 425, 441
    in first-order streams, 49, 50-51
    interaction with Atlantic salmon, 450
    interaction with brown trout, 439, 449-450
    interaction with cutthroat trout, 397, 412, 413, 421, 425, 427, 441
    introductions, 397
    in Lake Nipigon, 392, **395**
    migrations of, 513, 518, 520,
    naturalized in Europe, 397
    popularity of, 389-390
    record by angling, 395
    salters, 397, 522
    spawning of, 394-395, 400, 401
    as stenothermic fish, 50
    susceptible to angling, 426
Brown Dun, dry fly imitation of mayfly, 286
Brown, Jerry, governor of California, 548
BrownQuill, dry fly imitation of mayfly, 286

brown trout, 47, 51, 437-447, **437**, **521**
    displacing brook trout, 396, 397
    distribution of, 436
    feeding and invertebrate drift, 541
    hybrid with brook trout, 401, **401**
    incubation of eggs, 90, 91
    in Europe, 435
    interaction with Atlantic salmon, 439-440, 449-450
    interaction with brook trout, 449
    introduction to North America, 390, 438-440
    lake-living, 440
    lake-run, 436
    life history of, 436
    migration of, 435, 513, 514
    naming of, 435
    naturalized, in North America, 390
    naturalized, in world, 439
    parr, **437**
    resistance to angling, 426
    spawning of, 435-436
    zone, 47
Brulé, Étiénne, French exploer, 403
buffalo (fish), 62, 300
    angling for, 491
    bigmousth, 491
    distribution of, 491
    smallmouth, 491
Buffalo National River, Arkansas, 507, 508
Buffalo River, Arkansas, 505, 506
bugs, order Heteroptera, 209
bullheads, 48
Bureau of Land Management, 549

Bureau of Reclamation, 549
Burton, Sir Richard, explorer, 76
bull trout, 400

C

caddisflies, order Trichoptera 52, 303-320
  adult, 211, **308**
  annual production by, 309
  asynchronous, 304
  in benthos, 242
  biodiversity in, 303, 307, 310
  capture nets of, **208**, 298, 304, 309
  cases of, 303
  collecting cases of, 319-320
  common names for, 304, 318, 320
  day-active, 541
  diversity in case-making 304
  drift of, 155, 310
  ecological groups, 304
  ecological niches occupied by, 303
  functional groups of, 306
  feeding behavior of, 229
  filtering FPOM, 193, 200, 207, 304, 309
  as food for fish, 309
  food of, 166, 304, 307, 308, 309, 351
  habitat of, 304, 306
  holometabolous, 251, 304
  in hyporheic zone, 375
  as gatherers, 304
  in lake outlets, 309
  life cycle of, 304
  migrating upstream, 64-65, 90, **155**
  night-active, 535
  as omnivores, 304
  as predators, 208, 209
  in river continuum, 307
  as scrapers, 206, 307
  as shredders, 206, 304, 307
  use of silk by, 304
  in spiraling nutrients, 155
  "stick" caddis, 308
  in upper reaches, 307
  upstream flight of, 155, **155**, 545
  voltinism of, 247, 304
  in wood, 192
Caecidotea, genus of sow bugs, 331
  communis, 331
  lineatus, 332
  occidentatus, 332
Cahill, dry fly imitation of mayfly, 285
calcium, 98, 113, 114, 186
calcium bicarbonate, 114
calcium carbonate, 114, 115, 262, 344, 345, 368
calories, 125
California, 141
  chinook salmon in, 464, 468
  and coho salmon, 463
  endangered stocks, 471
  and pink salmon, 456
  trout in, 409, 410, 414, 417
Cambaridae, family of crayfish, 341
Cambarus, genus of crayfish, 341-342
  bartoni, 341
  hobbsi, 341
  robustus, 342
Campbell River, British Columbia, 464
Canada
  affected by acid rain, 160, 161
  sulfur deposition in, 159
Canadian Shield, 98
Canfield Creek, cave, **345**

canoeing
in Everglades, **180**
routes, and global climate
change, 325
Canthocamptus, genus of copepoda, 353
life cycle of, 353
capture nets, of filtering caddisflies, 207, **208**, 304,
309
carbon dioxide, 112, 115
as greenhouse gas, 321,
322, 323
increase in atmospheric
content of, 82, 323, 324
method for measuring
primary production
rate, 172
in photosynthesis, 115
from respiration, 197
carbonic acid
and caves, 344
in precipitation, 82, 114,
157
carnivores, 104, 164, 204, 205,
208, 231
carp
in large rivers, 48
in Mississippi River, 299,
301
carrying capacity, 544
Carter, President Jimmy, 548
Cartier, Jacques, French explorer, 66, 403
Cascade Mountains, 141
Caspian Sea, brown trout
in, 441
Castor canadensis, see beaver
catadromy, 514
catchment, 93, 94, **95**, 96, 98,
99, 100, 102, 198
catch per unit effort (CUE),
233
catfishes, 201, 485, 501-503
angling for, 503
blue catfish, 300
in caves, 347

channel catfish, , 49, 300,
301, 501-503, **502**
commercial fishing for,
502
distribution of, 502
in farm ponds, 502-503
feeding of, 501-502,
flathead catfish, 300
introductions of, 502
Catostomidae, sucker family,
429, 490-491
caves
animals in, 346
crustaceans in, 329
fish in, 347
Mammoth, Kentucky, 82
as source of streams, 82,
83, 343-348, **345**, 504
Cedar Creek, South Carolina,
200
Central Valley, California,
464, 468, 472
Centrarchidae, family of sunfishes, 483
Ceratopogonidae, family of
flies, 255
Champlain, Samuel de,
French explorer, 66
channelization, of streams,
364
Chaoboridae, family of flies,
255
char, 399
see also brook trout
chemistry
of acid rain 147
in catchment, 112
of stream water, 39, 62,
63, 83, 98, 99, 100, 217
chert, in Ozark rivers, 505
Chesapeake Bay, 379-380
Cheumatopsyche, 313
Chicago, Illinois, 43
Chihuahua, Mexican state of,
431
Chihuahuan Desert, 429
chimney, of crayfish, **340**

chinook salmon, 455, 463-
466, **465**, **517**
angling for, 463-464, 465
commercial catches of,
466
distribution of, 464
feeding of, 465
fry migration of, 515-
517, 518
introductions of, 464
spawning of, 464-465
Chironomidae, family of
flies,
246, 254-255
Chironomus, bloodworm, 267
chlorophyll, 171
chubs
Alvord chub, 494
bonytail, 494
Borax Lake chub, 495
Chihuahua chub, 494
creek chub, *see* creek chub
Gila, 494
horned dace, *see* creek
chub
humpback chub, 494
Hybopsis, 495
leatherside chub, 494
Nocomis, 495
Rio Grande chub, 494
Sonora chub, 494
roundtail chub, 494
tui chub, 494
yaqui chub, 494
chum salmon, 455, 459, 514
distribution of, 459
fry of, 459
hybridization, with pink
salmon, 459
migration of, 514-515
spawning of, 459
Chydoridae, family of cladocerans, 354
Cicadellidae, family of Homoptera, 253
Civilian Conservation Corps
(CCC), 22

cladocerans, 351, **353** ,
354, 535
in benthos, 328
drift of, 355, 543
as food of fish fry, 355
Cladophora, filamentous alga,
166
clams, 115, 264-266
and pollution, 266
Asian, 266
see also Bivalvia
Clark, William, explorer
and search for Northwest
Passage, 68-69
and cutthroat trout, 413
Clark Fork, Montana, 414-
415
classification
of invvertebrates, 205, 245
of lakes, 52
of particulate organic matter, 127-129
of streams and rivers, 28-
30, 32, 45
Clean Water Act, 301
Clearwater River, Idaho, 472,
473
Clemens, Samuel, steamboat
pilot, 296
climate
change, global, 157, 321-
326, **322**
as result of human activity,
102
Clinton, President William,
548
closed basins, 416-417
coal burning
as cause of global warm-
ing, 522, 552
as source of sulfuric acid,
157
coarse particulate organic matter (CPOM), 128-129,
153, 154, 188, 191,
192, 194, 195, 205-207,
307

Coastal Plain, southeastern
    United States, 198-199,
    201
coasters, 398, 455
coho salmon, 400, 455, 462-
    463, 514
    angling for, 463
    distribution of, 463
    food of, 462, 463
    introductions of, 463
    life history of, 462
    spawning, 463
cohort production interval
    (CPI), 248
coldwater fishes, 84, 388
coldwater streams, 45, 46, 48,
    50, 101
    see also coolwater streams
Coleoptera, order of beetles,
    254
collectors, 205
    food of, 206, 207
    and shredder ratio, 210
colonization cycle, in drift,
    542-544
colonization of organic matter
    by algae and fungi, 192
Colorado River
    Grand Canyon in, 421
    in Sonoran Desert, 429,
    430
    trout in, 421
Columbia River,
    and chinook salmon, 464
    coho salmon in, 463
    cutthroat trout in, 414-
    416
    and Bonneville Dam, 468
    and Grand Coulee Dam,
    469
    Hanford Reach in, 478
    pink salmon in, 460
    salmon and steelhead in,
    409, 410, 411
    and search for Northwest
    Passage, 67, 69
Columbus, Christopher, 66

commercial fishing,
    for chinook salmon, 465,
    467, 468
    overfishing by, 468
common shiner, **50**
conditioning of organic mat-
    ter, 129, 131-134, 186-
    188, 193
conifer forests, 130-132, **132,**
    133, 134, 174, 175,
    185, 189, 230, 231
continuum, in streams, 58,
    59, 63
    see also River Continuum
    Concept
coolwater streams, 485, 490,
    496
copepods, 351, 352-353, **353,**
    354, 535, 543
    in benthos, 329
    in caves, 346
    drift of, 543
Copper River, Alaska, **404**
Coregoninae, subfamily of
    whitefishes, 390
Corixidae, family of bugs, 253
Corps of Discovery, and
    search for Northwest
    Passage, 68
Corydalidae, family of
    Megaloptera, 256
Corydalus, **209**
    as predator, 208, 256
    in smallmouth bass
    streams, 247
Cottidae, family of sculpins,
    488
Cottonwood River, Minne-
    sota, **103**
Coweeeta Creek, North
    Carolina, 55
Coweeta Hydrologic Labora-
    tory, 53-56, **55**
CPI, *see* cohort production
    interval
CPOM, *see* coarse particulate
    organic matter

crane flies
  nymphs of, as shredders,
    206, 211
  as predators, 209
crappies, 300
crayfish, 115, 170, 245, 262,
    329, 338-343, 374
  in caves, 338, 346
  chimney of, 339, **340**
  as food for fish, 339, 341,
    342
  life cycle of , 338, 339,
    341
  migrations of, 339
  in Ozark and Appalachian
    mountains, 341, 505
  reproduction of, 340-341
  see also Decapoda
creek chub, 48,, 84, 393, 489,
    495
crenon, area of spring seeps, 77
crocodile, American, 179
Crossman, E. J., fishery bi-
    ologist, 455
crustaceans, 266, 327-343
  in caves, 328, 346, 347
  with exoskeletons, 115,
  as food for fish, 266, 328
  food of, 188, 257
  in hyporheic zone, 372,
    375
  in meiofauna,
    351
  as parasites, 328
Culicidae, family of flies,
    255
cultivation, effects of, 101,
    105, 110
Cumberland River, in Appala-
    chian Mountains, 235
Cummins, Kenneth W.,
    stream ecologist, 188
  and functional groups, 204
  and effect of dams, 476
  and sizes of particulate
    organic material, 127-
    128

Currrent River, Missouri, 505,
    506
Current River, Ontario, 457
cutthroat trout, , 50, 51, 82,
    455, 407-408, 412-427,
    513
  distribution of, 412, 415,
    421
  hybridization with rain-
    bow trout, 408, 414,
    419, 420, 421, 425
  interaction with brook
    trout, 397, 412, 421,
    425, 427, 441
  interaction with brown
    trout, 421, 423, 425,
    427, 441
  migration of, 518
  naming of, 435
  restoration of, 423
  spawning of, 413, 413
  subspecies:
    Alvord (extinct) 417,
      419, 420
    Bonneville, 417, 418
    coastal, 413, 414, 522
    Colorado River, 421,
      423
    finespotted, 416
    greenback 421, 423,
      424
    Humboldt, 417, 419,
      420
    Lahontan, 417, 418,
      419
    Paiute, 417, 419-420
    Rio Grande, 421, 423
    westslope, 413, 414-
      416, **415**
    Whitehorse, 417, 419,
      420
    yellowfin(extinct), 421,
      423-424
    Yellowstone, 414-416,
      421
  susceptibility to angling,
    426

cyanobacteria, 150
cyclomorphosis, 354
Cyclopoida, suborder of co-
    pepods, 353,
Cinygmula, 284
cypress swamps, in Everglades,
    178
Cyprinidae, minnow family,
    429
Cypridontidae, pupfish and
    springfish family, 432,
    433

D

dace
    blacknose dace, 496
    in desert Southwest, 496-
        497
    horned dace, see creek
        chub
    longnose dace, 496
    pearl dace, 495
    redbelly dace, 496
    speckled dace, 496
dams, 44-45, 62, 85, 410,
        433, 472, 475-482, 549
    and chinook salmon, 468
    on Clearwater River,
        Idaho, 472, 480
    on Colorado River, 478-
        479
    on Columbia River, 472,
        478
    and discontinuity in rivers,
        476
    Dworshak, 422, 479, 480,
        480
    Edwards, 481
    on Green River, 479
    on Kennebec River, Maine,
        481
    number of, 476, 478
    proposed on Eleven Point
        River, Missouri, 507
    removal of, 481-482

    on Snake River, 479, 481
    and tailwater fisheries, 477
    operations of, 473
damselflies, 208, 251, 527
    flight of, 258
    metamorphosis of, 258
darters, 48, 240, 374, 499-501
    as aquarium fishes, 500
    Etheostoma, 499, 500-501
    Iowa darter, 499,
    Johnny darter, 499, 500,
        501
    lacking gas bladder, 500
    logperch, 499-500
    in perch family, Percidae,
        499
    Percina, 499-500
    rainbow darter, 499
    sand darter, 500
    snail darter, 500
Dead Zone, in Gulf of
        Mexico, 301
debris dams, **154**, 193-195,
        194
    invertebrates in, 200
    microorganisms in, 151
    as patches in streams, 64
Death Valley, 429
Decapoda, 329, 338-343, *see
        also* crayfish
deciduous woodlands, 9, 133
    leaves of, **25**, 129, **130**,
        134, 137, 185, **186**,
        187, 191, 195
decomposers, 184, 186
denitrification, 151
denitrifying bacteria, 151
desert fishes, 428-434
    common names for, 429
    endangered species in,
        432-433
    species
        bluehead, 432
        bonytail, 431
        Colorado squawfish, 431
        desert sucker, 431
        flannelmouth sucker, 431

longfin dace, 432
Mexican stoneroller, 432
minnows, 433
razorback sucker, **430**, 431
roundtail chub, 432
Sonora sucker, 432
virgin spinedace, 432
woundfin, 432
speckled dace, 432
spikedace, 432
Yaqui sucker, 432
deserts
Chihuahuan, 429
Great Basin, 429
Mohave, 429
Sonoran, 429, 433
desert streams, 38, 210
Colorado River, 431
Bill Williams River, 431
Gila River, 431
Green River, 431
Little Colorado River, 431
San Juan Rivar, 431
Virgin River, 431
Des Moines River, Iowa, 41
detritivores, 204, 205, 260
detritus
as primary production, 104
leaves as, 104
pool, 170, 195, 198
diatoms, 98, 166, 306, 314, 316, 318
Dicosmoecus, 311
diel periodicity, *see* drift
Diptera, order of flies, 246, 254-256, 303
dispersal
defined, 510-511
of insects, 244
comparre migration
dissolved organic matter (DOM), 59, 127, 128, 131, 132, 188, 189, 190, 372, 373
Dixidae, family of flies, 255

dobsonflies, **209**, 247, 251
Dolly Varden trout, 400, 399
dolomite, 504, 505
Douglas, Marjory Stoneman, author, 177, 179, 181
dragonflies, 208, 251
flight of, 258
metamorphosis of, 258
migration of, 257, 526-527
drainage
for agriculture, 202
of Everglades wetlands, 181
drift, of algae, 150, 167, 207, 538
drift, of invertebrates, 59, 155, 167, 201, 229, 447, 535-547
alternans pattern in, 543
Baetis in, 538, 543
bigeminus pattern in, 543
colonization cycle in, 542
diel periodicity in, 536, **540**
effect of light, 536 **540**, 542, 543
effect of temperature, 536
excess production theory, 544, 545
and fish feeding, 135, 200-201, 538-541
of FPOM, 193
Gammarus in, 538, 543
of meiofauna, 542, 543
of microcrustaceans, 352,
of microinvertebrates, 543
as migrations, 512
nets, for sampling, 539, **539**,
night-active, 535
paradox, 545-547
seasonal pattern in, 543
as source of invertebrate recolonization, 376, 542, 543, 544
species involved in, 538

of stoneflies, 538
of terrestrials, 135, 517
Driftless Area, 342, 396
Drunella, 282
  coloradensis, 283
  doddsi, 283, 284
duckweed, 170
Du Luht, Sieur, French explorer, 66
Dworshak Dam, Clearwater River, 472, 479, 480, **480**
Dytiscidae, family of beetles, 254

E

Earth Day, 1970, 181
Earthquake, New Madrid, 235
Eastatoee Creek, South Carolina, **38**
ecological niche, 244, 268, **268**, 303
ecosystem management, 105, 482
ecosystem, stream, 25, 73, 74, 102, 106, 156, 163, 198, 202, 244
ecotone, 89, 105, 370
Edwards Dam, Kennebec River, 481
eel, American, 514, 524-526, **525**
  confusion with lamprey, 525
  distribution of, 525
  glass eel, 524
  migration of, 524-526
  spawning of, 525
effluent streams, 99, 153
electrofishing, **224**, 442, 490, 525
Elephant Butte Dam, Rio Grande, 480

Eleven Point River, Arkansas/Missouri, 505, 506, 507
Elkhair Caddis, dry fly imitatin for caddisfly, 318
Elmidae, family of beetles, 254
emerald shiner, 301
emergence
  of fish, 445
  of hyporheic insects, 374
  of insects, 135, 243, 244, 246-247, 248
  of mayflies in Mississippi River, 288, 289
  of *Tricorhythodes*, 249
  variations in, 252
endangered species
  of darters, 500, 501
  of desert fishes, 433
  in Everglades, 179
  among Pacific salmon, 393, 471-474
  paddlefish, in Mississippi River, 300
Endangered Species Act, 393, 433, 472
energy, 217
  allochthonous, 125-126, 131, 188, 191, 192, 193, 200
  alternative sources, 322
  autochthonous, 196
  in autumn leaves, 188, 196
  in biomass, 322
  budgets, 152, 218
  central to growth, 144, 183
  flow in stream ecosystem, 125, 233
  in food, 164
  in plant matter, 172
  in stream algae, 62
  in stream plants, 60
  in terrestrial organic matter, 60, 87, 96, 145
  in trophic pyramid, 104

sources of, 105, 372
spiraling of, 147
supply to streams, 106
from wind, 322
in wood, 193
engulfers, 209
Epeorus, 284, 285
Ephemera, 286, 287
Ephemerella, 277, 280, 282, 283, 286
dorothea, 283
invaria, 283
rotunda, 283
subvaria, 248, 283
Ephemerellidae, family of mayflies, 278, 281-283
Ephemeridae, family of mayflies, 278, 286
Ephemeroptera, order of mayflies, 245, 273-294, 303
Ephoron, 278, 291
album, 291
leukon, 291
epigean habitats, 346
epilithon, 167, 168, 307, 349, 372
erosion, 29
as factor in sculpting landscapes, 31, 63, 96
and meanders, 37
stream bank, **123**
of streams, 32, 45
from wind, 322
in wood, 193
eurythermic
reaches in streams, 49
fishes, 50, **50**, 390
invertebrates, 52
see also stenothermic
evaporation, 99
evapotranspiration, 99
Everglades, 177-182
birds of, 179, 181
Everglades National Park, **178**, **180**
exotic species
of fishes, 51

in Everglades, 179
extinctions of fish, 411, 419, 424, 433, 471-474

F

Farrar & Rinehart, publishers, 380
fecal pellets, as FPOM, 128, 207
feeding guild, 203
fencing
against livestock, 91-92, **122**
filamentous algae, 327
filterers
food of, 207
in RCC, 232
filter-feeding insects, 195
fine particulate organic matter (FPOM), 128, 153, 154, 170, 188, 190, 191, 192, 195, 196, 200, 201, 205, 208, 232, 255, 286, 304, 306, 371
Finger Lakes, New York, 392
Firth, Penelope, stream ecologist, 325
fish
in blackwater rivers, 201
distribution of, along stream, 43-44, 57, 386
food of, 23, 98, 154, 240, 347
fry, 241
methods for capture of, 43
migration of affected by stream sediments, 37
in Mississippi River, 299-301
omnivorous, 62
Fish and Wildlife Service, U.S., 213, 423, 549
Fisher, Stuart, stream ecologist, 325

fisheries management, 46, 233
Flaming Gorge Dam, Green
    River, 421, 479
Flathead Lake, Montana, 416,
    461
Flathead River, Montana,
    369
flood control
    in Everglades, 181
floodplains, 72, 90, 98, 110,
    111, 226
    and allochthonous mate-
        rial, 127
    along lower river reaches,
        232
    aquatic invertebrates in,
        136
    by blackwater rivers, 200,
        202
    and channel boundary,
        136
    hyporheic zones in,
        368, 378
    lakes on, 171
    in refuge, 211, 213
floods, 44, 72, 90, 99, 100,
    111
    in Mississippi River, 106-
        110, **109**
    in Red River, 363-366
    removal of leaf packs by,
        190
floodways, to divert floodwa-
    ter, 107
Florida Bay, 179, 180, 181
Florida Keys, 179
Fontinalis, genus of moss, 168
food
    in caves, 347
    from conditioned leaves,
        188
    of invertebrates, 159, 167,
    in lake outlets, 85
    as major factor in produc-
        tion, 220-226, 170, 194,
        196
fossil fuels, 162, 322

forests
    deciduous, 174
    coniferous, 174, 175
    boreal, 174
Forest Service, U.S., 507, 549
Forestville Creek, Minnesota,
    83
Fort Chipewyan, 67
FPOM, *see* fine particulate
    organic matter
Fraser River, British Colum-
    bia, 67, **383**,515,
    Hell's Gate in, 515, **516**
Fremling, Calvin R., river bi-
    ologist, 288, 314
freestone streams, 115, 131,
    132, 189, 220, **222**
    see also softwater streams
Fulton, Robert, steamboat
    builder, 235
functional groups
    203-216, 129
fungi, 185-196
    in caves, 346
    in conditioning of wood,
        133
    in cycling of nutrients, 148
    as food for meiofauna,
        349
    as food for invertebrate
        scrapers, 205
    in hyporheic zone, 371,
        374
    in periphyton, 166
    role of, in streams, 146
    255
fur trade, 403, 404

G

gallery forest, 63, 102, **103**
Gammaridae, family of scuds,
    334
Gammarus, 90, 170, **206**, 269,
    334, **335**, 538, 545
    in caves, 336

drift of, 335
fasciatus, 336
as food of trout, 424
lacustris, 336
life cycle of, 335, 336
minus, 336
pseudolimnaeus, 335, **335**
voltinism of, 336
in watercress and leaf
    packs, 335-336
Gastropoda, snails, 262-264
gatherers, 206, 207
genetics, of brook trout, 161
Geological Survey, U.S., 33
Georgia, 395
Germany, source of brown
    trout eggs, 438, 439
Gerridae, family of bugs, 253
Giardia lamblia, 357
Gibbs, Elizabeth, entomolo-
    gist, University of
    Maine, 292
Gila trout, 409
Ginger Quill, dry fly imitation
    of mayfly, 285
gizzard shad, 301
glacial beaches, in Red River
    valley, 364
glacial stream
    on surface of melting gla-
        cier, 86, **86**, 87
glacial deposits, 80, 96
Glacial Lake Agassiz, *see* Agas-
    siz, Glacial Lake
glacial lakes, 87, 212, 363-366,
    396, 417
Glacial River Warren, *see*
War-
        ren, Glacial River
glaciation
    in North America, 37, 39,
        42, 363, 418, 419, 469
glaciers
    melting of, 39, 86, 363
    mountain 86, **86**, 87
    thickness of, 40
    transporting soil, 112

Glen Canyon Dam, on Colo-
    rado River, 481-482
global climate change, 321-
    326
    and coal and oil industries,
        323
    Earth Summit conference,
        323
    General Circulation Mod-
        els in, 325
    from global warming,
        321-326
    Kyoto, Japan, protocol,
        323
    and streams and rivers,
        325, 324-325
Glossosoma, 316
Glossosomatidae, family of
    caddisflies, 309, 315-
    316
gold mining, in Alaska,
    470
gougers, 206
gradient, of streams, 35, 36,
    37, 60, 96, 201
Grand Cascapedia River,
    Quebec, 443
Grand Coulee Dam, Colum-
    bia river, 469, 478
grass carp, 170
gravel bars, **117**
grayling
    Arctic, 47, 469-471, 523
    angling for, 470
    European, 47, 471
    Montana, 469
    Michigan, 395, 469,
        471
    spawning of, 470, 523-
        524
    zone, 47, 48
gray wolf, 403
grazing
    by crustaceans, 328
    by invertebrates, 151, 170
    livestock, 472, 473

Great Basin, 416, 419, 420, 421
Great Bear Lake, 459
Great Lakes, 14, 159, 166, 287-288, 325, 336, 341, 342, 363, 390, 395, 400, 410, 435, 438, 458, 463, 464, 467, 470, 483, 488, 489, 491, 520, 521, 525, 526, 531
Great Salt Lake, 417
greenhouse effect, 321
greenhouse gases, 321, 326
Green River, Wyoming/Utah trout in, 421
Greer Spring, on Eleven Point River, 507
Grey, Zane, author, 409
Grizzly King, dry fly imitation of mayfly, 294
Groseilliers, Sieur des, French explorer, 66
groundwater
    in bedrock, 84, 97
    and brook trout spawning, 395, 402
    carrying biological by-products, 112
    chemistry of, 87, 100
    desert streams, 428, 433
    discharge area of, 80, 99
    and effluent streams, 153
    as fate of precipitation, 79
    and floods, 106
    in hydrologic cycle, 111
    outcrops, 79, 80-81
    recharge area of, 80
    as source of streams, 94
    temperature of, 46, 87, 90, 98, 100
    see also springs
Gulf of Alaska, 460
Gulf of California, 412, 429, 430, 431, 479
Gulf of Mexico, 41, 179, 297, 301, 430, 522, 525

Gulf Stream, 443
Gyrinidae, family of beetles, 254

H

Haig-Brown, Roderick, author, 464, 515
Hanford Reach, on Columbia River, 478
hardness of water, 83, 114
    from calcium, 115
    defined, 114
    and drift of microcrustaceans, 352
hardwater streams, **175**
    fungal growth in, 187
    see also limestone streams
Harlequin Duck, 451-452
Harpacticoida, suborder of copepods, 352
Hastaperla, 260, 538
hatcheries, fish, 161, 233, 387, 410, 411
    Caledonia, New York, 438
    Long Island Cold Spring, New York, 438
    as mitigation, 467-468
    Northville, Michigan, 438
    Newfoundland, 439
headwater reaches, 44, 48, 60, **61**, 63, 64, 90, 94
    Atlantic salmon in, 520
    and allochthonous inputs, 210
    bacteria and fungi in, 184
    brook trout in, 394, 397, 442
    cutthroat trout in, 421, 425
    with debris dams, 194
    in deciduous forests, 377
    heterotrophic, 197
    mosses in, 168
    of prairie streams, 102

return of anadromous fish to, 528
sculpins in, 489
and secondary production, 232
shaded streams in, **185**
spawning, fish, 514, 527
wood in, 192, 193
hemimetabolous insects, 251
Hendrickson, dry fly imitation of mayfly, 248, 250, 280, 283
Henry's Fork, Idaho, 414-415
Henryville Special, dry fly imitation of caddisfly, 319
Henshall, James A., author and fish biologist, 486
Heptagenia, 284, **287**, 286
Heptageniidae, family of mayflies, 277, 278, 281-286
voltinism of, 284
Heteroptera, order of aquatic bugs, 252-253
heterotrophy 183-262, 201, 350
defined, 127
Hetch Hetchy Dam, Tuolumne River, 481
Hexagenia, 247, 277, 278, 287-288, **287**
bilineata, 288, 289, 298
298
emergences of, 289
limbata, 288, 289
in Mississippi River, 298 301, 314
voltinism of, 289
Hibbing, Minnesota, 77
holometabolous insects, 251
horned dace, *see* creek chub
Horton, Robert E., developer of stream-order system, 33, 48, 77, 78, 82
Holt, Rinehart, and Winston, publishers, 380

Hudson River, New York, 235
Hudson Bay, 40, 42, 160, 336, 364, 395, 398, 412, 469, 470
Huet, Marcel, Belgian professor, 32, 47, 386
Humboldt River, Nevada, 236, 417, 420-421
Humpbacked Nymph, nymphal imitation of mayfly, 293
Hurricane Creek, Arkansas, 507
Hyalella azteca, 334
Hyalellidae, family of scuds, 334
Hydracarina, water mites, 268
hydrologic cycle, 78, 111
hydrologic sequence, 78, 79
hydrology, of catchment, 101
Hydrometridae, family of bugs, 253
Hydropsyche, 313
Hydropsychidae, family of caddisflies, 298, 309
annual production by, 313
below reservoir and lake outlets, 312
capture nets of, **208**, 312
emergence of, 313
feeding of, 313
in Mississippi River, 298, 313
retreats of, 312
voltinism of, 313
Hydroptilidae, family of caddisflies, 316, **317**, 319, 515
Hynes, H. B. Noel, stream ecologist, 24, 96, 191
and allochthony, 127
and fish, 388
and functional groups, 204
and hyporheos, 367, 376-377
and secondary production, 220

Hyphomycetes, class of fungi, 187
hypogean habitats, 346, 347, 348
hyporheic zone, 100, 367-378, **369**
hyporheos, 90, 226, 367-378, **371**

I

Ictaluridae, family of cat-fishes, 501-503
Idaho,
    endangered fish stocks in, 471
    trout in, 409
Illinois
    flood in, 109
    University of, 43
Illinois River, 109
imprinting, of migratory fishes, 529
Indiana, 41, 159
influent streams, 99, 153
Insecta, 245
insects
    aquatic, 60
    in biofilms, 192
    emergence of, 155, 242
    filtering, 193
    as food for fish, 187
    food of, 151, 166, 188, 190
invertebrates, aquatic
    in blackwater rivers, 199
    as food for birds, 453
    as food for fish, 187, 240
    food of, 151, 153, 184, 186, 189, 203, 241
    life history of, 243
    sampling of, **225**
Iowa
    flood in, 109
Isopoda, 329, 330-333
    see also sow bugs

Itasca, Lake, Minnesota, 76
Izaak Walton League, 213, 548

J

J.S., cruise steamboat, **236**
Jacks Fork River, Missouri, 88, 505, 506, **506**
jassids, 134, 253
Jefferson, President Thomas, 68-69
Johnson, President Lyndon, 546
Jordan, David Starr, ichthyologist, 423, 424

K

Kamchatka Peninsula, Russia, 409, 412
Kansas
    crayfish in, 342
    flood in, 109
karst topography, 81, **81**, 82, 84, 158, **158**, 344-345, 504
Kentucky River, 235
Kenya, 397
kettle lakes, 397
Kingfisher, Belted, 451, **452**
Kipling, Rudyard, author, 409
Kissimee River, Florida, 178
Kitchitikipi Spring, Michigan, 80
kokanee, 461-462, 514
    angling for, 461
    introductions of, 46

L

Labrador
    Atlantic salmon in, 448

Lady Beaverkill, dry fly imitation of mayfly, 283
Lahontan Basin, 417, 421
Lake Athabasca, 67
Lake Erie, 396
Lake Huron, 401, 461, 463
Lake Itasca, Minnesota, **296**,
302
Lake Michigan, 43, 48, 79,
463, 464
Lake Nipigon, Ontario, 394-
395
brook trout in, 395, **395**
Lake Okeechobee, Florida,
178, 179, 180, 181
Lake Pend Oreille, Idaho,
400, 461, 462
Lake Pepin, Minnesota/Wis-
consin, 288-289, 301
Lake Superior, 260, 325,
396, 398, 399, 403,
457-458, 463, 517,
523, 525-526
Lake Tahoe, Nevada/Califor-
nia, 260, 416, 417, 461
lake trout, 390, 399, 416, 467,
470, 521
largemouth bass, 44, 201,
299, 300, 301, 484
La Salle, Sieur de, 295
leaves, 187-191
conditioning of, 189
as CPOM, 129
deciduous, 129, 195, 197
decomposition of, 24, 25
and ecological niche, 269
energy in, 132, 196
as food for invertebrates,
24-25, 130, 310-311
and fungi, 188
in hyporheic zone, 372
leaching of, 130-131, **188**
in leaf packs, **25**, 129, **130**
151, 190, 242, 335-336
shredding of, 188
species of, 25, 130
leeches, 346

Lemna, 170
Leonard, Justin and Fannie,
authors, 282
Leopold, Aldo, 148, 531-534,
533
author of *A Sand County
Almanac,* 534
education of, 531, 534
work experience, 531
Leopold, Luna, 29
Leptohyphidae, family of
mayflies, 290
Leptophlebiidae, family of
mayflies, 286
Letort Spring Run, Penn-
sylvania, 330, **331**, 333
Lewis, Meriwether, explorer,
68-69, 413
life cycle
of *Baetis*, 250
of crustaceans,
327, 328
of hyporheic animals, 374
of invertebrates 244, 247,
248, 249
of *Tricorhythodes*, 250
life history
of Ephemeridae, 286
of invertebrates, 243, 244,
248
Liguus, 179
limestone, 84, 115, 131, 187,
190, 220,
bedrock, 38, 504
buffering against acid
rain, 158
caves in, 344
in oceans, 115
source of calcium, 114
streams, 81, **222**, 228,
333, 334, 368, 541
Limnephilidae, family of caddisflies, 310-311
adult and larva, **309**
Limnephilus, 311
Linnaeus, Carolus, originator
of binomial system

of naming organisms, 28-29

Lirceus, 331
  brachyurus 331
  fontinalis, 331
  hoppinae, 331
Little Red River, Arkansas record brown trout in, 441
Little River, Newfoundland, **448**
Little Tennessee River, 500
livestock grazing, 105, **122**, 411, 419, 420, 421, 423, 425
Loch Leven, strain of brown trout, 439, 440
logging
  near streams, 89, 99, 105
  and river drives, 138
  and sediment, 411, 472, 473
log marks, 138-142, **140**
Long Island Cold Spring hatchery, 438
Louisiana Waterthrush, 453-454
Lucky Dog Creek, Idaho, **45**
Lumbee River, North Carolina, Indian name, 202
Lumber River, North Carolina, 202, 551

M

Macan, T. T., English stream ecologist, 52, 547
MacDonald, Marshall, U.S. Fish Commissioner, 424
Mackenzie, Alexander, Scottish explorer, 67, 69
Mackenzie River, British Columbia, 456, 464

macrophytes, 166, 168, 169, **169**, 170, 171, 184, 195-196, 306, 307
Maine,
  Atlantic salmon in, 439-440
  brown trout in, 440
  logging in, 140
Manitoba, 87
Marinaro, Vincent C., author, 330
March Brown, dry fly imitation of mayfly, 283, 285
mayflies, 273-294
  adult life of, 274
  in benthos, 242
  common names of, 294
  drift of, 278
  ecological groups in, 275
  food of, 23, 24, 90, 98, 115, 166, 200, 278
  life cycle of, 274
  production by, 218
  reproduction by, 274
  as scrapers, 206
  voltinism of, 247
McCafferty, Patrick, professor of entomology, Purdue University, 277, 294
meanders, in streams, 35, 36, **36**, 37, 44
Megaloptera, order of insects, 256-257
meiofauna, 349-362
  in benthos, 240, 241
  cladocerans, copepods, and ostacods in, 29
  as food for fish fry, 361, 446, 515
  as food for invertebrates, 351
  in hyporheic zone, 369, 372, 374, 377
metamorphosis,
  complete, 251
  incomplete, 251

methane, greenhouse gas, 321, 323
Mexican golden trout, 409
Michigan, 140, 159, 397, 398, 469, 470
Micrasema, 315
    feeding on moss, 315
    as shredders, 315
microcaddis
    larvae of, in meiofauna, 361
    as plant piercers, 209, 316
microcrustaceans, 201, 351, 352, 353, **353**, 356, 373, 374, 446, 511
Micropterus dolomieu,
    see smallmouth bass
midges (Chironomidae)
    emergence of, 252
    in hyporheic zone, 373, 374
    larvae of, in meiofauna, 361-362, 446
    as scrapers, 206
    voltinism of, 247
midreaches, of streams, 48, 60, 61, **61**, 64, 90, 105, 197, 207, 210, 232
migration
    of American eel, 524-526
    of Arctic grayling, 521-522
    of Atlantic salmon, 447, 519-520
    of brook trout, 398, 520
    of caddisflies, 155, 311, 542-543
    of chinook salmon, 515-517
    of chum salmon, 514-515
    of coho salmon, 517-518
    of dragonflies, 526-527
    of Harlequin Duck, 451, 452
    of invertebrates, 154, 155, 244, 257, 354-355,

528-529, 542-543
    of lake trout, 520-521
    mechanisms of, 531-530
    of northern pike, 523-524
    odor of stream water in, 529-530
    of pink salmon, 514-515, 520
    reasons for, 510-511
    of sea lamprey, 521
    of sockeye salmon, 518
    of steelhead, 518-519
    of striped bass, 522-523
mining
    and grayling, 470
    and loss of trout species, 421
    source of sediment, 413, 473
Minneapolis, Minnesota, 299, 395
Minnesota
    brook trout in, 396, 397, 399
    floods in, 109
    logging in, 140
    prairies in, 174
    production in streams of, 174, 230-332
    salter brook trout in, 398
Minnesota River, 87, 109, 230, 363
minnow family, Cyprinidae, 201, 429, 492-499
    chubs, 494-495
    dace, 496-497
    shiners, 496, 496-498
    squawfishes, 493-494, **493**
    stonerollers, 496
minnows, common names of
    brassy minnow, 497
    fathead minnow, 497
    plains minnow, 497
minnows, family Cyprinidae, 492-499
    distribution of, 493
    introductions, 493

Mississippi River, 295-302
412
and American eel, 525
ancestral, 40, 41, 42
and brook trout distribu-
tion, 396
compared with Nile and
Missouri rivers, 32
crayfish in, 342
floods in, 106-110, **108**
Headwaters, 230, 296,
299
Lower, 42, 109, 297, 299,
300
mayflies in, 287-289
navigation system in, 213,
288, 297, **296**, 300
pollution in, 301
source, 76-77, **296**
steamboats on, 235
Upper, 109, 211-216,
296, 298, 300
wing dikes in, 297, 314
Missouri, 41, 109, 483
Missouri River
ancestral, 40, 41, **41**, 42,
109
and Arctic grayling, 469-
470
cutthroat trout in, 407,
413, 414
length of, 302
and search for Northwest
Passage, 68-69,
Three Forks, **69**
Mohave Desert, 429
Mollusca, phylum of clams
and snails, 115, 262-
266, 375
Monongahela River, Penn-
sylvania, 235
Montana
Arctic graylng in, 521
glaciation in, 41
trout in, 409
Morone saxatilis, see striped
bass

moths, 304-305
mountain whitefish, 489-
490, **489**
in Pacific Northwest, 489
as sport fish, 489
muddler, *see* sculpin
Muddler Fly, imitation of
sculpin, 488
Muir, John, naturalist, 481
Mulberry River, Arkansas, 507
Müller, Karl, German scholar,
542, 543
muskellunge, 49

N

Narraguagus River, Maine,
443
Nasturtium, genus of watercress, 170
National Environmental Protection Act, 481
National Park Service, 506,
507, 549
National Weather Service, 108
National Wild and Scenic
Rivers Act, 481, 506
Navaho Dam, on San Juan
River, 361
Nebraska
crayfish in, 342
flood in, 109
Needham, Paul R., trout biologist, 135, 541
nekton, 254, 257
nematodes, 359-360
in hyporheic zone, 375
life cycle of, 359
members of meiofauna,
359
Neophylax, 311
Nepidae, family of bugs, 253
neuston, 254
Nevada,
trout in, 412, 417

New England
    Atlantic salmon in, 439
    crayfish in, 341, 342
    and global climate change,
        325
    logging in, 140
    salter brook trout in, 399
    sulfur emissions in, 159
Newfoundland
    Atlantic salmon in, 395,
        435, 448, **449**
New Orleans, Louisiana, 108,
    109, 235, 299, 300,
    325
New Zealand, 397, 464
Nipigon River, 395, 489
nitrate, 187, 230, 302, 372
nitric acid, 157
nitrifying bacteria, 372
nitrogen, 112, 113, 115, 150,
    157, 161, 186, 189, 527
nitrous oxide
    as a greenhouse gas, 321,
        322, 323
North American Benthological
    Society, 241
North Dakota, flood in, 109
northern pike, 299, 300, 523-
    524
northern squawfish, **493**, 494
North Sycamore Creek,
    Arkansas, 507
North Umpqua River, Ore-
    gon, **6**
Northwest Passage, 66-70,
    403
Norway
    Atlantic salmon in,
        443, 448
Notonectidae, family of
    backswimmers, 253
nutrients, 147-156
    delivery to stream, 94,
        111-120
    in desert soils, 433
    in desert streams, 428
    and fish migration, 527

in hyporheic zone, 372
in organic matter, 185
and primary productivity,
    177
storage of, 153, 154
transport in stream
    156, 529
in wood, 192

O

Odonata, order of damselflies
    and dragonflies, 257,
    273
odor of streams, 293-294,
    529-530
Ohio, 159, 396
Ohio River, 109, 235
    steamboats on, 235
Oklahoma, 342
oligochaetes, 360-361
    in hyporheic zone, 375
    Naididae, 360
    Tubificidae, 360
Oligophlebodes sigma, **155**, 311
omnivores, 104, 204, 232,
    328, 339, 346
Ontario, 396, 399, 483
opossum shrimp, 462
orangespotted sunfish, 300
Orconectes, 342
    immunis, 342
    luteus, 342
    propinquus, 342
    punctimanus, 342
    rusticus, 32
    virilis, 342
Oregon, 141
    endangered fish stocks in,
        471
    trout in, 410, 417
organic matter, nonliving, 94,
    96, 170, 184, 185, 186,
    197, 200, 203, 217
ostracods, 351, **353**, 355-356
    as food for fish fry, 356

as food for invertebrate predators, 356
drift of, 356, 543
food of, 356
habitat of, 356
in benthos, 329
Otter River, Michigan, **185**
oviposition
  by insects, 244, 246, 248, 286
  synchronous, 249
Oxford Universisty Press, 534
oxygen, 122, 156
  in brook trout lakes, 398
  and browm trout, 441
  content in stream water, 172
  in Dead Zone, Gulf of Mexico, 302
  in hyporheic zone, 373-374
  in mayfly burrows, 286
  need for by ostracods, 354
  and stoneflies, 259
  and trout, 391, 402
  and *Tubifex*, 267
  and water currents, 242
  in wood cavities, 192
Ozark bass, 486, 505, 507
Ozark Mountains, 341
  rivers in, 504-508
Ozark National Scenic River-ways, 342, 505
Ozark Plateau, 114, 342, 483, 504
ozone depletion, 157, 162

P

Pacifasticus leniusculus, 341
Pacific Northwest, 140, 191, 210
Pacific Ocean, 455
Pacific salmon, 193, 393, 443, 455-474, 473, 478
paddlefish, 300

Pale Evening Dun, dry fly imitation of mayfly, 283
Paraleptophlebia, 286
parr, 528
  of Atlantic salmon, 436, **437**
  of brown trout, 436, **437**
parr marks, 436
particulate organic matter (POM), 127-128
patches, on streambed, 167, 196, 268, 307
P:B, *see* production-to-biomass ratio
Peace River, British Columbia, 409
Pecos River, New Mexico, **423**
  trout in, 423
Pedocopida, order of ostra-cods, 355
Pennsylvania, 140, 159, 160, 330, 331
Pentagenia, 286, 287
Pepin, Lake, Minne-sota/Wisconsin, 288-289
periphyton, 151, 159, 166, 167, 171, 189, 196, 205, 210, 232, 263, 307, 349, 371, 372, 536
Perlidae, family of stoneflies, 261
pesticides, from agricultural cultivation, 102
Petromyzon marinus, see sea lamprey
phantom midge, 511
Pheasant Tail, nymph imita-tion, 541
phosphorus, 113, 115, 149-150, 151, 186, 189, 527
photosynthesis, 94, 105, 112, 115, 125, 126, 144, 147, 150, 153-177, 183, 196, 323, 344,

346, 350, 371
allochthonous, 233
rates of, 171
in trout lakes, 398
Physis, 263-264
phytoplankton, 86, 170-171,
302, 312, 344
pickerel, 201
piercers, 209
Pink Lady, dry fly imitation
of mayfly, 294
pink salmon, 455, 456-458,
458
angling for, 457
distribution of, 456
feeding by, 457
fry of, 456
introductions of, 457
life history of, 457-458
migration of, 514-515
Plains, Central, 114
plastron, air bubble, 281
Plecoptera, order of stoneflies,
259-262, 303
Pleistocene Epoch, 101, 212,
329, 408, 416
pollution
anthropogenic, 157
and brown trout, 441
and clams, 266
by decaying fish, 156
in Mississippi River, 301
organic, 391
and sinks, 347
from St. Louis, Mis-
souri, 289
from Twin Cities, Minne-
sota, 288
Polymitarcyidae, family of
mayflies, 278, 291
POM, *see* particulate organic
matter
potamodromy, 514, 521, 523
Potamogeton, genus of macrophyte, 169
predation, 135, 208, 209, 229,
241, 243, 257, 261,

301, 328, 342, 346,
351, 403, 416, 511,
541
primary production, 148, 159,
163-177
in bl ackwater rivers, 200
in caves, 346
in desert wat ers, 428
in Minnesota streams, 231
in hyprorheic zone,
371
as trophic level, 230
Prince, nymph imita tion, 541
Prince Edward Sound,
Alaska, 412
production
of Atlantic salmon, 446
of fish, 220-222, 228-229,
231
downstream succession in,
232
of invertebrates, 222, 231
ecology of, 222
production-to-biomass ratio
(P:B), 248, 547
productivity, 217-238
affected by spiraling of
nurients, 152
biological, in streams, 115
and chemistry, 111
defined, 126
of invertebrates, 446, 449
protein, 151, 187, 190, 536
Protozoa, 357, 358
Amoeba, 357, **358**
as food for fish fry, 446
food of, 357
Giardia lamblia, 357
in hyprorheic zone, 372,
373
Paramecium, 357, **358**
secondary production by,
356
Psphenidae, family of beetles, 254
Pteronarcyidae, family of
stoneflies, 261

Pteronarcys, 247, 261, **261**
  emergence of, 261
  food habits of, 261
  californica, 261
Puget Sound, 456
pumpkinseed sunfish, 263,
    300
pupfish, 432-433, 434
  secondary production by,
    433
Pyramid Lake, Nevada, 417,
    418

Q

Quebec, 342, 443
Quetico-Superior wilderness,
    531
quillback, 300

R

Radisson, Pierre Esprit,
    French explorer, 66
rainbow trout, 408-412, 455
  in Alaska, 400
  in Appalachian Mountains,
    396
  hybridization with cut-
    throat trout, 408, 414,
    419-421, 425
  introduced, 395, 396, 408,
    419
  naming of, 435
  native, 51, 407-408, 409,
    513
  subspecies:
    California golden trout,
      412
    coastal rainbow trout,
      409, 411-412
    Columbia redband trout,
      409, 411
    Kern River rainbow trout,
      412

Litle Kern River golden
    trout, 412
  Russian subspecies, 409
  Sacramento redband
    trout, 411
  see also steelhead trout
razorback sucker, **431**
Reelfoot Lake, Tennessee, 235
redear sunfish, 263
redhorses, 48, 490, 505
red pine, 174
Red River of the North, Mani-
    toba, North Dakota,
    Minnesota
  ancestral, 40
  buffalofish in, 491
  floods in, 363-366
Red Rock Lake, Montana, 470
reset, of a river, 45, **103**
retreat, of filtering caddisflies,
    208, **208**
Rhithrogena, 282, 282, 285
rhithron
  upper reach of stream, 77
  zone, 48
rhododendron leaves, 130,
    131, **131**, 132, 189
Rhyacophila, 208, **318**
Rhyacophilidae, family of
    caddisflies, 318
  as free-ranging predators,
    318
  as scrapers, 318
rhythms, of biological proc-
    esses, 173
Ricker, William E., fisheries
    biologist, 221
Rinehart and Company, pub-
    lishers, 380
Rio Grande, New Mexico/
    Colorado, 407, 412,
    423, 430
riparian birds, 451-454
riparian zone, 85, 89, 92, 105,
    111, 210, 377, 405
    424
  of blackwater rivers, 200

and livestock grazing, 420,
protection of, 419
source of allochthonous
material, 127,
terrestrial invertebrates in,
136
river carpsucker, 300
River Continuum Concept
(RCC), 30, 58, **61**, 62,
96, 197, 201
and deciduous leaves, 190,
210, 547
fish production in, 2 32
inversion of, 102, **103**
primary production in,
165, 166
the River Group, authors
of, 58
terrestrial energy in, 104
as unifyng concept, 65,
river log drives, 138-142
Rivers of America book series,
177, 379-3 84
rock bass, 46, 48, 299, 343,
486-488
distribution of, 486
habitat of, 487
in Ozark streams, 505
Rocky Mountains, 67, 69,
140, 141, 421, 521
Roosevelt, Nicholas, steamboat captain, 235
rotifers, 358-359, **358**
derivation of name of, 358
feeding mechanisms of,
358
as food for meiofauna,
446
foods of, 359
in hyporheic zone, 372,
373
round whitefish, 489
distribution of, 489
Royal Coachman, dry fly imitation of mayfly, 294

S

Sacramento River, California,
236, 464, 468, 472
Salmo fario, old name for
stream-resident brown
trout, 440
Salmo gairdneri, old name for
rainbow trout, 408
Salmo lacustris, old name for
lake-living brown trout,
440
Salmo salar, see Atlantic
salmon
Salmo trutta, see brown trout
salmon, 513,
Atlantic, 443-450
Pacific, 455-475
see also individual
species
Salmon Fly, dry fly imitation
of stonefly, 247, 261
Salmonidae, family of fish,
390
see also individual species
Salmoninae, subfamily of
trout and salmon, 390
salters, 398
Salton Sea, 420
San Joaquin River, California,
464, 468
San Juan River, 267, 361, 421
San Juan Worm, nymph to
imitate sludge worm,
136, 240, 266-267, 361
Sargasso Sea, 524-526
Saskatchewan River, Alberta,
407
saw grass, in Everglades, 177,
178, 181
Scandinavia
Atlantic salmon in, 448
lakes affected by acid rain,
161
Schoolcraft, Henry, geologist,
76

Scotland, source of brown
    trout eggs, 438-439
Scott, W. B., fishery biologist,
    455
scrapers, 205, 210, 232
SCUBA, 228
scuds, 211, 242, 245, 251,
    329, 333-337, 373
    in caves, 333, 346
    color of, 337
    in drift, 333
    as food for trout, 333, 424
    life cycle of, 333
    voltinism of, 333
    see also Amphipoda,
        Gammarus
sculpin, 488-489, **488**
    in benthos, 488
    distribution of, 488
    spawning of, 489
    lacking gas bladder, 488
    in hyporheic zone, 374
    mottled, 488
    in North America, 46, 48,
        51
    Old World, 47
    slimy, 488
sea lamprey, 400, 463, 521,
    526, 526, 528
sea-trout, *see* brown trout
secondary production, 164,
    201, 217-238
    allochthonous, 134, 135
    by crustaceans, 328
    by fish, 220
    in hyporheic zone, 373,
    by invertebrates, 220
    methods for estimation of,
        220-222
    rates of, 183, 376
sedge, common name for
        caddisfly, 318
sediment, 89, 90, 94
    and brown trout, 441
    deposits, 241
    from eroding straam bank,
        123

from gold mining, 470
    in hyporheic zone, 374
    inorganic, 50
    from livestock grazing,
        411, 413, 425
    from logging, 411, 413
    in Mississippi River, 288,
        298, 301
    in prairie streams, 102
    in reservoirs, 477
    sorting of, by meanders
        and gradient, 37
    suspended, 62, 266
seston, 195, 207, 265
shadow bass, 486
Shelford, Victor E., professor
    of zoology, University
    of Illinois, 43, 44, 47,
    49, 57, 386, 495
shiners
    common shiner, **50**, 497-
        498
    eamerald shiner, 498
    golden shiner, 497-499
    pallid shiner, 496
shorthead redhorse, 300
Shoshoni Indians, 69
shredders, 210, 211, 232, 328
    food of, 206, 207
Sialidae, family of alder-
        flies, 256-257
Sierra Club, 481, 482, 548
Sierra Nevada mountains, 429
silicon, 98, 113, 150
Silver King Creek, California,
    419-420
Silver Springs, Florida, 80
silver trout, 392
silt
    and grayling, 470
    as habitat for burrowers,
        307
    in hyporheic zone, 369
    in salmonid spawning
        redds, 402
    trapped in macrophytes,
        169

Simuliidae, family of black
    flies, 255
sinks
    and caves, 347
    in karst terrain, 81, **81**,
        344
    leading to caverns, 81, 82
sinuosity of streams, 36
Siphlonisca aerodromia, 292
    life history of, 292
Siphlonuridae, family of may-
        flies, 278, 292
Siphlonurus, 292
Skinner, Constance Lindsay,
        author-editor, 379, 380
slime community, 167
Smallmouth Alliance, The
        486
smallmouth bass, 46, 48, 60,
        220, 341, 343, 388,
        483-486, 490, 525-526
    angling for, 485-486
    annual production by, 485
    black fry, 484, **484**
    distribution of, 483,
    management of, 486
    migration of, 524
    in Ozark rivers, 505, 507
    spawning of, 484
Smith, Robert H., author,
        387, 409
Smoky Mountains, 391, 392
snag habitat, 193, 201, 226
snails, 115, 206, 262-264
    spiraled shells of, 263-264
Snake River, Idaho
    chinook salmon in, 464
    coho salmon in, 463
    endangered stocks in,
        472
    pink salmon in, 460
    trout in, 410, 411, 414,
        416
sockeye salmon, 455, 460-462,
        514
    angling for, 461-462

distribution of, 460
food of, in nursery lake,
        460, 462, 518
life history of, 460
spawning of, 460
softwater streams, 132, 159,
        160, **175**, 189
Sonora, Mexican State of, 431
Sonoran Desert, 429
sources of streams and rivers,
        73, 75-92, 428
South Africa, 397
South Dakota
    Black Hills in, 98
    flood in, 109
    glaciation in, 41
South Platte River, trout in,
        423
sow bugs, 329, 330
    in caves, 330, 332, 346
    as food for trout, 330
    in Letort Falling Spring,
        330
    in limestone streams, 330
    voltinism of, 330
    see also Isopoda
space
    as major factor in produc-
        tion, 222-223, 227-230
Spain, brown trout in, 440
spawning
    of brook trout, 442
    of brown trout, 442
    of cutthroat trout, 92
    in lakes, 436
    of Pacific salmon, 92
    of steelhead trout, 92
speleology, 344
Speke, John, English explorer,
        76
Spheriidae, family of clams,
        264
    as food for fish, 265
spiraling, 147-162
    length of spirals, 148, 149,
        154
    loose, 148, **149**

of nutrients, 148
tight, 148, **149**
splake trout, 400-401
spotted bass, 487
   angling for, 487-488
   distribution of, 487
   in Ozark rivers, 507
Spotted Sandpiper, 453
springfish, 433
springs, 88, 89
   affecting temperature of
      streams, 91, 100
   Alley, in Ozark Moun-
      tains, **89**
   artesian, 81
   conduit, 82-83, 84, **84**
   diffuse, 86
   Kitchikipi, Michigan, 80
   in Ozark Mountains, 504
   Silver, Florida, 80
   as source of stream water,
      77, 99
squawfish
   Colorado, 494
   northern, 493, **494**
St. Anthony Falls, Minne-
   sota, 299, 396
St. Croix River, Minne-
   sota/Wisconsin, **547**
St. John's River, Florida,
   236
St. Lawrence River, 66, 67,
   363, 403, 458, 492,
   525-526
St. Louis, Missouri, 109,
   110, 288, 289, 296,
   297, 299
St. Louis River, Minnesota, 67
St. Paul, Minnesota, 109, 288,
   296
standing stock, 376
   see also biomass
steamboats, 234-238
   construction of, 236
   Golden Age of, 235, 237
   J.S., **236**,

New Orleans, 235
Sultana, wreck of, 237
steelhead trout, 193, 455, 478,
   513
   life history of, 519
   migrations of, 518-519
   feeding of, 519
   spawning, in Russian
      streams, 518
   spawning, in Pacific Ocean
      tributaries, 519-520
   in sporting literature, 409
   stocks of, 467
   see also rainbow trout
Steel River, Ontario, 160
Stenonema, 282, 284, 285
   vicarium, 285
stenothermic
   fishes, 50, **50**, 390
   invertebrates, 52
   reaches of stream, 49
stick caddis, 307, **308**
stocks, of fish
   Aurora trout, 393
   as concept, 391-393,
      410, 435, 437
   definition of, 392
   endangered, 471-474
   in Finger Lakes, New
      York, 392
   and genetic forms, 466-
      469
   and hatchery operations,
      392, 473
   in Newfoundland, 392
   among Pacific salmon,
      471-474
   silver trout, 392
   in Smoky Mountains, 392
stoneflies, 90, 259-262
   diapause in, 250, 259,
   drumming of, 270-272,
      271
   food habits of, 25
   hemimetabolous, 251
   voltinism of, 247

walking upstream, 545
stoneroller
 central, 496
stream ecology, 125, 184,
 202, 388, 538
stream ecosystem, 94, 217,
 370, 377
stream improvement, 22, 23,
 228
stream order, 33, **33**, 34, 35,
 48, 49, 50, 54, 58, 60,
 77-78, 82, 96, 193,
 197, 199, 206, 377,
 489
streams and rivers
 artificial, in laboratory, 25
 glacial, 85-86, **86**
 underfit, 86
striped bass, 492, 514, 522-
 524, **523**
 distribution of, 492
 fry of, 492, 523
 hybrid with white bass, 49
 in reservoirs, 492, 523
 introductions of, 492
 migrations of, 523
 naturalized populations,
  523
 spawning of, 492, 523
structure, of stream biological
 populations, 58, 59, 62
structures, flood control, 107
stygiobionts, 329
succession, downstream, 43-
 53
suckers, 490-491
 in desert waters, 429
 distribution of, 490
 in large rivers, 48,
  51, 62, 201
 shorthead redhorse, 490
 white sucker, 490
Sulfur, dry fly imitation of
 mayfly, 283, 284
sulfur emissions
 in England, 161
sulfuric acid, 157

summercool streams, 85, 89,
 101, 388, 390, 397
sympatry, in fishes, 449
synchrony, in life history, 249

T

Tabanidae, family of flies, 256
tailwaters
 trout fisheries in, 85, 314,
  361, 412, 416, 421
Tamiami Trail, Florida, 181
Tanzania, 397
Teays, West Virginia, 41
Teays River, ancestral river,
 41, 42
Tellico Dam, 500
Temperance River, Minnesota,
 97
Temperate Zone, in North
 America, 79, 85-86, 87,
 187
temperature
 air, 46
 and brown trout, 441
 and fish distribution, 388
 of groundwater, 46, 87,
  90, 98, 100
 of hyporheic water, 373,
  374
 increase in Earth atmos-
  phere, 324
 and invertebrates, 449
 and oxygen content, 172
 of spring water, 79
 of stream water, 39, 44,
  84, 105
 succession of, in streams,
  46
Tennessee River
 steamboats on, 236
terrestrials, imitations of, 135
territoriality
 in fish, 227, 229, 447
Thymallus arcticus, see grayling, Arctic

tiger trout, 401, **401**
Tipulidae, family of flies, 256
Tomah Stream, Maine, **136**, 292,
Torrent Duck, South America, 452
transpiration, in plants, 78, 99
tree species and leaf conditioning, 189
Trichoptera, *see* caddisflies
Tricorhythodes, 249, **249**, 278, 290-291
    asynchonous life history of, 290
    in meiofauna, 361
    voltinism of, 290
troglobites, 347
troglophiles, 347
trophic levels, 73, 104, 105, 164, 165, 173, 183
    carnivores in, 208, 232
    in caves, 347
    energy budget for, 219
    fungi and bacteria in, 184
    number of, 164
trophic pyramid, 104, 147, 151, 159, 164, 165, 197, 198, 205, 219, 346, 372
trout
    of deserts, 407-427
    distribution in streams, 44, 48, 60
    food of, 341
    of mountains, 407-427
    popularity of, 389
    see individual species
trout streams, 60, 88
    cave source of, **83**
    as coldwater streams, 50, 101
    from groundwater, 84
    number of fish species in, 46
    pools and riffles in, 229
    tailwaters, 85

temperature of, 101
    in winter, **46**, 247
Trout Unlimited, 387, 471, 481
Truckee River, Nevada, 418-419
true flies, 251
Truman, President Harry S, and Everglades National Park, 180
Tubifex tubifex, 267, 361
Tubificidae, sludge worms, 267, 360-361
    oxygen need for, 361
Tuolumne River, California, 491
turbidity
    of large river reaches, 62
Twain, Mark, 420, *see also* Clemens, Samuel
Twin Lakes, Colorado, 424

U

Uenoidae, family of caddisflies, 311
unifying concepts, 53, 62, 63, 64, 547
Unionidae, family of clams, 264, 265
Upper Mississippi River National Wildlife and Fish
    Refuge 211-216, **214**
    beaver ponds in, 215
    birds in, 213
    fishing in, 214, 215
    lakes in, 215
    locks and dams in, 215
    mammals in, 213
    map of, **212**
    navigation system in, 215
urbanization, 98, 101, 202
Utah, trout in, 412, 417

V

Vancouver, British Columbia, 461
Victoria, Lake, Africa, as source of Nile River, 76
Virginia
  streams in, affected by acid rain, 160
voltinism, 246-249
  of caddisflies, 304, 313
  of crustaceans, 328, 330
  of mayflies, 278-290
Von Behr, Baron, 439
Von Behr strain of brown trout, 439, 440
voyageurs from Montreal, 67

W

walleye, 49, 299
warmwater fishes, 200, 388, 390, 483-503, 507, 522
warmwater streams, 45, 46, 50, 343, 484, 524
Warren, Glacial River, 87, 212, 363, 364
water boatmen,
  food for smallmouth bass, 253
  winter migration of, 253
  see also Corixidae
Washington, 141
  endangered stocks in, 471
  trout in, 409, 410
watercress, 330, 331, 332, 334, 335, 442
water fleas, cladocerans, 353, 354
waterfowl, in Red River valley, 364, 366
water table, 79, 80, 153
water temperature
  and leaf conditioning, 189
  and primary production,

177
West Virginia, 41
wetlands, drainage of, 110
whiper, white bass/striped bass hybrid, 492
white bass, 491-492
  angling for, 491, 492
  distribution of, 491-492
  hybrid with striped bass, 492
  spawning of, 492
whitefishes, 390
White Fly, dry fly imitation of mayfly, 291
white pine, 140, 141, 174
White River, Missouri/Arkansas, 342, 441, 505
white sucker, 300
Whitewater River, Minnesota, **95**
Wild and Scenic Rivers System, National, 202, 481, 546-550
  act signed by President Lyndon Johnson, 546
  categories of wildness, 550
  passed by U.S. Congress, 546
  rivers in Alaska, 548, 551
  rivers in Boston Mountains, 507, 551
  rivers in California, 548, 551
  rivers in Michigan, 551
  rivers in Oregon, 548, 551
  rivers in Ozark Mountains, 506-507, 551
  rivers in Pacific Northwest, 551
  St. Croix River, **547**
  study streams in, 546
winter stoneflies
  diapause in, 260
Wisconsin
  coaster brook trout in, 399
  flood in, 109
  logging in, 140

trout lakes in,
University of, 532
woody debris, 59, 133, **133**
153, 163, 185, 191,
192, 197, 199, 200,
210, 226, 310
in hyporehic zone, 372
as large particles, 206
preconditioning of, 134
source of energy, 132,
137,
Woolly Worm
nymph imitation, 211,
262
Woolly Bugger
nymph imitation, 262

X

xylophages, 193

Y

year class, of fish, 238
Yellow Dog River, Michigan,
551

yellow perch, 299
Yellow Sally, imitation
of stonefly, 260, 538
Yellowstone Lake, 416
Yellowstone River, 40, 41,
414, **416**
Yugoslavia, 344

Z

zebra mussel, *Dreissena*, 266
zones, in streams, 29-30, 47-
48, 53, 58, 59, 386
barbel, 47
bream, 47
grayling, 47
trout, 47
zooplankton, 241, 312, 351-
352, 511
in large rivers, 62
in lake outlets, 86
in reservoir outlets, 477
and sockeye salmon, 460,
518
Zygoptera, suborder of damselflies, 257

608   Wildstream